TELEVISION FOR WOMEN

Television for Women brings together emerging and established scholars to reconsider the question of 'television for women'. In the context of the 2000s, when the potential meanings of both terms have expanded and changed so significantly, in what ways might the concept of programming addressed explicitly to a group identified by gender still matter?

The essays in this collection take the existing scholarship in this field in significant new directions. They expand its reach in terms of territory (looking beyond, for example, the paradigmatic Anglo-American axis) and also historical span. Additionally, while the influential methodological formation of production, text and audience is still visible here, the new research in *Television for Women* frequently reconfigures that relationship.

The topics included here are far-reaching; from television as material culture at the British exhibition in the first half of the twentieth century, to women's roles in television production past and present, to popular 1960s television such as *The Liver Birds* and, in the twenty-first century, highly successful programmes including *Orange is the New Black*, *Call the Midwife*, *One Born Every Minute* and *Wanted Down Under*.

This book presents ground-breaking research on historical and contemporary relationships between women and television around the world and is an ideal resource for students of television, media and gender studies.

Rachel Moseley is Director of the Centre for Television History, Heritage and Memory Research in the Department of Film and Television Studies at the University of Warwick, UK. She has published widely on popular television and film, with a particular interest in questions of history, address and representation. She is the author of *Hand-Made Television: Stop-Frame Animation for Children in Britain, 1961–1974* (2016).

Helen Wheatley is Associate Professor (Reader) in Film and Television at the University of Warwick, UK and co-founder of the Centre for Television History, Heritage and Memory Research. She has published widely on television history and aesthetics and is the author of *Gothic Television* (2006) and *Spectacular Television: Exploring Televisual Pleasure* (2016). She is also editor of *Re-viewing Television History: Critical Issues in Television Historiography* (2007).

Helen Wood is Professor of Media and Communication at the University of Leicester, UK and has published widely on television, audiences, class and gender. She is author of *Talking with Television* (2009) and, with Beverley Skeggs, *Reacting to Reality Television* (2012); she has also edited *Reality Television and Class* with Beverley Skeggs (2011) and is editor of the *European Journal of Cultural Studies*.

TELEVISION FOR WOMEN

New Directions

Edited by Rachel Moseley, Helen Wheatley and Helen Wood

LONDON AND NEW YORK

First published 2017
by Routledge
2 Park Square, Milton Park, Abingdon, Oxon OX14 4RN

and by Routledge
711 Third Avenue, New York, NY 10017

Routledge is an imprint of the Taylor & Francis Group, an informa business

British Library Cataloguing-in-Publication Data
A catalogue record for this book is available from the British Library

Library of Congress Cataloging-in-Publication Data
Names: Moseley, Rachel, editor of compilation. | Wheatley, Helen, 1974-
editor of compilation. | Wood, Helen, editor of compilation.
Title: Television for women : new directions/edited by Rachel Moseley,
Helen Wheatley and Helen Wood.
Description: London; New York: Routledge, 2017. | Includes
bibliographical references.
Identifiers: LCCN 2016021584 | ISBN 9781138914285
(hardback: alk. paper) | ISBN 9781138914292 (pbk.: alk. paper) |
ISBN 9781315690896 (ebook)
Subjects: LCSH: Women on television. | Women's television programs. |
Television and women–History.
Classification: LCC PN1992.8.W65T45 2017 | DDC 791.45/6522–dc23
LC record available at https://lccn.loc.gov/2016021584

ISBN: 978-1-138-91428-5 (hbk)
ISBN: 978-1-138-91429-2 (pbk)
ISBN: 978-1-315-69089-6 (ebk)

Typeset in Bembo
by Sunrise Setting Ltd, Brixham, UK

To our children, in the order they arrived during the *Television for Women* project: Rudy, Dora, Max, Ned, Arthur and Hannah

CONTENTS

ILLUSTRATIONS

Figures

Tables

PREFACE

The question of television for women

'Television for women', as a category, must always be a matter of debate. Each word of the three is much trickier than it may seem at first glance. If the obvious questions are 'which women?' and 'what is television in the twenty-first century?', there are also questions about the very constitution of the category. For it is a category of address, condensed in the single preposition, 'for', and textual address can be very difficult to specify. The notorious twentieth-century advertising-industry shorthand for a certain genre of commercial, '2 Cs in a K' ('two cunts in a kitchen'), referred to ads that both featured and were aimed at women. This was television for women which understood women as the main purchasers of cleaning and food goods, and situated them within the domestic – in the 'K', to be precise. But the Cs aren't only to be found in the K, and often watch and enjoy television which addresses its audiences quite differently. Nor is gender, in identity and representation, ever just gender. The Cs aren't just Cs: their dress, appearance, deportment, language, and the accoutrements of their kitchens will tell other stories about age, social class, desire, ethnicity and nationality. The determinants of identity are complex and imbricated with each other. Some television may be produced primarily 'for' a female audience, but that 'for' does not predict how that audience is conceived, who will respond to that solicitation or how the programming will be watched.

The trickiness of the category 'television for women' is also its appeal. It's a baggy, permeable category which can be disputed and challenged, and in those challenges much can be revealed about the history of television production, representation, criticism and taste cultures. And that's what this book seeks to do. This collection traces some of these complexities, some of its histories and some of the surprises of exploring what 'television for women' has been, is and might be.

Charlotte Brunsdon, May 2016

ACKNOWLEDGEMENTS

We would like to thank researchers Mary Irwin and Hazel Collie for all the work they put into the AHRC project 'A History of Television for Women in Britain' (AH/F017251/1) and for making it the success that it was. Thank you to the University of Warwick for funding the initial workshop that led to the setting up of the project, and all the participants who attended this and inspired our work: Charlotte Brunsdon, Christine Geraghty, Ann Gray, Joke Hermes, Michele Hilmes, Dorothy Hobson, Joanne Hollows, Deborah Jermyn and Janet Thumim. Thanks also to De Montfort University who funded a PhD project around the history of feminism on television, completed by Jilly Kay in 2015. Thank you to those who helped with various other aspects of the project: to our colleagues in Research Support Services at the University of Warwick who supported us throughout the project's life (Liese Perrin, Katie Klaassen, David Duncan and Nadine Lewycky), to the Phoenix Arts Centre in Leicester and the BFI Southbank for helping us to host events on 'Career Girls on Television' and to Laura Elliot at Coventry Arts Space for enabling our 'Pop Music TV Pop-Up Shop'. Of course we want to thank all those who attended those events, wrote valuable comments and invigorated our interest in television for women as cultural heritage. Thank you too to Kate Kinninmont and Tony Ageh for supporting the project and speaking at our final event. We would also like to thank colleagues at the Universities of Warwick, De Montfort and Leicester who supported us during the life of the project and beyond. Many thanks to all our contributors for bearing with us, and special thanks to Jilly Kay for her hard work in helping to prepare the manuscript.

And finally to our families, who have literally come into being and grown during the life of this project – you are amazing.

Rachel, Helen and Helen

CONTRIBUTORS

Vicky Ball is Senior Lecturer in Cinema and Television Histories, De Montfort University. She has published articles on gender and British television drama and is currently writing a book about the British female ensemble drama (Manchester University Press, 2017). She is co-investigator on the AHRC-funded project 'Women's Work, Working Women: A Longitudinal Study of Women Working in the Film and Television Industries (1933–1989)' and a member of the Committee of the Women's Film and Television Histories Network: UK/Ireland.

Munira Cheema holds a PhD in Media and Cultural Studies from the University of Sussex, where she also works as an Associate Tutor. She is also a Visiting Lecturer in Media, Culture and Language at the University of Roehampton. Her research interests include politics/representation of gender in South Asia, gendered citizenship and religion and the evolution of the mediated public sphere in Pakistan. Her forthcoming book, entitled *Women and TV Culture in Pakistan: Islam, Gender and Nationhood*, will be published by I.B.Tauris in 2017.

Hazel Collie is a Lecturer in Media Theory at Birmingham City University. Her research focuses on historical audiences, feminine cultures and the relationships that audiences enact with and through television.

Sara De Benedictis is an ESRC-funded PhD student in the Department of Culture, Media and Creative Industries at King's College London. Her thesis explores representations of and reactions to birth in British popular culture. Sara will soon begin a research associate/fellow position at the University of Nottingham to work on a Wellcome-funded project on televising childbirth. Sara's research interests include birth, class, reality television, television production and austerity.

Dana A. Heller is Eminent Scholar and Interim Dean of the College of Arts & Letters at Old Dominion University. She writes about film and television, has authored numerous articles on topics related to literature, popular culture, LGBT and American studies, and is the author/editor of eight books, most recently *Hairspray* (Wiley-Blackwell, 2011) and *Loving* The L Word: *The Complete Series in Focus.*

Vanessa Jackson is a former BBC series producer, and now course director of the BA (Hons) Media and Communication and degree leader of Television at Birmingham City University, teaching practical television production skills to undergraduates. Her research interests include the history of television, as well as the uses of social media in community history projects.

Jilly Boyce Kay is a Research Associate in the Department of Media and Communication at the University of Leicester. Her work on gender, class, television and media has been published in journals such as *Feminist Media Histories, Critical Studies in Television, Social Movement Studies* and *Journalism: Theory, Practice and Criticism.*

Moya Luckett teaches at NYU's Gallatin School of Individualized Study. She is the author of *Cinema and Community: Progressivism, Exhibition and Film Culture in Chicago, 1907–1917* (Wayne State University Press), and is currently writing two books: *Not Quite New Media: Celebrity, Social Mobility and the Historiography of Media Transition* and *Femininity in Popular Media.* Her essays on femininity, early film, television history, British cinema and celebrity have been widely anthologised and have appeared in *Screen, Feminist Media Studies, The Velvet Light Trap* and *Aura.*

Ruth McElroy is Reader in Media and Cultural Studies at the University of South Wales where she is Director of the Creative Industries Research Institute. Her research interests centre on the mediation of national, classed and gendered identities in contemporary television. She is co-editor of *Life on Mars: From Manchester to New York* (2012, University of Wales Press) and has published in journals such as *Critical Studies in Television, Television and New Media* and the *Journal of Popular Television.* She is editor of a forthcoming collection on *Contemporary British Television Crime Drama* (Routledge, 2016) and is Principal Investigator on an AHRC international network on television production in small nations.

Sarah A. Matheson is Associate Professor in the Department of Communication, Popular Culture and Film at Brock University in St. Catharines, Ontario, Canada. She is co-editor of *Canadian Television: Text and Context* and has published widely in the area of Canadian television studies. Her work has appeared in journals such as the *Canadian Journal of Film Studies* and *Film and History* and in anthologies such as *Programming Reality: Perspectives on English–Canadian Television, Parallel Encounters: Culture and the Canada–US Border* and *Detecting Canada: Essays on Canadian Detective Fiction, Film, and Television.*

Sujata Moorti is a feminist media studies scholar who has specialised in analysing the representations of race and gender. She has also published extensively about the transnationally circulating media of the South Asian diaspora and about Indian cinema. Her most recent book manuscript, *All-American Crime Drama* (co-authored with Lisa Cuklanz), examines the US television series *Law and Order: Special Victims Unit*.

Rachel Moseley is Director of the Centre for Television History, Heritage and Memory Research in the Department of Film and Television Studies at the University of Warwick, UK. She has published widely on popular television and film, with a particular interest in questions of history, address and representation. She is the author of *Hand-Made Television: Stop-Frame Animation for Children in Britain, 1961–1974* (Palgrave, 2016) and is writing a book on questions of region and landscape in film and television through a case study on Cornwall.

Cecilia Penati (PhD) is Adjunct Professor of International Media Systems at Università Cattolica del Sacro Cuore, Milan (Italy), Senior Researcher at CeRTA, the Centre of Research on Television and Audiovisual Media, at the same university, and Adjunct Professor of Media for Arts at IULM University of Milan.

Anna Sfardini (PhD) is Adjunct Professor of Intercultural Communication at Università Cattolica del Sacro Cuore, Milan (Italy) and Senior Researcher at CeRTA, Centre of Research on Television and Audiovisual Media, at the same university.

Helen Wheatley is Associate Professor (Reader) in Film and Television at the University of Warwick, UK and co-founder of the Centre for Television History, Heritage and Memory Research. She has published widely on television history and aesthetics and is the author of *Gothic Television* (2006) and *Spectacular Television: Exploring Televisual Pleasure* (2016). She is also editor of *Re-viewing Television History: Critical Issues in Television Historiography* (2007).

Helen Wood is Professor of Media and Communication at the University of Leicester and has published widely on television, audiences, class and gender. She is author of *Talking with Television* (2009) and, with Beverley Skeggs, *Reacting to Reality Television* (2012); she has also edited *Reality Television and Class* with Beverley Skeggs (2011). She co-edited the *Centre for Contemporary Cultural Studies Occasional Papers* (2007) for Routledge and is also editor of the *European Journal of Cultural Studies*.

INTRODUCTION

Television for women – what *new* directions?

Rachel Moseley, Helen Wheatley and Helen Wood

This collection of essays comes at the end of a twelve-year journey. In 2004, we organised a workshop at the University of Warwick, to which we invited key scholars to talk with us about the kinds of questions that might need to be asked were we to embark upon a project to reinvigorate the study of television *for* women.[1] Some of the key questions underpinning our subsequent AHRC-funded project 'A History of Television for Women in Britain, 1947–1989' (2010–14), and now in *Television for Women: New Directions*, came out of that two-day meeting: what were the parameters of the existing field and how might a richer history of women's programming inform that field? Why were we interested in television 'for' rather than television 'and' women, or television 'by' or 'about' women? What kinds of methodological approach would be needed, or preferable, in order to research television for women? It seemed to us that research on the relationship between women and television continued to proceed without an adequate history, and was based on key assumptions about the gendering of tastes. Our project picked up and moved on from the vital work on soap opera (Brunsdon, 1981, 2000; Modleski, 1979; Geraghty, 1981, 1991) and its audiences (Hobson, 1982, 2003; Seiter *et al.*, 1989) in the 1980s and 1990s which aimed to 'rescue' women's genres and women audiences from derision. Feminist work on 'women's genres' continued into the 1990s with the prominence of the talk show (Masciarotte, 1991; Moorti, 1998; Shattuc, 1997; Wood, 2009), but when the theoretical shifts into poststructuralism began to argue that we should move beyond researching stable gender categories (e.g. Ang and Hermes, 1991) and that the gendering of audience tastes was apparently less relevant than it had previously been considered to be (e.g. Gauntlett and Hill, 1999), there seemed to be a need to reflect. Was the field really stalling? Did we know all we needed to know about women's relationship to television? If not, what new or reframed questions, in relation to the terms 'woman', 'feminism' and 'television', would be generated by the shifting context of the 2000s? Surely there were lacunae in the existing field?

So many ideas came out of that original discussion, but, for us, despite the enduring understanding that television was a feminised medium, we kept coming back to the fact that there were key gaps in the critical work on television's address to women, and a series of absences in our historical understanding of this programming. The existing field of study then in the mid-2000s was remarkably contemporary to the moment of research and writing; while this work had been invaluable, it now seemed important to think further about the antecedents of contemporary programming, about genres watched by women which had not yet been considered (for example, non-fiction), as well as about the historical audience of women television viewers. Furthermore, the field of production was then a significant gap in the existing work on women and television, with some notable exceptions (Leman, 1987; Thumim, 2004). We thus wanted to ask: what kinds of decisions underpinned the production of programming addressed to a female audience? What was the discursive construction of that audience by the industry? What kinds of heretofore invisible (or under-attended) roles had been played by women in producing that programming?[2] In discussing the lack of historical study in the field, we also reflected at the workshop on questions of method. The classic approach which separated out the study of production, text and audience seemed too linear and over-determined; we needed a method which allowed for a multi-directional flow between these areas of research, not just because the fields of consumption and production were becoming blurred, but because those categories have always called for an interconnection in television history and analysis. Our textual objects of study might be defined as much through audience research as via production histories, for example. Ann Gray's suggestion, in our discussion, of a method built upon a 'contingent mosaic' approach (later taken up by Wheatley 2007, 2016), in which television historians draw together different strands of the production/text/viewer triumvirate according to the different needs of their research, or Spigel and Mann's notion of 'conjunctural histories' (1992: viii) seemed to offer a richer, and more flexible, approach to the study of women's television. In putting together an edited collection on this subject, we continue to draw these strands of research together, collecting research into viewers, programmes and producers of television which does not always delineate the contexts of production, text and audience into neat categories and sometimes works productively at the seams of their interconnection.

These, then, were the central questions upon which our work on television for women was built. Our project developed as a study of women's television in Britain, which reflected the national specificity of television history in this moment, though we were attendant to the need to remain in contact with researchers working on comparative histories around the world; indeed, this collection is a product of this ongoing conversation.[3] Across the life of the project, post-doctoral research fellow Mary Irwin and doctoral researcher Hazel Collie produced work based on the kind of 'contingent mosaic' described by Gray above, constructing a television history which looked for a more synchronous relationship between archival and audience research. In looking at British industrial history for the early period of our study, Irwin explored and demonstrated the significant role of Doreen Stephens, the BBC's first Editor of Women's Programmes, in producing television addressed specifically to a female audience (2011, 2013), and in the process brought to light the women's daytime arts programme *Wednesday Magazine* (BBC, 1958–63) (2015b). This programme was contemporaneous with the renowned *Monitor* (BBC, 1958–65) and rivalled it in terms of coverage and achievement, but had remained largely absent in academic enquiry, no doubt as a result of its daytime position in the schedule and its gendered address.[4] Collie's qualitative research with multiple generations of British women television viewers produced the first major study of the historical audience for women's television in Britain, and impacted significantly on existing understandings of the relationship between gender and genre. This oral history research allowed for a divergence of focus from the classic genres of soap opera, classic drama and talk shows to emerge, and, as a result, the importance of sport on television, pop music programming and desire as a viewing pleasure came to light (Collie, 2014, and see Chapter 12 in this volume). Collie's findings on the importance of pop music television took Irwin to the archives and, through programme listings research, the very clearly gendered address of this under-explored genre on British television was unveiled as a result of our 'mosaic' method (see Collie and Irwin, 2013). Alongside this, the investigators produced innovative historical work which thought about television for women in terms of material culture via its presence at the exhibition site (Wheatley, Chapter 11 in this volume) and provided evidence of the first British female audiences of television approaching this new technology with trepidation, given the pride in their new roles as 'housewives' in the late 1940s (Wood, 2015).[5]

In 2014, as the project came to a conclusion, we staged an international conference on the question of Television for Women. Our intention was to significantly expand our research agenda in order not only to develop the scope of our nationally specific project by bringing together related research from around the world (and in particular to diversify beyond the Anglo-American context), but also to multiply the range of questions needing to be asked about women's television – questions which typically are determined by geo-political positioning. We also hoped that the conference would reveal new histories to us and tell us something about what was happening to women's television in the contemporary moment, and whether television *for* women still played a central role in the contemporary digital television landscape. This collection of essays is a direct result of that conference and includes chapters developed from papers delivered there, as well as writing commissioned especially to address gaps that we perceived in the book's coverage. At the same time, the conference, and in particular the closing plenary, raised critical questions about the very terms upon which the project and the conference had been built: what did 'television' mean today, in a digitised and individualised landscape, and why should we desire to hold on to a term like 'women' which had been used, historically, in deeply exclusionary ways around race, class and sexuality? In what follows, we situate this collection, its agenda and its absences in relation to the existing field and indicate the questions emerging for future research on television for women.

Whose television? Which women?

Paradigmatically, the relationship between women and television has been couched in terms of a series of structuring assumptions: certain genres have been assumed, and later theorised, as 'belonging' to women through representation and content and/or form (soap opera, television talk, reality television), or have been adapted to address them specifically (the police series). In terms of scheduling, daytime television has also been understood (in the industry and in academia) as 'belonging' to women. Women's affiliation with television has been constructed as an intimate one, sometimes problematically so (Doane, 1991: 24), largely through the assumption of a close relationship between femininity and domesticity. Women have been understood as intimately related to practices of consumption, among which television viewership numbers one of many (and these are often related, particularly through lifestyle television and its focus on cookery, fashion and home-making). While existing scholarship has examined these relationships in relation to contemporary television (e.g. Moseley and Read, 2002; Akass and McCabe, 2003; Lotz, 2006), part of our objective in assembling this collection has been to expand upon and challenge these assumptions and approaches to the relationship, for example in terms of historical perspectives on women's relation to consumption and the home (Wheatley), or the relationship between feminism, femininity and genre (Ball, Luckett, Matheson). Some contributors to *Television For Women: New Directions* draw attention to the gendering of industrial landscapes, for example in relation to women's work in the production of television for women, historically and in the present (Jackson, McElroy), while also pointing to the changing television landscapes of particular national and political contexts (Cheema, Penati and Sfardini). Contributions bring to light the significance of desiring straight and queer female subjectivities in women's viewing pleasure (Collie, Heller), while the relationship between women, television and subjectivity remains central to this collection, and the essays here by De Benedictis, Kay and Wood and Moorti reframe that relationship in relation to new television genres, viewing attachments and visibilities.

It is perhaps this final question around the conjunction of subjectivity, identity and representation that remains the thorniest for this collection. The critiques offered at the conference around the continued usefulness of the category 'woman' in politicised intellectual work were the result of perceived absences in the conference programme. The raising of this issue in our closing discussion led us to actively seek out for this collection work which could speak more directly to questions of intersectionality than had been represented in the spread of submissions to the conference. While we wanted to address the importance of intersectionality in identities in our selections for this collection, we were also wary of letting go entirely of the category 'woman'. While Judith Butler (1990) questioned the 'etc.' which appears at the end of lists of social divisions as though the categories run out of steam, signalling their exhaustion, Nira Yural Davies (2006) instead argues for the centrality of the historical as a route out of this impasse. She argues that 'in specific historical situations and in relation to specific people there are some social divisions that are more important than others in constructing specific positionings' (2006: 188). It is in our notion of the 'contingent mosaic' that the category of 'women' emerges differentially in relation to particular conjunctions of time and space. For the work in this collection, this has meant that the femininity of those represented in, and addressed by, the television programming at hand has taken prominence, sometimes alongside other markers of identity (race, class, sexuality); we thus continue to hold on to the possibility of 'woman' as a stretchy and expansive, non-essentialist and queer-able term. In the turn towards intersectionality, we must not give up a platform from which to challenge the underpinning structures of capitalism and patriarchy: gender, and its accompanying exclusions and discriminations, does not simply disintegrate in the face of intersectionality. The 'Television for Women' project, conference, and indeed this collection were planned and largely put together before the debate about transgender femininities and feminism became so emphatically visible in the academy and the media; the meaning of the term 'woman' is more obviously expansive today than it has ever been, and as Heller acknowledges in this collection, women's programming has become an important forum for contributing to public awareness of the problems faced by trans women and the larger trans community. Therefore, the term 'woman', and the idea of women's programming, have not been emptied of their political significance in the contemporary moment, but have become significantly more inclusive. While the figure of the female viewer and the idea of 'woman' still matter so much in television production and scheduling, it is clearly impossible for historians and theorists of the medium to do away with the idea of programming *for* women altogether.

Television for women and the new landscape of television

Of course, 'television' itself requires some interrogation, as today this term would appear to mean something radically different than it did, for instance, in 1991, the year in which Andrea Press' *Women Watching Television* was published. Popular discourse suggests that we are in a radically new digital landscape, in which post-broadcast, post-network television is available across multiple platforms, devices and scales and, critically, is typically consumed in individualised ways (for instance via streaming services such as Netflix, Hulu and Amazon Prime). These new ways of consuming television, it is suggested, both bypass the tyranny of the schedule and lessen, if not entirely remove, the possibilities of co-present viewing, which was one of the cornerstone theories of broadcast television (see Jenner, 2016; Lotz, 2014; Newman and Levine, 2011; Spigel and Olssen, 2004). However significant these changes have been (as demonstrated by Faye Woods' work on online female television fan communities (2015) and by Heller, Moorti and Penati and Sfardini in this volume), it is important to remember that access to this new television landscape is contingent upon factors such as class position, generation and even region, and that long-standing gendered tastes and forms of consumption still abide. Furthermore, 'schedule-free' television is not democratically available to all, nor is it desired by all viewers, and focusing entirely on these new modes of viewing and new delivery platforms risks losing sight of the large majority of viewers and viewing practices. Figures show, for example, that in 2015, 92.4 per cent of the British population still watched broadcast television (Ofcom, 2015), and while Netflix now has some 4.3 million subscribers in the UK, only 31 per cent use the service to access original television programming (Jackson, 2015).

Subsequently, we argue that the hegemonic discourse which figures television as radically changed and individualised is not necessarily borne out in many women's everyday viewing; even casual discussion with our teenage students demonstrates the ways in which viewing is often still inextricably stitched to the family, home and the schedule (think of Saturday night viewing in the UK, for example), to even their own surprise. For viewers engaging with broadcast television on a regular basis (and for the industry, which spends significant amounts of money on researching and organising planned programme flows), the schedule certainly does still matter and continues to be organised around gendered forms of address. As we argued in the introduction to our special issue of *Critical Studies in Television* on afternoon television, there is a long-standing association between women television viewers and the afternoon schedule, where programming addressed to them has been located historically, and which persists despite the broad move from a mixed schedule with specific slots to genre-specific channels in the new landscape (Moseley, Wheatley and Wood, 2014). Thus while we have had to expand how and where we imagine television for women is located in the schedule, as well as in a variety of television on-demand platforms, older spaces, places and genres of women's television remain significant in this shifting landscape.

The organisation of the book

The book is structured into four sections. These sections, 'Women and work', 'Women and identity', 'Formations of women's television' and 'Women and the home', seem to us to capture a sense of the classical ways in which the relationship between women and television has been understood (identity, home), but also to indicate other important ways in which that relationship should be understood, for example in relation to women's labour on and in television, shifting notions of television genres 'for' women' and questions of television's relationship to geo-politics (work, formation). The neoliberal, postfeminist context in which this project was conceived and conducted also means that the stakes of the more traditional concepts through which women's relationship with television has been constructed have been transformed and need to be thought about differently, as we suggest above. At the same time, it is clear that there is meaningful overlap between the categories that we have constructed. Vicky Ball's essay on the female ensemble drama, for example, appears in the section on women, television and identity, but speaks to questions about the changes to the organisation of the home brought about by changes in the labour environment in the 1960s and 1970s. Similarly, while Munira Cheema's chapter on 'interactive genres' on Pakistani television is situated in the section on 'formations' of television for women, since it is working at the intersection of production contexts and textual content, it also contributes to debates across the book about identity, the home and women's labour. We hope that readers will make such connections across the book and consider the productive ways in which the chapters here reflect on earlier approaches to the question of women's television, as well as looking forward to new directions.

The section which opens the book, 'Women and work', brings together work which thinks about the relationship between women, labour and television, both on and behind the screen. A longer history of the relationship between working women and television – their representation and their roles in production – has been a significant finding of our AHRC-funded project (Irwin, 2015a), but here the focus of this work is expanded into both the realm of contemporary television drama and the production of daytime/lifestyle programming for women. In the opening essay, Moya Luckett examines the ways in which a range of contemporary television dramas, including *Mad Men* (AMC, 2007–15), *Call the Midwife* (BBC1, 2012–), *The Bletchley Circle* (ITV, 2012–14) and *Downton Abbey* (ITV, 2010–15), articulate postfeminism's emphasis on achieved gender equality even as they use the recent past to uncover more complex and potentially progressive histories that ground, rationalise, inspire and justify contemporary women's professional lives. Going beyond simple narratives of female progress, Luckett argues that these texts seek to puncture widespread illusions about the limited nature of female participation in the pre-1970s Anglo-American workplace. Next, Ruth McElroy's essay takes the production for television of British writer Sally Wainwright's work by Nicola Shindler's company Red Production as a case study through which to explore the dynamics of women working in contemporary British television. McElroy's research shows that the notion of 'television for women' needs to be understood as a category constructed in academic research which may not correspond to production discourse, and argues that intimacy with the complexity of women's lives has become central to quality mainstream drama. Vanessa Jackson approaches this question from a historical perspective through her work on the BBC's Pebble Mill studios in Birmingham, tracking the ways in which women's roles in television production have shifted since the 1970s. Jackson's work uncovers the fact that the women who rose through the ranks at Pebble Mill often found themselves making programmes predominantly viewed by women (working in 'gendered niches' like daytime and lifestyle programming), and were able to develop their programmes with a successful feminine address. In both McElroy's and Jackson's chapters, interview data signals a strong refusal, from the production perspective, of the notion of *making* television for the lucrative female audience, despite acknowledgement from Jackson's participants of the 'female-skewed' nature of the audience for daytime/lifestyle programming, and the evident centrality of women's professional and emotional lives to Wainwright's drama as argued by McElroy. This gap, between producer, an understanding of address, and audience, points not only to the ongoing lack of value attached to television for women, but also to the difficulty of drawing clear and direct lines between production and reception discourse in the classical production–text–reception triad. This is, we suggest, evidence of an area of scholarship that is in need of the kind of 'mosaic-ed' methodological approach to the study of television which we discuss above.

The essays in the next section, 'Women and identity', consider historical and contemporary television's construction of women's identities. Dana Heller's essay on the popular Netflix show *Orange is the New Black* (2013–) focuses on the significance of the catfight as a stylised performance of a shared stock of fantasies, anxieties, industrial techniques and intertexts out of which queerness, or its media affect, emerges. Through her engagement with histories of camp and the woman's prison drama, Heller argues that the catfight in *Orange is the New Black* is evidence of queer culture's perpetual presence as an intervention in media hierarchies of taste, a sustained and sustaining critique of what counts as 'tasteful' to television itself. Heller proposes that the catfight grants pleasure to savvy viewers who recognise the sordid cultural archive on which the series draws, at the same time as it dramatises the tensions and connections between queer and straight identities. Sujata Moorti writes about reactions to *The Mindy Project* and *The Good Wife* in terms of how the representational burden placed on 'brown girls' in viewers' investments can be seen across social media. Her piece concentrates on how key moments of reaction help to reconstitute the texts as 'for' women, but importantly these reactions reverberate precisely because figures like Mindy Kaling do not represent the figure of the brown girl who needs 'saving' which is resonant in the discourses of the third world girl. In this piece we see precisely television's ability to intervene in transnational and racial feminist politics. Sara De Benedictis' research into the factual programme *One Born Every Minute* considers the text as part of a growing interest in birth and birth stories across contemporary television. Her research into immediate audience reactions shows how women affectively respond to the visceral immediacy of the birthing moments. Here she discusses how audiences move through positions which both reassert and refute the ideological discourses of the 'good birth' which mirror those of the 'good mother' within contexts of neoliberal value. Finally in this section, Vicky Ball examines British female ensemble situation comedies of the 1960s and 1970s, through a focus on the much-loved and long-running series *The Liver Birds*. Through a particular focus on the articulation of classed femininities, Ball shows how the British television of this period used the female ensemble text to speak to changing notions of female identity through the scenario of single girls sharing a city flat. In this way, her chapter draws new attention to how such texts acknowledged changing and diversified understandings of female identity.

In 'Formations of women's television' we have brought together chapters which showcase new research on the history of producing television for women, and specifically women's brands and channels – and the take-up of that television. The essays here raise questions about generic identity, notions of gendered address and the construction of audience in production discourse. It seems significant that the essays which attend to these questions emerge from geo-political contexts which produce research agendas and thematic foci different from those which formed the earlier work in the Anglo-American-dominated field. Sarah Matheson explores the development, failure and reinvention of Canada's Women's Television Network from the 1990s, arguing that WTN's aim to make a generically differentiated 'television for women' was based upon a feminist politics which was too 'second-wave' to align with the historical development of feminism as 'post-' in the 1990s and its changed relationship with popular culture. Cecilia Penati and Anna Sfardini, on the other hand, discuss the success of women's television in Italy and the way in which a 'swarm' of channels grew that developed gendered arenas of lifestyle television. In their audience research with different generations of women from different regions of Italy, they discuss how older women viewers saw the idea of television addressing them directly as 'progress', while younger viewers who still took pleasure from lifestyle television were more critical of its traditional gendering around the home. They argue that the popularity of television's address to women in this context can thus be understood as a constant re-imagining of 'woman' between innovation and tradition. Munira Cheema's chapter, which concludes this section, is based on research with producers and audiences of 'interactive' television genres on Pakistani television since its liberalisation and diversification in 2000. Cheema's essay explores the important role played by ratings and viewing data on the production of television for women, drawing out assumptions made by producers about their female viewers but, at the same time, drawing attention to the way in which this ratings-driven genre can be understood as a significant 'mediated public sphere' in which gendered crimes such as rape and acid attacks are exposed and discussed.

The final section of the book returns to more familiar terrain in its turn to questions of the domestic and an understanding of women (and their viewing) in the home. However, the chapters in this section explore the domestic woman/viewer from new or re-emerging perspectives. Helen Wheatley's chapter in this section examines the ways in which the female consumer-citizen, as the figure at the centre of the ideal home, was targeted by broadcasters and set manufacturers alike through the displays of television at the mid-century exhibition (and the Ideal Home Exhibition in particular). Wheatley argues that this history outlines the ways in which television, as both spectacular exhibit and everyday technology, was figured as a gendered technology at the mid-twentieth century exhibition, and was central to discourses of domestic/gendered modernity. Hazel Collie's essay, on the other hand, draws on her research on the 'A History of Television for Women in Britain, 1947–89' project to construct a new and productive understanding of the under-explored but critical relationship between television, women and desire. Collie's interviewees articulate the role played by attraction/desire in relation to their television viewing in negotiating their domestic life. Importantly, Collie concludes in this work that the domestic arena represents a different space for attraction and desire to be played out, and that television's position creates a more everyday set of desirous-looking relations as compared to cinema. Finally, Jilly Kay and Helen Wood discuss the contemporary British television factual programme *Wanted Down Under* and how it returns us to ideas about the ideal female viewer as the 'worrying mother'. The text invites families to try out life in Australia and consider a move abroad by setting claims about a renewed family life and more time for children against the apparent worsening conditions of austerity in the UK. Being a 'responsible' migrant is set against strong affective attachments to home which anxiously figure the viewer/mother in a moment of 'cruel optimism' (Berlant, 2011) related to the colonial legacy of Britain and Australia.

This book by no means represents the full diversity of work on women's television or of feminist television scholarship. Instead it is an attempt to consider how television has spoken, and continues to speak, directly to women, putting the issue of 'address' at its core. Our project intended to consider the relationship between television's address and the pace of social and cultural change for women, since its development has coincided with key moments in women's history. That task can only really be gestured to, as the parts of the mosaic of the story of women's engagement with television are still being pieced together. What is clear, though, is that research into television's relationship to women continues to expand in new directions, both by conducting more rigorous histories *and* by attending to the new and shifting landscape of television. While television studies itself seems only renewed by the changing nature of television, feminist scholarship too can only be renewed by the changing figuration of 'woman' and her place in time and space.

Notes

1 Along with the editors, in attendance were Charlotte Brunsdon, Christine Geraghty, Ann Gray, Joke Hermes, Michele Hilmes, Dorothy Hobson, Deborah Jermyn and Janet Thumim. Joanne Hollows also sent us a valuable contribution in writing.
2 Some of this historical picture has begun to be addressed in the UK by the arrival of the Women's Film and Television History Network, which began to include television at the time of the duration of the project. See https://womensfilmandtelevisionhistory.wordpress.com/about-us/network-organisation/wfthn-founder/.
3 Historical research coming out of the EU Screen project (www.euscreen.eu) and elsewhere has more recently pioneered a welcome transnational approach to television history (e.g. Fickers and Johnson, 2012).
4 As a result of this research, a viewing copy of this important programme was made available for other researchers to consult and, hopefully, to teach.
5 The complete outputs of the project can be explored via Research Council UK's research-fish.com resource.

Bibliography

Akass, K. and McCabe, J. (eds) (2003) *Reading Sex and the City*, London: I.B.Tauris.
Ang, I. and Hermes, J. (1991) 'Gender and/in media consumption' in J. Curran and M. Gurevitch (eds) *Mass Media and Society*, London: Arnold, pp. 307–28.
Berlant, L. (2011) *Cruel Optimism*, Durham: Duke University Press.
Brunsdon, C. (1981) '*Crossroads*: Notes on soap opera', *Screen*, 22, 4: 32–7.
Brunsdon, C. (2000) *The Feminist, the Housewife, and the Soap Opera*, Oxford: Oxford University Press.
Butler, J. (1990) *Gender Trouble: Feminism and the Subversion of Identity*, New York: Routledge.
Collie, H. (2014) 'From Cathy "Queen of the Mods" to Paula "Pop princess"': Women, music television and adolescent female identity', in L. Mee and J. Walker (eds) *Cinema, Television and History: New Approaches*, Newcastle: Cambridge Scholars Press, pp. 47–66.

Collie, H. and Irwin, M. (2013) '"The weekend starts here": Young women, pop music television and identity', *Screen*, 54, 2: 262–9.

Doane, M.A. (1991) *Femmes Fatales: Feminism, Film Theory, Psychoanalysis*, London and New York: Routledge.

Fickers, A. and Johnson, C. (eds) (2012) *Transnational Television History: A Comparative Approach*, London and New York: Routledge.

Gauntlett, D. and Hill, A. (1999) *TV Living: Television, Culture and Everyday Life*, London and New York: Routledge.

Geraghty, C. (1981) 'Continuous serial – a definition', in R. Dyer (ed.) *Coronation Street*, London: BFI Publishing, pp. 9–26.

Geraghty, C. (1991) *Women and Soap Opera: A Study of Prime Time Soaps*, Cambridge: Polity Press.

Hobson, D. (1982) *Crossroads: Drama of a Soap Opera*, London: Methuen.

Hobson, D. (2003) *Soap Opera*, London: Wiley.

Irwin, M. (2011) 'What women want on television: Doreen Stephens and BBC television programmes for women, 1953–64', *Westminster Papers in Communication and Culture*, 8, 3: 99–122.

Irwin, M. (2013) 'Doreen Stephens: Producing and managing British television in the 1950s and 1960s', *Journal of British Cinema and Television*, 10, 3: 618–34.

Irwin, M. (2015a) 'Career girls: Women at work in *Compact* and *The Rag Trade*', *Feminist Media Studies*, 15, 5: 845–59.

Irwin, M. (2015b) 'BBC's *Wednesday Magazine* and Arts Television for Women', *Media History*, 21, 2: 162–77.

Jackson, J. (2015) 'Two thirds of UK's Netflix and Amazon users don't watch their original shows', *Guardian*, 6 August, www.theguardian.com/media/2015/aug/06/uk-netflix-amazon-users-online-tv-house-of-cards, accessed 19 April 2016.

Jenner, M. (2016) 'Is this TVIV? On Netflix, TVIII and binge-watching', *New Media & Society*, 18, 2: 257–73.

Leman, J. (1987) '"Programmes for women" in 1950s British television', in H. Baehr and G. Dyer (eds) *Boxed In: Women and Television*, London & New York: Pandora, pp. 73–95.

Lotz, A. (2006) *Re-designing Women: Television after the Network Era*, Urbana: University of Illinois Press.

Lotz, A. (2014) *The Television will be Revolutionized*. 2nd edn. New York and London: New York University Press.

Masciarrotte, G.J. (1991) 'C'mon, girl: Oprah Winfrey and the discourse of feminine talk', *Genders*, 11: 81–110.

Modleski, T. (1979) 'The search for tomorrow in today's soap operas: Notes on a feminine narrative form', *Film Quarterly*, 33, 1: 12–21.

Moorti, S. (1998) 'Cathartic confession or emancipatory texts? Rape narratives in *The Oprah Winfrey Show*', *Social Text*, 57: 83–107.

Moseley, R. and Read, J. (2002) '"Having it Ally": Popular television (post-) feminism', *Feminist Media Studies*, 2, 2: 231–49.

Moseley, R., Wheatley, H. and Wood, H. (2014) 'Introduction: Television in the afternoon', *Critical Studies in Television* (Special Issue on Afternoon Television), 9, 2: 1–19.

Newman, M. and Levine, E. (2011) *Legitimating Television*, London and New York: Routledge.

Ofcom (2015) 'Report: Changes in TV viewing habits', http://stakeholders.ofcom.org.uk/, accessed 20 April 2016.

Phoenix, A. (2006) 'Editorial: Special issue on intersectionality', *European Journal of Women's Studies*, 13, 3: 187–92.

Press, A. (1991) *Women Watching Television: Gender, Class, and Generation in the American Television Experience*, Philadelphia: University of Pennsylvania Press.

Seiter, E., Borchers, H., Kreutzner, G. and Warth, E.-M. (1989) '"Don't treat us like we're so stupid and naïve": Towards an ethnography of soap opera viewers', in E. Seiter, H. Borchers, G. Kreutzner and E.-M. Warth (eds) *Remote Control: Television, Audiences, and Cultural Power*, London and New York: Routledge, pp. 223–47.

Shattuc, J.M. (1997) *The Talking Cure: TV Talk Shows and Women*, New York: Routledge.

Spigel, L. and Mann, D. (1992) *Private Screenings: Television and the Female Consumer*, Minneapolis: University of Minnesota Press.

Spigel, L. and Olssen, J. (2004) *Television after TV: Essays on a Medium in Transition*, Durham and London: Duke University Press.

Thumim, J. (2004) *Inventing Television Culture: Men, Women and the Box*, Oxford and New York: Oxford University Press.

Wheatley, H. (ed.) (2007) *Re-viewing Television History: Critical Issues in Television Historiography*, London: I.B.Tauris.

Wheatley, H. (2016) *Spectacular Television: Exploring Televisual Pleasure*, London: I.B.Tauris.

Wood, H. (2009) *Talking with Television: Women, Talk Shows and Modern Self-Reflexivity*, Urbana: University of Illinois Press.

Wood, H. (2015) 'Television – the housewife's choice? The 1949 Mass Observation Television Directive, reluctance and revision', *Media History*, 21, 3: 342–59.

Woods, F. (2015) 'Girls talk: Authorship and authenticity in the reception of Lena Dunham's *Girls*', *Critical Studies in Television*, 10, 2: 37–54.

Yuval Davis, N. (2006) 'Intersectionality and feminist politics', *European Journal of Women's Studies*, 13, 3: 193–205.

PART I
Women and work

1

WOMEN'S HISTORY, WOMEN'S WORK

Popular television as feminine historiography

Moya Luckett

Over the past few years, several widely discussed British and American period television dramas have testified to public fascination with the history of working women. These series respond to the ways in which work increasingly dominates women's lives, exploring how paid employment might have shaped femininity in the past and, by extension, the present. In exploring work's impact on feminine identities, shows like *Mad Men* (AMC, 2007–15), *Call the Midwife* (BBC1, 2012–), *The Bletchley Circle* (ITV, 2012–14), *Mr Selfridge* (ITV, 2013–), *The Paradise* (BBC1, 2012–13), *The Hour* (BBC2, 2011–12) and *Downton Abbey* (ITV, 2010–15) directly address concerns held by women audiences. Seen collectively, these programmes articulate postfeminism's emphasis on achieved gender equality even as they use the recent past to uncover more complex and potentially progressive histories that variously ground, rationalise, inspire and justify contemporary women's professional lives. Going beyond simple narratives of female progress, these texts seek to puncture widespread illusions about the limited nature of female participation in the pre-1970s Anglo-American workplace. Rather than presenting their characters as surprising pioneers, they demonstrate working women's relative ubiquity, encouraging viewers to revise their understandings of feminine labour. Bridging past and present, they link work to female emancipation, agency, self-fulfilment and even glamour, all characteristics that conventionally attract women audiences. Avowedly feminine skills are shown as central for even the most markedly patriarchal and traditional workplaces, with these programmes consistently presenting women as the more visually literate sex and thus more perceptive to the visual cues key to a variety of tasks, including solving crimes, assessing medical emergencies and running successful modern businesses. Female audiences are consequently invited to see their spectatorship in similar terms as these programmes encourage identification with their protagonists' visual labour, something mirrored in the very act of viewing. The discourse on women's work mounted in these series reflects upon and extends to the labour performed by their female spectators.

Showcasing a variety of working women – retired 1940s code-breakers, 1950s midwives and TV executives, 1960s advertising professionals as well as domestic servants, shopgirls, nurses and elite professionals from the 1910s–20s – these dramas depict histories marked by varying degrees of female professionalisation, drudgery, emancipation and struggle. In focusing on non-iconic periods for female liberation – the 1910s, 1950s and early 1960s, years often associated with more 'traditional' domestic gender archetypes – these programmes effect more serious archeological investigations into women's working lives, ones consistently framed in terms of revelation. Throughout, femininity is presented as particularly suited to modern working life, with female characters often displaying greater, if at times unrecognised, mastery of their professions as well as the ambition necessary to succeed. Female audiences are courted through representations that ally work to feminine expertise, going beyond the more traditional private, domestic skills associated with nurturing and homemaking (*Downton Abbey, Call the Midwife*) to the more public domain of representation (advertising – *Mad Men*, television – *The Hour*, even the code-breaking/detective work of *The Bletchley Circle*'s women).

Although typically associated with liveness and 'presence', television's status as potential chronicle and archive – as well as its neo-Victorian postwar cultural roots and affiliations with domesticity and women's leisure – make it a particularly compelling, if fanciful, site for popular feminine histories/historiography. Besides offering a wide range of histories of women's work, these programmes employ varied modes of address. *Downton Abbey, The Paradise* and *Mr Selfridge* extend the romantic conventions associated with costume drama to the workplace and history itself. *Call the Midwife, The Hour* and *Mad Men* employ accurate mise-en-scène to develop a self-conscious historicity that stimulates audiences to reflect more critically on the past and practices of historical representation, particularly in terms of the ways these define femininity and frame women's lives. *The Bletchley Circle*'s address is in some ways the most interesting, inviting female audiences to share its leads' conventionally feminine visual literacy while signifying how, in this particular context, these skills cannot emancipate these women nor change the broader social climate. Taken together, these series all hail female audiences with their recognition of the contradictory pleasures and pressures of female labour, its potential for pleasure and its sense of suffocating entrapment, its links to identity and self-actualisation as well as its capacity to contain and limit self-expression.

Despite sometimes dubious claims to history, these programmes (and their surrounding discourses) perform a series of important historiographic functions. Besides contributing to a public history of women's work, they employ a series of rhetorical strategies, most notably presenting their working women as a revelation, unveiling a secret or hidden past. Here, these shows try to ally themselves with 'reputable' histories like BBC2's *Shopgirls: The True Life of Girls Behind the Counter* (2014) that bridge popular and 'academic' fascination with the 'unknown' history of working women, whether those deemed exceptional (like Bletchley's code-breakers) or more mundane (shopworkers, nurses and secretaries).[1] Marketing and promotions employ similar tactics: America's PBS website features an interview with a history professor at George Mason University who testifies to *Call the Midwife*'s accuracy ('Real Life History of *Call the Midwife*', n.d.), while Bletchley Park's website featured images from *The Bletchley Circle*. Self-consciously positioning themselves against prevalent conceptions of the past that typically occlude female participation in the workplace prior to (at least) the 1960s, the popular period dramas I discuss here position their interventions as significant even as they hone an ultimately well-established path of rediscovering (working) women's past. Real historical events (like the sinking of the *Titanic*, World War I, the Suez crisis, the assassinations of John F. Kennedy and Martin Luther King) and these series' own much-touted visual authenticity, their attention to details of clothing, sets, design, etiquette and each period's signature representational practices, further validate these representations of working women, embedding them in the popular historical record.

In the process, these shows position femininity as particularly dependent on history and time, helping account for its myriad variations. Unlike masculinity, which is conventionally seen in terms of an illusory (and false) stability, the feminine is upheld as historically variable and contingent, making period drama a rich site for exploring popular understandings of womanhood while effectively parsing its relationship to the present. Similar ideas saturate much feminine popular culture, including magazines, popular fiction and fashion, inviting women audiences to reflect on their position as profoundly historical subjects, even if this historicity depends more on variations in work experience and appearance. Lynn Spigel's discussion of *Mad Men* and other related programmes such as *Pan Am* (ABC, 2011–12) and *The Playboy Club* (NBC, 2011) highlights this particular contemporary feminine sensibility, one that is forward-looking but dependent on history. These series imagine 'a future where feminism never happened, but where somehow miraculously, without political struggle, everyone gets a great job, great clothes and great mixed drinks' (Spigel, 2013: 275). In recognising contemporary women's desire for a past that 'validates the present by giving postfeminism a heritage', she speaks to femininity's peculiar need for history, here its desire to revise the past to license both the present and hopes for the future (ibid.: 273). While presenting historical women who already aspired 'to be postfeminists, independent, career-focused, yet hyperbolically "feminine" in their embrace of fashion, shopping and dating', *Mad Men*'s otherwise meticulously reconstructed past erases feminism, omitting a history that facilitated the professional lives of both its characters and the female audience (ibid.: 272–3). Arguably the British shows discussed below are more cognisant of feminism, possibly because they are more willing to deal with issues of struggle rather than utopian possibility. Still, they often gesture to feminism with a revelatory flourish, suggesting its history – like that of working women themselves – is less well known. *Downton*'s Sybil and Edith both engage with first-wave feminism, educating audiences about its goals, while *The Bletchley Circle* shows how the absence of a postwar feminism, even one that is largely compatible with femininity, silences these women and removes them from the workplace and from history itself.

As such, amnesia pervades popular histories of working women, whose pre-1970s forebears are typically presented as unusual pioneers or novelties. Although the working woman is widely seen as a recent phenomenon, making her an avatar of modernity, women have always worked, even during periods of backlash like the Depression, the late 1940s and the 1950s. The removal of women from the workplace in the immediate postwar years has denaturalised working women, recasting them as inherently political – an often inaccurate generalisation. Correspondingly, popular histories largely position the workplace as entirely male until the 1960s, 1970s or even 1980s, despite the reinvention of the secretary as a preeminently female job during the late nineteenth century.[2] Lost, then, is the nineteenth-century legacy of female professionalism, administrative, factory and retail work, the increased female college enrolments of the 1910s and 1920s and working-class and single women's unbroken history of labour. From the late nineteenth century, urbanisation, consumerism and industrialisation opened up a range of occupations for women. New careers as shop assistants, typists, secretaries, factory workers, telegraph and telephone operators complemented established positions in service, childcare, nursing and education. High-profile female professionals like the young American lawyer Inez Milholland Boissevain (1886–1916); the first British female MP to take her seat, American Lady Nancy Astor (1919); and screen, stage and print celebrities captured the public imagination during the 1910s, glamorising work and linking it to greater self-actualisation. A better understanding of this history might help us disarticulate and complicate the relationships between feminism and working women. Work may have helped open up the public sphere, but it was often not on feminine terms – plenty of women were aware of distinctions between necessary drudgery and self-fulfilment. More varied representations of work would perhaps resonate with contemporary female audiences for whom work is a necessity, not a choice, and thus not a political act (Moseley and Read, 2002: 247).

Based on Jennifer Worth's bestselling memoirs – books heralded for their authenticity, realism and historical accuracy – *Call the Midwife*'s style and address exemplify a feminine historiography centred on revelation and recurrent amnesia. Particularly conscious of its historical narration, *Call the Midwife* alternately presents a sometimes dreamlike, lost past and uses its more authentic details to assert its distance from the present. While the show's opening credits vary, they typically feature black-and-white images of handwriting, signifying its written origins and relationship to a lost past. Several episodes, including the pilot, use black-and-white photos to establish a historical gap that is compounded by the clearly reconstructed Poplar streets and docks, which are sometimes shrouded in a dreamlike mist. Here the past is alternately presented in terms of nostalgia and stylisation, suggesting that the show performs history rather than reconstructing it. Vanessa Redgrave's voice-over as the older Jenny Lee compounds this sense as it echoes her work in Joe Wright's *Atonement* (2007), another text that self-consciously deals with history, memory and women's work. *Call the Midwife*'s forgotten world becomes animated via recollections, recasting difference along axes of class, work/motherhood, paid and unpaid labour. The series' first words – from the older Jenny Lee – highlight the importance of women's work, ambitions and professional choices in this unlikely time and setting. She recalls: 'I could have been an air hostess, a model, concert pianist, seen the world, followed my heart', establishing this young, attractive, upper middle-class woman's privilege via her investment in work. While her words link other occupations to glamour and mobility, her profession takes her to an unfamiliar but hardly alluring locale. The topic of working women in this historical period is ultimately introduced as both central and as something of a revelation – we do not expect work to define such a woman nor to find her in this place or time, nor are we aware of the skills and knowledge her work demands.

Amnesia and revelation: television and the history of working women

Despite lacking historical rigour, popular beliefs about women's entry into and acceptance in the workforce have social and cultural effects, shaping public understanding of work's value and perceptions about female autonomy. Notably self-conscious about their historical interventions, these contemporary television dramas point to continuities across change, asserting visions of capable, progressive femininity, even though these may be more ambivalent than they first appear. Highlighting the forgotten, the unpredictable and the unexpected – particularly in terms of women's lives – they gesture to limitations in contemporary understandings of the past.

Historical TV dramas typically have a greater impact on public understandings of the past than books, costume movies and non-fictional television because they are more widely seen, often more emotionally engaging and accessible and of longer duration, prolonging public interest and debate (Landsberg, 2015: 61–110). Their structurally complex but easily understood multi-perspectival realist and verisimilar narratives foster identification, helping bridge past and present, while their visual details both foreground historical gaps and attract female viewers by evoking their presumed competence in emotion, understanding of fashion and overall visual literacy. This strategy has migrated to daytime, with dramas like *Land Girls* (BBC1, 2009–11) focusing on a group of women in the Women's Land Army during World War II. The first period drama on BBC daytime television, *Land Girls* testifies to broadcasters' shifting conceptions of their female audience, even in time slots catering to traditional homemakers. This commission recognised women's interest in work, history, the politics of race and class – even as they were domesticated within costume drama's more conventional investments in romance, family, friends and interactions with the aristocracy. Part of the public commemoration of the seventieth anniversary of the start of the war, *Land Girls* presented women as central historical agents, despite its much criticised historical inaccuracies that offended surviving WWII veterans, including members of the WLA. Its teatime slot and 'two dimensional' and clichéd narrative (Khan, 2009; Viner, 2009) arguably limited its status as popular history even though it remained successful, drawing nearly two million viewers each week, many of them young women. One blogger, Miss Rosie

Beau (2012a), a self-described 'lover of vintage living', raved about the programme, her comments indicating that vivid historicity did not always require accuracy. She enthused: 'I actually feel this may be what it would have been like as a Land Girl. I love the scenery and costume too, oh of course the costume!'. After acknowledging the 'real trials' the girls face in their work and pointing to their 'juicy relationships', Beau posted her own version of a Land Girl's outfit, complete with loafers recently purchased from Tesco.[3] Her reflections suggest that female audiences might read these dramas much like traditional daytime staples, as inspirations for makeovers and spectacles of romantic dysfunction and excess. History remains the central attraction for these audiences, animating and reviving feminine possibilities whether real or imaginary, as seen in the vintage community's own progressive and quasi-feminist reworking of the past.

Unlike film, whose fascination with the exceptional extends to working women, television presents itself as more typical, more mundane and more accessible. Its contributions to myths about women's absence from the workforce are thus doubly significant. Television participates in this historiography of revelation and amnesia via the medium's treatment of working women. American TV has even reshaped its own history along these lines. It has, for example, become a truism that *The Mary Tyler Moore Show* (CBS, 1970–7) was the first American programme focused on a working woman, despite earlier hits such as *Our Miss Brooks* (CBS, 1948–58), *Private Secretary* (CBS, 1953–7), *Julia* (NBC, 1968–71) and *That Girl* (ABC, 1966–71). Although outnumbered by domestic dramas, these sitcoms presented working women as both a social reality, if not the dominant one, and a source of identification/aspiration. Similar figures lurked in the background of television shows – the husband's secretary, the daughter's teacher, sales assistants at department stores as well as maids, cooks, shopkeepers and other sundry workers. While these dramas are not historical, they constitute an archive that can be used to counter historical myths about women's absence from the workforce.

Despite not receiving the same degree of attention, British television likewise featured women working, whether in women's magazines (*Compact*, BBC1, 1962–5), in factories (*The Rag Trade*, BBC, 1961–3, LWT/ITV, 1977–8), as typists (*The Bed-Sit Girl*, BBC1, 1965–6), as detectives (*The Avengers*, ABC/ITV, 1961–9) or in the sundry working- and middle-class jobs featured in anthology dramas like *The Wednesday Play* (BBC1, 1964–71).[4] Here work was often collapsed into questions of class, shattering gender ideals and establishing a work–class relationship that continues in the British series discussed in this chapter. These programmes in turn complicate generalisations about work, agency and emancipation, problematising relationships between feminism and women's work. In a screen landscape where lowly forms of labour like cleaning, factory work, tending a corner shop or working in a local pub were commonplace, not all employment could be enlisted into utopian narratives of aspiration or histories of women's choice. The need and desire to work are often separated – roughly speaking, the working-class women in British shows like *The Rag Trade* have little say in the matter, with their jobs offering little self-actualisation. On the other hand, more elite women's professional activities are often recast as adventures, forays into public life or a search for pleasure, with fashionable young protagonists performing activities that might be considered work – espionage, crime-fighting – sometimes without pay or any formal employment. This archetype, seen in shows like *The Avengers*, resists most formal designations of work, linking privileged women's activity to self-fulfilment.

In associating work with feminine fulfilment and agency, the period dramas analysed here all nod to some kind of feminism, although this relationship is often ambivalent, with consequences for their attendant historiographies and visions of the past. Some programmes, such as *Mad Men, The Hour, Masters of Sex* (Showtime, 2013–) and *The Bletchley Circle*, sympathise with a broadly defined feminist project as they explore women's efforts to achieve professional status and secure respect in less 'enlightened' times. *Call the Midwife* draws on a more radical nostalgia for the newly created welfare state even as it explores how class, domesticity and their own anatomy limited women during the early postwar years. Others, like the short-lived *Pan Am*, are more accepting of their period's values, positioning work as part of a utopian female fantasy of style, independence, play and mobility while pointing to the era's glamour and potential for fun (*Mad Men* addresses the seductive ambivalence of these very characteristics). Markedly more conservative, *Downton Abbey* romanticises cross-class relations and domestic work. It uses working women to render the past benign, obviating the need for feminism while depicting figures like Mary (Michelle Dockery), Edith (Laura Carmichael), Sybil (Jessica Brown Findlay), Gwen (Rose Leslie) and even Daisy (Sophie McShera) in these very terms. In negating or dis-avowing fundamental struggles, these more conservative shows evoke postfemin-ism's more benign patriarchy, one linked to beliefs that second-wave feminists helped create an unnecessary gender war.

While some programmes, such as *Downton Abbey* and *Pan Am*, present women's work as the result of unbroken historical progress, others, such as *Mad Men* and *The Bletchley Circle*, foreground discontinuities, suggesting a less utopian process invol-ving cycles of return, stasis and retreat. *The Bletchley Circle* is most explicit here, with its first episode establishing a wartime workplace filled with highly intelligent, skilled female code-breakers before cutting to 1952 where these women are alternately mired in domesticity or working in thankless jobs (waitress, librarian). Reuniting to solve a complex series of murders, its four protagonists face unsupportive husbands and hostile authorities, even though they alone perceive and decode patterns that uncover the killer. *Bletchley* highlights women's tenuous place in the workforce – this world would rather see a serial killer escape justice than listen to women. The friends' differences – Susan's (Anna Maxwell Martin) quiet strength and uncanny ability to perceive and decode patterns, Millie's (Rachael Stirling) defiant glamour, working-class Lucy's (Sophie Rundle) gift for recall and Jean's (Julie Graham) severe book-ishness – uphold variations in female intelligence and demonstrate the costs of these women's removal from the workplace, both for these individuals and for society more generally. By pointing to women's contingent and tenuous position in the labour market, *Bletchley* refutes simple narratives of historical progress, a position with implications for contemporary and future womanhood.

Work, class and social mobility

While not a typical working-women show, *Downton Abbey* is important because most of its female protagonists work, establishing relationships between women's work, class and social (im)mobility. Besides framing domestic service as (somewhat romanticised) work rather than the inevitable destination for underprivileged women, *Downton* addresses women's employment in fields rooted in a variety of feminine skills – social work, secretarial work, nursing and even writing – while raising the spectre of female ambition. In season 1, for instance, housemaid Gwen secretly trains as a secretary, a choice supported by Bates (Brendan Coyle), Anna (Joanne Froggatt) and future radical Lady Sybil, but not the other servants. In the 2011 Christmas special, Daisy is told she has the skills to be a sous chef at a top London restaurant or a cook at a large house, awaking ambition and developing her self-confidence. Similarly ambitious, the cook Mrs Patmore (Leslie Nichol) downplays the maid's ability, taking the credit for training her and testifying to the competition among the servant class. Daisy stays at Downton and ultimately becomes assistant cook just as she is offered the chance to run her late husband's family farm. *Downton*'s women are typically more ambitious than the men, even the servants, with only Thomas (Rob James-Collier) – tellingly, a closeted gay man – rivalling his female counterparts' drive.

Downton consistently presents women's approach to work as more up-to-date than that of upper-class men, although its working women are not avatars of modernity – that would be cousin Rose (Lily James), a flapper-type figure who ultimately follows a more conservative trajectory as a young bride and mother. Although Mary and Matthew's (Dan Stevens) progressive strategies save the estate, Robert, the Earl of Grantham (Hugh Bonneville), is angered by this usurpation of his power. After working on a farm during World War I, then as a convalescent nurse, Lady Edith writes to *The Times* about diminished options for full female suffrage (outraging her father). Her letter is published and leads to a post as columnist for the *Daily Sketch*. Lady Sybil qualifies as a nurse while her big sister, Mary, tends to patients when Downton houses convalescing soldiers in the war's final months (like Edith, she is untrained). Here and elsewhere, women's desire to work allies them to the most successful professionals, the middle class (Matthew Crawley, Michael Gregson [Charles Edwards]), creating a series of associations between femininity, work, modernity and social mobility. Two ideological tendencies emerge here: a self-consciously modern one where work makes upward mobility possible for servants (like Anna, Daisy and Gwen) and a more conservative version where work dismantles aristocratic women's social standing, seen in Lady Sybil and Lady Edith's experiences as nurse and journalist. These professions bring these women into contact with the unglamorous side of life – injuries, infections, bodily fluids in the one case, and the underbelly of urban life and its sordid politics for the other. Work also inadvertently imperils them: her stint in journalism, itself a response to the trauma of being left at the altar, leads Edith into another ill-fated romance that results in extra-marital pregnancy. Sybil's training as a nurse furthers her radical sympathies, giving her the courage to marry her true love, outspoken socialist and republican Tom Branson (Allen Leech), the family's Irish chauffeur. While both women's professional lives are linked to their battles for independence and express their strong will, their fates are couched in terms of tragedy and melodrama respectively – death shortly after childbirth (Sybil) and forced renunciation of one's child (Edith). Meanwhile, Branson's unlikely rise into the Crawley family presents romance, not work, as a more accepted form of upward mobility (significantly and ironically, Branson is opposed to class privilege). But this counter-narrative is highly gendered and less available to women. Ethel (Amy Nut-tall), the ambitious servant who preferred reading about Hollywood to domestic work, is a more cautionary feminine equivalent. She becomes pregnant as a result of an affair with Major Charles Bryant (Daniel Pirrie), who dies in World War I. Destitute after her dismissal from Downton, she approaches Bryant's family for help. They are prepared to take her son, but only if she renounces all contact. She ultimately takes her child back, forsaking his inheritance and her dreams of upward mobility for motherhood.

Downton effectively creates a genealogy of female work which it in turn associates with a somewhat bourgeois way of life, anchored through Matthew's more (upper) middle-class mother, Isobel Crawley (Penelope Wilton), formerly a nurse and then a quasi-social worker tending to fallen women. As with *Call the Midwife*, nursing evokes an under-acknowledged history of working women and signifies the fudging and potential erasure of female professionalism, with unqualified attendants given the same title despite lacking the necessary training, knowledge and expertise. Something similar happens with social work, with untrained upper-class women adopting the term to justify their interventions into lower-class life. Like secretarial work, dom-estic service and some forms of teaching, nursing exemplifies widespread under-standing of women's work as sometimes necessary but often overlooked under the banner of care, embodying a history that voids or minimises the contribution of professional women. Possibly the ultimate 'gendered profession', nursing epitomises how women's work is often devalued, cast aside, sexualised or sentimentalised, as Julia Hallam has shown, with mass media participating in these misconceptions that lead to diminution of its status (Hallam, 2000: 7, 11, 20).

In *Call the Midwife*, nursing exposes women to other classes, something seen in the women's own varied backgrounds and through their encounters with Poplar's largely working-class (and sometimes destitute) women. Nursing *may* lead to social mobility, but, as with the Crawley sisters' professional ventures in *Downton Abbey*, it often diminishes women's status: Jenny Lee (Jessica Raine) is introduced as working below her class (and her looks), as is the aristocratic (but unglamorous) Chummy (Miranda Hart), whose marriage to a working-class police constable, Peter Noakes (Ben Caplan), consolidates her new middle-class rank. While her mother, Lady Cholmondeley-Browne (Cheryl Campbell), despises both her choice of career and husband, Chummy's happiness is enhanced by the birth of her baby son, although we see little of her new life on-screen.[5] Nursing, and by extension the other pro-fessions, are shown as having the power to obscure social backgrounds, something that can either be potentially empowering or dangerous. Season 4's Nurse Phyllis Crane (Linda Bassett) is one of several midwives whose background is not as it first appears – her outspoken modern views, her new car and her seemingly snobbish approach mask her background as an illegitimate child.

Work, glamour and visibility

Popular culture usually presents working women in terms of their visibility, used by women's forms and genres to establish their agency and subjectivity following modernity/postmodernity's preeminently visual logic (Conor, 2004: 16–35). This visibility associates women's work with glamour, a trait not linked to male labour. While these images may attract female audiences and capitalise on women's putative visual literacy – especially when it comes to understanding and judging female appearances – they potentially contribute to cultural amnesia around working women by diverting attention away from their labour and professionalism. Dialectics of visibility and invisibility consequently mark both historiographic and representational practices, as seen in the strategies of revelation discussed above. Independent working girls are widely seen as creations of the 1960s–70s, particularly in their glamorous incarnation, which is often linked to Helen Gurley Brown's 1962's *Sex and the Single Girl* and its sequel, *Sex and the Office* (1965), masking a much longer history (Enstad, 1999: 1–47; Radner, 1999: 4–20). Indeed, the working woman defines much women's media from the late nineteenth century, appearing in dime novels and silent and classical Hollywood women's pictures, as well as shaping discourses on film stardom (Bean, 2002; Enstad, 1999: 48–83; Hallett, 2013: 3–26, 69–102). Women's magazines, including film- and television-related titles, further developed associations between glamour, agency and women's work, both in terms of putatively ordinary young women's experiences as well as through the figure of the star as female worker.

This fusion of work, glamour and feminine progress has historically attracted women audiences. It defines the pre-1960s American working women's magazines which focused on fashion, work, narratives of upward mobility, women's fiction, Hollywood stars, domestic tips and childcare. Many of these forgotten titles predate Gurley Brown's rise to prominence. One early antecedent, *Excella* (1924–6?), alternately bore the tag lines 'Stories from Real Life' and 'A Magazine of Fashion, Fictions and Housekeeping', perhaps indicating its efforts to balance the glamorous with the mundane. Spun off from Excella Patterns (later taken over by Simplicity), each issue featured a free pattern as well as a reproduction of a work of art, gifts that attest to the magazine's concurrent domestic address as well as its emphasis on self-improvement. Features included 'Personal Stories of Successful Women', 'Doris Kenyon's Fashion Talk' (September 1925) and 'How I Learned the Rigid Rules of New York Society' (March 1925). Further testifying to feminine ambitions and desire for visibility, the magazine launched a star-search contest in 1925 in conjunction with Famous Players-Lasky, tantalising readers with the promise of the ultimate glamorous job (advertisement, *Photoplay*, July 1925: 13).

The first American magazine explicitly devoted to working women, Condé Nast's *Charm*, emerged out of the ashes of *Picture Play* in 1941, finally merging into *Glamour* in 1959. Created by three women – Estelle Rubenstein, Helen Valentine and Cipe Pineles – it was aimed at the 'increasing numbers of women entering the workforce' not catered to by any other publication.[6] Its high-fashion covers prominently featured the tag line 'The Magazine for Women who Work'. *Charm* is important for several reasons: it has disappeared from the historical record, more so than its contemporary, *Mademoiselle*, repositioning *Cosmopolitan* and thus the early 1960s as *the* period when ordinary (young) women appeared in the workplace and availed themselves of its glamour. It is ripe for recovery as another document testifying both to pioneering glamorous female professionals and to that legacy of an unknown female workforce whose existence can now be revealed to a more sympathetic (postfeminist?) world. Several blogs have commented on the surprising presence of ambitious, glamorous women that this publication seemingly evidences, significantly linking them to figures like Peggy from *Mad Men*.[7] These bloggers generally see these attractive images as self-evident proof that such women existed, rather than considering these representations' more complex relationship to reality. As utopian images, they likely shaped some period conceptions about successful womanhood, affecting female aspirations and self-judgment, rather than mirroring an unmediated historical reality. Blogger Amy Albert Bloom of the World of Undine (2011) employs what has become a standard rhetoric of revelation when discussing this kind of material, writing that

> This magazine find was a wonderful surprise . . . the [January 1956] issue devotes an amazing amount of space, for a fashion-oriented pictorial, to a celebration of improvements in the working world for women [including] 'Women at Work', a mini-history of work for women in America.[8]

Unlike *Ms* or *Spare Rib*, *Charm* showcased the glamour, spectacle and pleasures of femininity, presenting images of working women very much in sympathy with more contemporary youthful feminine ideals while challenging prevailing concepts of the recent past. These images signify something to contemporary audiences – even if it is only the traces of a much longed-for, more progressive, professional feminine past. The popularity of *Charm* covers on Pinterest (itself a feminised digital archive) speaks to this yearning for a sense of commonality with the past, presenting a utopian vision of the 1940s and 1950s where strong, glamorous working women flourished and did not have to choose between femininity and ambition, a history that is then used to bolster, justify and support the present. The contemporary recirculation of these covers recalls Spigel's argument, positioning *Charm* as another 'teleology for postfeminism' that 'portrays postfeminism as a form of inevitable progress: a female future perfect circa 1962' (Spigel, 2013: 273). The magazine's rediscovery again promises a form of feminine success that reconciles contradictions inherent in both work and femininity, suggesting answers lie in a seductive past that is now ready for rediscovery.

Television's historical dramas also link glamour to working women's past, most notably in *Mad Men* and department store dramas like *Mr Selfridge* and *The Paradise*.

Mad Men's Joan (Christina Hendricks) flirts with and distracts male coworkers on her route to social and professional progress, while Peggy (Elisabeth Moss) crafts persuasive and surprising advertisements but generally refuses to apply these talents to her own image. These two figures point to a dichotomy that structures many popular representations of working women – as visible, decorative, potentially powerful and distracting or as invisible, ignored, insignificant or strategically working for power by downplaying their gender. *Mad Men* is not alone in teasing out this duality, or in making it so central to its representation of working women. In the first episode Joan tells Peggy how to maximise her looks (as the camerawork and narrative highlight both women's visibility), advice that the young secretary fails to follow. She opts instead for tactical invisibility, rejecting the preeminent male gaze and refusing to conform to its power (allowing her to hide her pregnancy and maintain her job and status during season 1). Peggy's occasional efforts to stand out are designed to prevent her potential exclusion from key business decisions conducted outside the office. Most notably in season 2, episode 6 ('Maidenform'), she dresses up in a stunning (and out-of-character) low-cut teal dress to join the men and their lingerie client in a strip club after work in order to participate in the decision-making process, even subjecting herself to their flirtations. The scene is decidedly ambiguous – Peggy successfully performs as a different kind of woman, which her colleagues enjoy (she may even be having fun). It is not, however, a strategy she repeats, particularly as she gains more authority. While Joan uses her body/appearance to signify her power and to achieve greater executive and managerial goals, her greatest advance into the realm of partner involves effectively prostituting herself for Sterling Cooper Draper Pryce, the advertising agency. After this promotion, she does not change her mode of dress or self-presentation but annexes her glamour to her professional ambitions, signified via her removal of her trademark pen pendant that linked her to the secretarial realm. *Mad Men*'s commentary on professional women's visibility and their use of glamour is not straightforward – especially given its knowing references to the period's sexual mores, where many such gestures can be recuperated in terms of male pleasure and the male gaze. This glamour is, however, generally divorced from the conspicuous consumption that usually surrounds portrayals of working women's investment in self. Ironically for a show dealing with advertising and consumption, neither Peggy nor Joan work to shop, nor are they overly invested in fashion – characteristics that allow *Mad Men* to position glamour and self-presentation not in terms of pleasure but primarily in terms of agency and as a route to workplace power, whether through heightened visibility or tactical invisibility. Such glamour may empower and possibly resonate with aspects of lived experience, but it is not available to all women at all times. The more functional woman may not have chosen her status, nor the invisibility that potentially limits her agency in a preeminently visual world – the older nuns in *Call the Midwife*, for instance, or the older members of *Downton Abbey*'s staff, are shown as often indistinguishable and have few options to change their status.

Call the Midwife further addresses the tensions surrounding the decorative function of female workers, most notably through its reference to the lavender puffed-sleeve Norman Hartnell uniforms seen in season 2, with their huge sleeves, crisp white aprons, starched white collars and lacy caps, worn when Jenny is seconded to the London hospital. As women audiences well know, fashion and glamour are not simple matters, particularly in this context – the Hartnell uniforms gesture to a whole history of nurses' caps, belts, buckles and dresses that tried to mask contradictions between the decorative and the functional that are central to the profession's history and have further ramifications for all working women's attire. As Hallam points out, nursing's early image, with its connotations of purity, drew on the 'power of white femininity . . . used by Nightingale in her attempts to persuade the male-dominated Victorian public sphere to support her programme of reform', an image underscored in the whiteness of aprons, collars and cuffs (Hallam, 2000: 20). Despite obstructing the wearer's movement and vision, Hartnell's uniform challenges, but does not compromise, Jenny's efficiency, even as she complains about the size of its sleeves and the limiting structure of its collar. Its very glamour – she is told it is 'practically couture' – effectively places its wearer in *conflict* with a workplace defined by its proximity to disease, injury and bodily discharge, but the nurses here overcome these challenges, testifying to their professionalism while maintaining a certain glamour (in an unrealistic move, we never see a dirty nurse's uniform). Their skills undermine efforts to cast these women as purely decorative, positioning their uniforms as superficial, unnecessary and imposed upon them by others (Norman Hartnell, hospital management – largely masculine forces). Jenny is not like some of the women Hallam discusses, who welcome a smart uniform as a way to be fashionable in a world where clothing is rationed and expensive (Hallam, 2000: 134–5). She can afford to dress well and can thus choose fashion on her own terms, as well as selecting the space where she elects to display herself. In putting Jenny in an impractical outfit and increasing her contact with male doctors, the London hospital puts her into a setting that the series associates with sexual harassment and nurses' diminished control over their work.

The difference between Joan and Jenny's decorative functions is telling – the former signifies a feminine perspective where women initiate and inhabit glamour to advance professional and social standing; the latter confronts more traditional understandings of objectification and the male gaze. Women may have used dress to fit into the workplace – or been advised to do so – but fashion's very status as a feminine competence linked to masquerade, identity and self-creation demonstrates its potential to undermine singular, fixed professional roles, as seen in *Mad Men*, where women use dress to create new incarnations of self – Peggy the coquette at the strip club; Betty (January Jones) the *soignée* Italian tourist; Megan (Jessica Paré) the ever-changing actress. These costume dramas play to feminine knowledge of fashion's capacity to potentially undercut or circumvent patriarchal and workplace strictures – all in full view of presumably oblivious male coworkers and audiences. Joan uses fashion in this way, communicating messages that only fashion-literate and presumptively female (or gay male) audiences are likely to pick up: wearing purple, for instance, when she is feeling vulnerable or secretly dating office coworkers.[9] Besides embodying aspirations of feminine power and literacy, fashion acquires a greater visibility as women enter professional life – not least through the very publications and mass media addressing this new target audience. Effectively a historical discourse primarily available to female audiences, fashion contributes to these shows' popularity and their economic success (both *Mad Men* and *Downton Abbey* have had their own clothing and accessory lines).[10]

The Bletchley Circle offers a particularly complex meditation on women's work, glamour and decoration. From the very start, its women are linked to intricate and elaborate patterns – both through the clothing they wear as 1940s code-breakers and via their ability to decode difficult messages. This latter quality is upheld as almost entirely feminine – women dominate at Bletchley and the four protagonists employ these same skills postwar to solve elaborate crimes that confound the (male) police. While not identical, patterns and glamour are linked as particularly feminine visual forms, affiliated to women's professional competence but also inherently ambiguous. The complex patterns *Bletchley*'s women study mask dangers – to nation (in the case of war) and to women (in terms of peacetime crime) – while glamour likewise both empowers and endangers the show's professional women. In particular, the serial killer's crimes highlight this ambivalence as victims are seemingly lured to their deaths via the promise of hard-to-find perfumes and cosmetics (both heavily rationed postwar). In an image that shockingly underscores glamour's complex associations with both female agency and women's objectification, police officers find a pin-up poster at a presumptive crime scene and laugh, signifying their reductive view of female sexuality and aligning them against victims of sexually oriented crimes. This find further endangers women as it prematurely ends their official search, allowing the killer to murder his young, pretty captive. To bait the suspect, who appears to be using black-market cosmetics and accessories to lure young working women, Millie makes over the youngest member of the group, Lucy, using make-up and clothing acquired with difficulty and through subterfuge. A more feminine power is, however, evidenced in Millie's later use of a lipstick to map out the train line where the killer worked – a gesture that highlights glamour as a form of feminine communication, affiliated with careful perception and deduction. This lipstick becomes Millie's signature, embodying a feminine mode of analysis marked by acute perception. Similar evocations of feminine literacy occur later in the series when the girls refer to knitting and cake-baking as skills, like code-breaking, that need practice to work – directly leading them to the recognition that the patterns they have traced were effectively distractions, patterns within a pattern that signified earlier killings. The murders they investigate are effectively decoys, extraneous decorations designed to lead investigators elsewhere, fabricating the past while masquerading as truth. These serial killings and the women's investigation further highlight struggles over glamour, juxtaposing prurient masculine gazes and danger with feminine empowerment, detection, professionalism and the right to self-presentation. Furthermore, the women's ability to navigate the killer's traps and expose his use of decorative patterns posits another kind of feminine historiography – pointing to battles over the interpretation and use of the past.

Beyond sacrifice

Despite work's undeniably privileged position in both feminist and postfeminist discourses of equality, without private and/or self-oriented pleasures it becomes mere drudgery (Enstad, 1999: 19–20, 73–4). Couched in often sacrificial terms, women's work may even verge on the monastic, as seen in *Call the Midwife*'s setting, Nonnatus House, a convent where the midwives live, some of them ordained nuns. Even when women are passionate about their jobs – as evidenced in the flashbacks to Bletchley's code-breaking or during the heights of Peggy and Joan's ambition and success – representations of a life defined largely through work often approximate the self-sacrifice associated with maternal melodrama. *Mad Men*'s women find marriage and work hard to reconcile, often sacrificing one for the other, and typically have limited social lives. Despite her Vassar education, Betty does not work after marriage, while Joan divorces her weak and abusive husband, returning to work and putting her career ahead of motherhood. Joan is unhappy when she leaves Sterling Cooper Draper Pryce after her marriage – and her ambition is one factor in the marriage's demise (viewers realise it is a bad move and that she belongs in the workplace). Although the younger Peggy wants it all, she prioritises her career, experiencing a series of breakups, flings and loneliness along the way: after the failure of one romance, she follows her mother's advice and buys a cat, seemingly accepting the costs of a career – romance and children (she gives her son up for adoption at birth). She is finally gifted with a utopian resolution – a workplace romance with Stan (Jay R. Ferguson), with love fittingly presented in the form of professional devotion. Megan's ambitions help destroy her marriage to Don (Jon Hamm), which falters after she returns to acting, leaving behind the copywriting job he secured for her. Her brief career success corresponds with a diminution in his affections, a situation symbolised in her miscarrying their child, a pregnancy she was unsure she wanted until it was over. Even in *Downton Abbey*'s highly romanticised world, being a servant curtails life choices. 'Normal' marriage is difficult, illustrated by Anna and Bates' struggle for domestic stability and Daisy and William's (Thomas Howes) failed union; families are seen infrequently, and motherhood is almost impossible. As these examples attest, the self-sacrificial mode often mitigates working women's agency and self-fulfilment, with presentations of a solely career-oriented womanhood skirting close to servitude or infantilisation, seen in the way Bletchley's women live together like schoolgirls in a dormitory. Here work is linked to regression and the evasion of maturity, something that positions it as predominantly a liminal stage in women's lives, but one, like youth, that is highly valued in fantasies of ideal modern femininity.

Conclusion

Although these working-women narratives have an unquestionable feminist charge, they are not without a certain ambivalence. Women's professional successes validate their struggles to establish themselves as workers, as *Mad Men* and *The Bletchley Circle* evidence, and cement their value for employers, a message that is aimed as much at contemporary audiences and their neoliberal workplace. While representations emphasising work's associations with glamour may belie the reality of many mundane, poorly paid, low-prestige and boring jobs, they suggest a certain feminine agency, moving women beyond the domestic, albeit setting up horizons that are often too utopian. As Angela McRobbie has pointed out, women's 'wage earning capacity . . . functions symbolically as a mark of respectability, citizenship and entitlement', traits that often substitute for the kind of full social and political participation feminism might offer (McRobbie, 2008: 2). Glamorisation further diminishes or masks labour's discipline, drudgery, exploitation and submission to authority and its temporary renunciation of self, creating a discourse that potentially lures women into employment that is often not well paid, not satisfying and sometimes exploitative.[11]

Questions about women's work and agency are relevant in a postfeminist, neoliberal society that stresses the importance of a flexible workforce – arguably feminising employment, albeit at the expense of the worker's own agency, stability and pleasure (McRobbie, 2008: 56, 125, 168; Hearn, 2008: 495–504). Produced and consumed in a contemporary social and political context that resituates women's relationship to work, these programmes' efforts to open up working women's hidden past can arguably be used for more conservative ends, even as they authenticate and legitimate women's place in the workforce. Elsewhere, Helen Wheatley has shown how popular costume dramas work through contemporary women's issues, countering the thesis that these programmes merely salve uncertainty in times of transition by looking back at a more 'settled' past (Wheatley, 2005: 149–50). Like her example, *Upstairs Downstairs* (LWT/ITV, 1971–5) and its mediations of second-wave feminism, the series under consideration here participate in 'a kind of public thinking' about women's work, its benefits, its costs and its links to popular feminine fantasies about self-realisation (ibid.: 149). For more than two decades, both American and British governments have curtailed welfare payments for single and stay-at-home mothers, disincentivising those who stay at home, even as salaries and working conditions stagnate/decline and good jobs become harder to find. Although these period dramas help naturalise working women by recovering seemingly lost histories of women's work, we might still ask: who benefits from their labour? Such questions are difficult to answer but important to parse, especially given postfeminist tendencies to emphasise progress and to laud developments/texts/popular discourses that point to an already achieved equality.

Notes

1 *Shopgirls* was hosted by Pamela Cox, a social historian at the University of Essex. Cox co-wrote the tie-in book, *Shopgirls: The True History of Life Behind the Counter* (2015), with TV producer, Annabel Hobley. Cox is just one of the younger, telegenic academics used to host historical documentaries and lifestyle programmes on British TV, including Kate Williams of Royal Holloway and Oxford's Janina Ramirez. This trend even caught the *Daily Mail*'s attention: see Hilton, 2013.

2 Most popular origin stories (emanating from popular culture rather than academic history) date women's emergence as workers from the 1960s–80s, with full acceptance, including the ability to balance professional and domestic life, coming later (the 1970s, 1980s or even

1990s – again, this timeline keeps shifting to later decades). This revisionary history rearticulates earlier periods of female emancipation, largely erasing women's work – the 1920s flapper, for example, is largely perceived in terms of leisure, mobility and limited sexual autonomy.

3 *Land Girls* producer Roland Moore commented twice on this blog entry, appreciating her comments and agreeing to an interview, which was posted on 19 June (Beau, 2012b). Here he discussed production and preproduction, primarily emphasising the historical research involved (reading academic histories and interviewing surviving Land Girls), noting that he had to take dramatic licence (the girls worked 12–14-hour days, making for dull TV, and there was a need to conform to viewers' perception of a period rather than its reality). Moore reinforces themes found throughout these historical working women dramas, noting 'I wanted to write a drama about the Land Girls because it was a time of change for so many women . . . I was really interested in the themes of independence and empowerment and these friendships forged through adversity'.

4 See Vicky Ball's chapter in this volume.

5 Much of their life together occurs off-screen (Chummy conducts missionary work in Africa) due to Miranda Hart's other television commitments.

6 See Theresa from Blue Velvet Vintage (2010)'s 'Flashback: *Charm* Magazine', April 1947, published on the website *Jezebel*. See also Robert Newman (2014), '*Charm*: "The Magazine for Women who Work"'.

7 See 'This Vintage Beauty Magazine was Made for Peggy' (Rennells, 2014), and World of Undine, 'Charm Magazine: A Sassy Suffragette's Style File' (NeverIsSacred, 2011).

8 See World of Undine (2011).

9 See Tom and Lorenzo (2010, 2013) 'Mad Style', particularly S3, part 2; 'Mad Style: The Better Half', www.tomandlorenzo.com/2010/07/mad-style-joan-holloway-s3-part-2-2.html; www.tomandlorenzo.com/2013/05/mad-style-the-better-half.html.

10 *Mad Men* merchandise includes a range of Barbie dolls from 2010 (Joan, Betty, Don and Roger); Banana Republic offered three women's and men's collections, including clothing, jewellery, shoes and accessories (2011–13) as well as a record turntable, albums, cocktail shakers, flasks and glasses. Meanwhile *Downton Abbey* tie-ins include official mugs with vintage-style decoration, jewellery, ornaments, music CDs, fabric imprinted with Highclere Castle and the show's logo, Edwardian-style curtains and shower curtains, aprons, cookery books, tea towels, vintage-styled lamps, candles and character-themed teddy bears, Farrow and Ball paint and wallpapers and even specially rebranded boxes of Aunt Bessie's frozen Yorkshire puddings for the show's final season (autumn 2015) labelled as Mrs Patmore's Yorkshires. A clothing line announced in 2013 would not come to fruition, despite much internet enthusiasm for the idea.

11 Contemporary culture clearly recognises work's less attractive features, as seen in the emergence of a feminised celebrity culture that seeks the consumerist rewards of work and the public standing it might offer without engaging in either dull, time-consuming or unpleasant labour.

Bibliography

Bean, J. M. (2002) 'Technologies of Early Stardom and the Extraordinary Body', in J. M. Bean and D. Negra (eds) *A Feminist Reader in Early Cinema*, Durham: Duke University Press: 404–43.

Beau, R. (2012a) '*Land Girls* on BBC One'. http://everything-unfinished.blogspot.com/2012/03/land-girls-on-bbc-one.html. (Last accessed 2 February 2016).

Beau, R. (2012b) '*Land Girls* Interview'. http://everything-unfinished.blogspot.com/2012/06/land-girls-interview.html. (Last accessed 2 February 2016).

Conor, L. (2004) *The Spectacular Modern Woman: Feminine Visibility in the 1920s*, Bloomington: Indiana University Press.

Cox, P. and A. Hobley (2015) *The True History of Life Behind the Counter*, London: Penguin Random House.

Enstad, N. (1999) *Ladies of Labor, Girls of Adventure: Working Women, Popular Culture, and Labor Politics at the Turn of the Twentieth Century*, New York: Columbia University Press.

Gurley Brown, H. (1962) *Sex and the Single Girl*, New Jersey: Barricade Books.

Hallam, J. (2000) *Nursing the Image: Media, Culture and Professional Identity*, London and New York: Routledge.

Hallett, H. (2013) *Go West, Young Woman! The Rise of Early Hollywood*, Berkeley: University of California Press.

Hearn, A. (2008) 'Insecure: Narratives and Economies of the Branded Self in Transformation Television', *Continuum: Journal of Media and Cultural Studies*, 22:4: 495–504.

Hilton, L. (2013) 'The History Girls: Meet the Women Building a Bright Future from the Past', *Mail Online*, 3 November. www.dailymail.co.uk/home/you/article-2479096/The-History-Girls-meet-women-building-bright-future-past.html. (Last accessed 1 September 2015).

Khan, U. (2009). 'BBC *Land Girls* Drama Slammed for Historically Inaccuracies' [sic], *Daily Telegraph*, 4 November. www.telegraph.co.uk/culture/tvandradio/5940130/BBC-Land-Girls-drama-slammed-for-historically-inaccuracies.html. (Last accessed 2 February 2016).

Landsberg, A. (2015) *Engaging the Past: Mass Culture and the Production of Historical Knowledge*, New York: Columbia University Press.

McRobbie, A. (2008) *The Aftermath of Feminism: Gender, Culture and Social Change*, London and Thousand Oaks: Sage.

Moseley, R. and J. Read (2002) 'Having It Ally: Popular Television (Post-) Feminism'. *Feminist Media Studies*, 2:2: 231–49.

NeverIsSacred (2011) 'Charm Magazine: A Sassy Suffragette's Style File', 15 June. https://neverissacred.wordpress.com/2011/06/15/charm-magazine-a-sassy-suffragettes-style-file/. (Last accessed 19 August 2015).

Newman, R. (2014) '*Charm:* "The Magazine for Women who Work"', 28 July. www.robertnewman.com/charm-the-magazine-for-women-who-work/. (Last accessed 18 August 2015).

Radner, H. (1999) 'Queering the Girl', in H. Radner and M. Luckett (eds) *Swinging Single: Representing Sexuality in the 1960s*, Minneapolis: University of Minnesota Press: 1–31.

'Real Life History of *Call the Midwife*' (n.d.) www.weta.org/tv/program/call-midwife/history. (Last accessed 3 February 2016).

Rennells, L. (2014) 'This Vintage Beauty Magazine was Made for Peggy', *Bobby Pin Blog*, 30 December. www.vintagehairstyling.com/bobbypinblog/2014/12/this-vintage-beauty-magazine-was-made-for-peggy.html. (Last accessed 19 August 2015).

Spigel, L. (2013) 'Postfeminist Nostalgia for a Prefeminist Future', *Screen*, 54:2: 270–8.

Theresa from Blue Velvet Vintage. (2010) 'Flashback: *Charm* Magazine', *Jezebel*, 21 April. http://jezebel.com/5520757/flashback-charm-magazine-april-1947. (Last accessed 18 August 2015).

Tom and Lorenzo (2010) 'Mad Style'. http://tomandlorenzo.com/2010/07/mad-style-joan-holloway-s3-part-2-2. (Last accessed 25 May 2013).

Tom and Lorenzo (2013) 'Mad Style: The Better Half'. http://tomandlorenzo.com/2013/05/mad-style-the-better-half. (Last accessed 25 May 2013).

Viner, B. (2009) 'Last Night's Television', *Independent*, 7 September. www.independent.co.uk/arts-entertainment/tv/reviews/last-nights-television-land-girls-bbc1-the-restaurant-the-winners-story-bbc2-clever-v-stupid-bbc3-1783369.html. (Last accessed 2 February 2016).

Wheatley, H. (2005) 'Rooms Within Rooms: *Upstairs Downstairs* and the Studio Costume Dramas of the 1970s', in C. Johnson and R. Turnock (eds) *ITV Cultures: Independent Television over Fifty Years*, Maidenhead and New York: Open University Press: 143–56.

World of Undine (2011) 'Charm Magazine's Feminist Issue, 1956', 29 January. http://worldofundine.blogspot.com/2011/01/charm-magazines-feminist-issue-1956.html. (Last accessed 18 August 2015).

2

THE FEMINISATION OF CONTEMPORARY BRITISH TELEVISION DRAMA

Sally Wainwright and Red Production

Ruth McElroy

As scholars we need better to understand what television means for the women who make it as well as for those who watch it. This chapter contributes to that project by examining the gendered production contexts out of which some of the most popular contemporary British television drama has emerged. By drawing together analysis of the production and writing of television drama by women with close textual analysis of television popular with women viewers and critics on-screen, this essay offers a multi-method approach to understanding the feminisation of contemporary British television drama. Particular attention is given in the essay to the output of Sally Wainwright, one of the UK's foremost writers of mainstream contemporary television drama, and Red Production, an independent production company established in Manchester in 1998 by Nicola Shindler.

Although television has long been considered a feminine media form and women constitute the majority of television viewers, remarkably few women writers in British television have earned significant scholarly attention or indeed have attained substantial recognition from the industry itself in the form of major awards. In her study of BAFTA awards, Julia Hallam notes that only two women have won the BAFTA Dennis Potter award for contribution to screenwriting (Kay Mellor and Lynda La Plante), as against nine male writers. Feminist scholars, both as researchers and as teachers of the next generation of academics and TV workers, are in the privileged position of being able to correct the neglect of women writers, their output and collaborations. For example, Manchester University Press' 'The Television Series' has made an important contribution to our knowledge of individual writers and producers who have helped shape British television, yet only one volume, Julia Hallam's (2011) *Lynda La Plante*, has a woman as the main focus of study. Academic books are themselves susceptible to the vagaries of publishing fashion and it may be that editors perceive volumes on women television writers as having no market either at home or abroad. Unless both 'writing for television' and 'women in television' are made areas of concern in our teaching, there can be little hope for viable publishing in the field. But the absence of women writers in the academic literature also implies a devaluing of women's scripts *both* in terms of their careers *and* the stories they tell. This chapter directly emerges from my concern to address these dual aspects of contemporary television drama and to demonstrate that we can only fully appreciate television's contribution to how women as workers are understood in popular culture if we attend to women's labour both on- *and* off-screen. It is precisely because 'there have been few attempts to understand the ways in which female creatives . . . influence the depiction of female characters and their issues and concerns on the small screen' (Hallam, 2013: 2) that this chapter sets out to explore the nuanced, rather than reductively mimetic, relationship between the status of women in television drama production and the award-winning output of one such team of creatives. My selection is guided by the distinct collaboration between Sally Wainwright as a writer and Red as a female-led indie producer, and the unique opportunity it affords to explore how women's relations to one another as workers and managers in television can help shape the stories we watch on-screen. Moreover, my focus on drama from beyond London, which remains the workbase of 42 per cent of the UK creative media industries workforce (see Skillset, 2012: 13), deliberately attends to the importance of place in contemporary British drama and to the importance of ensuring that stories are told from a diversity of places in the UK.

The chapter begins by establishing some of the main concerns of women who have worked in the television industry, and argues that we need to understand the challenges women faced historically in making television alongside the experience of women in post-war labour markets more generally. Television's distinct characteristics as an industry are outlined and their significance for women workers discussed critically, but the emphasis is on understanding labour conditions in television production as part of wider developments in the story of women's changing worklives. The rise of women as senior figures in contemporary television is detailed and set within a wider theoretical analysis of the feminisation of British television, understood as an ideological rather than purely empirical process. The essay then turns to Sally Wainwright's drama output as a case study, providing the first detailed analysis of her work and its appeal to women as viewers and critics.

Women in television drama: voices from the workplace

> [T]he only one he made sign a contract was me, and I was quite taken aback. It was that very day that I realised I had a value. It was quite odd. I had never thought of it.
>
> *(Beryl Virtue cited in Ian Potter, 2008: 27)*

> 'Let's get one thing straight from the start. There is no question of equality between us.'
>
> *(Irene Shubik, 2014: 45)*

In this section, I want to listen to the voices of a select number of women who have worked in television drama production, so as to hear in their own words the kind of negotiations they have undertaken in order to make television. The starkly different quotations above from two of the most significant women in British television production remind us that there *is* a history of women working in British television, albeit a neglected one, and that listening to the voices of women who have made television is an important feminist activity for television scholars. Vicky Ball and Melanie Bell's current AHRC-funded project 'Women's Work, Working Women: A Longitudinal Study of Women Working in the Film and Television Industries (1933–1989)' promises to make a significant contribution to our understanding of a period during which significant historical change was taking place for women. Importantly, though, that history is diverse, as are the experiences of women working in television. Beryl Virtue's career began as secretary to Associated London Scripts (initially a writers' collective established in 1954 including Eric Sykes, Spike Milligan, Ray Galton, Alan Simpson and Frankie Howerd), though she quickly became, in effect, the agent for these writers. The contract to which she refers was the outcome of a merger between Associated London Scripts and the Robert Stigwood Organisation, and under Virtue as Managing Director, ALS pioneered the sale of UK television abroad (see Potter, 2008). That she only appreciated her own significance when valued contractually, and over and above the male writers with whom she worked, tells us something of how self-deprecating women workers have been in the television industry and how important the authority of public, named positions can be in conferring value upon their labour. Meanwhile, Irene Shubik's words above recount her first meeting with Peter Luke (story editor for *Armchair Theatre*[1]) at ABC on her first day and remind us of how pervasive sexism and class prejudice has been in British television workplaces. This history not only binds women television workers to the history of women's labour in general, but also reveals how the particular structure of television production can itself both help and hinder women's progression within the industry.

Television production is notoriously risky, dynamic and fragmented, with short-term contracts the norm for most workers, and networking – knowing the right people and being able to transform contacts into contracts – a vital skill that demands considerable effort and cultural capital. The processes of deregulation that reshaped the media landscape during the 1980s and 1990s have left many marks, among them a workforce that has considerably less security of employment or coherent career training and progression. Instead, these have been replaced by the realities of a freelance existence in which the worker's own self is held responsible for the generation of paid work while being lauded as an autonomous creative agent (see Ursell, 2000). Some of the craft roles in which women dominate (make-up design, hairdressing and costume, for example) are also those in which some of the highest concentration of freelances are to be found (see Skillset, 2012). In his analysis of media work, Mark Banks, for instance, argues that

> the pressure to conform and compete in a more market-led and *individualized* economy may bring with it the corollary of social atomization and a more

pronounced need for self-coping as a consequence of disembedding from collectivized environments and structures of support.

(2007: 43)

In this environment, it is unsurprising that so much campaigning attention has fallen on how women, despite initial career success in their twenties, tend to fall from view in their mid-thirties and forties, when family responsibilities compete for their attention. Attrition rates of women in this age group and at this career stage mean that men are over-represented in the older (and often more senior) TV workforce. For example, a 2009 Skillset report, produced with Women in Film and Television, noted that among their respondents

the prevailing view was that the majority of men are comfortable working with or for women, but that the industry operates within a culture that makes it very difficult for women to sustain a long term relationship or start and bring up a family, and that women should be mindful of the sacrifices they may have to make before entering the industry.

(Skillset, 2009: 3)

The constraints of a workplace that makes family lives difficult to sustain have led to the creation of several professional network organisations, including Women in Film and Television (UK), geared to supporting women working in the creative media and part of an international network of over 10,000 women worldwide. Media Parents is an organisation with an active social media and web presence that seeks to

pull all the short-term, regular hours, job share and part-time jobs in media into one place along with standard contracts, to help freelance working parents – or anyone experienced who wants to work flexibly – and to make it easier for employers to find this highly skilled and experienced part of the media workforce.

(Media Parents, 2015)

According to Media Parents' own website, 5,000 women and 750 men left television over the three years preceding the writing of this chapter – a considerable loss of talent which the organisation wants to arrest. Both Women in Film and Television (UK) and Media Parents have developed tangible initiatives including mentoring schemes, exploiting social media for sharing job opportunities and supporting return to work through networking events. Such interventions are evidence of an activist aim to try to reinsert collective support for workers, while at the same time illustrating how pervasive the demand to manage one's own professional self and opportunities for paid work has become in the television marketplace. Media Parents' own exchanges of labour opportunities seem perfectly to illustrate Gillian Ursell's argument that television

freelance workers have taken onto themselves the task of organising their own labour markets. This has involved both a much strengthened role for the self-referential and partially closed occupational communities which have always characterised television workforces, and also an intensification of the self-commodification process by which each individual seeks to improve his/ her chances of attracting gainful employment.

(2000: 807)

Trade unions such as BECTU have advocated flexible working for their members in an environment where long days on set are the norm, especially in drama. While many accounts of work in the creative industries emphasise the shift away from unionised labour, it is important that scholars understand the enduring efforts made by trade unions for their members; this is not a space that has been evacuated. In my recent research examining the development of the BBC's new specialist drama studios at Roath Lock, Cardiff, for example, the realities facing those women who work on set was a major issue of concern for trade union representatives:

> A lot of sound have said, 'I just can't do it any more. I just don't want to work eleven-day fortnights, sixteen-hour days and be away from my family'. With women as well what we're having, 'What do I do? Do I have a child or a career?' And one thing that we try to discuss with BBC . . . is to talk to them about job sharing, about flexible working. It can be complicated in some areas of drama, but I think they've been successful in *Pobol y Cwm* [Welsh-medium soap opera made by BBC for S4C] because it's a series where one person does one block and the one the other . . . there needs to be more imagination in terms of how can we be a more accessible workforce for people with childcare . . . or other caring responsibilities because otherwise, we're losing the talent.

> *(BECTU interview, Cardiff 2013)*

Television fares significantly better than many creative media sectors in that 45 per cent of its workforce is female (Skillset, 2012). This may be one reason why some have argued that from the late 1990s onwards, British television has undergone a process of feminisation (see Ball, 2012). A diverse array of evidence has been marshalled to support this analysis, ranging from changes in genre and the emergence of lifestyle and reality formats in prime-time (see Brunsdon, 2003; Moseley, 2000), to the emergence of new scripts articulating emotional and reflexive approaches to life management (see Lewis, 2008; Creeber, 2004), to personnel changes. From the late 1990s onwards, an increasing number of women have occupied senior roles in British broadcasting, including Dawn Airey (Chief Executive of Channel 5 from 2008 to 2010), Jana Bennett (Director of Vision at BBC from 2006 to 2011), Kay Benbow (Controller CBeebies, 2010–), Julie Garner (Head of Drama, BBC Wales, 2003–9 and Controller of Drama Commissioning at BBC Television, 2006–9; Executive Producer BBC Worldwide, 2009–15), Sally Haynes (Controller of Drama Commissioning at ITV from 2007 to 2013), Janice Hadlow (Controller BBC2, 2008–14), Lorraine Heggessey (Controller of BBC1, 2000–5), Laura Mackie (Director of

Drama at ITV from 2007 to 2013), Jane Root (Controller of BBC2 from 1999 to 2004), Kim Shillinglaw (Controller of BBC2 and BBC4, 2014–16) and Jane Tranter (Controller of Fiction at BBC from 2006 to 2008). In their different roles, these women had direct control of a significant percentage of public service broadcasters' commissioning during a period of major change in the history of television which saw the development of an increasingly multi-channel, competitive digital market in television production, and one in which an increasing proportion of television was getting made by independent production companies, many of whom had women in senior leadership roles. Kudos, for example, appointed Jane Featherstone as its head of drama in 2000, where she remained until 2014. It became one of the foremost producers of popular and award-winning British TV drama, making series such as *Broadchurch* (Kudos/Imaginary Friends for ITV, 2013–), *Hustle* (AMC/ BBC, 2004–12), *Life on Mars* (Kudos/BBC/Red Planet Pictures, 2006–7), *Ashes to Ashes* (Kudos/Monastic Productions/BBC, 2008) and *The Hour* (Kudos/BBC/ BBC America, 2011–12). While these dramas may not ostensibly, I think, be seen as television for women, it is certainly the case that women have been integral to the rise of drama in British television as a privileged genre marking the terrain of 'quality television' itself – one of the BBC's main strategic defence measures against political critics who regard popular entertainment as superfluous in public service broad- casting. Both Lorraine Heggessey and Jane Tranter exploited one of the major shifts in the BBC's scheduling, transmitting many of these dramas in the weekday 9 pm slot which emerged following the controversial decision to move BBC1's main evening news to 10 pm.

The accomplishments of these women are considerable and genuinely reveal the feminist gains made by women workers, especially when contrasted with Shubik's experience above. Feminist activism of the second wave was able to produce the considerable social and industrial change which has made these women's senior careers possible. Nonetheless, it is misleading when individual prominent women in managerial roles are used metonymically to stand for the whole workforce. When I asked Nicola Shindler, producer and founder of Red Production, in interview if this feminisation of television accorded with her own experience, she said:

> My experience over twenty-five years is that there are so many more women in senior roles, in commissioning, in decision roles, producing roles and that might be why TV people say these things about feminisation but I don't think that, I'm not aware of that.

In her sophisticated analysis, Vicky Ball makes the argument that 'discourses of success circulating in culture privilege neo-liberal discourses of choice and individualism, and evade deep and pernicious gender inequalities that continue to affect women' (2012: 250). The overall figure of a 45 per cent female workforce obscures the gendered division of labour in television, where many areas of craft and technical remain male-dominated and where the highest representation of women is in office-based (rather than set-based) activities such as commissioning, development or legal work.

Thus while 'women represent 66% of legal roles, 48% of strategic management roles and creative development (each), 61% of broadcast management and 56% of production', they account for just 26 per cent of studio operations, 20 per cent of audio/sound/music, 19 per cent of editing, 16 per cent of lighting, 15 per cent of camera/photography and 3 per cent of animators (Skillset, 2012: 13). A single homogeneous narrative of progress toward a feminist tradition of making British television seems to me something of a red herring, a venture that, were it to be embarked upon, would end up silencing some of the most important female voices in television. As the head of an independent production company, Shindler noted that balancing work and family

> depends on what you do. So the job that I do and the fact that I run my own business and can choose my own hours and be flexible so therefore it's fine, I can be a mother and do this job. Were I to work on a film set as part of a crew then it would be virtually impossible.

This perspective was echoed in a separate interview with Karen Lewis, producer of several Red dramas written by Wainwright, including *Happy Valley* (Red Production for BBC, 2014–), *The Last Witch* (Red Production for Sky, 2013) and *Last Tango in Halifax* (Red Production for BBC, 2012–). Lewis became a producer having worked as a script editor at BBC Wales, following an earlier career working as a fiction and non-fiction reader for publishers Jonathan Cape and Bloomsbury. 'Production', she told me, is 'very hard for women . . . when you're in production and you have to work these ridiculous hours; when you're filming you work twelve-hour days and there could be nights'. As in the Shindler interview, these patterns of work were recounted by Lewis as a norm around which all workers were expected to shape their lives. The financial crisis and the cuts to public service broadcasting undertaken by the 2010–15 Coalition government review of public spending have further added to the sense of precarious employment and competitive market for work in television production. However, both women commented on the gendered nature of women's experience, with Lewis noting that 'obviously lots of men have children, but many of them have wives, so it's just absolutely not the same'. Implicitly, the working assumption remains that wives will accomplish far more by way of domestic labour for their husbands than vice versa; working women cannot expect to be fully relieved of what is often termed the 'second shift' at home. The physical and emotional labour such working practices demand of women making television was strikingly exemplified by Lewis' discussion of a female colleague:

> A make-up designer. She's got two small children six and four. Make-up and costume have to get in even earlier than everybody else to prep the artists, so imagine she could be on a normal day getting up at 5:30 am, leaving her children there, has to have someone looking after the children, and then she'll work eleven hours on camera, and then if it's period they have to de-rig all the

artists and things like that, so she'll get home at what 8, 9 pm. They have to travel as well and often the industry doesn't do five-day weeks. *Last Tango* [sic] is going to be one, so that's brilliant. I can't remember the last time that ever happened to me. So usually it's eleven-day fortnights and so you don't really get much chance to see your family.

Writing about her research with women in the magazine industry, Andrea Press (2011) has argued that feminist media studies needs to pay closer attention to how female professionals themselves understand feminism and the operation of gender in their own workplace and professional practice. We should not assume that workers in the creative industries – whose bread and butter is, after all, the management of meaning across a range of symbolic levels – are not themselves well able to identify many of the major gendered forces affecting their own working lives. My interviews at Red, unlike the more expansive creative industry-wide research conducted by Gill (2014) and Ursell (2000), do not paint a picture of women in television eschewing gender as a structural inequality. This contrasts with Anne O'Brien's (2015) research on the contemporary Irish television industry in which she reports a tendency to frame inequality through the lens of personal responsibility, a tendency which, she argues, is characteristic of the postfeminist, neoliberal work ethic. My differentiated findings may be because Lewis and Shindler are both more established in their careers than many of O'Brien's more junior interviewees and are of a generation that experienced political critiques of gender and collective politics first-hand, in contrast with many of O'Brien's younger workers, whose working lives have taken shape in a postfeminist age. But it strikes me, too, that Lewis and Shindler's experience of being able to sustain a close working relationship with each other, and with Wainwright as a writer committed to writing women's lives over a period of several years, may also mean that they have been able to create an environment that supports women's creative work more fully, albeit still working within the precarious realities of project development, drama commissioning and contract working that govern television production today (almost all the non-core office staff at Red were freelance). The highly selective, reputational marketplace that characterises such work may also provide the tools, for women who have the power and inclination to do so, to choose to work with other women and sustain their careers in doing so. Still, as Ursell (2000) and O'Brien (2015) argue, the operation of power in such a marketplace elicits a considerable degree of self-responsibility from workers who have become habituated to a régime that demands their endless accommodation or else their departure from the sector altogether. The emotional costs borne by women working long hours on set, often at a distance from family, are known and, as here, acknowledged as terribly demanding by other women working at different levels of television production. This accords with research undertaken by O'Brien, who found that:

> Women in television production in Ireland are expected to constitute the perfect neoliberal subject by subscribing to traditionally masculine practices

of long working hours, a rigid separation of career and life, and a lack of workplace flexibility. For most of the women interviewed, long working days, antisocial hours, and weekend work were very normal.

(2015: 268)

My own research suggests that there is no direct correlation between an understanding of the gendered realities of work in making television drama on the one hand, and a conviction that inequalities behind the camera shape what viewers see on-screen on the other. This was especially notable in interview with Shindler. When asked if she believed that these gender realities shaped the programmes we see on-screen, she insisted that this was not the case:

> I don't, because with a lot of the development process and commissioning process, it is possible to have a normal life and there are a huge number of women in those roles. So I think it's a shame there aren't more women DoPs [Director of Photography] but I don't think that impacts on what you see on-screen. I think it's terrible for women and for women who want to be DoPs, but I don't think that impacts what you see on-screen.

For Shindler, the influence of gender as a potential determinant of output is negligible because of the hierarchical position occupied by the gatekeeping roles of commissioners and developers, many of whom are women. What appears on-screen is shaped by them, not by the crew on set. In other words, it is the commissioners (occupying more permanent posts within the broadcasters) and executive producers (often business partners in the independent production companies making contemporary drama) who are understood to wield greatest power in shaping televisual representation because it is they who all other workers, male and female, must please if they are to remain in work. When asked if her collaboration with a writer like Sally Wainwright means that she considers herself to be making television for women, Shindler replied:

> Oh, I don't think so at all! I would be mortified if anyone thought that was the case! We don't make telly for women and we don't think about audiences in those terms, we don't specify the audience. *Broadcasters* [my emphasis] might, but we don't.

Feminist television scholars need to appreciate how internal professional structures and hierarchies, together with the ways in which women inhabit them, may contribute to how women workers themselves understand what gender, feminism and indeed television for women might mean. In the context of this collection, my research seems to suggest that 'television for women' is a category constructed in academic discourse, and was not familiar to any of the women whom I interviewed. This speaks to a kind of dissonance between how television scholars might conceptualise television output and the very different conceptualisation of their work by female professionals, in terms both of individual texts but also of the context of independent production. In other words, there is a lack of recognition of the term's currency in the business discourse they use to describe their own work and output, but this disjunction is also suggestive of the differences between how different workers and agents within the industry conceive of their work. Hence Shindler talks about audiences and the possibility of television for women being a commissioner/broadcaster concern rather than a concern for her as an indie producer, whereas Wainwright as a writer articulates a more personal vision of her interests in writing women's lives. Such distinctions between how women working as writers, producers and commissioners might conceive of and articulate their work in relation to gender are an important reminder that roles within television are diverse and distinct from, for example, the literary field. As noted above, women in British television have succeeded in gaining access to some of these very positions over recent years, but having more women in such positions does not itself mean that the hierarchical structure of television as an industry is being altered. As many feminists have argued, with reference to numerous industries and professions, it is not enough to have women in senior positions; change needs also to be made to the very structure of organisations and the wider social values which underpin their environments. It is with this more explicit feminist concern to examine the broader cultural conditions of women's professional labour in mind that I now turn to Sally Wainwright, as one of the most successful writers of British television dramas which attend directly to women's working lives today.

Sally Wainwright: writing women's working lives

> Women are more heroic, I think. Women are braver and more complex than men. I am just not as excited by men.
>
> *(Wainwright in Keene, 2011)*

Sally Wainwright is one of the most accomplished and well-regarded writers of contemporary television drama working in the UK today. She is known for writing drama that places contemporary female protagonists centre-stage, and it is their lives and experiences that principally drive the narrative trajectory of her fiction. Her credits include *At Home with the Braithwaites* (Yorkshire Television for ITV, 2000–3), *The Amazing Mrs Pritchard* (Kudos Productions for BBC, 2006), *Unforgiven* (Red Production for ITV, 2009), *Last Tango in Halifax* (Red Production, 2012–), *Scott & Bailey* (Red Production for ITV, 2011–) and *Happy Valley* (Red Production, 2014–). In 2015 she won a BAFTA Best Writer (Drama) award for *Happy Valley*, having won the same award in 2013 for *Last Tango in Halifax*, and in 2009 the Royal Television Society Writer of the Year award for *Unforgiven*. Echoing Hallam's critical analysis, Wainwright has nonetheless spoken openly about the timing of her BAFTA success many years after she first started to pen her own series:

> It brings up a lot of emotions. And one of them for me was, 'Why haven't I won this before now?' To win it last year, after I wrote the Braithwaites 14 years

ago . . . you do think: 'Why haven't I been noticed before now?'

(Wainwright in Frost, 2014)

Wainwright began her career, as many British writers have done, working as part of a soap opera team, first with BBC Radio on *The Archers* (1951–) and then at ITV on *Emmerdale* (Yorkshire Television, 1972–) and *Coronation Street* (Granada, 1960–), during the 1990s. She has spoken publicly of how important this experience was for her development:

> I think it's [writing scripts] something you're born with – you can either do it or you can't. I think being able to write dialogue oddly we all speak it but very few of us can actually write it, which is a funny thing. But I think story is something that doesn't necessarily come easy. I think it's something that you've really got to work at. And it was only when I started to work on team shows like *The Archers*, urm particularly *Coronation Street*, really seeing how stories evolve and develop and the amount of work that goes into them. That was fascinating. And I couldn't be doing what I do now on my own had I not been through that kind of apprenticeship on shows like *Coronation Street*.
>
> *(Wainwright, 2012)*

Long-running serial fiction is one of the principal training grounds for writers, who hone their technique and learn to negotiate the pressured realities of the intensive television production system while benefiting from some continuity of employment, a scarce commodity in the industry. In the UK they have also provided some of the earliest and most enduring spaces for representing working-class lives in the English regions, and, as a considerable body of feminist scholarship has traced (Brunsdon, 1997, 2000; Geraghty, 1990; Hobson, 1982, 2003), the role of soap operas in offering a space in popular culture for women actors and viewers to see women's changing work and domestic lives being worked through on-screen has been significant. Consideration of Wainwright's own working history acts as a counter to the tendency within television studies to gravitate toward high-concept, often imported from the US, supposedly 'quality TV' dramas that have come to be regarded with considerable admiration, as if their own inventive form of long narrative arc was unique. Arguably, reality television and 'quality' imported drama have dominated the analysis of television in recent years, with homegrown, prime-time drama yet to benefit from the considered analysis of both the nature of its own craft production and its distinct aesthetic and narrative concerns. It is not just a problem of gender that explains the relative dearth of critical analyses of women writers in television, but a problem of British television drama and a critical unease or disinterest in analysing the characteristics of the kind of television writing that produces some of our mainstream domestic dramas. As Alison Huber (2013) has demonstrated, the concept of the mainstream is more commonly deployed in the negative than used either as a positive descriptor or as a well-developed analytic category. Yet the taken-for-granted nature of the mainstream belies its own force and the work necessary for its own production. My own use of the term 'mainstream' should alert the reader to questions here of value and taste (see Brunsdon, 1997 and Geraghty, 2003), and to the conceptual challenge posed when trying to account for broad, popular dramas on the main terrestrial channels that gain the 6–7 million viewers which broadcasters such as the BBC and ITV require as a staple of their evening schedules. Wainwright's capacity, as a writer, to deliver such audiences is central to her success within the industry. It is here that debates about mainstream television drama and the feminisation of television meet, and it is in the stories of women's lives – many of them ensemble pieces that examine both women's entry into and success in the workplace and their family and personal lives – that the mainstream finds contemporary force. Television for women precisely *is* mainstream in contemporary Britain, inasmuch as many of the prime-time dramas on the large, popular terrestrial channels, BBC1 and ITV, make the exploration of women's work and personal lives central to their fictional narratives. In itself, this is not a new phenomenon. Writing more than a decade ago, Dorothy Hobson pointed out how soap operas simultaneously deliver

> two functions of television programmes. For the audience they are entertainment; for the producers and broadcasters they are business. The two needs are inseparable and mutually compatible . . . More than any other genre the soap opera speaks to the audience, and for this reason, it is a form which is invaluable to broadcasters.
>
> *(2003: xii)*

Even if this claim of generic uniqueness no longer quite holds, the tensions of balancing work and home lives have become the very stuff of contemporary neoliberal life scripts which are dramatised in prime-time TV fiction. Even historical series such as the BBC's immensely popular *Call the Midwife* (Neal Street Productions for BBC, 2012–) use the female ensemble drama to explore the changing aspirations and preoccupations of women's lives in the mid-twentieth century, before the advent of second-wave feminism.

In strictly commercial terms, the production of fiction likely to appeal to women viewers is unsurprising given the higher hours of television viewing women undertake compared with men. In his analysis of the rebranding of ITV, for example, Ross Garner argues that the broadcaster's renewed commitment to television drama is closely tied to its commercial strategy to brand itself as being at the heart of popular culture, a branding strategy epitomised by its 'Where Drama Lives' series of trailers. ITV1's viewership is skewed toward female viewers in their mid-thirties and upwards. But the mainstreaming of such women-led dramas is indicative not only of a perceived commercial advantage in securing women viewers as consumers, but also of a perception that the relationship between women's emotional labour and their paid work is *itself* central to contemporary popular culture. Indeed, I would go further and argue that women's intimate lives have become a *preoccupation* of popular culture in ways that reflect not only the new forms of consumerism that have emerged with women's increasingly central place in the workforce, but also the new forms of emotional management which have accompanied these fundamental changes in post-industrial societies' labour markets. Eva Illouz puts this succinctly when she argues: 'never has the private self been so publicly performed and harnessed to the discourses and values of the economic and political spheres' (2007: 4). Illouz's analysis of what she terms emotional capitalism – 'a culture in which emotional and economic discourses and practices mutually shape each other' – reveals how an older binary between the public, rational self and the private, emotional sphere has been unmade by the increasing demand that the self and its emotions be well-managed in the service of the economy. It is my contention that one of the reasons for Wainwright's popularity with both commissioners and viewers is precisely her capacity to examine these very tensions through compelling characters and well-plotted scripts.

I want briefly to illustrate this argument by reference to the second of Wainwright's recent crime dramas, *Happy Valley*, a police procedural set in the semi-urban Calderdale valley in West Yorkshire and centred upon its compelling protagonist, uniformed Sergeant Catherine Cawood (played by Sarah Lancashire). Like Suranne Jones, who plays Rachel Scott in *Scott & Bailey*, Lancashire worked for a long time on *Coronation Street,* playing the character Raquel Wolstenhulme for five years. Lancashire is one of British television's most accomplished and versatile actresses, with roles ranging from soap opera to costume drama, as well as stage and musical performances. In 2000, Lancashire starred alongside Lesley Sharp in one of Red Production's earliest drama hits, *Clocking Off* (2000). In July 2000 she made British television history by being the first actress to win a golden-handcuff deal with a major UK broadcaster, ITV. Writing in the *Observer*, Tina Ogle noted that

> Lancashire joins John Thaw, Robson Green, David Jason and Ross Kemp in the gang of five handsomely rewarded thespians who will work only for ITV in the foreseeable future. This is the elite among television actors; the top-rank stars that the ITV network is confident can pull in audiences time after time.
>
> *(Ogle, 2000)*

As Mark Lawson (2014) noted in reviewing *Happy Valley*, Lancashire's versatility allows her to deliver the nuance of a script while eliciting empathy from viewers. Lancashire's own emotional labour – her capacity to make us *feel* – is vital to her appeal. This combination of qualities has brought her both popular and critical acclaim; Lancashire is thus a recognised name who brings with her a measure of quality and audience appeal likely to suit both producers and broadcasters.

We are introduced to Catherine in the opening scene of the first episode when she steps out alone from her police car, lights flashing, and walks into a local newsagent asking for a fire extinguisher. She joins her younger female police constable colleague, who has obviously called for back-up, and the two women walk alongside one another to the scene of the potential crime (see Figure 2.1) – a young, drunk man who is threatening to set himself alight. She strides along the playing field in her full uniform,

FIGURE 2.1 Sergeant Catherine Cawood (Sarah Lancashire) strides into action with junior sidekick WPC Kirsten McAskill (Sophie Rundle)

the sheer bulk of her vest jacket adding to her physical presence, to where he has situated himself. Catherine looks like nothing so much as a confident cowboy, the sheriff arriving in a violent small town where she's in charge.

Adhering to the generic conventions of uniformed police procedurals, she is disdainful of the specialist senior officers who, she knows, are unlikely to arrive in time; 'Basically, it's you and me, kid', Catherine says sardonically to her colleague. With her dark glasses on and quipping to her colleague 'well, he can send himself to paradise but he's not taking my eyebrows with him', Catherine exudes professionalism, confidence and physical prowess – her occupation of space, the calm and darkly comic nature of her dialogue and her pronounced local accent all giving a rich depiction of her place in this fictional world.

A great deal of storytelling is achieved in these few moments. When Catherine arrives at the young man, she sets down the large fire extinguisher and asks, 'How's it all come to this then, lad?', a friendly vernacular style of speech establishing contact with the precarious young man. In the moments that follow, we see her engage him in dialogue, explaining to him the danger he's in, in no uncertain terms:

> You're upset. I understand that. The point I'm making is that with all these fumes – and frankly I don't know how you're staying conscious – you could go up any second whether you intend to or not and once you go up, you won't just go up a bit, you'll go up a lot. And the other big thing to say is it hurts. Three seconds in you'll be screaming at me to put you out, seven seconds in you'll be begging me to shoot ya.

This detail, and the deadpan tone of Lancashire's pitch-perfect delivery, concisely betray Catherine's experience and the horrors she has witnessed as a police officer in this troubled town. Notwithstanding her familiarity with violence and suffering, her approach is genuinely personable and her choice of language, while seeming effortless, works effectively to establish a rapport with the young man. The point that this is second nature to Catherine is made satirically as the camera cuts to the younger female officer receiving a message on her walkie-talkie from the hostage response unit, who patronisingly tell her to 'keep the subject engaged in conversation', to which she nods ironically and says: 'I think we've got that covered.' Both uniformed women, working together, are in control of a potentially deadly situation, and their camaraderie against the absent officers and with one another wins the viewer's admiration. This is a female workforce able to support one another and professionally take control.

But Catherine is no perfect heroine; instead, she introduces herself to the young man and to the viewer, announcing: 'I'm Catherine, by the way. I'm forty-seven, I'm divorced, I live with me sister, who's a recovering heroin addict. I've two grown-up children, one dead, one who dun't speak to me, and a grandson, so . . .'. This litany of messed-up private life directly enters the public, professional realm of Catherine's work and it is this very emotional and personal reality that enables her to bring this potentially fatal situation to a safe conclusion. In one sense, her professional management of the situation epitomises the emotional competence which Illouz cites as a principal requirement of the modern workplace: 'professional compet-ence', she writes, comes to be 'defined in emotional terms, by the capacity to acknowledge and empathise with others. Such emotional capacity to forge social relationships has become synonymous with professional competence writ large' (2007: 22). Catherine's class position – uniformed and rooted in the community rather than elevated to the more socially distant detective ranks – also means that the detached, managerial tone of her superiors is routinely undercut with a more immediate and impassioned sense of not wanting or not being able to separate herself from the town and the people she serves. The series' set design and camerawork commonly place her in everyday social locations that are integral to the series' own gritty realist style. Wainwright herself has said that 'the location was hugely important. It was like another character, it informed the whole show' (Wainwright, 2015). Rather than separating herself from the local population of drug dealers, petty criminals and hopeless cases, Catherine proclaims herself to be one of them. Like them, she is also the victim of violence, both through the suicide of her own daughter and ultimately by the searing physical attack upon her by her daughter's rapist, Tommy Lee Royce, who is released from prison, unknown to Catherine, in the first episode. The power of the state to intrude upon ordinary working lives and recklessly ignore their feelings is writ large here and exemplifies a distinctly classed sensibility, the drama deriving precisely from the tremendous disempowerment felt by Catherine as the mother of a victim, contrasted with her significant authority as a confident police officer and made dramatic through her considerable on-screen presence. Much of the series' emotional intensity comes from the oscillation in the plot between Catherine's investigative powers in trying to capture Royce and his accomplices on the one hand, and on the other, the psychological narrative that gradually reveals the depths of the harm done to Catherine and her whole family by Royce's initial sex crime.

Happy Valley recaptures the social agenda of earlier British police dramas – what Sue Turnbull regards as their tendency, 'instead of attributing crime to individual acts of moral failure', to focus 'on the underlying social causes of crime' (2014: 46) – but is distinguished from them by the centrality of women's lives in the narrative and in the particular violent and sexual crimes perpetrated by men against women. Wainwright has spoken of how her writer's instinct to excavate a character's backstory can develop when a second or third series gets commissioned:

> It's an increasing pleasure to write because you really feel you know these people, you're telling the audience more and more about them. You know good storytelling is about telling things backwards as well as forwards. Especially in Series Three we started telling the story of Rachel's bad relationship with her mother . . . it's bad things in Rachel's past that allow us to know more about who she is and why she is like she is.
>
> *(Wainwright, 2012)*

Wainwright's social commitment as a writer is precisely to understand the lives of her often working-class or recently middle-class characters. In both *Scott & Bailey* and *Happy Valley*, Wainwright adapts the generic conventions of the police procedural (in which the investigative hero is often personally troubled) to her own narrative aims, which are to explore the social and professional worlds which her contemporary female professional characters inhabit. In this regard, Wainwright's different crime dramas suggest a significant development since British police procedurals of the 1980s and 1990s such as *Prime Suspect* (Granada for ITV, 1991–2006) or *The Gentle Touch* (London Weekend Television for ITV, 1980–4), and the isolated exceptionalism of their respective protagonists, Jane Tennison and Maggie Forbes. Instead, Wainwright's female police officers are surrounded by other women at ranks both above and below themselves. As Lesley Sharp has said,

> We're at pains to show women as good, cooperative and supportive colleagues . . . There's no unpleasant skulduggery or bitching. They both want to succeed, but it's a healthy depiction of two women in the workplace rather than an archetypal telly catfight.
>
> *(Sharp, cited in Brown 2014)*

These women have spent their working lives in the force; individually and collectively, they have a history. *Scott & Bailey* is a quite different police procedural, based upon the fictional Greater Manchester Police Major Incident Unit, which centres on three female detectives: DCI Gill Murray (Amelia Bulmore), DS Janet Scott (Lesley Sharp) and DC Rachel Bailey (Suranne Jones). One of the most distinctive characteristics of the series is its use of the traditional police ensemble in procedurals to explore women's professional lives while avoiding reductive forms of sexual competition between the women. In very different ways, both Murray and Scott are shown balancing their professional responsibilities as detectives and mothers, while Bailey's emotionally fragile relationship with her troubled mother exemplifies how family life intrudes upon even this highly ambitious and aspirational woman's professional career. Part of the series' appeal rests on this deft balance between the personal and professional, which speaks precisely to the real anxieties evident in our culture about women's domestic and professional labour.

One of the most striking visual representations of the multiple demands on women's time comes from the use of mobile phones, where time and again the requirement to balance long professional working hours in the force with the emotional labour and availability of family life is captured in the detectives taking personal calls. These numerous mid-shots pepper the series and vividly portray the realities of women's management of self and work. In this respect, *Scott & Bailey* seems like a very different iteration of the police procedural from those examined by Charlotte Brunsdon (2012) in her discussion of the genre's relation to post-feminism. Talking of ITV's *Murder in Suburbia* (Carlton, 2004), Brunsdon writes that 'in dramatic terms, putting young women into traditionally male character slots works as long as they stay young (i.e. without responsibilities to families)' (2012: 15). Instead, Wainwright's interest is precisely in women of all generations, and there is a sustained examination in her writing of the figure of the working woman, be that a professional police officer, as in *Happy Valley* and *Scott & Bailey*, or an Oxbridge-educated headmistress, as with Caroline Dawson (Sarah Lancashire) in *Last Tango in Halifax*. As a working mother who has developed her writing career during this historic period of change in women's place in the workforce, it is unsurprising that women's labour and its complex existence across private and public, professional and domestic spheres has provided such fruitful material for Wainwright's character-driven fiction. As Máire Messenger Davies has argued, writers' own work histories,

> their personal accounts of how they worked – have a value for us scholars. Not only are they witnesses to the historical conditions of production at the time they were working, but these accounts also give revealing insights into how to read the texts, the stories we see on screen.
>
> *(2007: 173–4)*

Conclusion

Contemporary British television drama, like popular culture more broadly, seems preoccupied with women's intimate and working lives. Rather than signalling the accomplishment of feminism, debates about the feminisation of British television testify to the ambiguous and ideologically complex relationships which the industry, as well as the culture, have with women's occupation of the workplace. Women writers, directors and producers in turn occupy quite variegated positions within this industry and their own work merits further extensive and consistent academic enquiry. This chapter has argued that the way to advance our understanding of the imbrications of gender in television drama is not by trying to establish a direct, essentialist correlation between women's work on- and off-screen, but instead by exploring how broader changes in women's structural working lives, the templates for which can be found in the bigger apparatus of the cultural economy, may find themselves on-screen. It is my contention that one of the best places to begin original investigative work is with prominent writers such as Sally Wainwright and successful production companies such as Nicola Shindler's Red Production. What this chapter has demonstrated is that a nuanced appreciation of the complex relationship between the working lives of women in television and the fictional representation of women's labour on-screen can lead feminist scholars to a fuller understanding of the difference women's writing specifically makes to the stories told in contemporary British drama about how women live and work today.

Note

1 *Armchair Theatre* ran on Sunday evenings from 1956 to 1974 and was a series of single plays shown on the commercial public service broadcaster, ITV. In British television history, it occupies a privileged position as an example of the golden age of innovative, contemporary television drama.

Bibliography

Ball, V. (2012) 'The "feminization" of British television and the re-traditionalization of gender', *Feminist Media Studies*, 12(2): 248–64.

Ball, V. and Bell, M. 'A history of women in British film and television production, 1933–1989', https://research.ncl.ac.uk/womensworkftvi/ (last accessed 7 July 2016).

Banks, M. (2007) *The Politics of Cultural Work*, Basingstoke: Palgrave Macmillan.

Brown, D. (2014) 'Scott & Bailey: Lesley Sharp, Suranne Jones and Amelia Bullmore reveal all about the new series', *Radio Times*, 10 September, www.radiotimes.com/news/2014-09-10/scott–bailey-lesley-sharp-suranne-jones-and-amelia-bullmore-reveal-all-about-the-new-series (last accessed 7 July 2016).

Brunsdon, C. (1997) *Screen Tastes: Soap Opera to Satellite Dishes*, London: Routledge.

Brunsdon, C. (1998) 'Structure of anxiety: Recent British television crime fiction', *Screen*, 39(3): 223–43.

Brunsdon, C. (2000) *The Feminist, the Housewife and the Soap Opera*, Oxford: Oxford University Press.

Brunsdon, C. (2003) 'Lifestyling Britain: The 8–9 slot on British television', *International Journal of Cultural Studies*, 6(1): 5–23.

Brunsdon, C. (2012) 'Television crime series, women police, and fuddy-duddy feminism', *Feminist Media Studies*, 13(3): 375–94.

Creeber, G. (2004) *Serial Television*, London: BFI.

Frost, V. (2014) 'Sally Wainwright: "I like writing women, they're heroic"', *Guardian*, 6 June, www.theguardian.com/tv-and-radio/2014/jun/06/sally-wainwright-i-like-writing-women-theyre-heroic-happy-valley (last accessed 11 October 2016).

Garner, R. (2017) 'Crime drama and channel branding: ITV and *Broadchurch*', in R. McElroy (ed.) *Contemporary British Television Crime Drama*, London and New York: Routledge: 139–53.

Geraghty, C. (1990) *Women and Soap Opera: A Study of Prime Time Soaps*, Cambridge: Polity Press.

Geraghty, C. (2003) 'Aesthetics and quality in popular television drama', *International Journal of Cultural Studies*, 6(1): 25–45.

Gill, R. (2014) 'Unspeakable inequalities: Post feminism, entrepreneurial subjectivity, and the repudiation of sexism among cultural workers', *Social Politics*, 21(4): 509–28.

Hallam, J. (2011) *Lynda La Plante*, Manchester: Manchester University Press.

Hallam, J., (2013) 'Drama queens: Making television drama for women 1990–2009', *Screen*, 54(2): 256–61.

Hobson, D. (1982) *Crossroads: The Drama of a Soap Opera*, London: Methuen.

Hobson, D. (2003) *Soap Opera*, Cambridge: Polity Press.

Huber, A. (2013) 'Mainstream as metaphor: Imagining dominant culture', in S. Baker, A. Bennett and J. Taylor (eds) *Redefining Mainstream Popular Music*, London: Routledge: 3–13.

Illouz, E. (2007) *Cold Intimacies: The Making of Emotional Capitalism*, London: Polity Press.

Keene, D. (2011) 'Sally Wainwright Talks to Danuta Keene', *Mslexia*, 51: 51–4.

Lawson, M. (2014, 3 June) '*Happy Valley* TV Review – Sarah Lancashire gives her best performance', *Guardian*.

Lewis, T. (2008) *Smart Living: Lifestyle Media and Popular Expertise*, New York: Peter Lang.

Media Parents (2015) www.mediaparents.co.uk/ (last accessed 7 July 2016).

Messenger Davies, M. (2007) 'Quality and creativity in TV: The work of television storytellers', in J. McCabe and K. Akass (eds) *Quality TV: Contemporary American Television and Beyond*, London: I.B.Tauris: 158–170.

Moseley, R. (2000) 'Makeover takeover on British television', *Screen*, 41(3): 299–314.

O'Brien, A. (2015) 'Producing television and reproducing gender', *Television and New Media*, 16(3): 259–74.

Ogle, T. (2000) 'We can't get enough of TV's famous five', 23 July, *Observer*.

Potter, I. (2008) *The Rise and Rise of the Independents: A Television History*, London: Guerilla Books.

Press, A. (2011) 'Feminism and media in the post-feminist era', *Feminist Media Studies*, 11(1): 107–13.

Shubik, I. (2014, orig. 2000) 'Television drama series: A producer's view', in J. Bignell and S. Lacey (eds) *British Television Drama*, Basingstoke: Palgrave Macmillan, 2nd edn: 45–51.

Skillset (2009) 'Why her? Factors that have influenced the careers of successful women in film and television', www.wftv.org.uk/sites/default/files/Why%20Her%20full%20report_0.pdf (last accessed 18 July 2016).

Skillset (2012) 'Creative Skillset employment census of the creative media industries', http://creativeskillset.org/assets/0000/5070/2012_Employment_Census_of_the_Creative_Media_Industries.pdf (last accessed 7 July 2016).

Turnbull, S. (2014) *The TV Crime Drama*, Edinburgh: Edinburgh University Press.

Ursell, G. (2000) 'Television production: Issues of exploitation, commodification and subjectivity in UK television markets', *Media Culture and Society*, 22(6): 805–25.

Wainwright, S. (2012) 'Manchester Literature Festival 2012: Sally Wainwright Q&A', www.bbc.co.uk/blogs/writersroom/entries/fd6c1e4c-0f54-3905-99b7-7d3e027a3c60 (last accessed 7 July 2016).

Wainwright, S. (2015) 'Sally Wainwright (Happy Valley), Writer Drama Winner, BAFTA TV Craft Awards', www.youtube.com/watch?v=C0HKHpytgCE (last accessed 7 July 2016).

3

'WOMEN PUSHED THEIR WAY FORWARD AND BECAME QUITE A FORCE WITHIN THE BBC'

Women's roles in television production and the production of programmes for women

Vanessa Jackson

Introduction

This chapter explores how the position of women working at the BBC changed from the 1970s onwards. It examines the extent to which gendered production teams meant that television produced for women was also television produced by women. The chapter presents the results of empirical research carried out in 2013, which forms part of the Pebble Mill Project: a history of broadcast production at BBC Birmingham, centred on the iconic Pebble Mill building, which opened in 1971 and was demolished in 2005. It was the first purpose-built television and radio broadcast centre in Europe. The research consisted of an online survey of fifty-six women, with four in-depth interviews with female television production workers active in the BBC between 1965 and 2012.

There is a body of existing research, both produced by the industry and within the academy, which examines the position of women within the television workplace, considering the potential inequalities and challenges they faced historically, and continue to face today. Significant studies include the *Patterns of Discrimination against Women in the Film and Television Industries* report carried out by the Association of Cinematograph and Television Technicians (ACTT) in 1975, and the *Television Industry Tracking Study* carried out by the British Film Institute (BFI) between 1994 and 1998. The literature identifies several key factors which impact on women's careers in television production, including gendered roles within television production, potential inequalities of opportunity and the casualisation of employment.

The ACTT report highlights the position of women within the television industry in the mid-1970s. The union notes that 60 per cent of its female members were concentrated in 3 out of 150 television grades: those of Production Secretary, Continuity Girl and Production Assistant (ACTT, 1975: 1). While the Association of Broadcasting and Allied Staff (ABS) was the union recognised by the BBC, and ACTT membership was predominantly within the ITV broadcasters, there is no reason to assume that the pattern of employment was markedly different at the BBC. Women tended to work in relatively low-status secretarial or administrative, rather than creative or managerial, roles. The BBC was aware of the small number of women in senior posts, and acknowledged the need for change. In 1973 it issued a statement saying '[s]teps will, therefore, now be taken to make quite certain that the potential of women members of staff is always as positively encouraged and developed as is that of their male colleagues' (ACTT, 1975: 42). The ACTT report asserted that the roles undertaken by women in television were largely 'dead-end'. The ABS also remarked on the lack of career progression available to women within the Corporation, stating that many female graduates were recruited as secretaries, with promises of production careers, which seldom materialised (Fogarty et al., 1981: 158). Women seemed to encounter a 'glass ceiling', which proved difficult to break through, given the gendered roles within the broadcasters.

This bleak state of affairs has undoubtedly improved since the 1970s, but the literature also highlights some contemporary challenges facing women television workers. The pressure of the women's movement led to equality legislation in the 1970s and equal opportunities initiatives in the 1980s, but the casualisation of the industry from the 1990s presented further uncertainties (Antcliff, 2005). Despite the difficulties in gaining promotion in the 1970s and early 1980s, television offered secure employment. This security was in contrast to the freelance culture and short-term contracts which became the norm from the 1990s onwards. For the BBC, this was in the context of John Birt's internal market reforms, leading to Producer Choice in 1993, and the rise of the independent sector, with the 25 per cent guarantee agreed in the 1990 Broadcasting Act (Paterson, 2001). Today's television workplace is dominated by short-term work often acquired through informal networks, which some academics have asserted disadvantages women. A study carried out by Grugulis (2012) concluded that women, along with working-class and black and minority ethnic workers, were less likely to secure work in television. The members of these groups who succeeded tended to have been employed for long periods by terrestrial broadcasters, or have served long apprenticeships. It was not that they networked less actively than white men, but that their networks did not have access to high-quality productions (ibid.). While the study finds that terrestrial broadcasters, like the BBC, are providing a greater equality of opportunity than the independent sector, the fact that women and other groups seem to be disadvantaged in the wider industry is worrying, and bodes ill for the future. This view was echoed by Women in Film and Television Board Director Nicci Crowther, quoted in *Broadcast*, the UK television trade newspaper: 'our workforce will be increasingly made up of people who are under 35, male, childless, white and increasingly well-heeled' (Conlan, 1999). While equal opportunities legislation has undoubtedly helped women working in television, industry practices, including increased casualisation, appear to have had the opposite effect.

The factor that runs through much of the literature around women's employment, irrespective of era, is the difficulty of combining motherhood with a career in television. Paterson, citing the BFI study from the mid-1990s, notes the high proportion of women over 40 working in the industry who were childless (Paterson, 2001: 499), while Hesmondhalgh and Baker's research emphasises a lack of women in their late thirties and forties in the industry (2011: 147). In examining why women leave media work, O'Brien (2014) asserts that it is the gendered nature of media work cultures, together with increased casualisation and the difficulties women have in participating with networks – rather than a positive desire to care for families – that is the cause (ibid.: 1209). It seems that the long hours, demand for flexibility and extremely high levels of commitment make it difficult for women to continue in television production once they have children.

The literature provides a useful context particularly about the nature of women's employment in the television industries and the challenges they encounter, but frequently it concentrates on the cultures of employment, rather than the cultures of production. It provides a valuable snapshot of particular periods, tending to examine the current, or then current, experiences of women, rather than asking the participants to reflect back on their careers and consider how practices have changed. Very little work seems to have been carried out into identifying the particular programmes on which women were working, whether these programmes were produced with a particularly gendered audience in mind and if, consequentially, this impacted on the production process.

Context of the study

The research carried out into the experiences of women at BBC Birmingham is part of a larger body of work I am undertaking: a historiography of BBC Pebble Mill (http://pebblemill.org), the broadcast centre in Birmingham which opened in 1971 and was demolished in 2005, with production moving to a central Birmingham location. At its height Pebble Mill produced around 10 per cent of BBC television and radio output, employing around 1,500 staff. BBC Pebble Mill was renowned for its production of what Frances Bonner (2003) terms 'ordinary television', especially daytime magazine programming, which had a predominantly female address (Moseley and Wheatley, 2008). Such television was frequently live and daily, such as *Pebble Mill at One* (BBC1, 1972–86) and *Good Morning with Anne and Nick* (BBC1, 1992–6); it was seen as ephemeral and 'low status' (Moseley *et al.*, 2014: 15). In addition to its daytime programming, Pebble Mill was a well-respected drama production centre, and also produced long-running factual series such as *Gardeners' World* (BBC2, 1968–), *Top Gear* (BBC2, 1977–2001) and *Countryfile* (BBC1, 1988–).

Methodology

The Pebble Mill Project consists of a website, http://pebblemill.org, and an associated Facebook page: www.facebook.com/pebblemillstudios. The Facebook community

FIGURE 3.1 BBC Birmingham, Pebble Mill building 2003, photograph by Benedict Peissel

is active, with more than 1,390 members, many of whom worked at BBC Pebble Mill (see Figure 3.1). In conducting the study I posted a link to an online questionnaire on the Pebble Mill Facebook page and on my personal Facebook profile. As a former series producer at BBC Birmingham, I am in touch with many colleagues, and therefore it was sensible to approach people from within my own networks, as well as contacts from the wider Pebble Mill group. A total of fifty-six women responded to the survey request. The sample was self-selecting and relatively small, and is not necessarily representative of the views and experiences of all women who worked at BBC Pebble Mill, nor necessarily the broader population of female television workers within the BBC or United Kingdom. However, the structures and working practices that operated at Pebble Mill were the same as those employed across the BBC, and were similar to those in the ITV production hubs. The changes seen across the industry from the 1990s onwards, with the increase of freelance working, made experiences of working for the large broadcasters more similar to those in the independent sector. Therefore, although the survey reveals the experiences of particular female workers at a particular workplace, the themes emerging are likely to be more generally applicable to the industry as a whole.

The survey was demanding, with the majority of questions requiring open-ended written responses. Respondents were asked their age bracket, dates they had worked at BBC Birmingham, which departments and programmes they worked on, their job titles, whether there were women in senior roles, the gender breakdown of production teams, whether they were conscious of some Pebble Mill programmes having a female-skewed audience and whether in their opinion this affected how the programmes were made. The survey also asked what were the biggest challenges facing women television workers at BBC Birmingham, and whether they perceived a glass ceiling. In quoting individual respondents, I am providing their most senior job title while at BBC Birmingham, and the dates they were employed. The survey was followed up with semi-structured, video interviews with four female production team members, from different age groups, who were active within BBC Birmingham in different eras, in order to gain more qualitative data. These interviews were transcribed, and the data derived will also be drawn on. I have included the first names of the interviewees and their job roles.

Data: generational shifts

The survey data illustrates a generational shift in production practices over time in the television industry. Respondents were asked what their first job was upon joining BBC Pebble Mill. Joiners in the 1970s–80s had very similar experiences. The vast majority started work at the BBC in clerical or secretarial grades; the starting jobs of joiners from the 1990s onwards, however, were markedly different: the secretarial and clerical grades had largely disappeared, due to advances in technology, and most women were entering as runners or researchers. This finding is consistent with observations by Grugulis, who noted that prior to 1990, entrants, who were often graduates, usually started in lowly jobs and worked their way up the hierarchy, learning on the job (Grugulis, 2012: 1314). The women in the survey tended to be entering at a low level and then working their way up.

The earliest joiners tended to spend their whole career at the BBC; they were a stable workforce, with staff jobs and the security of employment which that brought. They were working during the duopoly period prior to the 1980s, in which most domestic programming was made by permanent staff at the BBC or ITV (Thynne, 2000: 66). This position conferred advantages on female staff, such as paid maternity leave, on-the-job training and potentially the chance to develop through in-house schemes, such as the BBC Attachment Scheme (ibid.).[1] The benefit of having a paternalistic employer, job security and the possibility of some career progression is probably reflected in the long periods of service seen in the early joiners, although their ability to progress in their careers is explored later in this chapter.

From the late 1980s the workforce became increasingly fluid, with the rise of the independent sector and the impact of Producer Choice within the BBC, resulting in more freelance and contract work. Producer Choice was part of the financial reforms and restructuring of the BBC in the 1990s under John Birt. It gave in-house producers the freedom to book crews and facilities outside the Corporation, and resulted in many craft positions being made redundant and staff becoming freelance. The industry changed from employing staff on continuous contracts to employing mostly freelance workers (Willis and Dex, 2003: 121). This observation is supported by Skillset's data which suggests that almost 60 per cent of television production staff were freelance by the turn of the millennium (Skillset, 2001). The proportions of freelance staff working in a broadcast centre, like Pebble Mill, might be lower than in other television workplaces, particularly independents, but the trend is still apparent in a reduction of years of BBC service observable in the survey responses from younger respondents.

Respondents were asked about the gender split of staff in their programme teams or craft areas. Of joiners in the 1960s and 1970s, 64 per cent reported that their department was male-dominated. This contrasted with joiners from the 1980s, where over half said their team was female-dominated. This proportion grew further with the 1990 and 2000s joiners, where over 80 per cent reported either equal numbers or a female-dominated team. This data suggests more women were working in BBC Birmingham from the 1980s onwards. The growth of daytime programming made at Pebble Mill during this era might account for some of these changes, as the respondents were clear that this production area was largely staffed by women.

Where women worked

The interviews and survey data provide considerable detail about the jobs women were carrying out at Pebble Mill, and the programmes they were working on. Stephanie, one of the interviewees – who joined the BBC as a secretary in 1965, and rose to be Managing Editor Daytime by the time she left in the early 2000s – summed up the changing position of women in television:

> Women didn't have careers and they didn't have career aspirations, when I started . . . But during the course of my long career it did change and the horizons broadened and opened . . . it was very rewarding to see channel controllers and heads of Vision who were women, because I think at the beginning of my career I wouldn't have considered it as a possibility.
>
> *(Stephanie)*

The positions to which women were able to rise improved within the BBC during Stephanie's career, although there was never a female Head of Building, Head of News or Head of Drama at Pebble Mill. The widening roles for women reflected societal changes, including the rise of feminism and equal opportunities legislation, meaning that most women *do* now have career aspirations.

In the late 1960s, Stephanie says, 'the real glamour job was the television PA [Production Assistant], because there was nothing else on offer to women'; this echoes the ACTT report's observations that women were concentrated in a few, relatively 'dead-end' roles – those of Production Secretary, Continuity Girl and Production Assistant (1975: 1). Stephanie was able to undertake PA training, working in the clumsily titled Immigrants' Programme Unit at Pebble Mill on both studio and location shows, and then found herself stuck for a number of years until

> This new grade of Researcher . . . emerged [in 1970] and there was finally a post which offered women a stepping stone between being a PA and being an Assistant Producer. Because previously it was too big a leap and it was a whole new ball game once researchers were on the books.
>
> *(Stephanie)*

Prior to this PA had been the ceiling for many women, particularly in factual production. Stephanie talks about a critical mass of talented women – notably on *Pebble Mill at One* (BBC1 1972–86), where she was working in the early 1970s – wanting careers, being very aware of the rise of feminism and pushing to become Assistant Producers, while there were few vacancies and 'all the posts were held by men'. In time, several well-qualified women, including Stephanie, secured these positions, and almost immediately acted up as Producers.

The situation in Television Drama appears to have been better from a female perspective. Like Stephanie, Jenny, one of the other interviewees, joined BBC Birmingham as a secretary in the late 1960s, becoming Secretary to David Rose, Head of English Regions Drama, from 1971. She states that there were always female producers and directors, often freelance, who would come and work on a show, and therefore women in junior positions knew that the possibilities were there. For Jenny, Drama had 'less of the macho-ness' that was apparent in other production areas, where some of her friends worked. She did not perceive the glass ceiling in the way Stephanie had:

> I think it was partly an expectation, that people expected the boss to be a male, but also partly self-inflicted, because when you rise beyond a certain point, do you happily stick there, rather than bang against it and start dealing with the serious stuff?
>
> *(Jenny)*

She observed that women might particularly enjoy being producers or directors and not want to take the next step into more senior positions, because you then stopped doing what you actually enjoyed, and had to take on difficult decision-making. There is probably some truth in this argument, although the important issue would seem to relate to equality of opportunity.

In other areas, the position was very different. One of the survey respondents, who worked in Regional News, wrote that only 'one out of three or four TV News Editors were female', and that women 'never progressed far and judgements on them were always more severe' (Presenter and Reporter, 1987–92). This view suggests there was some truth in News being considered as a more 'macho' environment, and one which resisted the promotion of women to senior positions. Another respondent who worked in News noted that female producers had to work harder than men, in order to prove themselves.

Several respondents remarked on the lack of women in key craft areas, such as camera, sound and editing. There was one female Camera Operator during the entire period in which Pebble Mill was open – a woman who went on to become a director. She was one of the survey respondents, and talked about the challenges of 'being sexually stereotyped' and 'looked down upon' (Camera Operator, Director 1985–93). It was clearly difficult to be accepted as an equal when working in a traditional, male-dominated area. In editing, there were always a few female Film Editing Assistants, who became Offline Editors when computerisation of editing arrived in the early 1990s, but there were no women Videotape Editors or Engineers. These observations accord with Thynne's research, which concluded that key craft roles on the comparatively well-resourced programmes of terrestrial broadcasters remain 'almost entirely a male preserve' (Thynne, 2000: 69).

One of the survey respondents summarised the gendering of roles across craft and production thus:

> In craft areas there are still frighteningly few women. In nearly twenty years I've only worked with four female Editors. In production I think there were always a roughly equal number of women at researcher and AP [Assistant Producer] level and I'm not sure that's changed much . . . It seems to be at PD [Producer/Director] level where there are fewer women. In BBC Birmingham at one time there were nine staff PDs and I was the only woman. At SP [Series Producer] and Executive level I think it evens out again.
>
> *(Producer/Director, 1994–present)*

From this response it seems that women predominated in less technical production roles, both junior and senior, whereas roles like directing were seen as more of a male preserve. A different respondent talks about the move to 'self-shooting' being a turning point for women. Self-shooting became increasingly important in the late 1990s and early 2000s, with advances in camcorder technology, and was a cost-effective way of making programmes, particularly for high-volume, low-budget Daytime series. The respondent mentions how production roles changed:

> It was no longer enough to be a good Researcher/AP/Producer/Director – you also had to self-shoot. I enjoyed self-shooting which possibly at that time led to increased opportunities, but there was definitely a perception that men could handle the cameras better than women.
>
> *(Assistant Producer, 1999–2004)*

From the survey and interviews, it was clear that the Daytime production teams were predominantly female, especially from the 1990s onwards, and to an extent became a gendered silo: 'women at Pebble Mill were largely stuck in Daytime while men held the prime-time positions. *Top Gear, Countryfile, Country Tracks* – mostly men in charge' (Series Producer, Daytime, 1990–2002). The resentment inherent in this comment is obvious, with the use of 'stuck' being striking. Another respondent makes a similar comment:

> Daytime programming was dominated by women because men tended to 'look down' on it and the type of content (lifestyle) did not always appeal to men, so it was actually a good place for a young female to work in and to progress up the career ladder.
>
> *(Producer, Daytime, 1989–95)*

From this comment it is clear that working in Daytime could be a paradox: from one perspective an unappealing feminised production area, but conversely a good place to progress quickly, without too much male competition. Daytime programming required higher volumes of episodes but with smaller budgets than prime-time, resulting in lower production values. Shows tended to be transmitted daily rather than weekly, so the pressures on production teams to produce episodes quickly were high, with less room for creativity. This, combined with content that was sometimes perceived as frivolous or ephemeral – for example, room or fashion makeovers – and aimed at a predominantly female viewer led some in male-dominated departments – for example, the Motoring unit, which included *Top Gear* – to 'look down' on Daytime. The production teams in Daytime usually included more women than men, although frequently there was a male Editor.

One of the questions posed in the survey was whether respondents perceived a glass ceiling for women, which prevented their promotion. For joiners to Pebble Mill in the 1960–80s, around 35 per cent said that they thought there was a glass ceiling, while 22 per cent thought there was not; 43 per cent of the respondents felt that there had been a barrier, but that it had improved over the course of their careers. The following comment typifies that perspective: '[w]omen pushed their way forward and became quite a force within the BBC' (Production Manager, 1983–2012). The vast majority of joiners from the 1990s and 2000s did not perceive any inequality of opportunity. Many of the younger participants were conscious of the pioneering work of women before them:

> I know that the generation before me found it tough, but I think we were very lucky, those who entered at the beginning of the nineties and onwards, we were treated pretty equally actually.
>
> *(Caroline, Producer, Daytime 1989–95)*

These results support the view that female workers' ability to reach senior roles in television production improved during the operating period of Pebble Mill, although women still tended to be working in gendered silos.

Women in management

The survey asked respondents whether they knew of female managers in the BBC. For joiners in the 1960s, 1970s and 1980s, around two-thirds knew a few women managers during their time at the BBC, but around 12 per cent did not know of any. Stephanie, one of the interviewees, said when she joined the BBC in 1965, there were no women in senior positions. This was in contrast to joiners in the 1990s and 2000s, who all knew of female managers, with around 70 per cent observing that there were quite a number. The responses point to the successful implementation of the BBC's objective to appoint women to managerial positions, which was articulated as early as 1973 (see ACTT, 1975; also Fogarty *et al.*, 1981), although it seems to have taken a considerable period of time for this to have been realised.

Two of the interviewees, Stephanie and Jenny, had been among the first female managers at BBC Pebble Mill. In the mid-1990s Stephanie was appointed Managing Editor Daytime, making her the first female Managing Editor at Pebble Mill. By that stage the culture at the BBC was changing, and Stephanie noted that being a woman was certainly not a disadvantage; she talks of the corporate 'Brownie points' that would be awarded to her male bosses for appointing her, although she notes, with a smile, that she was 'the best man for the job'. This view is echoed by Jenny, who became Head of Planning and Programme Services in 1990, negotiating budgets and transmission schedules and managing Design, Costume, Graphics and Scene Crew staff. When Producer Choice was brought in, in 1993, she had to make one-third of those staff redundant – including her own post – and subsequently became Head of Commissioning and Scheduling. She left the BBC in 2000. Like Stephanie, she talks about the positive encouragement she was given to enter management, perhaps cynically to increase the equal opportunity statistics:

> I was rolled out on all the posh occasions, you know, here she is, here's this woman, because at the time, I was what, late thirties. So it was a kind of unique thing then, because they didn't usually have female managers.
>
> *(Jenny)*

Producer Choice – John Birt's restructuring of the BBC, including reform of the internal market – was an era of uncertainty mentioned by both women. Stephanie highlights the vulnerability she felt:

> The higher up the ladder you went, the more expensive you were to retain. So you did feel vulnerable to being picked off, or being made an offer you couldn't refuse.
>
> *(Stephanie)*

Moving into management might therefore be seen as both a blessing and a curse. For Stephanie, the happiest time of her career was when she was a producer. Jenny shared this ambivalence:

> I was given opportunities and I took those opportunities and in the main, I probably don't regret them. I probably did regret them a few times in my career. There was a point when the ownership of my position, I was pushed to

be run through the Resource department and the management there was very, very different from working in a production department and quite difficult to deal with at times.

(Jenny)

She alluded to a 'macho' culture within Resources which she had never felt in Drama, and this perhaps belies the fact that there were so few female workers in the craft areas of television. The women's comments seem to reflect changes during the 1990s in women's positions in the television industry as observed by Georgina Born in *Uncertain Vision*, her ethnography of the BBC:

> The most remarkable result of the equal opportunities initiative was a transformation over the decade of women's position within the BBC, with a steady rise in the proportion of women in senior and middle management.
>
> *(Born, 2004: 202)*

The push from the BBC centrally to increase the number of women in management rippled through to regional centres like Pebble Mill, in the shape of women like Stephanie and Jenny. Melanie, a producer, raised the widely shared view that the female managers 'weren't necessarily the women you could identify with very well, they were kind of very strong women, women who didn't have children': women who had had to fight hard to achieve their position. Of the female managers I interviewed, Stephanie had one child, and Jenny was childless. Several respondents noted a lack of empathy from women in positions of power: 'I noticed that women would often perceive other intelligent women as a threat, and would make life as difficult for them as possible' (Assistant Producer, 1985–2013). This might be symptomatic of the struggle that women in positions of power had undergone to achieve those positions.

One survey respondent noted that

> Women in management seem to dominate certain genres – Daytime, Features – the 'softer' genres that concentrate on lifestyle and the home. I think the challenge is to be a woman taken seriously in the male-dominated areas like journalism and hard factual.
>
> *(Series Producer, 1994–ongoing)*

This comment points to the fact that there is still room for further progress in terms of women's appointments within the BBC, and indeed the television industry more widely.

Television for women

An area which is currently under-researched in the field of television production studies is whether programmes that are addressed to a particularly gendered audience also have gender-skewed production teams, and whether the gender of production teams has an impact on the production of television itself. This research sought to address this question.

The survey highlights some interesting points about the production teams' response to the audience. The vast majority of respondents were able to identify Pebble Mill programmes they thought had a predominantly female audience; the list included many Daytime titles, some Drama output and even evening leisure shows such as *Gardeners' World* (BBC, 1968–). However, when participants were asked whether they thought that having a predominantly female audience affected how the programme was made, only around 40 per cent felt that it did, with an equal percentage disagreeing. This was pursued further in the interviews, where one interviewee tangibly resisted acknowledging that having a largely female audience might affect the programme-making. Stephanie, who had worked in production from 1965 until the 2000s, agreed that the majority of the available audience for a Daytime series like *Pebble Mill at One* was female, being largely made up of older people and young mothers, but also including shift workers, students and others. In her interview she remarked: 'although the subject matter was for women I didn't downgrade, in my view, in any way, the content or the balance of the accuracy, or the integrity of the programme.' The defensive nature of her response is surprising; particularly notable is the view that programmes aimed towards a female audience might be less rigorous, less balanced or of a lower quality. Stephanie was resistant to the notion that having a predominantly female audience would affect how the programme was made. The gender skew of the audience was not reflected in the demographics of the production team at the time to which she was referring. In the early 1970s the production team of *Pebble Mill at One* contained no women in senior positions; all the directors and producers and the Editor and Deputy Editor were male, and all but one of the researchers were female.

A researcher who was working on *Pebble Mill at One* from 1981 mentions the programme including

> lots of cooking, authors, safe fashion, male crooners, little chart pop music, no youth topics, nothing controversial. However, there were big events like the SAS storming the building, which appealed to everyone . . . The feel of the show was always driven by the Executive Producer, who, with one exception, was always male.
>
> *(Researcher, Assistant Producer, 1979–88)*

The production team of the series included many more women at Producer level by the early 1980s, although it is clear from this comment that the overall content and tone was dictated by the male Editor. It is arguable that this resulted in a show which was more gender-neutral than some later Daytime series, for example the makeover series which became popular in the 1990s such as *Style Challenge* (BBC1, 1996–8), *Real Rooms* (BBC1, 1997–2003), *Real Rakeovers* (BBC1, 2000), *Big Strong Girls* (BBC1, 1999–2001) and *Big Strong Boys* (BBC1, 2000–4), which included a predominantly female address.

Other participants in the study, most of whom were working in the 1990s and 2000s, were much more cognisant of catering to a female audience and the effects this had on both the subject matter and style of productions. Melanie, who is still a producer in the industry, talks about the tone of Daytime makeover shows from the 1990s and early 2000s, such as *Housecall* (BBC1, 2000–3), as being 'chatty', 'informal' and 'colourful'; she notes that the presenters would be 'good-looking younger men' or 'non-threatening', 'next-door neighbour-type' women. She describes this approach as 'quite sexist at times', meaning that assumptions about which presenters – particularly men – would appeal to the imagined female audience were often made by the commissioners and producers on the basis of looks. In terms of the structure of the shows, she was conscious of the audience dipping in and out, which made 'magazine' formats ideal, with their short segment lengths. While the production team knew that the majority of the audience was made up of older people, she mentions feeling that the audience being targeted when ideas were pitched was the 30–40-year-old woman who wanted aspirational quick tips to improve her home, rather than the older audience. In her opinion, the shows being made for a predominantly female audience affected their content, tone and presentational style, as well as the structure. Although she does not mention the 'integrity' or 'balance' that Stephanie described, her observation of sexism could refer to the same perception of 'downgrading' to which Stephanie was resistant: a feeling that Daytime programming was of a lesser quality than prime-time. This is borne out by the observation of the tone being light, the content often superficial, and presenters being selected on the basis of their looks rather than their expertise. For the production teams making them, this did not feel like programming that was considered serious or important by the BBC; it was not programming that was going to win awards, or change viewers' perceptions of the world.

Several subjects in the study mentioned that having a predominantly female audience was rarely talked about within the programme teams. Melanie remarks, 'I don't think I ever had a conversation where someone told me this has got to be aimed at a female market, I think that that was just a general feeling', and Caroline notes that 'I think we knew subconsciously that our audience was female'. A survey respondent also articulates this view:

> I was aware that none of my brother, boyfriends, father etc., were remotely interested in most of the programmes I worked on, as they would tell me how 'girly' they were. This was never talked about at work.
>
> *(Production Co-ordinator, 1991–ongoing)*

The fact that the subject was never discussed is telling, and fits with the ambivalent response to the survey question about whether having a female audience affected the production process. It seems as if catering to a predominantly female audience was perceived as a negative, as a factor that would limit the tone, structure and content of the show. That the audience was assumed but not discussed is perhaps surprising, but echoes the sentiments mentioned earlier about Daytime programming being perceived as 'down-market', and working on it being poorly regarded.

Another recurring subject in the responses was the use of attractive men in shows aimed at a female audience. Melanie mentions the use of a 'sex symbol chef' in *Housecall* and carpenters with 'a few muscles', while a production manager talks about attractive male presenters as 'a bit of eye candy for the bored housewife at home'. Caroline, one of the interviewees, booked celebrity guests for shows like *Daytime Live* (BBC1, 1987–90), and mentions choosing 'male heart-throbs' much of the time. Dramas, such as *Dangerfield* (BBC1, 1995–9), were also identified as using actors who 'were considered eye candy'. The notion of female viewers experiencing an often secret desire through their watching of television is explored much more fully in Chapter 12 in this volume by Hazel Collie. It is interesting that the importance of desire as a motivation to view was understood by the television production teams, and was deliberately addressed in the casting of many shows. This aspect may warrant further research in future.

The research data suggests that the differing opinions towards the production of programmes with a female-skewed audience are dependent on the age of the respondents and the period during which they were working, with younger women being more open in acknowledging the effects of the assumed audience on the tone, presentation and subject matter. A possible interpretation is that this reflects a change in the culture of production, as women television workers occupied senior positions and felt more integrated from the 1990s onwards. The response that comes through most strongly is that for many respondents, catering for a female-skewed audience often involved casting attractive men in key on-screen roles, and there was a common perception of 'downgrading' or making the content more superficial for this audience.

Children

As noted earlier in this chapter, the challenge of combining television production and motherhood has been well documented since the early 1970s, and it was a theme that emerged strongly in both the interviews and survey responses. Stephanie, who went on to become Managing Editor, Daytime, by the end of her career returned to work in the early 1970s, as a researcher with a young child:

> [I]t was my approach to present a professional working image. I rarely mentioned the fact that I had a child. It was known, but I didn't talk about it . . . I didn't want anyone to think that I was a weak link. Anyone who is on a freelance contract is somewhat vulnerable and certainly being a working mother, I felt, added to my vulnerability.
>
> *(Stephanie)*

That having a child might add to a female worker's sense of vulnerability suggests inherent sexual discrimination within the organisation, as does the fact that talking about her status as a mother might make her seem less 'professional'. Stephanie was working on a freelance basis then, which was quite unusual when working for a large broadcaster at that time. Her comment relates to the 1970s, when consciousness about equal opportunities was in its infancy – although similar issues were described by other participants still working in the industry, such as Melanie, a producer:

> There was actually a female Executive, who told me in confidence that she wished she hadn't taken the year out [when she had a baby], because she really felt it had a detrimental effect . . . she actually told me she wouldn't even put maternity leave on her CV – that to almost try and not mention that you had children, if you went for an interview. And I certainly felt that by having children I was being treated in a very different way.
>
> *(Melanie)*

These women perceived that motherhood could potentially damage one's career. Melanie went on to explain in greater detail:

> I was aware that the minute I decided to have children my career might take a slight nose-dive . . . And I was worried about that because I had seen it happen to quite a lot of women in the industry . . . I think TV is the sort of industry that does demand a lot from you. It expects you to be flexible, it doesn't really have set hours. If you're on a shoot and something goes wrong then it's not a case of it's five o'clock, let's all go . . . it's very, very difficult to manage that lifestyle with children.
>
> *(Melanie)*

Many of the survey respondents mentioned the incompatibility of combining motherhood with a career in television. The following sentiment was echoed by several women: 'I stopped working when I had children – there was no way I could do the hours expected of me and have any normal family life' (Drama Continuity, 1976–81). However, one of the interviewees, Caroline – who worked on live studio programmes in the early 1990s, and had risen to producer by the time she left – held a different view:

> I think it was actually an incredibly supportive workplace and probably pioneering in the way that it supported its female workers. It had a crèche, very early on, and I don't think there was any problem. I had colleagues who were mothers and in some ways being a live daily show going out at lunchtime, you were kind of OK, because if you had to pick up the children late in the afternoon, your job was done . . .
>
> *(Caroline)*

That Pebble Mill had a crèche for staff's children was noted in the ACTT report in 1975, at a stage when the London premises did not; it could therefore be considered as a progressive workplace (ACTT, 1975: 35). The crèche at Pebble Mill was active in the mid-1970s but then closed; it reopened in the late 1980s, and remained open until the building closed in 2004. However, it had standard opening hours, closing at 6 pm in the evening, which made it difficult for production staff to rely on this facility. Such a service was valued by staff, though, and demonstrates that regional centres sometimes led the way in innovations over the metropolitan headquarters.

Caroline makes the point that working on a daily live studio show was relatively practical for a working mother, a factor emphasised in the ACTT report: it was easier for women with families to take a permanent studio job rather than cope with location filming (ibid.: 1). This would have contributed to the 'gendered niches', such as 'Children's' and 'Education', which Fogarty *et al.* (1981) identifies. Daytime studio shows would also seem to qualify as a 'gendered niche', where staff were predominantly female, and where increasingly there were women in positions of seniority.

A comparison of television listings from 1995 and 2015 reveals that fewer Daytime studio programmes are now being transmitted on the BBC. The BBC1 morning schedule for the week Monday 16 to Friday 20 January 1995, which was a typical week, lists *Kilroy* (BBC1, 1986–2004), followed by *Good Morning with Anne and Nick* (BBC1, 1992–6), then *Pebble Mill* (BBC1, 1991–6) – all studio shows – while the listing for the corresponding week in 2015, from Monday 19 to Friday 23 January, includes only location-based programmes. While the change from studio to location-based series is not universal, with ITV and Channel 4 still producing a number of studio shows, it does potentially contribute to the challenges women continue to face in combining television production and motherhood. One of the most disheartening conclusions to emerge from this research is that the difficulties facing mothers working in television production seem to have become more acute in recent years, rather than less. Here is the view of one respondent:

> It seemed over time more difficult for women with children to work in production . . . It was interesting to see the number of working mums who have accepted redundancy over the years.
>
> *(Assistant Producer, 2002–12)*

With the benefit of hindsight, the relatively stable employment situation at BBC Pebble Mill from the 1970s to the 1990s – an enlightened employer providing relatively generous maternity leave and pay, an on-site crèche, together with a number of live daily Daytime shows to work on – was a real benefit for working mothers. Changes in programme tastes, resulting in fewer live studio shows, increased casualisation and reduction in work benefits such as crèches, has made combining motherhood and television production more problematic.

Conclusion

The results of this study suggest that while there have always been women in television production, their roles have changed markedly since the 1970s. In the 1970s and early 1980s women were concentrated in a few heavily gendered roles, with little chance of progression. A combination of the introduction of the Researcher grade in the early 1970s and a positive desire to increase opportunities for women within the

BBC has enabled women to progress to senior production and managerial positions. Women make up the majority of the workforce in many production teams, especially in gendered niches like Daytime, but there are still relatively few women in craft and more technical areas.

Several issues impact on women's ability to work in television production. They continue to encounter sexism, but the most frequently cited challenge was the difficulty of combining motherhood with the demands of television production. With increased casualisation and the move away from studio to location programming, the position for working mothers is arguably worse now than in the late 1980s and 1990s. Staff contracts, in-work benefits such as maternity leave and crèches and the ability to work on studio programmes made it easier to organise childcare when the large broadcasters dominated programme production, before the growth of the independent sector.

The majority of respondents were able to identify programmes made at BBC Pebble Mill which appealed to a predominantly female audience, especially Daytime series, but this seems to have rarely been discussed within the production teams. In the 1970s, and early 1980s, the senior positions on these programmes were almost exclusively male, but this changed markedly in the subsequent decade.

There are a number of diverse factors which, in combination but not individually, contributed to the rise of women to senior television roles. These women often made programmes predominantly viewed by women, and developed a successful feminine address. Women tended to work in 'gendered niches' like Daytime and lifestyle programming – areas which were often 'looked down on' by those working on better-resourced prime-time series, which were deemed more serious and important, and which received more critical acclaim. Daytime programming was often limiting for production teams because of tight formats, quick turnaround and small budgets, which left less room for creative freedom and, therefore, job satisfaction than prime-time. It is significant that women were able to dominate production team roles, including senior positions, in areas like Daytime: these were programme areas which were less coveted by male colleagues, and where it was therefore easier to carve out a niche for themselves. The programmes where women made up the majority of the production team were also the programmes which had a predominantly feminine address, and which appealed less as a workplace to male competitors.

Note

1 The Attachment Scheme allowed permanent staff to join a different department for a specified time period, usually of several months. The scheme gave many individuals the opportunity to develop production skills and gain promotion within the BBC.

Bibliography

ACTT (1975) *Patterns of Discrimination against Women in the Film and Television Industries.* London: Association of Cinematograph, Television and Allied Technicians.

Antcliff, V. (2005) 'Broadcasting in the 1990s: Competition, choice and inequality?' *Media, Culture & Society,* 27(6): 841–59.

Bonner, F. (2003) *Ordinary Television: Analyzing Popular TV*. London, Thousand Oaks and New Delhi: Sage.

Born, G. (2004) *Uncertain Vision: Birt, Dyke and the Reinvention of the BBC*. London: Secker & Warburg.

Conlan, T. (1999) 'Survey cites "slave labour" in TV'. *Broadcast*, December 10. www. broadcastnow.co.uk/survey-cites-slave-labour-in-tv/1225762.article (Last accessed 5 August 2015).

Dex, S., J. Willis, R. Paterson, and E. Sheppard (2000) 'Freelance workers and contract uncertainty: The effects of contractual changes in the television industry'. *Work, Employment & Society*, 14(2): 283–305.

Fogarty, M.P., I. Allen, and P. Walters (1981) *Women in Top Jobs: 1968–1979*. London: Policy Studies Institute, Heinemann Educational Books.

Grugulis, I. (2012) 'Social capital and networks in film and TV: Jobs for the boys?' *Media, Culture & Society*, 33(10): 1311–31.

Hesmondhalgh, D. and S. Baker (2011) *Creative Labour: Media Work in Three Cultural Industries*. London and New York: Routledge.

Lee, D. (2011) 'Networks, cultural capital and creative labour in the British independent television industry', *Media, Culture & Society*, 33(4): 549–65.

Moseley, R. and H. Wheatley (2008) 'Is archiving a feminist issue? Historical research and the past, present, and future of television studies', *Cinema Journal*, 47(3): 152–8.

Moseley, R., H. Wheatley, and H. Wood (2014) 'Television in the afternoon', *Critical Studies in Television*, 9(2): 1–19.

O'Brien, A. (2014) '"Men *own* television": Why women leave media work', *Media, Culture & Society*, 36(8): 1207–18.

Paterson, R. (2001) 'Work histories in television', *Media, Culture & Society*, 23(4): 495–520.

Pettigrew, N., J. Willis, and R. Paterson (1995) *The British Film Institute Television Tracking Study, the First Year: An Interim Report*. London: BFI.

Pettigrew, N., J. Willis, and R. Paterson (1997) *The British Film Institute Television Tracking Study, Second Interim Report*. London: BFI.

Sheppard, E. and S. Dex (1998) *Analysis of Attrition in the Longitudinal Television Industry Tracking Survey*, unpublished document, London: BFI.

Skillset (2001) *Skillset Freelance Survey 2000–1*. http://creativeskillset.org/assets/0000/6243/Skillset_Freelance_Survey_2000-01.pdf (Last accessed 25 April 2016).

Thynne, L. (2000) 'Women in television in the multi-channel age', *Feminist Review*, 64 (Spring): 65–82.

Willis, J. and S. Dex (2003) 'Mothers returning to television production work in a changing environment', in A. Beck (ed.) *Cultural Work: Understanding the Cultural Industries*, London: Routledge: 121–41.

PART II
Women and identity

4

CATFIGHT! CAMP AND QUEER VISIBILITY IN *ORANGE IS THE NEW BLACK*

Dana A. Heller

It is difficult to talk, let alone write, about catfights without exclamation points. That's because the catfight is one of visual culture's loudest and most sensational materializations of gender excess. As mass media convention, the catfight owes as much to the twentieth-century industrial development of popular film and television genres and the loosening of censorship laws in the 1960s as it does to consumer capitalism's spectacularization of femininity, which produced the figure of the "Modern Woman." Indeed, not unlike the visual display logic of modern womanhood, the catfight is staged as pure spectacle and is constitutive of what Liz Conor has termed the "Modern Appearing Woman," a new embodiment of feminine subjectivity (2004: 2). For this reason, the catfight occupies a unique place in the overlapping historical evolution of cultural scholarship and feminist film theory, both as a stock commercial feature of "pulp" genres deemed low (comedy, melodrama, pornography, exploitation films) and as a perennial register of woman's visual objectification and exploitation in the mass media. While feminist theories of cinematic spectatorship have undergone significant revision in acknowledgement of the nuance, complexity, and fluidity that mediate the organization of the gaze and blur the boundaries of gendered identifications and desires, the catfight has remained largely ignored and mocked. It has either not been taken seriously at all, or it has been taken seriously for the wrong reasons. It has certainly never been dignified in the way that Judith Butler's (1990) *Gender Trouble* gave intellectual currency and cachet to the role of drag performance. It is time to give the catfight its due.

My interest in catfights arises in part from my sense that they are making a comeback in the era of television's post-*Ellen* assimilation of queer communities and histories. More on this will follow. For now, I want to make one thing clear: when I use the term "catfight," I do not refer to verbal sparring between women, professional rivalries between women, or any indiscriminate use of the term, which only serves to dilute the catfight's clarity and grandeur: the trumped-up Twitter feud between

Nicki Minaj and Taylor Swift has no relevancy here. When I talk about a "catfight" I refer to the hardcore throwdown, the spectacle of two women engaged in a wild, extravagant physical altercation that typically involves (but is not limited to) scratching, biting, slapping, strangling, straddling, kicking, and hair-pulling. In its soft-porn variety, it may also involve the shredding and/or yanking off of clothing as the fight intensifies. Catfights have no truck with sophisticated weaponry. By defi-nition, they are battles of instinctive physical proximity—*mano a mano*. No matter the tactics, all catfights share one thing in common: they are always in bad taste, uproariously and by design. Catfights are unapologetically taboo-breaking, not because they reinforce or undermine cultural scripts of gender and sexuality but because they compel us to think critically—even daringly— about the brutal con-tradictions that make gender and sexuality televisible.

The term "catfight" is itself brutal, with etymological origins that trace back, surprisingly, to an 1854 study of the domestic organization of Mormon polygamy. In *Utah and the Mormons: The History, Government, Doctrines, Customs, and Prospects of the Latter-Day Saints, from Personal Observation during a Six Months' Residence at Great Salt Lake City*, author Benjamin G. Ferris notes that Mormon homes were built so as to separate the household's multiple wives, in an effort to "prevent those terrible cat-fights which sometimes occur" (Ferris, 1854: 308). From these origins, the catfight gained mainstream popularity in the context of postwar fetish photography (particularly the work of Irving Klaw), low-budget exploitation movies, and Russ Myers' campy cinematic obsession with large-bosomed, ass-kicking biker chicks. However, it was the golden age of 1970s television that brought the catfight into our living rooms, thanks largely to the American prime-time soap operas *Dallas* (CBS, 1978–91) and *Dynasty* (ABC, 1981–9), the latter of which adopted the catfight as one of its signature conventions in an all-out effort to boost its first season's lackluster ratings. And it worked. Viewers began tuning in to watch Krystle Carrington—the perfect wife of oil tycoon Blake Carrington—slug it out with his conniving ex-wife and über-bitch, Alexis. Over the course of the series, the rivalry between Krystle and Alexis produced eleven catfights, which established, according to *Entertainment Weekly*, "the gold standard of scratching and clawing" (Stack, 2008). The fights also helped establish the gold standard for a certain brand of deliriously trashy, blow-dried 1980s camp, which reveled in the performative excesses of Reagan-era status-seeking, conspicuous consumption, and greed.

Clawing and trashiness are only part of that which has made the catfight a highly problematic and politically charged image for feminist critics and scholars. For example, in the essay "Catfight: A Feminist Analysis," cultural critic Rachel Reinke argues that the catfight, which represents women fighting in "erotic, humorous, and ineffective ways," serves to affirm the negative cultural stereotype that "women tend to be overly competitive with one another" (2010: 164). She claims that the per-vasiveness of the catfight image is symptomatic of a "catfight culture," which dehumanizes and disempowers women. In *Where the Girls Are: Growing Up Female with the Mass Media*, media scholar Susan J. Douglas sees the catfight as a larger metaphor "for the struggle between feminism and antifeminism," or as a patriarchal means of repudiating and ridiculing the myth of feminism's collaborative aims, its organization around the trope of universal sisterhood (1994: 233). In *Catfight: Rivalries among Women—From Diets to Dating, from the Boardroom to the Delivery Room*, social critic Leora Tannenbaum blames the derailment of the contemporary feminist movement on petty competition between women themselves and seeks to reveal, in large part through a critique of popular culture, the "roots of this competition, which at best makes one woman covet another woman's designer handbag and at worst thwarts her in the development of her career and her ability to raise children with sanity" (2003: 34). Yet, even more than a cultural caricature or real social manifestation of ruthless female competition, the catfight has been written off by liberal mainstream feminism as a source of cheap entertainment for the male gaze, which, by defining femininity in terms of narcissism, envy, and erotic spectacle, denies women the right to autonomously define their own gender and sexuality.

Implicit in these analyses is the assumption that the erotic spectacularization of intense competition between women is not only damaging to women but also ideologically objectionable—an affront to the legitimate goals of feminism. These analyses arise out of a certain moralistic strain of feminist identity politics that adheres to mainstream cultural codes of feminine politeness and decorum, seeks to sanitize non-vanilla, non-reproductive female sexuality, renders taboo representations of female abjection and the unequal distribution of power among women, and denies women the capacity to enjoy cultural fantasies that eroticize same-sex rivalries or explore links between power and pleasure. Such analyses, as limited as they are limiting, suggest that the catfight has been largely misread as a result of its co-option by a mode of straight, white middle-class feminist thinking that is out of sync with queer theory's interventions into practices and representations of normative sex and gender construction, inattentive to the expansion of analytic possibilities exemplified in the work of feminist scholars and activists of color, and neglectful of the politically charged performance artistry of feminist sexecologists, such as Annie Sprinkle. It is also at odds with the catfight's unique status as an exercise in popular comedic camp, which holds the potential to serve as a formidable critique of neoliberal feminism's investments in consolidating politics and aesthetics, or habits of class, gender, and taste.

Catfights invite us to engage with television images of women differently by drawing our attention to the rules that govern women's engagements with one another. I think this is important for understanding the long evolution of what is often sanguinely referred to as "queer television"—meaning television that has become progressively inclusive of LGBTQ characters and content—and equally important for understanding the ways that LGBTQ consumers are hailed by programming branded with terms such as "edgy," "sophisticated," and "groundbreaking." This is not to say that catfights have become trendy or chic in an age of expanding LGBTQ visibility. Rather, as a mode of performance and unit of discourse, the catfight has evolved into a critique of normative taste hierarchies and their historical organization around admissible embodiments of gender, sexuality, race, and class. More than a tabloid brawl between hot girls enacted for the salacious entertainment of male viewers, catfights scramble the codes of heteronormative, middle-class femininity by staging chaotic conflicts between standards of high culture and low culture, domination and resistance, power and subordination, good girls and bad girls.

If the catfight appears to be making a comeback it may be because one of its most familiar venues, the women-in-prison drama, is also resurgent. Indeed, the catfight has long been a staple of this exploitation subgenre, which explores the social, political, and affective dynamics of captive women isolated from the outside world and forced to live in close physical proximity as they undergo surveillance and rehabilitation by the state. The women-in-prison narrative has its origins in 1930s pulp fiction paperbacks and cinema melodramas that commonly featured a young female protagonist's conversion to moral righteousness through the hardship of imprisonment (*Paid* [1930], *Ladies They Talk About* [1933], *So Young, So Bad* [1950]). However, as film scholar Judith Mayne (2000) notes, the subgenre blossomed in the 1950s and revealed a more complex fascination with how women relate to one another, sexually and across boundaries of race and class, when left to negotiate their own desires. Mayne's argument that films such as *Caged* (1950) and *Chained Heat II* (1983) constitute subversive feminist texts makes sense when we consider their "raw energy" and "celebration of female revolt" (2000: 116). Moreover, by inviting viewers into a world of social outcasts, sexual deviants, and relentless internal ogling and surveillance, women-in-prison films helped assimilate lesbian characters into the conventions of popular cinema. The lesbian presence, whether explicit or implied, complicates "the strict dichotomy of the man who surveys the woman" by emphasizing the leering interest with which women watch women (ibid.: 118). And although they are typically classified as tawdry B-movies, many early women-in-prison films register progressive aspirations in their exploration of real social problems and institutional injustices that ensnare women and leave them little choice but a life of crime.

Indeed, it is fair to say that there has always been something queer about the very idea of a woman's prison. As Heather Love (2014) argues, prisons (along with medical hospitals and psychiatric institutions) have played a vital role in the popular denotation of modern lesbian identity as lawless, unstable, and violent. The history of homosexual criminalization positioned correctional facilities as key locations for the containment of lesbianism, but even more importantly as sites for the cultural imagining of lesbian sex, engaging fictional "sites for the production of fantasies about sexual excess and disorder, desire, and domination" (Love, 2014). No wonder, then, that women-in-prison films have

> produced some of lesbianism's most familiar stock images (the violent and possessive butch dyke; the spiteful, sexually frustrated warden; the naive straight woman) as well as key elements of plot (the corruption of an innocent; dramas of sexual ownership; and psychotic overinvestment).
>
> *(Love, 2014)*

Heavily formulaic, women-in-prison films habitually feature catfights, all-female strip searches, sexual bullying, group shower scenes, consensual lesbian sex with inmates and/or guards, and the constant threat of rape by inmates and/or guards, both male and female.

While production of women-in-prison films appears to have ebbed in contemporary Hollywood, the conventions of the subgenre continue to shape popular culture fantasies of homoerotic seduction and violence.[1] Lady Gaga's extended music video for the pop hit "Telephone" (2009) pays homage to the subgenre with its flamboyant references to lesbian homoeroticism, sadomasochism, and female buddy films such as *Thelma and Louise* (1991). Speaking of Lady Gaga, *Saturday Night Live* (NBC, 1975–) staged what could be considered the ultimate fantasy catfight in a 2009 comedic sketch that pitted the pop diva Madonna against Gaga in a satirical MTV duet that rapidly devolves into a clawing and hair-pulling match. The catfight circulates ubiquitously in contemporary culture through its use in television advertising (e.g. the controversial bikini catfight advertisement for Miller Lite beer, which aired during the US 2003 National Football League Playoffs; situation comedy (*Seinfeld* [NBC, 1989–98]; *Friends* [NBC, 1994–2004]); ensemble drama (*Desperate Housewives* [ABC, 2004–12], *Xena: Warrior Princess* [WTVZ, 1995–2001], *Gossip Girl* [CW, 2007–12]); and reality programming (*The Jerry Springer Show* [FOX, 1991–], *Celebrity Apprentice* [NBC, 2011–], *The Bachelor* [ABC, 2002–], *The Real Housewives of . . .* [Bravo, 2006–]), not to mention the countless websites devoted to connoisseurs of the catfight's pornographic appeal (catfightcentral.com, fightingfelines.com, latincatfights.com). Meanwhile, prisons have reemerged as a locus of dramatic television storytelling. The British series *Bad Girls* (ITV, 1999–2006) and the Australian series *Wentworth Prison* (SoHo, 2013–), a remake of the popular 1980s soap opera *Prisoner: Cell Block H* (Network Ten, 1979–1986), have drawn large international audiences and positive reviews for their gritty realism and compelling characters. Showtime's popular series *The L Word* (Showtime, 2004–9), the first show in US television history to feature lesbian, genderqueer, and bisexual women as lead characters, staged a tongue-in-cheek parody of the women-in-prison genre. In "LGB Tease" (Season 5, Episode 1), Helena Peabody's (Rachel Shelley) conviction for theft results in her incarceration and an invocation of the iconic shower rape scene when a friend warns her: "Whatever you do, don't drop the soap." Once in jail, of course, Helena promptly proceeds to drop the soap, and her need for protection leads her to fall in love with a fellow inmate, Dusty (Lucia Rijker), whose name is itself a satirical riff on prison nicknames.[2]

When television writer Jenji Kohan, best known as the creator of the dark Showtime comedy *Weeds* (2005–12), approached both Showtime and HBO with an idea about a women-in-prison series, they turned her down. She took the project to Netflix and the rest, as they say, is television history. After four successful seasons, *Orange is the New Black* has captured the entertainment industry spotlight, enjoyed superlative praise from critics, sent social media all atwitter, and won numerous prestigious recognitions, including Primetime Emmy Awards, People's Choice Awards, Screen Actors Guild Awards, an NAACP Image Award, and the GLAAD

Media Award for Outstanding Comedy Series. Based on Piper Kerman's memoir of her incarceration in the Federal Correctional Institution at Danbury, Connecticut, *Orange is the New Black* has been crowned by Netflix as the "most watched" original series on their streaming service, having surpassed the Emmy Award-winning series *House of Cards*. *Orange is the New Black* has been described as a "TV revolution for women"—a show created by women, written by (mostly) women, and driven by a female cast of talented actors of different ages, sizes, shapes, colors, and genders (Rorke, 2014). Not surprisingly, the series has also garnered a faithful following of queer fans by casting self-identified LGBT actors in central, recurring roles that portray lesbian, transgender, genderqueer, and bisexual characters and their relationships in a realistic and humanizing light. Additionally, it has garnered accolades—more than any previous women-in-prison film or television series —for bringing intersectional female identities to the fore, with a wide range of racially, ethnically, and sexually diverse characters whose individual histories are conveyed through flashback sequences that illuminate what their past lives were like on the outside and how they wound up in the correctional system.

For the remainder of this chapter, I want to further explore what *Orange is the New Black*'s alleged "revolution for women" suggests, not only in terms of the series' identification with the women-in-prison topos but in terms of what might make investments in queer visibility productive for content producers as a cultural branding tool. Additionally, I'm interested in the ways that queer performance speaks to audiences who are attuned to the history of what Quinn Miller calls "television camp," an oppositional strategy through which media industries have satirically circulated "queer culture in forms that elude assimilation" (2014: 143). My argument is double-pronged: Firstly, I argue that *Orange is the New Black* has virtually nothing to do with the reality of women's experiences in prison, or the current US crisis of mass incarceration, or the privatization of a prison–industrial complex that has come to view both male and female inmates as a source of indentured labour and profit, although the series does superficially acknowledge these realities in the interests of relevancy and for promotional purposes.[3] Secondly, I argue that *Orange is the New Black* has much to do with the collective cultural memory of women's (mis)representation in film and television history. More specifically, *Orange is the New Black* hails content consumers as savvy and sophisticated taste-makers through its use of popular camp conventions that maneuver around the representational politics of its prison setting by paying homage to a catalogue of self-reflexive tropes referencing the insider knowledge, rituals, and pulp cultural properties through and against which minority audiences fashion a sense of history and community. My claim is that nowhere throughout the series is the convergence of camp, parody, and gender performativity rendered more hyperbolically than in the recurring trope of the catfight.

In the promotional trailer for Season Three of *Orange is the New Black*, main character Piper Chapman (Taylor Schilling) offers advice to some new inmates at Litchfield Penitentiary: "People think all we do is have lesbian sex and strip searches and naked catfights in the shower," she explains. She then pauses thoughtfully before adding, "We *also do other things.*" Her remark places emphasis on the fact that *Orange is the New Black* is not a show about what women do in prison, but a show about what women do in women-in-prison movies and television shows. It also demonstrates how series writers have craftily maneuvered around one of the main criticisms of the show, which is that *Orange is the New Black* eroticizes the experience of incarceration and fails to accurately reflect the boredom, drudgery, and depression of daily life in a women's correctional facility. Obviously, real prison is not funny. At the same time, boredom, drudgery, and depression make for bad television. In this sense, Piper's description of life at Litchfield is directed less to the prison newbies than to fans and potential Netflix subscribers as an affirmation of the series' commitment to pulpy serialized entertainment. It is an acknowledgement of the debt the series owes to sexual fantasies and fetishes that are part of queer pop culture history, as well as a sideways reference to the camp sensibilities and blue humour that fuelled the production of early "mainstream" television comedies. To those who would ascribe a social justice mission to the series or expect adherence to realist aesthetics in its rendering of prison life, Piper's words place the very possibility of representational authenticity in quotation marks, acknowledging it to be contradiction, a mythical construct that has been largely perpetuated by a historical iconography of cinematic melodrama and exploitative erotic imagery that have become the properties of certain exaggerated, stylized television performances.

Orange is the New Black refers compulsively to this shared stock of fantasies and anxieties about situational prison lesbianism through camp practices that serve as a homage to women-in-prison films of the past and as a wink to viewers, who learn from the premiere episode's opening montage that Piper was a lesbian, or at least bisexual, even before her arrival at Litchfield. "I've always loved getting clean," Piper says in voice-over in the pre-credits sequence, as we see the baby Piper bathing contentedly in a sink full of suds. We next see the adult Piper making love in the shower with her former drug-dealing girlfriend, Alex Vause (Laura Prepon), then canoodling in a bathtub with her under-employed writer fiancé, Larry (Jason Biggs), and then alone, naked, anxious, and wary as she negotiates the notorious communal shower. When fellow inmate, Tasha "Taystee" Jefferson (Danielle Brooks), complains that she is taking too long, Piper apologetically surrenders the shower stall while awkwardly trying to cover up with a too-small towel. Without a moment's hesitation, Taystee yanks the towel off to expose Piper's breasts. "Ooooh, you got some nice titties," she appreciatively observes. "You got them TV titties. They stand on their own, all perky and everything." Taken aback, Piper thanks her, modestly readjusts her towel and scurries away, but not before we see her glance down appraisingly at her own chest and smile.

The obvious pleasure that Piper takes in the compliment reinforces the series' self-reflexive status as TV—real women don't have tits like that, after all. It also reinforces the series' depiction of Piper as a narcissistic, privileged white woman who initially sees her fourteen-month prison sentence as an opportunity to improve her abdominal muscles. "I'm gonna get ripped," she tells Larry. "Jackie Warner ripped."

Her reference to the openly gay fitness guru and star of the Bravo reality series *Work Out* (Bravo, 2006–8) indicates Piper's extreme naïveté about prison life and also delivers a shout-out to viewers of Bravo, a cable channel with a prominent LGBT consumer base. "There are lesbians here," Chief Officer Healy (Michael Harney) warns Piper during their first counseling session. Determined to keep her past a secret, Piper feigns apprehension as Healy advises her to keep to herself and avoid making friends. "You do not have to have lesbian sex," he assures her. However, Piper's repressed erotic history inevitably returns during her first two days at Litchfield. When guard Wanda Bell (Catherine Curtin), commands Piper to "strip" during intake processing, the scene immediately cuts to a flashback of Piper dancing a seductive striptease for Alex. Later, when Piper encounters lesbian lothario Nicky Nichols (Natasha Lyonne) going down on Lorna Morello (Yael Stone) in the bathroom, she is visibly unnerved, although not uninterested. The first episode concludes with Piper's innocent delusions about her status as "a nice white lady" shattered after she is subjected to starvation for inadvertently insulting the prison cook, Galina "Red" Reznikov (Kate Mulgrew), and after witnessing a vicious catfight between two inmates over a half-eaten ice cream cone. Just as Piper reaches the breaking point, Alex—who, unbeknownst to Piper, is also serving time at Litchfield—appears before her in the flesh.

By the end of Season One, Piper has become hardened to the extremes of prison conditions after losing favor with Alex (who dumps her when she learns of her engagement to Larry), Larry (who breaks off their engagement when he learns that Piper has rekindled relations with Alex), and Healy (who abandons Piper when she reveals her penchant for lesbian prison sex, which earns her a period of solitary confinement in the "SHU"). When Tiffany "Pennsatucky" Doggett (Taryn Manning) embarks on a paranoid holy mission to murder Piper there is nobody left to protect her. Poussey (Samira Wiley), Black Cindy (Adrienne C. Moore), and Taystee provide Piper with a brief lunchtime lesson on mastering the prison catfight. Later, at the annual Christmas pageant, Pennsatucky confronts Piper with a sharpened wooden crucifix. With nothing but a stolen screwdriver to defend herself, Piper snaps and unleashes her pent-up rage using the brutal survival techniques that she learned from her fellow inmates. The final bloody battle between Piper and Pennsatucky functions without irony or eroticism as the conclusion to a season otherwise rife with comic references to the fine line between lesbian sadism and lesbian sex. The spectacle of Piper losing control of her emotions, relentlessly pounding Pennsatucky's face with her fists, brings the series back to its grounding in character. The fight scene functions less as a register of Piper's transformation and initiation into prison society than as evidence of an innate capacity for ruthlessness and self-preservation that was always a part of who she is. "I'm scared that I'm not myself in here," Piper admits to Dina (Adrienne Warren). "And I'm scared that I am." At Litchfield, Piper has a self-actualizing experience.

Catfights frame Season One of *Orange is the New Black*, marking Piper's development from a timid, bourgeois innocent who voluntarily surrenders herself to Litchfield because it is the "right thing" to a cutthroat manipulator who'll do anything to better her circumstances and stay alive. If this bleak scenario sounds familiar, it may be because we've seen it countless times before:

> A delicate blonde is incarcerated after she serves as an accomplice in her significant other's crimes. The blonde forms ambivalent bonds with the other women in prison, a process that is implicitly linked to her relationship with lesbianism. After traumatic clashes with prison authorities, including a spell in solitary confinement, she reveals a startling capacity for violence.
>
> (Berlatsky, 2014)

While this may sound like an accurate summary of *Orange is the New Black's* first season, it is actually a summary of the 1950 women-in-prison film *Caged*. In fact, *Orange is the New Black* so closely resembles this "virtually forgotten" classic that Noah Berlatsky suggests Netflix lifted the series' first season plot "practically wholesale." However, the generic plot is not unique to any one original source. The summary aptly describes a wide range of twentieth-century fictions that capitalize on the theme of women needing to be caged and/or controlled by chains. More than enabling a realistic exploration of a broken justice system, the women-in-prison motif condenses femininity itself to its "startling capacity" for sex and violence. The prison setting is largely a pretence that caters to a broader cultural fascination with femininity as essentially treacherous and female sexuality as threateningly animalistic. Regina Spektor's theme song, "You've Got Time" (2013), acknowledges *Orange is the New Black's* debt to *Caged* and the many imitations it spawned by referencing the fundamental metaphorical linkage of women to wild animals:

> The animals, the animals
> Trapped, trapped, trapped, until the cage is full
> The cage is full, the day is new
> And everyone's waiting, waiting on you
> And you've got time . . .

Orange is the New Black's "revolution for women" thus begins with its positioning of Piper Chapman as the antithesis to feminine ferocity, an embodiment of civilized white feminist ethics and sophisticated class entitlement, all of which starts to unravel once she is inside Litchfield's alternate organization of power and privilege. "My mom told friends I was doing volunteer work in Africa," Piper explains when asked how her family is handling her incarceration. Upon receiving her regulation canvas prison shoes, Piper approvingly observes, "These are kinda like Toms." Her reference to the trendy shoe company that provides free footwear to impoverished children is lost on Officer Bell, who looks at Piper warily. "Who's Tom?" she asks. "Toms are shoes," Piper explains, condescendingly. "When you buy a pair, the company gives another to a child in need. They're great. And they come in lots of different colors . . ." The moment is keenly illustrative of the ethical consumerism that Piper retains when she enters Litchfield, a marker of class privilege that Officer

Bell regards with droll indifference. Initially, Piper approaches prison as though she were a tourist in a third world country with dull-witted natives and limited shopping options. However, after offending Red, it doesn't take long for the reality of Litchfield to break down Piper's pretensions. "How am I supposed to prison-fight an old Russian lady with back problems," she sobs during Larry's first visit to Litchfield. Chief Officer Healy tries to put her at ease. "This isn't *Oz*," Healy informs Piper, referring to the grisly HBO drama series (1997–2003) about a men's maximum-security prison. "Women fight with gossip and rumors." Miss Rosa (Barbara Rosenblat), an inmate who suffers from terminal cancer, later sets the record straight by explaining the actual rules of engagement to Piper. "It's how we settle things," she says, matter-of-factly. "We brawl." However, the women of Litchfield also protect one another by concealing their brawls from the guards. In an attempt to prove her insider mettle and make amends for insulting Red's cooking, Piper marches into the kitchen and passively offers herself to Red to be punched. "You want me to hit you?" Red asks, contemptuously, as Piper readies herself for a blow to the face. Instead, Red denies Piper the satisfaction of a beating, assuring her that she will leave prison a skeleton in a body bag. In this instance, we see that prison catfights are not merely outlets for suppressed violence but expressions of intimacy and affiliation, constitutive of kinship bonds and tribal alliances; catfights establish and affirm one's place in an all-female social order, access to which is itself a privilege that Piper has not yet earned.

In this manner, *Orange is the New Black* relies on queer practices of disidentification (Muñoz, 1999) by situating itself within and against the reified meanings that were ascribed to catfights in earlier representations of women in prison. By producing dissonant values, *Orange is the New Black* rehabilitates the encoded social and political value of the prison catfight. More than a cheap formulation of comedic homoerotic spectacle, the catfight helps contain and manage affective complexities that arise from the series' evolving development of character. Moreover, catfights are used to signal key moments in the advancement of plot by upsetting an oversimplified dominant narrative of female rivalry and lesbian malevolence, and by opening up subversive possibilities for non-normative relations among women whose rivalries are conditioned by their mutual dependencies. If catfights are prohibited and punishable by solitary confinement, if they must be conducted under a veil of secrecy, it is not because they deny female inmates agency and power; it is because they appropriate and redistribute agency and power in defiance of the systemic bureaucratic violence of the patriarchal state.

At the same time, *Orange is the New Black* incorporates practices of queer identification into its marketing and branding, thus opening up subversive possibilities for pleasurable intertextual readings and community-building among fans. With more than thirty regular and recurring characters, *Orange is the New Black*'s sprawling ensemble cast undergirds the series' valuing of feminist community and permits writers to explore relationships and storylines that develop independently of any single central driver. Piper's storyline serves principally as an anchoring point-of-view: audiences enter the prison with Piper, acclimatize to the harsh realities of Litchfield with her, and then begin forming attachments elsewhere, as Piper's narrative becomes one of many interconnected stories, and as she becomes increasingly fixated on her fraught erotic entanglement with Alex and their never-ending game of sexual–juridical one-upmanship. Ensemble casting also enables Netflix to cast a wide net for consumer identifications and to appeal directly to queer fans through casting choices that reference a shared archival history of popular LGBT media imagery. Natasha Lyonne, who plays Nicky, has accumulated a long list of credits in queer-themed film and television projects, most notably as the innocent schoolgirl who is sent to gay conversion camp in the indie comedy *But I'm a Cheerleader* (US, 1999). Lori Petty, who appears in Season Two as Lolly Whitehill, is recognizable as the star of the 1995 movie adaptation of the post-apocalyptic comic book series *Tank Girl* (US, 1995), a film lauded for its radical feminist themes. The real-life butch comedian and performer Lea Delaria, whose 1993 breakout performance on *The Arsenio Hall Show* (Paramount, 1989–94) made her the first openly gay comic to appear on late-night television, is deftly cast as the archetypal sinister prison dyke, Carrie "Big Boo" Black. Australian genderqueer model and DJ Ruby Rose Langenheim plays Stella Carlin, Piper's androgynous rival love interest in Season Three. The casting of transgender actor and LGBT spokesperson Laverne Cox as transgender lesbian inmate Sophia Burset marks an important first for trans visibility and intersectional representations of gender, sex, and race. The role has provided *Orange is the New Black* (and Cox) with a valuable forum for contributing to public awareness of the problems faced by trans women and the larger trans community. And in a much-publicized instance of life imitating art, Samira Wiley (who plays Poussey) and Laura Morelli (one of the series' writers) lit up social media in the autumn of 2014 by going public with their romantic relationship after Morelli divorced her husband and came out as gay.

Orange is the New Black's social media team, cast members' presence on Twitter and Instagram, and socially connected fans have been central to the show's successful branding and promotion via the hashtag #OITNB. The creation of *Orange is the New Black* emojis; the circulation of commanding visuals across mobile networks; and social promotions that invite comments, sharing, and real-time interactions forge compelling connections between the show and its viewers. Above all, #OITNB uses campy photo memes that play coyly with the homoerotic conventions of women-in-prison films as a means of addressing fans as cultural insiders and potential partners in *Orange is the New Black*'s celebration of queer lust. "I'll be your prison wife," reads the caption of one widely shared photo of Alex, whose tomboyish looks and badass persona have made her a lesbian heartthrob. An Instagram promotion invites fans to upload photos of themselves wearing regulation prison orange, with the hashtag #OnWednesdaysWeWearOrange!, to demonstrate their devotion to the series. Twitter chats @AskOrange feature different guest characters that fans can communicate with directly during "Global Visiting Hours." A Pinterest promotion for *Orange is the New Black*'s second season included a "Litchfield Love Map" which charts Litchfield's mazy network of sexual relations in a graphic that recalls *The L Word*'s famous chart, which Alice Pieszecki created to prove that all lesbians are inevitably connected to one another "through love, through loneliness, through one tiny lamentable lapse in judgment" ("Let's Do It," 1.2).

Season Two of *Orange is the New Black*, which Netflix released for streaming on June 6, 2014, builds on this notion of interconnected histories as it traces a serial gang catfight. The fight arises out of a contest for dominance among three powerful women, all of whom function as maternal proxies for queer families who form kinship relations based on reciprocity, tribal loyalties, racial and ethnic common-alities, and promises of protection. Red, who is fired as Head Chef for smuggling illicit goods, leads a ragtag group of elderly inmates known as the "Golden Girls." Gloria Mendoza (Selenis Leyva), who takes over the kitchen, leads a group of Latina inmates known as "Spanish Harlem." Yvonne "Vee" Parker (Lorraine Toussaint), a sociopathic heroin dealer and repeat offender, returns to Litchfield, which sets off a battle with Red and Gloria for control over the traffic in contraband. As the pri-mary antagonist of Season Two, Vee uses her charisma to exploit every perceived weakness in her fellow Litchfield inmates while instigating hostilities across racial, ethnic, and sexual lines in an effort to seize power. Vee's backstory reveals that she has committed horrible abuses, enticing abandoned children to push heroin, making sexual advances on a young man whom she takes in as a foster son, and then having him murdered by a crooked cop when she discovers that he is competing with her business. Vee has a long history with Taystee, who grew up a ward of the state, living in group homes. In flashback, we see Vee's first encounter with Taystee at a "black adoption fair," where Vee tells her that she's too big, her hair too "ratsy," her desperation to be loved too obvious, and her skin too dark for anyone to adopt her. Eventually, Vee takes Taystee in and puts her to work as an accountant for her drug trade. Vee's emotional and psychological manipulation of Taystee's need for pro-tection is a constant theme in their relationship. When Vee returns to Litchfield she immediately offers her protection and affection once again, fomenting distrust and tension in Taystee's relations with her crew—Crazy Eyes (Uzo Aduba), Black Cindy, and Poussey.

Vee also has a long history with Red, which began as a friendly business part-nership—funneling illegal goods through the kitchen—and ended when Red refused to cede control of the operation and was beaten nearly to death. In Season Two, Red, Gloria, and Vee form a toxic political triumvirate that is animated as much by their mutual hostilities and grievances as by their mutual trepidation and intimate knowledge of one another's capacities for cunning. Their storyline evolves as a series of artful deceptions, seductions, and betrayals, as Vee and Gloria lock horns in a turf battle over bathroom access, while Gloria and Red continue their struggle over control of the kitchen. At the same time, another storyline follows a somewhat different contest for authority. Big Boo and Nicky compete to see who can have sex with the most women at Litchfield based on a scoring system that attributes point value to each of the inmates. Piper's annoyance upon learning that she is ranked a mere "3" is a clear indication of the extent to which *Orange is the New Black* turns the history of lesbian representation on its head: while the women-in-prison genre framed lesbian desire as a threat to the appearance of the "new girl," *Orange is the New Black* frames the "new girl" as threatened by lackluster lesbian interest in her appearance.

Season Two culminates in a brutal confrontation between Red and Vee that similarly alters the rhythms of the conventional prison fight. The confrontation takes place in the barren prison greenhouse, which Healy permits Red to revive after her expulsion from the kitchen leaves her without allies, influence, or purpose. Red works in the greenhouse under the pretense of gardening; however, her main interest is a forgotten sewer grate that leads from the greenhouse floor to the outside world, enabling her to recommence smuggling in goods. Emboldened by their new status as Red's posse, recognizing the threat that Vee poses and knowing first-hand the violence that she is capable of, one of the Golden Girls, Taslitz (Judith Roberts), decides to stab her with a sharpened toothbrush. However, due to her failing eyesight, she accidentally stabs the wrong inmate. Vee is alerted to their plot, and so Red must either take action or be killed. When a hurricane strikes, Litchfield experiences a widespread power outage. As the storm rages in the background, Red and Vee happen to meet in the greenhouse. When an argument ensues and Vee threatens to harm Red's family on the outside, Red loses control. Taking Vee from behind, she wraps a twisted cord of cellophane around her throat and attempts to strangle her. "You have more balls than I thought," says Vee, gasping for air. Red's rage proves too much for Vee to handle. They wrangle intensely, groaning and straining as gradually Vee goes slack and submits to her fate. Red knows what she must do but something stops her. Almost imperceptibly, Red and Vee's cries turn to laughter as they collapse onto the ground. Red releases Vee. "Oh, god," Red sighs, exhausted and dazed. "This place is getting to me." "Oh, yeah," Vee agrees. "You just tried to strangle me with plastic wrap so that you can sell mascara in jail."

The catfight between Red and Vee is discontinued when Red becomes conscious of her actions and recognizes that she's not behaving like herself. In reality, she cannot kill anyone; it is prison—"this place"—that compels her. Red's eruption of histrionic violence leads to a truce, as she and Vee agree to share power. "You'll keep yours, I'll keep mine." Soon afterwards, however, Vee returns to the greenhouse and beats Red unconscious with a slock (a heavy lock tucked inside a sock). And so it goes, as *Orange is the New Black* reworks the dynamics of the catfight to fit within a serialized, and highly self-conscious, prison comedy-drama. Catfights are episodic, as frequent as they are frequently interrupted or deferred as storylines develop and as characters' relationships and alliances change. Red's realization that prison is making her behave like someone else—like, perhaps, a character in a women-in-prison movie—is part of *Orange is the New Black*'s strategy of Catfight Interrupta—a withholding technique that sustains narrative tensions across the breadth and length of a full season. In *Orange is the New Black*, catfights are produced for the season rather than the episode. In this way, *Orange is the New Black* brings a new structural integrity to the catfight, which is used to dramatize the long arc of complex entanglements that make Litchfield inmates irreducible to stereotypical caricatures. At the same time, *Orange is the New Black* exploits the iconic theatricality and over-the-top sensationalism of the catfight as a convention that stages women's prison conflicts in the present as the sum total of images gleaned from pop culture's queer archives.

In its preoccupation with representational tropes of the past, Katrin Horn argues that *Orange is the New Black* seeks to provide queer pleasures in the present through its backward-glancing return to earlier structures of lesbian desire and criminalization. Unlike other contemporary "quality" television shows that are set in the past (e.g. *Downton Abbey, Mad Men*, etc.), Horn (2015) argues that *Orange is the New Black* generates its affective impact and registers its progressive aspirations through nostalgia for "a shared queer canon" and a longing to reimagine the cinematic trope of the criminal dyke. When Red claims "this place is getting to me," she refers not only to her disoriented psychological state but also to the status of the women's prison as "the kind of stigmatized place where forgetting (particularly shame, criminalization and discrimination) is impossible and where the pain and ignorance of past representational regimes can therefore be rewritten" (Horn, 2015). Indeed, part of what draws queer viewers to *Orange is the New Black* is its self-conscious engagement with this process of rehabilitating past representations of queer women and same-sex desire. In this sense, Litchfield can be considered a "correctional" facility in more ways than one, as it appropriates the past for the purposes of imagining a utopian future. Not only does *Orange is the New Black* humanize queer characters such as Big Boo and Sophia, but it also traces the evolving queer political consciousness of homophobic caricatures, such as Pennsatucky, whose Season Two transformation as a result of new teeth and a stint in the psych ward leads to an unlikely alliance with Big Boo. In a dialogue that could have been lifted out of the mimeographed pages of Valerie Solanas's 2004[1967] *SCUM Manifesto*, Pennsatucky asks Boo to explain how "the gay agenda" works. "Are you gonna let all the men die out," she asks, with naive curiosity. "Oh, fuck, no, we need slaves," Boo says. "You know, bookkeeping, janitorial, fetch and carry, that kind of shit." Pennsatucky asks whether sex with men will be permissible once the "agenda" is in place. "Well, maybe," Boo speculates, "but when you're done, you gotta toss 'em away like trash. I mean, the whole point of this is chicks digging each other and being in charge."[4]

Boo's facetious tone is humorously contrasted with Pennsatucky's puerile earnestness about the "gay" future. Nevertheless, Boo's utopian vision of an all-female society where men are disposable and women "rule the universe" (Solanas, 2004: 70) feels queerly retrospective, an invocation of Solanas's radical call for "responsible, thrill-seeking females . . . to overthrow the government, eliminate the money system, institute complete automation and eliminate the male sex" (ibid.: 35). Such moments arguably evoke lesbian-feminist nostalgia as a specific form of social melancholy and collective longing for an idealized past that has gained considerable resonance in the critical formation of a contemporary queer imaginary (Padva, 2014: 3–7). In this way, *Orange is the New Black* looks both backward and forward—backward towards a (re)membering of lesbian-feminism's radical separatist revolution and forward toward what Muñoz designates as "queer futurity," "an ideality that can be distilled from the past and used to imagine a future" (2009: 1). At the same time, *Orange is the New Black* is very much rooted in the affective tensions of the present, as elation over LGBT civil rights victories is wistfully measured and balanced against the loss of queer histories and communities. These tensions have produced, in Love's estimation, a feeling of "backwardness" that has become "a key feature of queer culture" (2009: 7). Camp practices, which demonstrate "a tender concern for outmoded elements of popular culture," are key to understanding the temporal dissonance of contemporary queer identity (ibid.). In this way, *Orange is the New Black*'s "revolution for women" is discursively situated somewhere between Boo's cynical cheekiness and Pennsatucky's gullibility. *Orange is the New Black* taps into these contradictory currents by evoking images from a traumatic queer past, images that continue to structure hope for the future.

Finally, we should acknowledge that *Orange is the New Black* stands at the forefront of another contemporary revolution, as methods of consuming media content undergo rapid transformation through the growing market penetration of online streaming services and multi-platform devices for accessing television content. One of the largest and most ambitious streaming services, Netflix has pioneered a distribution model that enables and encourages "binge-viewing" by making full seasons available to subscribers at once. Promising subscribers freedom, immediacy, mobility, and control—in addition to staging release dates as newsworthy cultural events—Netflix is banking on a production formula that caters to very specific viewer tastes and habits quite differently than broadcast networks or premium subscription cable channels. Unlike networks and basic cable channels that view programs as delivery vehicles for advertising, relying on pilot episodes and ratings information to test audience interest and attract advertising revenue, Netflix claims that it has no need for arbitrary tests or ratings data as part of its business model. And while the broadcast networks remain focused on the individual episode as product and revenue source, Netflix claims that it has chosen to focus on the longer arc of a story, with multi-layered plots and complex character development, rather than generic commercial contrivances with built-in pauses for commercial breaks and artificial cliff-hangers designed to keep viewers tuning in.

But how genuine are these claims? *Orange is the New Black*, like all of Netflix's original shows, functions chiefly as an advertisement for Netflix, or as a lure designed to entice viewers to subscribe to their streaming service for licensed, non-original content, which is their primary source of profit. Moreover, despite the company's postulation that it has no need for numbers, Netflix is notorious for monitoring viewer habits and mining "big data" to determine what viewers want to watch and how they watch it. It is equally notorious for refusing to share that data with content producers, product licensers, and the general public. This makes it difficult, if not impossible, to analyze demographic data in the conventional sense, thus complicating any scholarly effort to fully evaluate *Orange is the New Black*'s appeal to women or queers. But perhaps demographics no longer matter. "Taste is becoming more global," says Todd Yellin, Netflix's Vice President of Product Innovation. "What we've learned over time is: it's not who they are in a superficial sense—like gender, age, even geography. It's not even what they tell you. It's what they do" ("Netflix Goes Beyond Demographics," 2015). One thing we might take from this emphasis on viewer behaviour is that television's (re)production of queer sensibility has no meaningful relation to ideologies of identity, community, or visibility—no relation, even, to an imagined or wished-for "television for women." Rather, television operates according "to imperatives other than those valued by academic tastes" and political priorities (Villarejo, 2009: 51). Television is responsive to itself and to its own logic of encoding differences across "a broader array of intertexts, paratexts, extratexts, and auxiliary texts that, in drawing out cross-pollinations and meanings that exceed standardization, draw out the networks of meaning within which representation comes to life in its queerest manifestations" (Miller, 2014: 143).

In conclusion, feminist critics have not been entirely wrong in arguing that the catfight luxuriates in images of femininity as wanton eye candy, an erotic fantasy composed of soft-porn clichés and crude homoerotic sensationalism, or an enactment of damaging feminine competition. However, by engaging with histories of camp, we see that the stylized performative nature of the catfight has always functioned as an acknowledgement of the shared stock of fantasies, anxieties, industrial techniques, and intertexts out of which queerness—or its media affect—becomes manifest. The catfight is evidence of queer culture's perpetual presence as an intervention in media hierarchies of taste, a sustained and sustaining critique of what counts as "tasteful" to television itself. While catfights undoubtedly grant pleasure to *Orange is the New Black*'s viewers who recognize the sordid cultural archive on which the series draws, these fights are also part of much larger historical and industrial scaffolding, strategically—even tenderly—positioned within the series as a means to television's own survival in the present. The "revolution for women" will most likely not be streamed, but with Netflix's announcement that *Orange is the New Black* will be returning for a fifth season, one can always wait and hope. After all, we've got time.

Notes

1 Exceptions include Jared Cohen's direct-to-video "mockbuster" *Jailbait* (2014), the DVD collection *Nymphos Behind Bars* (2006) and, most notably, Rob Marshall's award-winning movie adaptation of the long-running Broadway musical, *Chicago* (2002), which featured Queen Latifah in the highly suggestive role of the butch lesbian warden, Matron "Mama" Morton,

2 Ilene Chaiken, the creator of *The L Word,* had hoped to follow up after that series ended with another series set in a women's prison. But she could not sell it to Showtime.

3 On June 13, 2014, one week following the release date of Season Two of *Orange is the New Black*, the *New York Times* posted sponsored content, paid for by Netflix, about the US prison system's failure to accommodate the needs of female inmates. The story had all the features of a well-researched editorial—replete with expert quotes, illustrations, and statistics—except for a banner ad and overline that trumpeted the story's status as brand-sponsored content (Bloomgarden-Smoke, 2014).

4 Solanas further writes, 'The female, whether she likes it or not, will eventually take complete charge, if for no other reason than that she will have to—the male, for practical purposes, won't exist' (2004: 67).

Bibliography

Berlatsky, N. (2014) 'Orange is the New Caged.' Virtual Roundtable on *Orange is the New Black*. Public Books, May 15, www.publicbooks.org./artmedia/virtual-roundtable-on-orange-is-the-new-black#berlatsky. (Last accessed September 2, 2015).

Bloomgarden-Smoke, K. (2014) 'Orange is the New Sponsored Content.' *New York Observer*, June 13, http://observer.com/2014/06/netflix/. (Last accessed September 2, 2015).

Butler, J. (1990) *Gender Trouble*. New York: Routledge.

Conor, L. (2004) *The Spectacular Modern Woman: Feminine Visibility in the 1920s*. Bloomington: Indiana University Press.

Douglas, S. J. (1994, 1995) *Where the Girls Are: Growing Up Female with the Mass Media*. New York: Three Rivers Press.

Ferris, B. G. (1854) *Utah and the Mormons: The History, Government, Doctrines, Customs, and Prospects of the Latter-Day Saints, from Personal Observation during a Six Months' Residence at Great Salt Lake City*, New York: Harper & Brothers, https://archive.org/details/utah-mormonshisto00ferrich. (Last accessed September 2, 2015).

Horn, K. (2015) 'Longing for a Future Past? Nostalgia and Queer Women in Media.' Paper presented at Console-ing Passions: International Conference on Television, Video, Audio, New Media, and Feminism. June 20. Dublin, Ireland.

Love, H. (2009) *Feeling Backward: Loss and the Politics of Queer History*. Cambridge: Harvard University Press.

Love, H. (2014) 'Made for TV.' Virtual Roundtable on *Orange is the New Black*. Public Books, May 15, www.publicbooks.org./artmedia/virtual-roundtable-on-orange-is-the-new-black#love. (Last accessed September 15, 2015).

Mayne, J. (2000) *Framed: Lesbians, Feminists, and Media Culture*. Minneapolis: University of Minnesota Press.

Miller, Q. (2014) 'Queer Recalibration.' *Cinema Journal*, 53 (2): 140–4.

Muñoz, J. E. (1999) *Disidentifications: Queers of Color and the Performance of Politics*. Minneapolis and London: University of Minnesota Press.

Muñoz, J. E. (2009) *Cruising Utopia: The Then and There of Queer Futurity*. New York: New York University Press.

Padva, G. (2014) *Queer Nostalgia in Cinema and Pop Culture*. Houndmills: Palgrave Macmillan.

Reinke, R. (2010) 'Catfight: A Feminist Analysis.' *Chrestomathy: Annual Review of Undergraduate Research, School of Humanities and Social Sciences, School of Languages, Cultures, and World Affairs, College of Charleston*, 9: 162–85.

Rorke, R. (2014) 'Orange is the New Black Ignites a TV Revolution for Women.' *New York Post*, June 4, http://nypost.com/2014/06/orange-is-the-new-black-ignites-a-tv-revolution-for-women/. (Last accessed September 2, 2015).

Solanas, V. (2004[1967]) *The SCUM Manifesto*. Introduction by Avital Ronnell. London: Verso.

Spektor, R. (2013) 'You've Got Time.' Producer: Rob Cavallo. Sire Records.

Stack, T. (2008) 'TV's Latest Catfights.' *Entertainment Weekly*, October 24, www.ew.com/article/2008/10/24/tvs-latest-catfights. (Last accessed September 2, 2015).

Tannenbaum, L. (2003) *Catfight: Rivalries among Women—From Diets to Dating, from the Boardroom to the Delivery Room*. New York: First Perennial Publications.

Villarejo, A. (2009) 'Ethereal Queer: Notes on Method,' in G. Davis and G. Needham (eds), *Queer TV: Theories, Histories, Politics*. Abingdon and New York: Routledge: pp. 48–62.

Warc.com. (2015) 'Netflix Goes Beyond Demographics,' March 27, www.warc.com/Latest News/News/Netflix_goes_beyond_demographics.news?ID=34519#. (Last accessed September 2, 2015).

5

BROWN GIRLS WHO DON'T NEED SAVING

Social media and the role of 'possessive investment' in *The Mindy Project* and *The Good Wife*

Sujata Moorti

> The only thing that separates women of colour from anyone else is opportunity. You cannot win an Emmy for roles that are simply not there.
>
> *(Davis, 2015)*

This poignant assertion by acclaimed actor Viola Davis, star of the series *How to Get Away with Murder* (ABC, 2014–), during her Emmy acceptance speech went viral and became the flashpoint for heated discussion about contemporary television's representational practices. The statement draws attention to questions of taste, what is acknowledged by the industry and audiences as quality television and the political economy of the contemporary industry. This moment in television history, with its attendant social media afterlife, captures the key elements I wish to explore in this chapter: representations of women of colour, production practices and viewer responses. As Viola Davis notes in the quote above, the contemporary US television landscape offers limited roles for people of colour. The few shows starring people of colour have become the focus of intense social media exchanges. In this chapter, I will explore how televisual women of colour have become a key site from which viewers assert a possessive investment of racialised identity. By focusing on social media responses, I delineate the ways in which viewers invest symbolic and literal ownership over these representations. Through such a multifaceted examination, this essay aims to elaborate how women of colour are accommodated within the concept of television for women, a term interrogated in this volume. In addition, I illustrate the ideological instability of the term 'women of colour' and the capaciousness of the concept 'television for women'.

In the US, television representations of women or people of colour gain media attention seemingly only in two registers: critics either lament the paucity of images or celebrate the efflorescence of innovative figures (Barr, 2015; Dockterman, 2014; Paskin, 2013). Both responses evoke the spectre of a forgotten but more diverse past.

Media critics thus tend to repeatedly look back to a golden age of television against which the present is compared unfavourably. Tapping into different archives and different temporalities, media critics often lament the present to privilege the past. Thus for instance, a *New York Times* review essay reminded readers that celebrations of the Shonda Rhimes franchise[1] or other women-authored shows such as *30 Rock* (NBC, 2006–13) tend to forget that television programming in the 1980s was replete with popular women-authored shows such as *Designing Women* (CBS, 1986–93) and *Murphy Brown* (CBS, 1988–98) (Scovell, 2015). In media accounts, feminist celebrations of women and people of colour in contemporary television rest on the erasure of past feminist productions. These cultural critics gloss over the content of the shows or the salience of their narrative arcs. In sharp contrast, social media platforms offer the general viewer as well as the professional journalist an opportunity to intervene in these trends. Celebrating or criticising individual actors and specific episodes, social media conversations operate in a seemingly ahistorical space, a place saturated with present-ness and with no reference to a television past. The polarised distinction I am drawing is not as stark or clearly defined as I have laid out, but my aim is to draw attention to the different textures in conversations about television that occur on these different platforms. As I illustrate in the analysis that follows, social media conversations focus on the minutiae, and it is this attention to detail that permits these platforms to facilitate a possessive investment over the programmes and actors.

I elucidate these trends by focusing on women of colour who appear in two very different television series: *The Mindy Project* and *The Good Wife*. *The Mindy Project* features the Indian American Mindy Kaling and aired on Fox for three seasons before it was cancelled. The series has now found a home for twenty-six additional episodes in the streaming service, Hulu.[2] *The Mindy Project* as a series, and the responses it has generated on various social media platforms, draw attention to the changing media ecology. I also tap into the figure of Kalinda Sharma (played by Archie Panjabi), the leather-clad private investigator from *The Good Wife* (CBS, 2010–16), to outline how audience responses have transformed a mainstream legal drama into one that addresses issues particularly salient to women. In the process viewers' voices and critics' opinions have helped to significantly shift some storylines. The presence of these two women on prime-time television is symptomatic of the new roles occupied by people of South Asian origin in US popular culture (Thakore, 2014).[3] It is of equal significance that in both instances the figure of the brown actor has become the site of contestation and primary node for audience identifications and disidentifications. I explore these responses against the backdrop of the Girl Effect campaign, the other mainstream media discourse which brings the brown female body into visibility in popular culture. I suggest that it is the invisible subtext of the Girl Effect that makes these prime-time programmes, and in particular the figures of Kaling and Panjabi, sites where a definition of television for women is crafted. As I describe later in the chapter, the Girl Effect is a millennial initiative designed in the first world to rescue the third-world female subject from the burdens of traditional femininity.

I have a dual purpose in this chapter: first, to tease out how and by what means some shows earn the designation 'television for women', and second, to highlight the limits to women of colour's visibility by exploring the representational quagmire that they experience. Heeding the call of feminist scholars such as Casper and Moore (2009) and Kozol (2005), I remain attentive to the politics of visibility and how audiences' ways of seeing shows are embedded in larger webs of cultural politics. Thus, Kaling and Panjabi emerge as hypervisible figures whose televisual presence is carefully monitored and read through a lens that reflects the specificity of US-based identity politics. In the pages that follow I do not offer an analysis of either television series. Rather, I focus on a few key moments when social media attention centred on Kaling and Panjabi. By paying attention to these social media flare-ups I will explore how the logics of neoliberal multiculturalism shape the contemporary mediascape and how these impinge on feminist imaginings.

The Mindy Project

Mindy Kaling entered network television in a dual capacity as writer and actor for the US adaptation of the British comedy *The Office* (Fox, 2005–13). Scripted as a bit player in the ensemble cast of *The Office*, Kaling's Kelly Kapoor became one of the bodies through which the series offered a searing critique of existing race politics: a hypervigilance and simultaneous disavowal of the colour line. The ditzy, celebrity-loving, boy-crazy character of Kapoor permitted the series to mock mainstream multiculturalism, which cannibalises culture and consumes difference (hooks, 1992). More significantly, the series offered Kaling the opportunity to hone her writing and production skills. Some of the episodes she scripted and co-produced were nominated for awards.[4] Even before *The Office* concluded its run, Kaling had negotiated with the Fox network to produce and act in a scripted weekly series. As the first South Asian showrunner, Kaling joined a small group of women who were producing prime-time episodic television programming. *The Mindy Project* (Fox, 2012–15; Hulu, 2015–16) features Kaling as a successful New York City gynaecologist who is a partner in a medical practice. The protagonist's name, Mindy Lahiri, riffed off the name of the acclaimed Indian American writer Jhumpa Lahiri, thereby hinting at the literary characterisations of the South Asian diasporic experience. But apart from throwaway references to Lahiri's Indian origin, the series does not thematise diasporic issues. The series' provenance, however, was firmly entrenched in mainstream popular culture. Tapping into key tropes of the romcom film and the workplace situation comedy, such as *Ally McBeal* (Fox, 1997–2002), the series highlighted Mindy's ineptitude in romance and set it in contrast to her professional proficiency. By the end of the third season, Mindy's romance with a co-worker had been secured, and once the series migrated to Hulu she started to navigate the twin pulls of motherhood and workplace responsibilities. The setting, in an ob/gyn practice, seems to lend the series a proclivity to address concerns pertaining to women's health. However, as I illustrate in the analysis below, *The Mindy Project* is structured to address a mainstream audience. It is through viewer engagements that the series comes to address women's concerns.

Even before the first episode of *The Mindy Project* had aired, Kaling had drawn a significant amount of attention. She was hailed in the media, notably on self-avowed feminist social media sites such as Jezebel and Racialicious, as a trailblazer.[5] She was celebrated for joining a small cadre of women of colour showrunners, especially in the comedy genre. Equally importantly, Kaling was praised for her physical appearance, for not fitting the narrow mould of white hegemonic beauty norms. Indeed, her refusal or inability to present herself as a skinny person became a key signifier of Kaling's feminist credentials. Viewers lauded her for not adhering to a postfeminist sensibility where 'the body is presented simultaneously as women's source of power and as always already unruly and requiring constant monitoring, surveillance, discipline and remodelling in order to conform to ever narrower judgments of female attractiveness' (Gill, 2007: 149).

At the institutional level, *The Mindy Project* was part of a stable of programming that the Fox network had signed to regain audiences. During the 2000s, propelled by the success of a range of reality shows, Fox was vying with CBS for top ranking in audience ratings. However, by the end of the decade, as the popularity of reality shows waned, Fox turned to a new batch of programming to regain its popularity among young viewers, the demographic coveted by networks for the advertising revenue they generate. The success of the musical drama *Glee* (2009–15) was accompanied by several other ensemble scripted shows. *The Mindy Project* was paired with an already successful comedy, *New Girl* (2011–), and helped showcase back-to-back programming with female leads. Nominally, these two shows represent television *by* women, but their address was not necessarily gendered.

Kaling gained fame for her award-winning writing on *The Office*. However, among fans and cultural commentators, she is more often recognised for being a dark-skinned Indian American with a figure that goes against the thin stereotype.[6] She has repeated in numerous interviews that she did not aspire to be a 'spunky role model' (Nussbaum, 2014). Yet audience engagements with the show reveal the burdens of representation her character has to assume, satisfying the desires of South Asians to see themselves in prime-time programming and also those of a range of people who would like to see complex ideas of intersectionality worked out through her persona. Before the end of the first season, the same social media sites that had lauded Kaling as a feminist started to call into question her casting choices and the storylines. Social media developed into one of the primary sites through which audiences, especially those who self-identified as feminist, engaged directly with Kaling/Lahiri. In the analysis below I isolate three such moments to explore how these audience engagements pushed at redefining a programme *by* a woman into television *for* women. I deploy the terms 'audience' and 'viewers' broadly to encompass the voices of cultural critics, professional journalists and people who participate through comments sections or respond directly on Twitter. While it is easier to identify the gender and racial identities of critics and journalists, I have used only those audience responses where they either self-identify as a woman or a minority or their online handle suggests they are women. These multifarious voices permit me to illustrate how viewers transform *The Mindy Project* into television for women.

The Good Wife

It seems intuitive to draw a lineage for the Mindy Lahiri character from the figure of Kelly Kapoor. However, I contend that *The Mindy Project*'s salience in US popular culture draws on the energies generated by *The Good Wife* (2009–16), aired on the rival CBS network. A hybrid legal drama and procedural, the series was created by Robert King and Michelle King, and its production team includes Ridley Scott.[7] With its ensemble cast of acclaimed actors and familiar television faces, its complex narratives and excellent production qualities, critics hailed *The Good Wife* as quality television.[8] The series centres on the life of a politician's wife, Alicia Florrick, who supports her husband in public even after his sexual infidelities result in a media scandal. Alicia however returns to practising law, and the drama of the series derives from its exploration of the blurred lines between private and public spheres and the ways in which new media technologies complicate understandings of intimacy and sexuality (Leonard, 2014). The nuanced depiction of the 'good wife' as a capable, contradictory woman and mother has led critics to praise the series as feminist (Dove-Viebahn, 2010). Critics have also praised *The Good Wife* as a rare instance of a network television programme displaying the 'kind of emotional and character complexity' associated with quality television (Kirkpatrick, 2011). However, it is the figure of the private investigator Kalinda Sharma, played by British actor Archie Panjabi, who became the rich node of audience identification.

From the first episode, Sharma is depicted as an ingenious and capable investigator who helps the legal firm successfully conclude its cases. Over the first two seasons the storylines carefully trace a growing friendship between Sharma and the figure of Alicia Florrick, a relationship that permitted fans of the show to proclaim their allegiances with the pithy #TeamKalinda or #TeamAlicia slogans (Lahiri, 2012). Viewer responses, however, seemed to coalesce around Sharma's enigmatic sexuality, or what critics have termed her queer persona (Kohnen, 2011). Always clad in her signature boots, short skirts and leather jackets, Sharma is presented in the series as a sexually promiscuous character who refuses to be categorised as lesbian or bisexual and instead declares herself to be 'private'. In the analysis that follows, I use audience responses to the figure of Kalinda Sharma as a counterpoint to those evoked by *The Mindy Project*. The ambivalences constitutive of the Sharma persona are central to audience, especially feminist, identifications. Her corporeal presence as a brown woman becomes one of the vectors through which a programme geared toward a prime-time audience gets recrafted as television for women of colour.

In her analysis of contemporary television representations of race and ethnicity, Beltran points out that networks use the rainbow skin tones of the cast to evoke the youthful and cosmopolitan currency of their shows (Beltran, 2010). However, these representations, Beltran contends, do not constitute 'meaningful diversity'. In this project I am interested in the ways in which the characters must carry the weight of representational politics such that they spark in their viewers new dialogues across social media. In the analysis that follows, I think through how and why these two women of colour have become sites of social media conversations not just about the representation of women but about the forms of feminism they engender. I also explore how these social media interactions shift definitions of quality television and make them contingent on particular understandings of feminism. In addition, I consider how these images of the multicultural world citizen are produced in the interstices of larger discourses about third-world women, most notably those that have coalesced around the Girl Effect phenomenon.

Saving Mindy

Feminist media scholars have long disabused us of the idea of the passive audience. Instead, they have highlighted the ways in which television viewers actively engage with programming and sometimes mobilise activist movements. D'Acci (1994), for instance, has documented how fans helped restore the cop drama *Cagney and Lacey* (CBS, 1982–88) after it was cancelled. Fan-studies scholarship has elaborated on the audience's intense affective investments with particular programmes. In each of these instances, scholars home in on how audiences interpret and interact with particular texts (Jones, 2002). Much of this discussion about active audiences has been altered by social media platforms which permit viewers and producers to interact with each other. My analysis of *The Mindy Project* and *The Good Wife* is informed by this rich body of scholarship.

Long before Kaling was anointed a television star, she had gained a significant following on social media. Early in her television career, Kaling used Twitter, Snapchat and Instagram to catapult herself into visibility and to craft a network-activated celebrity persona (Karpel, 2012). Today, she has over three million followers on Twitter, where she circulates information on her activities, her reactions and those of her friends, such as Aziz Ansari, Lena Dunham, Amy Schumer and other actors. Rather than function as paratexts, these digital traces have helped constitute Kaling's persona – one that allowed her to move from Kelly Kapoor, a member of *The Office* ensemble cast, and a script writer to the showrunner, producer and star of *The Mindy Project*. As an adept social media user, Kaling has deployed Twitter and Snapchat to respond to viewers' and critics' comments about her show or her persona. The accelerated pace of these social media exchanges (Payne, 2013) has modified conventional understandings of call-and-response patterns of communication, a term associated with vernacular traditions of public engagement. Call-and-response exchanges involve spontaneous syncopated interactions between speaker and listener in which statements made by the speaker are punctuated with responses from the listener. But even in these social media-constituted call-and-response spaces, Kaling is bound by racialised tropes of the female celebrity as well as digital discourses of intersectionality and feminism.

To capture the structural conditions that enable white hegemony to prevail even as legal reforms and social policies attempt to undo centuries of racism, George Lipsitz (1999) has coined the term 'the possessive investment in whiteness'. Elaborating on the dual connotations of investment – 'invest in' and 'a state of being invested' – Lipsitz contends that white people have benefited the most from policies emerging from mid-twentieth-century identity-based politics. Simultaneously, white people have laid claim to whiteness, literally and symbolically. In my analysis of three snapshots of social media engagements, I mobilise a similar structure of feeling to characterise audience responses to the character of Mindy Lahiri. I contend that audiences have turned to social media to articulate their possessive investment in this character in a manner that overdetermines her racialised identity as well as her non-normative appearance. These audiences lay literal and symbolic claim to Lahiri/Kaling as a woman of colour and invest her persona with expectations that she does not and cannot uphold.

Snapshot 1

In February 2014, *Elle* magazine opted for four different covers for its women in television cover story, each featuring an actor from a contemporary hit series: Allison Williams from *Girls*, Amy Poehler from *Parks and Recreation*, Zooey Deschanel from *New Girl* and Mindy Kaling. Social media users were quick to point out that while the three white women were featured in colour and full-length photos, Kaling's cover 'ran in black-and-white and was cropped just above the actress' waist' (Gopalan, 2014). Offering a sophisticated critical reading of the practice of framing, some of the sites argued that 'institutionalised inequality' accounted for the editing choices (Levine, 2014; Schumann, 2014). In particular, they argued that it was Kaling's non-normativity, both in terms of her skin colour and her 'size 8, not a size zero' body, which accounted for the stylistic differences, a practice they termed 'reverse-objectification' (Davis, 2014). Bloggers enumerated the reasons why readers should be offended by *Elle*'s image of Kaling, most frequently calling the magazine racist and fat-ist or fat-phobic (Duca, 2014). People responding to these posts in the comments section averred these sentiments even as they proclaimed how much they loved Kaling's cover and her beauty. In rapid sequence, these social media discussions transferred to mainstream media, and soon outlets as diverse as CNN, the *Washington Post* and the *Wall Street Journal* were each addressing the magazine cover and the cultural politics underpinning the differences (Turner, 2014; Butler, 2014; Little, 2014). Kaling too addressed this issue in her Twitter feed. She defended the cover in several tweets, including one which read 'I love my @Ellemagazine cover. It made me feel glamorous & cool'. In supplementary tweets she responded with humour, all the while promoting her series. 'And if anyone wants to see more of my body, go on thirteen dates with me'. Or 'wishing for more skin on my @ElleMagazine cover? Chris Messina and I are naked on a brand new #themindyproject tonight'. Kaling responded to the contestations that had occurred over her image with wit. Appearing on *The Late Show with David Letterman*, she proclaimed that the fashion magazine cover was a first in her career and that 'it felt great . . . I feel like I look like a movie star on it' (Rivera, 2014). The social media protestations, in contrast, implied that her body was 'big, fat and grotesque'.

In *The Mindy Project*, Kaling's character acknowledges and exaggerates her corporeal difference from normative femininity. Her non-skinny body is the fodder for much of the humour generated by the narrative. However, the series also depicts Lahiri's consumption of food as joyful and unapologetic. She alludes sometimes to diet and exercise, but she is too busy working, dating and participating in New York City life to bother with a disciplining regime. Kaling imbues her character with ironic girliness; the character conforms to the features Dejmanee (2016) has identified as central to the intimacies of the postfeminist subject. Yet the persona is also depicted as mocking the postfeminist masquerade of empowerment through self-surveillance.

Social media responses to the cover were at radical odds with Kaling's, and even the character Lahiri's, presentation of the self. The *Elle* cover positioned Kaling's achievements and popularity with other stars, as one of several successful women in contemporary television. However, social media responses to this image highlighted the finesse needed to simultaneously proclaim equality and difference. While Kaling tried to use the publicity surrounding the magazine cover to mobilise viewership for her project and to deflect criticism, cultural critics used this opportunity to address a broader set of social practices. Bloggers criticised Kaling for defending *Elle*. They accused her stance of promoting the idea 'that even unintentional discrimination is kinda okay. And, you know, it's not' (Gopalan, 2014). The controversy surrounding the magazine cover exceeded Mindy Kaling and the television series she produces. Social media participants were using the 'semiotic raw materials' the magazine cover provided to offer critiques that addressed how the possessive investment in whiteness is enacted (Jenkins, 1992: 49). These social media voices laid claim to Kaling as a woman of colour and highlighted the mechanisms through which popular culture scripts her as other. They read the *Elle* cover design choices as a literal and symbolic claim to whiteness as normative femininity. These interlocutors represent what Nussbaum (2014) has called the 'female bad fan' – those who respond to shows with female protagonists and who crave empowerment from the roles. Mindy Kaling's responses sidestepped conversations about postfeminism and instead redirected attention to new regimes of surveillance being mobilised by viewers against female showrunners and stars.

Snapshot 2

At the end of the first season of *The Mindy Project* some bloggers, such as Jethro Nededog and Dodai Stewart, homed in on a narrative pattern. Lahiri dated numerous men during that first season; she suffered heartbreak repeatedly but remained unwavering in the narrative quest that is central to the romcom genre: requited love. However, viewers quickly pointed out that all of the men Lahiri dated were Caucasian. Others highlighted the absence of diversity in the casting choices of the series as a whole (Stewart, 2013). Apart from Lahiri, all other recurring female characters were assigned bit parts and the eponymous protagonist was the only recurring character of colour. Social media platforms became the primary site through which these ideas were developed; some viewers took to Twitter to directly address Kaling about her 'white guy obsession' (Nededog, 2013).

Criticisms of Kaling's casting choices were similar to those levelled against Lena Dunham's *Girls* for not featuring any people of colour (Berman, 2013) and those made about the 'post-racial' politics of Shondaland productions (Parham, 2013). Highlighting *The Mindy Project*'s shared resonances with other women-authored programming, one commenter proclaimed that the casting choice

> does matter and that the message being sent to young minority women who watch "The Mindy Project" – whether they realise it or not – is that the measure of success is not just working your way to the top of your profession but that the ideal signifier for that success is a white partner. And as for non-white men watching the show, it only reinforces the prevailing standard of attraction that ranks them lower on the desirability scale in our culture.
>
> *(Nededog, 2013)*

Others went a step further and described these casting choices as reflecting Lahiri's ethnic self-hatred (Gopalan, 2014). (It is worth noting that fellow Indian American comic Aziz Ansari is depicted as dating only white women on his Netflix series, *Master of None* (2015), but he has received little criticism for these casting choices.) Some Indian American bloggers, however, praised Kaling for not offering token ethnic characters or trafficking in stereotypes. Instead they suggest that Kaling's series 'makes a statement about race without needing to explicitly on screen' (Chittal, 2012). Lahiri's character refutes the stereotype that South Asians only date other South Asians, and also, more significantly, any number of assumptions about Indian American women which these bloggers aver.

These polarised responses to the representations of people of colour were allayed by the presence of a brother figure for the protagonist. Although he appeared in only two episodes, critics praised the aspiring rapper as a complex portrayal of an Indian American man, with punchlines that 'make mainstream misunderstandings of minorities the butt of the joke, not the minority Indian Americans' (Xia, 2013).

In the accelerated pace of call-and-response exchanges characteristic of the contemporary media ecology, Kaling turned to Twitter as well as media interviews to contest criticisms of her casting choices and her lack of attention to intersectionality. She tried to deflect criticisms by pointing out that the calls for greater racial representation are not levelled against mainstream network programming, but rather that viewers have made her show the primary site for racial reparations (Braxton, 2014). Nevertheless, these discussions have had an impact on *The Mindy Project* narrative arc. In an episode entitled 'Mindy Lahiri is a Racist', Kaling folded in key ideas circulating in social media about her show's refusal to engage with intersectionality in casting choices. In the episode Lahiri's medical practice is singled out for praise by a white supremacist mommy blogger, which results in a protest outside the office building. During the episode, Lahiri exclaims, 'I am Indian. I can't be racist', and one of her co-workers responds: 'Oh please. You only hook up with white guys'. Re-citing comments that had been voiced in social media, this episode ends with Lahiri behaving condescendingly toward her African American employee, moments after she propositions an African American politician, who claims he is already dating Tyra Banks. Kaling's critics remained unmoved by these gestures of direct response to her viewers because these narrative shifts did not promise a person of colour as a romantic partner for the protagonist (Mora, 2013). Over the four seasons these concerns over Lahiri's brown–white interracial romances have not eased, as she seemed to settle into a relationship with her colleague and partner, Danny Castellano (Chris Messina). Viewers have characterised Lahiri's romantic relationship with her white partner as conventional. In contrast, scholars such as Washington (2012) have documented the minimal representation of interracial romances in television narratives. In these scholarly accounts, cross-racial relationships are the progressive evolution of racial representations and race relations. Yet by drawing a through line between the producer's racialised identity and the series she produces, social media users have demanded a qualitatively different depiction of race relations on *The Mindy Project*. This snapshot is illustrative of the burdens of representation that women of colour experience as they come into visibility. In this instance, the interventions of viewers, most of whom appear to identify as women, seek to transform a prime-time programme into one that addresses concerns central to intersectional feminism, and thereby challenge liberal understandings of race and equality.

There are a number of other such instances in which *The Mindy Project* has provoked polarised responses from social media users and bloggers for its depictions of racial differences. I have singled out the instance of casting choices as a snapshot of the possessive investment viewers have in Mindy Kaling because it speaks to larger concerns about production practices and the politics of race in the contemporary US mediascape. As I indicated in the opening section of this chapter, *The Mindy Project* appeared on the programming schedule at a moment when there are a number of other productions by women, people of colour and gender-nonconforming people. While critics have contested the novelty status of these shows, television scholars have investigated the cultural politics that are embedded in what seems to be a response to shifting demographics and the result of various social justice movements. For instance, Shonda Rhimes, the very successful head of Shondaland Productions, has averred that she blindcasts her projects – a process where race is not written into the script (Nussbaum, 2012). However, Warner (2015) has documented that despite Rhimes' proclamations of postracial television, her series' mobilisation of bodies of colour is strategic and tactical. The central conceit of blindcasting is that it acknowledges racial difference in a manner that causes 'the least amount of discomfort to white audiences' (Warner, 2015: 645). Almost all Shondaland productions feature people of colour, but they seldom address racism or racialising processes. Thus these programmes feed into the belief that the visibility accorded to people of colour signifies historical progress in the struggle of televisual racial representation. *The Mindy Project* enters televisual representations of race and racial politics from a different angle of vision. The series does not characterise Lahiri's romances as crossracial affairs, but at the same time the narratives underscore her identity as South Asian American. Most televisual representations of race tend to be binarised along the black–white axis. *The Mindy Project*, on the other hand, opens the space from which brown can be considered as a signifier of somatic difference and as integral to racialised histories of the US (Sharma, 2010). This is a fraught project, which seems destined to fail. For instance, the pilot episode featured Lahiri treating a burqa-clad patient, whose son acts as translator. After the patient leaves the office, the episode showcases the stereotypes that have come to accrete around the figure of the Muslim woman. Lahiri tells her front-desk staff not to assign her 'non-English speaking pregnant immigrants with no health insurance', while the assistant confesses she mis-read the Muslim patient as someone rich, with oil money. The segment concludes with the assistant clarifying, 'So, more white patients? Done'. Many bloggers did not find this exchange humorous and advised Kaling that 'jokes about races other than your own are difficult to pull off' (Wakeman, 2012). Each of these moments when viewers, with online handles such as herbs31 and jakaydx, turn to social media to confront and challenge Kaling reveal audience investments in the series and the different avenues through which they claim it as a project of their own. Muñoz's (1999) term 'disidentification' seems an appropriate way in which to characterise social media narratives about Kaling. In *Bodies that Matter*, Judith Butler describes the experience of misrecognition, 'this uneasy sense of standing under a sign to which one does and does not belong', as disidentification (1993: 219). Muñoz elaborates on this concept as a process of recycling and rethinking encoded meaning:

> The process of disidentification scrambles and reconstructs the encoded message of a cultural text in a fashion that both exposes the encoded message's universalizing and exclusionary machinations and recircuits its workings to account for, include, and empower minority identities and identifications. Thus, disidentification is a step further than cracking open the code of the majority; it proceeds to use this code as raw material for representing a disempowered politics or positionality that has been rendered unthinkable by the dominant culture.
>
> *(1999: 31)*

I contend that the social media participants I examined seek to transform *The Mindy Project* for their own cultural purposes, working on, with and against its representations of race and gender. Rather than misrecognise its representations, they use Lahiri's persona as raw material to articulate the concept of intersectionality.

Snapshot 3

While the first two instances I have described centre on Mindy Kaling's capacity to navigate the terrain of identity politics, this third instance is focused on the series' capacity to espouse a feminist politics. In a September 2014 online magazine interview, Kaling declared that it would be demeaning to address the political contestations over abortion in a half-hour sitcom. In the original interview this comment was relegated to a parenthetical remark; however, in its circulation, the statement became the flashpoint for a social media conversation about Kaling's feminist credentials. Critics and bloggers pointed out that as a series centred on an ob/gyn practice, the storylines had engaged with a number of women's health concerns. Avoiding a discussion of abortion, they argued, was succumbing to the pressures exercised by mainstream political figures. Citing past shows such as the Norman Lear production *Maude* (CBS, 1972–8) and *Roseanne* (ABC, 1988–97), these critics rebutted Kaling's claim that the topic does not lend itself to the sitcom format (Gupta, 2014). These discourses evidence the prevailing sensibility among critics that television's past was more feminist than its current state. This was one of the rare instances where social media conversations moved beyond the immediate present to offer a historical background to television representations.

As was true in the two earlier snapshots, Kaling took to Twitter to engage her interlocutors. Faced with lists of comedies that had addressed abortion, Kaling conceded that she misspoke. She has not found a way to address the topic of abortion with humour, but this was not a limitation of the genre, Kaling clarified. The debate about abortion was renewed at the end of the third season when Lahiri declares that she is pregnant. Much to the consternation of social media inter-locutors, although the pregnancy was unplanned, Lahiri proceeds with the preg-nancy and gives birth to the child in the fourth season. As was the case with the exchanges about identity politics and the politics of representation, in this instance too Kaling's show was drawn into a discussion about a broader set of conversations animating the political sphere.

In each snapshot Kaling has complicated the labels of female and/or feminist producer that have been bestowed upon her. She has rejected the stances her viewers have expected her to espouse, even as she has navigated carefully the tensions between femininity and feminism. In discussing *Roseanne*, Rowe (1995) uses the trope of the 'unruly woman', a figure drawn from Bakhtin's analysis of the carni-valesque, to present the protagonist as a feminist icon. In that series the unruly woman defies patriarchal authority by being everything that respectable women are not: loud, abrasive, large and out of control. In *The Mindy Project*, the persona of Lahiri updates this archetype of the unruly woman, yet it is the social media interactions that help recast Kaling as not quite feminist enough.[9]

Notwithstanding Kaling's intentions, the social media conversations that have emerged around *The Mindy Project* have allowed viewers to claim the series as tele-vision for women. The topics that ignited the most comment and feedback from social media users were those that expanded the ways in which television has charac-terised programming for women. These comments have recast the comedy series into 'television *for* . . . women' (Moseley *et al.*, 2013); the three snapshots I have discussed effectively rescue the show from the mainstream and make it accountable to feminist and female concerns. In each instance social media has become a key node through which viewers have demanded the inscription of a particular kind of racialised (feminist) woman in television culture.

The debates in which viewers and critics engaged with *The Mindy Project* are also reminiscent of the conversations surrounding 'quality television' productions, such as *The Sopranos* (HBO, 1999–2007) and *Mad Men* (AMC, 2007–15), not those that are associated with either network programming or comedies (McCabe and Akass,

2007). Kaling has overtly positioned her series as engaging with the romcom – a feminine genre par excellence – subverting its norms even as she taps into its features. The artistic and storytelling devices associated with each of these televisual forms do not lend themselves to the term 'quality television'. Nevertheless, the contestations that have arisen in the social media space are reminiscent of the intellectual ferment McCabe and Akass (2007) describe as central to conversations about quality television. Kaling's social media presence allowed her show to become the fulcrum for a range of conversations about feminism, diversity and representational politics (more so than Shondaland productions). These multiply mediated conversations accord to *The Mindy Project* and Mindy Kaling qualities of distinction that both repeatedly fail at achieving. Kaling has inadvertently become the poster girl for 'real women' on television (Zolis, 2014).

Recasting characters

Viewer responses to the figure of Kalinda Sharma on *The Good Wife* were radically different. As I mentioned previously, audiences used the handles #TeamKalinda and #TeamAlicia to assert their allegiance to one of the two female protagonists in the series. Viewers celebrated Sharma's enigmatic persona as well as her uncategorised sexuality. Kohnen (2011) argues that Sharma's depiction teeters on the edge of Orientalist tropes of the unknowable Other. However, what rescues Sharma is

> the agency inherent in her active refusal to identify herself to others. This refusal simultaneously disallows us from neatly categorising her identity (thus leaving room for queer ambiguity) and it suggests a rich inner life (an interiority about which the viewer is invited to speculate).
>
> *(Kohnen, 2011)*

The only time this character came under attack from viewers was during the fourth season, when the series decided to flesh out her backstory. The storylines included an estranged husband who was violent, menacing and physically abusive. Critics and viewers took to social media platforms to complain about the narrative turn and the producers wrote the ex-husband out of the script mid-way through the season. Co-creator Robert King agreed that 'some characters you don't actually want to see that much backstory' (Robinson, 2015).

Archie Panjabi had participated in an impressive list of independent films and television shows in the UK before she was cast in the CBS show. Her roles in films such as *Bend It Like Beckham* (Gurinder Chadha, 2002) and *East is East* (Damien O'Donnell, 1999) centred on the South Asian diasporic experience in the UK. Until the introduction of the ex-husband, *The Good Wife* offered little background information to her persona. The narrative arc of the series however develops her in the contemporaneous present as a seducer whose libidinal energies are multidirectional. In contrast to Mindy Lahiri's promiscuous quest for romance, Sharma's sexual energies are presented as carefully controlled and often mobilised in the interests of her professional interests. The series presents Sharma as not adhering to the prime-time female sexual standard. She returns the objectifying gaze in a manner that queers the colour line. Viewers took to social media platforms such as Tumblr to respond very enthusiastically and positively to these depictions. Importantly, Archie Panjabi's persona seemed to deftly navigate the terrain of intersectionality.

Once Sharma quit the series in 2015, she took to social media, particularly Twitter, to contest and challenge the explanations for her exit that were proffered by the series' producers. While the series suggested that Panjabi had other pressing assignments, the actor clarified that it was because of a personal antagonism with Julianna Margulies, the actor and producer of the series, that she quit. The quarrel between the two actors became the focal point of viewer responses as well. Viewers started to keep track of the on-screen interactions between the two female characters, noting that for at least thirty episodes, since season three, the two women had only interacted on the phone or through another person (Orley, 2014). Following Sharma's last appearance on the series, viewers debated whether Alicia and Kalinda were physically present in the same space or if body doubles were used to produce the aura of physical proximity (Garcia, 2015). These viewer discussions of 'Kaliciagate' offered a sophisticated understanding of the editing strategies and production practices that go into making a series such as *The Good Wife* (Ausiello, 2015). They articulated the deep sense of betrayal audiences experienced when their suspicions about the editing strategies were confirmed. Viewers lamented the fact that televisual friendships between women were rare, and especially cross-racial friendships, so the loss of the Alicia–Kalinda friendship was one that produced considerable anguish (Yahr, 2015). Initially it was the friendship between the two women on-screen and the viewer responses it generated that allowed us to consider *The Good Wife* as television for women. However, the social media conversations about the feuding actors transformed the terms on which we can understand the concept of television for women. Viewers punctuated and simultaneously objected to the relationship between the two actors as a catfight. They contested the categorisation of their acrimonious relationship in sexist terms. The complex terrains of identity politics and intersectionality were notable for their absence in viewer discussions of Kalinda Sharma's persona. Many viewer comments were antagonistic toward Julianna Margulies and believed that she had wronged Panjabi. Racial difference, however, was never addressed in the context of the feud between the two actors. Strikingly, viewers celebrated Archie Panjabi's nomination for a NAACP image award in 2015, but contested a similar nomination for Mindy Kaling that same year.

Both Mindy Kaling and Archie Panjabi became stand-ins for the multicultural world citizen that Melamed (2006) identifies as central to racial politics in the era of neoliberal governmentality. In contemporary culture, race is carefully separated from biological markers and instead embedded in 'historic repertoires and cultural, spatial and signifying systems that stigmatise and depreciate one form of humanity for the purposes of another's health, development, safety, profit or pleasure' (Singh, 2005: 223). The colour line of the twentieth century is now overlaid by new categories of privilege and stigma so that some people of colour can occupy both sides of the privilege/stigma divide. We see this complex understanding of race and privilege being enacted in the social media conversations that viewers conducted.

The Girl Effect backdrop

As numerous cultural critics have noted, there has been a steady increase in the presence of South Asian American actors in US television. This visibility rubs against the other prevalent image of South Asian women in the West: that mobilised by the Girl Effect initiative.[10] Over the past decade, development efforts around the world have shifted their focus from the third-world woman to the third-world girl. While mid-twentieth-century discourses of development argued that controlling third-world women's fertility would be the solution to poverty, in the twenty-first century the figure of the third-world girl has emerged as the point where the interests of feminism and neoliberal capitalism have come to reside. In this discourse, the South Asian or African girl (any female below the age of twelve) has emerged as the primary site of global gender justice. Within such a discourse, the figure of the brown girl has emerged as a site of our anxieties about futurity (MacDonald, 2015).

A project started by the philanthropic arm of Nike has now been embraced by almost every international NGO, including the World Bank and the UN. The highly visible brown girl has become the site of transnational rescue and investment. These efforts pivot on the argument that education is the best available prophylactic and that high-school education for third-world girls will equip them with the skills needed to participate in the global economy. The third-world girl-child can become a pro-ductive, caring, and educated woman only with the help of westerners, who can enable the education needed.

Feminist scholars contend that the Girl Effect is an assemblage of transnational policy discourses, novel corporate investment priorities, biopolitical interventions, branding and marketing campaigns which target girls in affluent societies as the allies and saviours of their 'Southern sisters' (Murphy, 2013). Koffman and Gill (2013) contend that these discourses produce the third-world girl as an entrepreneurial subject-in-waiting. She is thoroughly heterosexualised; the investment in her requires her to be compliant with expectations to serve her family.

I contend that in a cultural imaginary that has come to see the brown girl as someone to be rescued through education, Mindy Kaling and Archie Panjabi are their grown-up versions. I am not arguing for a simple cause–effect relationship between the prevalence of the Girl Effect discourse and the possessive investments of viewers. Rather, I contend that even within the accelerated call-and-response nature of contemporary social media, the identifications and disidentifications engendered by the two actors, the manner in which racial difference is simultaneously hypervi-sible and unspoken, gain greater salience when we take into account the invisible subtext of the Girl Effect. In the US televisual context Panjabi's persona is perched between the figure of the multicultural world citizen and the domestic woman of colour, while Kaling is firmly located as a woman of colour who has to be schooled in her feminisms and identity politics.

Notes

1 Technically a media franchise refers to several (derivative) products developed from a single work. However, media commenters often use the word 'franchise' to discuss Shonda Rhimes' various productions, all of which hinge on strong, professional women, a diverse ensemble cast and narratives that tend to centre on the workplace. Rhimes' *Grey's Anatomy* (ABC, 2005–) and *Private Practice* (ABC, 2007–13) hew to the original understanding of franchise but her other shows, *Scandal* (ABC, 2012–) and *How to Get Away with Murder* (ABC, 2014–), share a familial resemblance by featuring black women protagonists.
2 See Akass (2015) for more on the impact on mainstream television programming of original programming produced by streaming services such as Netflix and Amazon Prime.
3 Actors of South Asian origin appear on several prime-time television programmes, such as *Community* (NBC, 2009–15), *Glee* (Fox, 2009–15), *Parks and Recreation* (NBC, 2009–15), *Big Bang Theory* (CBS, 2007–present), *Royal Pains* (USA, 2009–present), *Outsourced* (NBC, 2010–11) and *Lost* (ABC, 2014–10).
4 'Niagara', from 2010, is one of the episodes Kaling wrote with Greg Daniels; it was nominated for an Emmy award in the Outstanding Writing in a Comedy Series category.
5 Kaling was named one of *Time* magazine's 100 most influential people in the world in 2012. In 2014, she was named one of *Glamour* magazine's women of the year.
6 In an analysis of Melissa McCarthy's celebrity status, Meeuf (2015) has argued that while her comedy hinges on stereotypes of vulgar, low-class obesity, her star persona is that of a polite middle-class everywoman, epitomising narratives of self-confidence and self-acceptance. McCarthy thus becomes a site where neoliberal discourses of self-governance are amplified.
7 Julianna Margulies, the star of the show, assumed the role of producer in 2011.
8 Critics such as Ryan (2014) and Jensen (2013) have praised the series as constituting quality television and as comparable to *Breaking Bad* (AMC, 2008–13) or *Mad Men* (AMC, 2007–15).
9 If *Roseanne* had been first aired in a media ecology analogous to the contemporary one, it is possible that viewer responses on social media may have cast Roseanne, much as they have Kaling, as not feminist enough. It is worth noting though that in her stand-up comedy career prior to her television series, Roseanne Barr disassociated herself from feminism and feminist ideas; Kaling has not distanced herself from the term feminism.
10 See www.girleffect.org

Bibliography

Akass, K. (2015) 'The show that refused to die: the rise and fall of AMC's *The Killing*', *Continuum: Journal of Media & Cultural Studies*, 29 (5): 743–754.
Ausiello, M. (2015) 'Julianna Margulies and Archie Panjabi did not shoot that *Good Wife* finale scene together – and it's not OK', *TVLine*, 15 May, http://tvline.com/2015/05/15/good-wife-alicia-kalinda-finale-scene-julianna-margulies-archie-panjabi/ (Last accessed 15 October 2015).
Barr, M. (2015) '2015: The year women subtly took over TV', *Forbes*, 17 November, www.forbes.com/sites/merrillbarr/2015/11/17/women-on-tv-supergirl-jessica-jones-blindspot-unreal-orphan-black-girl-meets-world/#686351bc77cc (Last accessed 10 December 2015).

Beltran, M. (2010) 'Meaningful diversity: exploring questions of equitable representation on diverse ensemble cast shows', *Flow*, 12 (7), www.flowjournal.org/2010/08/meaningful-diversity/ (Last accessed 15 December 2015).

Berman, J. (2013) '"I'm a white girl": why "Girls" won't ever overcome its racial problem', *The Atlantic*, 22 January, www.theatlantic.com/entertainment/archive/2013/01/im-a-white-girl-why-girls-wont-ever-overcome-its-racial-problem/267345/ (Last accessed 15 December 2015).

Braxton, G. (2014) 'On diversity, Mindy Kaling finds herself held to higher standard', *LA Times*, 29 March, http://articles.latimes.com/2014/mar/29/entertainment/la-et-st-mindy-project-diversity-20140329 (Last accessed 20 October 2015).

Butler, B. (2014) 'Mindy Kaling loves her *Elle* cover, but should we?' *Washington Post*, 9 January, www.washingtonpost.com/blogs/she-the-people/wp/2014/01/09/mindy-kaling-loves-her-elle-cover-but-should-we/ (Last accessed 20 October 2015).

Butler, J. (1993) *Bodies that Matter: On the Discursive Limits of 'Sex'*, New York: Routledge.

Casper, M. and L. Moore (2009) *Missing Bodies: The Politics of Visibility*, New York: New York University Press.

Chittal, N. (2012) 'A reaction to the backlash against Mindy Kaling', *Jezebel*, 21 September, jezebel.com/5945075/a-reaction-to-the-backlash-against-mindy-kaling (Last accessed 7 July 2016).

D'Acci, J. (1994) *Defining Women: Television and the Case of Cagney & Lacey*, Chapel Hill: University of North Carolina Press.

Davis, M. (2014) 'Mindy Kaling's *Elle* cover looks different than the others', *Jezebel*, 6 January, http://jezebel.com/mindy-kalings-elle-cover-looks-different-from-the-othe-1495859348 (Last accessed 20 October 2015).

Davis, V. (2015) 'Viola Davis' Emmy speech', *New York Times*, 20 September, www.nytimes.com/live/emmys-2015/viola-daviss-emotional-emmys-acceptance-speech/ (Last accessed 15 October 2015).

Dejmanee, T. (2016) 'Consumption in the city: the turn to interiority in contemporary postfeminist television', *European Journal of Cultural Studies*, 19 (2): 119–33.

Dockterman, E. (2014) 'Is it really a "wonderful time" to be a woman on TV?' *Time*, 26 August, http://time.com/3181773/emmys-2014-women-on-television/ (Last accessed 15 October 2015).

Dove-Viebahn, A. (2010) 'Stand by your man?', *Ms.* (Spring): 47.

Duca, L. (2014) 'Here's why you should be upset over Mindy Kaling's Elle cover, even if she isn't', *Huffington Post*, 8 January, www.huffingtonpost.com/lauren-duca/mindy-kaling-elle_b_4561454.html (Last accessed 20 October 2015).

Garcia, P. (2015) 'Everything you need to know about *The Good Wife* feud', *Vogue*, 5 October, www.vogue.com/13357483/the-good-wife-feud-julianna-margulies-archie-panjabi/ (Last accessed 20 October 2015).

Gill, R. (2007) 'Postfeminist media culture: elements of a sensibility', *European Journal of Cultural Studies*, 10 (2): 147–66.

Gopalan, N. (2014) 'I understand why Mindy Kaling is defending her much-criticised Elle cover, but it's still hard to watch her do it', *xojane*, 14 January, www.xojane.com/issues/mindy-kaling-elle-cover (Last accessed 20 October 2015).

Gupta, P. (2014) 'Mindy Kaling says half-hour sitcoms cannot take on abortion – but these shows did', *Salon*, 3 September, www.salon.com/2014/09/03/mindy_kaling_says_half_hour_sitcoms_cant_take_on_abortion_but_these_shows_did/ (Last accessed 15 October 2015).

hooks, b. (1992) *Black Looks: Race and Representation*, Boston: South End Press.

Jenkins, H. (1992) *Textual Poachers: Television Fans and Participatory Culture*, New York: Routledge.

Jensen, J. (2013) 'The Good Wife', *Entertainment Weekly*, 16 December, www.ew.com/article/2013/12/16/good-wife (Last accessed 11 July 2016).

Jones, J. (2013) 'The Good Wife and the problem of too much good TV', *Entertainment Weekly*, 14 November, www.ew.com/article/2013/11/14/the-good-wife-and-the-problem-of-too-much-good-tv (Last accessed 20 October 2015).

Jones, S. (2002) 'The sex lives of cult television characters', *Screen*, 43 (1): 79–90.

Karpel, A. (2012) 'How Mindy Kaling is tweeting her way to cultural domination', *Co. Create*, 12 September, www.fastcocreate.com/1681575/how-mindy-kaling-is-tweeting-her-way-to-cultural-domination (Last accessed 20 October 2015).

Kirkpatrick, N. (2011) '*The Good Wife*', *In Media Res*, 10 October, http://mediacommons.futureofthebook.org/imr/2011/10/10/good-show-broadcast-cable-quality-and-good-wife (Last accessed 11 December 2015).

Koffman, O. and R. Gill (2013) '"The revolution will be led by a 12-year-old girl": girl power and global biopolitics', *Feminist Review*, 105 (1): 83–102.

Kohnen, M. (2011) 'The queerness of Kalinda Sharma', *In Media Res*, 13 October, http://mediacommons.futkohneneureofthebook.org/imr/2011/10/13/queerness-kalinda-sharma (Last accessed 15 December 2015).

Kozol, W. (2005) 'Marginalized bodies and the politics of visibility', *American Quarterly*, 57 (1): 237–47.

Lahiri, A. (2012) 'Why I am Team Kalinda: a new face for desi women on TV', *Racialicious: The Intersection of Race and Popular Culture*, 25 January, http://racialicious.tumblr.com/post/16469900689/whyiamonteamkalinda (Last accessed 7 July 2016).

Leonard, S. (2014) 'Sexuality, technology, and sexual scandal in *The Good Wife*', *Feminist Media Studies*, 14 (6): 944–58.

Levine, R. (2014) 'Mindy Kaling, *Elle* cover controversy continues', *Hollywood Take*, 7 January, www.hollywoodtake.com/mindy-kaling-elle-cover-controversy-continues-responding-critics-magazine-says-comedian-looks-sexy (Last accessed 20 October 2015).

Lipsitz, G. (1999) *The Possessive Investment in Whiteness: How White People Profit from Identity Politics*, Philadelphia: Temple University Press.

Little, L. (2014) 'Mindy Kaling defends her controversial Elle cover', *Wall Street Journal*, 8 January, http://blogs.wsj.com/speakeasy/2014/01/08/mindy-kaling-defends-her-con-troversial-elle-cover/ (Last accessed 15 October 2015).

McCabe, J. and K. Akass (eds) (2007) *Quality Television: Contemporary American Television and Beyond*, London: I.B.Tauris.

MacDonald, K. (2015) 'Calls for educating girls in the third world: futurity, girls and the "third world woman"', *Gender, Place & Culture: A Journal of Feminist Geography*, 23 (1): 1–17.

Meeuf, R. (2015) 'Class, corpulence and neoliberal citizenship: Melissa McCarthy on *Saturday Night Live*', *Celebrity Studies*, http://dx.doi.org/10.1080/19392397.2015.1044758 (Last accessed 15 October 2015).

Melamed, J. (2006) 'The spirit of neoliberalism: from racial liberalism to neoliberal multiculturalism', *Social Text*, 24 (4): 1–25.

Mora, C. (2013) 'The Mindy Project's controversial episode on race didn't clear up any concerns', *Bustle*, 20 November, www.bustle.com/articles/9309-the-mindy-projects-controversial-episode-on-race-didnt-clear-up-any-concerns (Last accessed 15 October 2015).

Moseley, R., H. Wheatley, and H. Wood (2013) 'Television for women dossier introduction: why "television for women"?' *Screen*, 54 (2): 238–43.

Muñoz, J. (1999) *Disidentifications: Queers of Colour and the Performance of Politics*, Minneapolis: University of Minnesota Press.

Murphy, M. (2013) 'The Girl: mergers of feminism and finance in neoliberal times', *The Scholar and Feminist Online*, 11 (1–2), http://sfonline.barnard.edu/gender-justice-and-neoliberal-transformations/the-girl-mergers-of-feminism-and-finance-in-neoliberal-times/ (Last accessed 15 October 2015).

Nededog, J. (2013) 'What's with Mindy's white-guy obsession on "The Mindy Project"', *The Wrap*, 17 September, www.thewrap.com/fox-mindy-project-season-2-premiere/ (Last accessed 20 October 2015).

Nussbaum, E. (2012) 'Primary colours', *New Yorker*, 21 May, www.newyorker.com/magazine/2012/05/21/primary-colours (Last accessed 15 October 2015).

Nussbaum, E. (2014) 'The female bad fan', *New Yorker*, 17 October, www.newyorker.com/culture/cultural-comment/female-bad-fan (Last accessed 15 October 2015).

Orley, E. (2014) 'Alicia and Kalinda haven't shared a scene in 30 episodes', *Buzzfeed*, 28 August, www.buzzfeed.com/emilyorley/kalinda-and-alicia-relationship-on-the-good-wife#.ru74MM5J2 (Last accessed 20 October 2015).

Parham, J. (2013) 'Why does "Scandal" keep avoiding the race question?' *Complex*, 17 May, www.complex.com/pop-culture/2013/05/shonda-rhimes-and-scandal (Last accessed 20 October 2015).

Paskin, W. (2013) 'Network TV is broken: So how does Shonda Rhimes keep making hits?' *New York Times Magazine*, 9 May, www.nytimes.com/2013/05/12/magazine/shonda-rhimes.html (Last accessed 15 October 2015).

Payne, R. (2013) 'Virality 2.0: networked promiscuity and the sharing subject', *Cultural Studies*, 27 (4): 540–60.

Rivera, Z. (2014) 'Mindy Kaling on Elle cover controversy', *New York Daily News*, 11 January, www.nydailynews.com/entertainment/gossip/mindy-kaling-elle-cover-beautiful-fat-body-article-1.1576298 (Last accessed 20 October 2015).

Robinson, J. (2015) 'How *The Good Wife* failed one of its best characters', *Vanity Fair*, 27 April, www.vanityfair.com/hollywood/2015/04/why-kalinda-left-the-good-wife (Last accessed 15 October 2015).

Rowe, K. (1995) *The Unruly Woman: Gender and the Genres of Laughter*, Austin: University of Texas Press.

Ryan, M. (2014) 'The Good Wife brings fun to quality TV', *Huffington Post*, 6 October, www.huffingtonpost.com/2014/10/06/the-good-wife-cbs_n_5939844.html (Last accessed 20 October 2015).

Schumann, R. (2014), 'Mindy Kaling Elle magazine cover attacked for "racist" cropping controversy on Twitter', *International Business Times*, 7 January, www.ibtimes.com/mindy-kaling-elle-magazine-cover-attacked-racist-cropping-controversy-twitter-photos-1530430 (Last accessed 20 October 2015).

Scovell, N. (2015) 'The "Golden Age for Women in TV" is actually a rerun', *New York Times*, 12 September, www.nytimes.com/2015/09/13/opinion/sunday/the-golden-age-for-women-in-tv-is-actually-a-rerun.html (Last accessed 15 October 2015).

Sharma, S. (2010) 'Taxicab publics and the production of brown space after 9/11', *Cultural Studies*, 24 (2): 183–99.

Singh, N. P. (2005) *Black is a Country: Race and the Unfinished Struggle for Democracy*, Cambridge: Harvard University Press.

Stewart, D. (2013) 'Mindy Kaling only makes out with white guys on *The Mindy Project*', *Jezebel*, 9 June, http://jezebel.com/mindy-kaling-only-makes-out-with-white-guys-on-the-mind-504732390 (Last accessed 15 October 2015).

Thakore, B. (2014) 'Must-see TV: South Asian characterisations in American popular media', *Sociology Compass*, 8 (2): 149–56.

Turner, N. (2014) 'Elle under fire for Mindy Kaling cover', *CNN*, 8 January, www.cnn.com/videos/showbiz/2014/01/08/nr-turner-mindy-kaling-elle-cover.cnn (Last accessed 15 October 2015).

Wakeman, J. (2012) 'On "The Mindy Project's" squicky jokes about race', *The Frisky*, 29 August, www.thefrisky.com/2012-08-29/on-the-mindy-projects-squicky-jokes-about-race/ (Last accessed 20 October 2015).

Warner, K. (2015) 'The racial logic of *Grey's Anatomy*: Shonda Rhimes and her "post-Civil Rights, post-feminist" series', *Television & New Media*, 16 (7): 631–47.

Washington, M. (2012) 'Interracial intimacy: hegemonic construction of Asian American and Black relationships on TV medical dramas', *Howard Journal of Communications*, 23 (3): 253–71.

Xia, C. (2013) '*The Mindy Project*'s Rishi and the call for more POCs in charge', *Racialicious*, 16 May, theaerogram.com/the-mindy-projects-rishi-and-the-call-for-more-pocs-in-charge/ (Last accessed 7 July 2016).

Yahr, E. (2015) 'Do "Good Wife" stars Julianna Margulies and Archie Panjabi hate each other?' *Washington Post*, 11 May, www.washingtonpost.com/news/arts-and-entertainment/wp/2015/05/11/do-good-wife-stars-julianna-margulies-and-archie-panjabi-hate-each-other-inside-the-alicia-kalinda-conspiracy/ (Last accessed 20 October 2015).

Zolis, S. (2014) 'Why I love Mindy Kaling', *Canadian Living*, 8 January, www.canadianliving.com/blogs/life/2014/01/08/why-i-love-mindy-kaling/ (Last accessed 15 October 2015).

6

WATCHING *ONE BORN EVERY MINUTE*

Negotiating the terms of the 'good birth'

Sara De Benedictis

Introduction

Birth has been firmly placed in the cultural spotlight. Among a broader contemporary interest in maternity, in the UK Channel 4's BAFTA award-winning television programme *One Born Every Minute* (Channel 4, 2010–) underscores that women's birthing experiences are receiving an unprecedented amount of airtime. The show presents itself as a documentary, purporting to reflect birthing experiences to entertain and educate viewers. Yet, despite claims of neutrality and education, these representations are highly contradictory and constructed, offering 'good'/'bad' birthing processes and bodies, which contribute to power relations and social inequalities.

Within a broader interest in the new visibility of 'public' birth, Tyler and Baraitser (2013) argue that what is peculiar about representations of televisual birth like *One Born Every Minute* is that this signifies a distinct break with cultural and psychosocial traditions of Western birth representations. Tyler and Baraitser note that historically in Western religious and philosophical traditions, birth has been depicted through a masculine lens, which obscures women's role in birth. The concealment of women's role in birth in cultural sites is part of the 'foundational "matricide" that inaugurates Western culture' (Tyler and Baraitser, 2013: 4). This 'matricide' underscores the constructed notion that the cultural and psychic repudiation of the maternal body (the primary abject) is necessary for individuation, which a number of feminists have critiqued (ibid.). Tyler and Baraitser argue, however, that televisual birth goes against this history, as women's role in birth is fundamental to these recent depictions of birth. And despite the inconsistencies and commercialisation of televisual birth, the significance of women's roles in this still needs further exploration as it 'poses a challenge to the abjection of maternal subjectivity from cultural space, by symbolically "returning birth to women"' (ibid.: 10).

Taking my cue from Tyler and Baraitser, I consider the implications of televisual birth through an exploration of the audience of *One Born Every Minute*. This chapter explores themes that emerged from an audience reception study of *One Born Every Minute* with eighteen women, to argue that to further understand the significance of televisual birth, it is important to explore televisual birth alongside viewers' reactions. This chapter looks to ask questions such as: how is birth constructed in *One Born Every Minute*? How is this construction framed by broader sociocultural structures and power? And how is the 'returning birth to women' that *One Born Every Minute* underscores experienced and reacted to by female viewers? This chapter traces my participants' negotiation and resistance to three themes that emerged through the study: birth as unknown; birth as abject and awesome; and birth as a vehicle for moral judgements.

Neoliberal maternity, 'childbirth TV' and *One Born Every Minute*

One Born Every Minute is surrounded by an array of broader maternal representations that have surfaced since the 1990s (Tyler, 2011b). In the British context, one only has to consider the cultural obsession with soon-to-be celebrity mothers ('bump watch'), the tweeting and Instagramming of celebrity and 'ordinary' women's births or the policy debates on the benefits or drawbacks of breastfeeding, homebirths or parenting classes, among many other examples, to see this recent 'maternal publicity' (Tyler, 2011a). A growing body of scholarship explores the cultural politics of these maternal representations, evidenced by, for example, investigations into the sexualisation of pregnancy (Tyler, 2011b) or the consumer-orientated 'yummy mummy' (Littler, 2013). As Shani Orgad and I note elsewhere, this body of literature emphasises that maternal femininities are increasingly created through neoliberal mentalities of consumerism, individualisation and self-responsibilisation (Orgad and De Benedictis, 2015). The literature also highlights deep social distinctions, as those who are upheld as successful maternal subjects are predominately white, heterosexual, able-bodied and middle-class, pitted against working-class mothers who are constructed as failing and abject, which serves only to highlight broader sociocultural inequalities.

Tyler (2011a) argues that British reality television occupies a crucial role in this foregrounding of maternal representations. She notes that 'maternal TV' is 'a proliferating reality subgenre', which includes '"correctional" parenting shows', such as *Supernanny* (Channel 4, 2004–12), '"teen" parenting' shows, such as *16 and Pregnant* (MTV, 2009–) and 'hospital-based childbirth reality shows', such as *One Born Every Minute* (Tyler, 2011a: 214). Elsewhere, Tyler and Baraitser explore televisual birth, arguing that 'birth as entertainment' proliferates into what they term 'childbirth TV' (Tyler and Baraitser, 2013: 9). Childbirth depictions are now evident in various British television genres, such as reality television, celebrity reality television, docusoaps, soaps and period dramas. Shows such as *One Born Every Minute*, *Call the Midwife* (BBC1, 2012–) and *Extraordinary Births* (Channel 4, 2015) have commanded large primetime audience shares over the past decade. Arguably, the most commercially successful programme that places birth in the spotlight is *One Born Every Minute*. At the time of writing, the ninth series of the show is airing in the UK. The show's visualisation of birth, showcasing of intimacy and glamorisation of midwifery has seen it retain its popularity. As such, *One Born Every Minute* is a rich site to explore neoliberal maternity and televisual birth, and how viewers engage with and negotiate this new maternal visibility.

The study

This chapter emerges from my doctoral research, an audience reception study of *One Born Every Minute*. I was interested in exploring what the increase in televisual birth through *One Born Every Minute* tells us about current understandings of birth, the maternal, gender and class, and how this is entangled within neoliberal notions of the self.[1] At the heart of this research was a commitment to listen to women and take their media experiences seriously. As such, I drew upon Skeggs and Wood's (2012) methodological framework of exploring reality television through interviews, focus groups, text-in-action sessions and textual analysis.[2]

From March 2013 to May 2014, I obtained data by recruiting eighteen participants who lived in Greater London. Once I had recruited key participants, I used the snowballing technique to form groups for the text-in-action sessions, and nine participant streams surfaced.[3] Participants were from various class backgrounds with different maternal identities and subjectivities, but were mainly white, middle-class and heterosexual. In all, twelve self-defined as middle-class, one self-defined as working-class, one self-defined as working-class and middle-class, two self-defined as working-class in the UK but middle-class in their birth country and two did not answer. All participants self-defined as heterosexual and white (either British, Slovakian, Italian or Argentinian), bar one participant who self-defined as British Pakistani. Recruiting participants for the study was challenging, especially regarding working-class participants. I attempted to recruit participants multiple times through various means, such as through acquaintances, friends, family, colleagues or social media forums, but people either were unresponsive or withdrew. This mirrors difficulties that other reality television audience reception researchers, such as Jensen (2013) and Skeggs and Wood (2012), have encountered when recruiting participants; both studies relate to the increasing observation of the working classes in the UK from government institutions and agendas. Furthermore, there was an overall whiteness of the participants in this study related to these recruitment difficulties and, retrospectively, how I recruited. This speaks to a broader power structure of whiteness as an 'unmarked norm' of audience reception studies (see Mayer, 2005). In Jensen's (2013) study of parenting reality television, she sees the issues she faced in recruitment and the overall whiteness of her participants as bound up in the implicitness of whiteness in parenting culture, which could be applied to birthing reality television shows too. It is essential to explore the racialised components of televisual birth and audience reception; however, there is not space to discuss this here.

The participants' engagement with *One Born Every Minute* varied; some had watched every series, others dipped in and out of episodes and others had only watched a few episodes. The research process did not require the participants to be 'fanatics', which much audience research leans towards; rather, it looked to exploring different types of viewers, such as the 'non-fan' (see Gray, 2003). While the research aims lay in exploring women's engagement with televisual birth, men's engagement still featured in the participants' narratives, especially of those in heterosexual relationships. *One Born Every Minute* is presented as 'women's TV' due to the content of birth and intimacy, but male control was still evident in some participants' engagement with the programme. Many of the participants' partners' opinions of *One Born Every Minute* would often stop them watching, even though the women usually regularly watched and enjoyed the programme. For example, Alina had watched every episode of *One Born Every Minute* but stopped watching the show when she met her boyfriend. She stated that this was because 'he doesn't like watching it' as he 'finds it disturbing' and 'scary' (Alina, Interview). This emphasised how a male presence in the private sphere still exerts control over women's cultural engagement, preferences and practices in explicit and implicit ways, perhaps surprisingly corroborating findings in older studies on gender and audiences (e.g. Gray, 1992). But this also underscores how gendered and classed cultural hierarchies around 'television for women', 'reality television' and value (see Biressi and Nunn, 2005; Skeggs and Wood, 2012) come into practice through intimate relations, signalling broader inequalities and power structures.

One Born Every Minute as revealing the 'reality' of birth?

One Born Every Minute heavily capitalises on revealing the 'insights into the reality of birth' (Channel 4, 2013). Although the show follows the conventions of the modern docusoap, aligned with public broadcasting remits, *One Born Every Minute* defines itself as documentary.[4] This documentary claim is offered through a modern twist of heightened surveillance due to the show's 'fixed-rig' production.[5] This enables the presentation of *One Born Every Minute* as a 'neutral', and implicitly educational, authority about birth experiences and processes. The show establishes itself as a higher form of 'truth' from the outset through the combination of this surveillant shooting style and the generic documentary convention of the 'voice of God' commentary (see Nichols, 1983). In the opening sequence, the voiceover states:

> Every minute, of every hour, of every day, a baby is born in Britain. To find out what it feels like to bring new life into the world we put forty cameras into a bustling maternity hospital. To the front desk, to the operating theatre, from the birthing pool, to neonatal, capturing new lives beginning and others . . . changing . . . for ever.
>
> *(One Born Every Minute, 2010)*

This voiceover links a montage of mothers in the throes of childbirth, fathers nervously watching, medics chaotically ensuring birth occurs smoothly and a brief moving CCTV camera, overlaid with women screaming, women stating baffled wonderment over impending motherhood and eerie repetitive sounds of medical equipment, until the words 'for ever', at which the soothing, non-diegetic music commences with faces of newborns and parents cooing. Humdrum hospital life is juxtaposed with intense birth experiences. Low-quality shots and cameras focusing and zooming allow surveillance to become a ghostly yet unquestioned omnipresence in *One Born Every Minute*. This establishes surveillance to show the 'happenstance' of the hospital (Dovey, 2000), creating the 'illusion of transparency: the attempt to capture life "as it happens", unedited and unmediated' (Clissold, 2004: 49). Moreover, the voiceover's use of the word 'every' with the charting of time links *One Born Every Minute* temporally to real events, creating a sense of 'liveness' (Couldry, 2003). The show's format furthers this claim to represent the 'reality' of childbirth and women's experiences. Fixed cameras are placed in National Health Service hospitals, intermingled with 'confessional' camera shots, as each episode follows the narratives of mothers entering the hospital to give birth, their families and the midwives who assist them. Kavka (2008) notes that truth claims in reality television are made through actuality, which 'strengthens the effect of immediacy; immediacy strengthens the effect of social community' (Kavka, 2008: 19). This 'truth' claim through actuality states that births are occurring *now* in Britain and those broadcast on *One Born Every Minute* could represent any of these.

Perhaps unsurprisingly, across all of my audience participants *One Born Every Minute* was considered a site to discover the unknown elements, overcome the mystique and increase their knowledge of birth. For example:

> I'm just always searching for a – a fuller picture and [. . .] I think birth is one of those really unique cases where you're never going to really have one. 'Cos you'll never know what's it's like for every person. [. . .] So I think that's what like *One Born Every Minute* keeps you hooked on.
>
> *(Alina, Interview)*

Underlying this quote is the sense that birth is unknowable and uncertain, which makes it 'unique'. Others described how *One Born Every Minute* can 'prepare you to not be so scared' as you cannot 'imagine the whole situation' (Sandra, Interview). The broader sociocultural attitude that birth is an experience that can never be *fully* understood unless it is experienced was reiterated in participants' accounts. Alina and Sandra had not given birth, but the benefits of watching *One Born Every Minute* to get the 'fuller picture' of birth were also stressed by those who had. For example, Rose described a 'vested interest' (Rose, Interview) in watching *One Born Every Minute* as she was considering having another child. What these extracts highlight is the gendered contradiction of being positioned as a subject who is perceived to have the capacity to birth, but who is unable to ever fully 'know' about birth, even for those who have experience. Birth as the 'great unknown' was a discursive trope in the construction of birth and accounts were peppered with anxiety, trepidation and fear. *One Born Every Minute* was seen to alleviate this fear by offering the 'fuller picture' of birth. These discussions of *One Born Every Minute* uncovering the unknown fell alongside many participants stressing that the show was an educational documentary. Watching *One Born Every Minute* was presented as a tool to demystify birth, allowing participants to be responsible, prepared citizens learning about birth through reality television, arming themselves with the knowledge required to give birth in the future.

However, simultaneously, many participants considered *One Born Every Minute* to be an unverifiable source of birth knowledge. For example:

> It's not particularly . . . well it's a little bit educational I guess you know but that's not why you watch it, you don't watch it to be educated, you'd go to NCT [National Childbirth Trust] classes if you wanted to be educated on having a baby. And I think it's very realistic.
>
> *(Rose, Interview)*

Rose, a middle-class mother, positions herself here as a 'knowing' audience member (that is, she sees through the guise that *One Born Every Minute* is educational), rather pointing to the intrigue lying in the realism of the show. This quote also highlights that she validated her own maternal experiences over *One Born Every Minute* by drawing on middle-class values of increasing knowledge about birth through control, preparation and classes (see O'Brien Hill, 2014: 189). This rejection of *One Born Every Minute*'s educational merits and validation of one's own maternal experiences also featured with some working-class participants. For example, Tracey stressed that she gained knowledge about birth from her family members. This difference in how some participants validated their experiences over *One Born Every Minute* in the research encounter corroborates Skeggs and Wood's (2012) argument that participants in their research used their own social position to assert their value in relation to television texts. Stressing that one gains birth knowledge through family, rather than through NCT, in rejecting *One Born Every Minute*'s birth knowledge could point to how alternative value-systems shaped by class see these women acquire and validate maternal knowledge.

In addition to this rejection of *One Born Every Minute* as educational, the text-in-action sessions with some participants highlighted a further contradiction to the assertion that *One Born Every Minute* increased birth knowledge. Clarification of medical terms and processes that episodes raised, but did not adequately explain, prompted questions like 'what's normal gestation?' (Jess, Text-in-action) or 'what exactly is a contraction?' (Carole, Text-in-action). These types of questions were common from the middle-class participants who had not given birth. Therefore, despite *One Born Every Minute*'s claim to demystify birth and indirectly educate viewers, for some the show engendered more questions than answers. Despite the participants' reflexive statements in interviews about how *One Born Every Minute* increased knowledge and education of the birthing process, this was contradicted within interviews and the text-in-action sessions.

Thus, there were ambiguities between what the participants initially communicated about why they liked *One Born Every Minute* (educational, increases knowledge, demystifies birth) versus the rejection of *One Born Every Minute* as birth knowledge and the ambiguity of gaining birth knowledge in the text-in-action sessions. Skeggs and Wood (2012) note that '[t]alking about television was connected to [what their participants] told us as researchers about their value' (Skeggs and Wood, 2012: 119). However, the immediacy of reality television in the text-in-action sessions 'positions viewers to locate themselves and their experiences within the drama/narrative' (ibid.: 107). Thus, the different methods highlighted the different subject positions the participants took up through *One Born Every Minute*. Reflexively stressing in interviews that *One Born Every Minute* was an educational documentary and a source of birth knowledge in the research encounter enabled the participants to elevate their cultural habits and justify watching the show as increasing educational capital. Simultaneously, the participants were aware of *One Born Every Minute*'s low cultural status more generally, and rejecting the way in which birth was represented enabled a validation of their own maternal knowledge through derision of *One Born Every Minute* as the 'bad' object. However, birth itself was still seen as unknowable and constructed through fear, and these complex negotiations and struggles over the validation of different forms of knowledge and value worked as attempts to quell this uncertainty and resolve ambivalences.

The rollercoaster ride of birth: from abject to awesome

A baby's head crowning was an emotionally powerful moment and met with reluctant fascination by the participants in the text-in-action sessions. Participants described feeling simultaneously transfixed and horrified. Some discussed watching with 'morbid fascination' (Alina, Interview); others described crowning as 'not necessarily something I want to see but it's the kind of thing where I'm [. . .] half looking away but actually I can't stop looking' (Amelia, Interview). In the text-in-action sessions participants communicated these reactions paralinguistically (for example cringing or gasping), through phrases like 'oh my god' and 'oh fuck' and by peering through half-closed fingers. Skeggs *et al.* (2008) note that from their text-in-action sessions, such responses represent when 'affective noise was translated into judgement through mediating statements such as "oh my God", which were then converted into moral judgements' (ibid.: 17). The participants' judgements were marked by disgust. As Ahmed (2004) notes, through disgust reactions, the 'process of both casting out and pulling away means that disgust works to align the individual with the collective at the very moment both are generated' (Ahmed, 2004: 95). The participants were reacting to the moment of crowning, when the birthing body is discursively constructed at its most 'taboo' (Tyler and Clements, 2009: 134).

Watching crowning emphasised an ambivalent relationship between birth and femininity. Alina highlighted this powerfully immediately after her text-in-action session:

> I just like kind of empathise with the woman [in *One Born Every Minute*]. I think it just reminds me when my mum talks about being a mother a lot and I remember her saying something about like your mum like will [. . .] never have any shame in [. . .] defending you or being a mother or protecting you because from the moment that she becomes your mother it's like the most shame that you could ever feel. Like she's given up all kind of like modesty or whatever in that moment because you've literally just like pooed and bled and stuff in front of loads of people, you're in an awkward position, you're sweaty and disgusting and like it – that's the moment when you become a mother. I dunno. I I think I empathise with them because it's kind of their – it's kind of like part of them is – is died. But then at the same time it's like a whole new start.
>
> *(Alina, Interview)*

In this extract, Alina adopts an intergenerational notion of maternal inter-subjectivity through considering how her mother discussed giving birth, to relate this back to *One Born Every Minute*. This extract highlighted a subject who has been exposed through giving birth. Alina described a number of maternal abject bodily processes – excretion, bleeding, sweating – that are immodest and shameful, as the maternal body is exposed to many people. Importantly, she describes this process through death: part of a woman dies during birth, but simultaneously a new chapter starts. What this extract highlights is how giving birth is constructed as a necessarily shameful, sacrificial act of femininity, which is a digression from constrained, restrained (middle-class) femininity. Birth is dis-cursively seen as an abject experience that, while necessary to retain life, offers a complex scenario whereby the maternal figure is disavowed and lost in order for this to occur. But Alina also attempted to discursively evaluate crowning to value her mother's experience and constructed sacrifice. More generally, there was something quite poignant about how the participants, including Alina, described the loss of self through the birthing process; it was a great source of anxiety for all the participants. In the context of postfeminist, neoliberal requirements for the pregnant body to be contained, controlled and sexual (Tyler, 2011b), crowning is a significant moment that challenges ideals of the sexual female body. I will return to this important point later in the chapter. However, it is important to note that crowning is seen to represent the peak of birth; the reactions to this in the text-in-action sessions carried great normative weight, marked by intensities and competing values around femininity.

In *One Born Every Minute,* however, a baby being placed on a mother's chest is often swiftly represented as juxtaposed against crowning. This moment is the emotional reward following crowning; the show takes the viewers on a rollercoaster from pain to relief to sentimentality. In the text-in-action sessions this moment of narrative closure was imbued with affective charge, met with 'awww' and 'how cute'. In the text-in-action sessions (and many of the other episodes in *One Born Every Minute*), after all the pain, sweat and labour, mothers are left in, by and large, heterosexual two-parent situations with newborn babies. The pay-off to the anxiety and fear around birth that the participants felt through *One Born Every Minute* was soothed, and naturalised, by 'traditional' family units; 'order' was restored through (largely) nuclear families.

A striking angle when discussing this climactic scene with the participants was the significance of taking this journey with the women on the episodes. For example, Tracey described that it felt like 'you're there living it with them, and you're going through the whole, like, wars. And I think when you've had a child you're thinking, "oh, I remember how that felt, oh, I remember that"' (Tracey, Interview). Other participants described visceral responses, as Elena eloquently explained:

> [I]t's tense and they're just like, 'oh my god, it's coming, it's coming now, it must be'. Oh, the first thing, like the head pops out it's like 'oh my god, oh my god', it's like tense, like, your muscles are like, yes, you feel like, 'my god, my god, my god', and then when you see the baby's completely out you say, 'ahh, how cute' and you really [. . .] feel the whole thing with her.
>
> *(Elena, Interview)*

These examples emphasise how the participants placed themselves into the drama, and for some participants this shifted them back to the memory of giving birth. Skeggs and Wood argue that the 'affect-producing technology' (Skeggs and Wood, 2012: 68) of television entices audiences to position themselves into moments of drama: the positioning of oneself into the proceedings of reality television, or refusing to do so – the 'as if' or 'as not' – saw their participants '*perform* the increasing mediation of experiences whereby public understandings of distinction, disgust and social in/difference are repeatedly produced' (ibid.: 160, original emphasis). Inherent to this was that the 'performance of labour (work, emotion and domestic) became immanently subject to performance review, as if our respondents were under the same demands as the television participants' (ibid.: 41). Similarly, the participants in this research emotionally (and sometimes physically) laboured with the women on their birth journeys, which saw them perform labour and align themselves with notions of the 'good' heteronormative subject.

'Good' and 'bad' birthing subjects and births

Birth as potentially threatening to norms of femininity was a notion that was (re)produced in *One Born Every Minute* and in the fieldwork. The attempt to control birth was ever-present. O'Brien Hill argues that 'it is the issue of control during labour within the hospital setting that is at the heart of each episode of [*One Born Every Minute*]'

TABLE 6.1 Text-in-action session 1

Visual	Audio	Participants
Close-up of the face of the birthing woman, Sam, as she cries.	Joyce: There. You take it. You know where it is. You hold it. Slow down with it.	
Close-up of the father, Ed, looking nervous.	Sam's mum: Steady.	Leah: [inaudible] Charlotte: She's panicking. Yeah.
Close-up of Sam breathing in gas and air rapidly.	Joyce: Right, come on. You're really not helping now.	
Medium close-up of midwife, Kay, as she takes a long sip of tea standing in the staffroom.	Midwife in the background: Yes. Yeah, very irregular.	Leah: Mmmm. She'll pan the property.
Long shot of the hospital corridor as Kay walks out of the staffroom.	Kay: Lovely.	Orla: Yeah.
		Leah: I guess that's the thing with staying calm. If you calmly have contact with people around you, I guess. Charlotte: Mmm. Orla: Yeah.

(O'Brien Hill, 2014: 189). Remaining stoic and modest when giving birth was important to the participants and made evident through imparting moral judgements as they watched women give birth. If the women giving birth deviated from maternal stoicism or a family member would glimpse at the birthing woman's vulva during crowning, these moments were met with great disapproval and shock. Transgressing stoicism was often shown through excess. See Table 6.1 for an example.

In this episode Sam is depicted not only as being too loud and flouting notions of femininity, but also as attention-seeking, weak-willed and a nuisance to medical staff. Sam is also depicted as irresponsible, spoilt and unwise to the reality of bringing up children, largely because she is unemployed and became pregnant. Sam is implicitly positioned as the young, working-class 'chav mum' who is created as irresponsibly 'leeching' off the state, rather than delaying motherhood and contributing to the labour market like her middle-class counterpart, creating class distinctions through disgust and humour (Tyler, 2008). The participants saw Sam as uncontrolled: as my research participant, Leah, uttered in watching the above, 'she'll pan the property'. Sam's birth ends in an emergency caesarean, and an unspoken link is made that this occurred because she did not 'try' hard enough in the show. The participants in this text-in-action session are disparaging of her behaviour as she did not remain 'calm' during birth. As another participant, Katy, stated about *One Born Every Minute*:

> [T]here's almost something philosophical about like women who seem to be like 'this is the most pain I've ever gone through but I'm just, you know, that's just the process and you have to'. Whereas you know the younger one that we saw in that programme, it was like 'why?!' you know just like fighting it and you know, blaming other people or just not facing up to the fact that she had to just go through with it. [I]t seems like, you know, [a] character divide sometimes.
>
> *(Katy, Interview)*

Underlying this extract are notions of individual mastery and conquering pain through birth. Labouring of the body, and the mind, was fundamental to give birth. The marker of the 'good' birthing subject is someone who can 'handle' this labour, which proves a woman's character. Or, as Katy further elaborated, giving birth vaginally separates 'the wheat from the chaff' and, oddly, 'the men from the boys' (Katy, Interview). This highlights that in birth discourses women must be *physically* strong and *subjectively* strong (the 'right' frame of mind and 'character'), which echoes the controlled and restrained postfeminist, neoliberal subject. O'Brien Hill notes that discourses around birth in *One Born Every Minute* are linked to control, the 'good mother' myth and neoliberal notions of self-discipline over pain relief; 'working with pain' is necessary in the transition to motherhood, as 'being prepared to suffer for your child during labour is regarded as a necessary rite of passage into motherhood' (O'Brien Hill, 2014: 190). Thus, this 'good mother' discourse is entwined with discourses around the 'good birth'.

O'Brien Hill further notes that *One Born Every Minute* 'makes a spectacle of the female body in pain, and part of that spectacle stems from focussing on how the expectant mother is perceived to be coping (or failing to cope) with that pain' (ibid.: 192). Through the ridicule of certain mothers featured, the show puts forth 'correct' ways to give birth. Any transgression from the restrained, stoic birthing body is policed, as was the case with Sam in the text-in-action session above. More generally, the women on *One Born Every Minute* are shown feeling shame and remorse for their behaviour during birth. Being unrestrained and uncontrolled, and apologising for this, highlights that birth does not enable women to behave without judgement; rather, birthing bodies are self-policed and expected to maintain, or show remorse for any transgressions of, middle-class notions of femininity. Apologising to – or being ridiculed by – partners and midwives for being too loud, too foul-mouthed or too self-centred during the birthing process is par for the course in *One Born Every Minute*. Beverley Skeggs (2004) notes that excessive dispositions and conduct have been historically constructed as the domain of working-class femininity in order to define middle-class notions of restraint. Furthermore, Gill (2007) notes that self-control and bodily discipline (usually attained through consumption) are features of the postfeminist subject. As the working-class woman is often figured as excessive and uncontrolled, this postfeminist requirement is out of reach. Although a mixture of mothers are featured, the show more often represents working-class mothers. The show leans on this class history that is re-enacted through postfeminist corporeal norms; thus, behaving 'badly' during birth becomes classed. Or, as one participant commented when watching a screaming birthing woman the day after Kate Middleton gave birth: 'Bet Kate didn't do that!' (Carole, Text-in-action).[6]

However, participants also saw birth norms broken if the women giving birth were, paradoxically, too quiet and calm. See Table 6.2 for an example.

This group felt that the birthing woman in this episode (Series 5 Episode 6), Cody, was inauthentic and 'weird'; she was not giving birth 'right', as she acted like she had 'stubbed a toe'. With other groups, judgement was passed on 'too' quiet women who cared too much about their presentation during birth. The importance of authenticity in reality television has been explored elsewhere (e.g. Allen and Mendick, 2013; Hill, 2005). As Allen and Mendick stress, notions of authenticity are integral to ideas of the 'inner self', as 'the ability to overcome obstacles to "knowing oneself" is central to the neoliberal project of self-actualisation' (Allen and Mendick, 2013: 2). Thus, even though the show goes to great lengths to enforce 'good' controlled birthing subjects, the judgement from the participants highlighted that there was an impossibility to get birth 'right': if the woman was 'too' loud she was unruly; if the

TABLE 6.2 Text-in-action session 2

Visual	Audio	Participants
Medium close-up of the father, Daniel, smiling and looking off shot.	Midwife: That's it. Ah look!	Sarah: She's not even screaming.
		Alex: Why you looking? Don't look down there!
Close-up of crowning.	Midwife 2: Oh, there she is.	Sarah: She's not even screaming.
Medium shot of the birthing woman, Cody, pushing, lying on her back with everyone around her.		Alex: She's in water.
		Kristy: I mean this is what's so weird.
Close-up of the baby being lifted out by the midwife.	Cody: Ow!	Sarah: She just went ow as if she'd stubbed a toe.
	Midwife: Look. Look. There she is.	Kristy: Yeah. Yeah it was exactly like that. That's what I thought.
		Sarah: Yeah.
Medium shot of the midwife handing Cody the baby.		Alex: But why's the mum still there?!

woman was 'too' quiet she was inauthentic. Furthermore, in reality television, authenticity is linked to a wider imperative to showcase emotion (Aslama and Pantti, 2006). Thus, the participants were also reacting to a visual lack of emotion as a lack of authenticity and emotional labour.

The extract above illustrates another birth digression in Alex's utterance of 'why you looking? Don't look down there!' Across the fieldwork all participants objected to a 'humorous' trope of *One Born Every Minute* whereby a partner or family member glances during crowning. This shot was always met with intense apprehension and rejection; it was a moment filled with shock and laughter. Statements like 'Oh, why's he looking!', '[laughs] They looked!' or 'He's not looking down?!' were common. Some participants attempted to stop the men looking at the women by demand. As Nicole urged, 'Don't you look, don't you look!' (Nicole, Text-in-action).

This rejection of 'peeping' by the participants could indicate conflating issues surrounding the construction of mothers' bodies. Littler (2013) argues that mothers are no longer expected to subscribe to asexual ideals of Christian maternity; rather, in neoliberal times, driven by consumerism and a 'fetishization of the maternal' (Littler, 2013: 233), the white, middle-class, heterosexual figure of the 'yummy mummy' sees mothers constructed as a 'desired object rather than desiring subject' (ibid.: 231). Discourses around the sexualisation of mothers shift how mothers' bodies are policed and, as such, the peeping birth partner, largely a birthing woman's boyfriend or husband, in *One Born Every Minute* sees the woman at her most vulnerable – and, importantly, abject – moment, which contradicts this new imperative of a mother's body being solely for sexual pleasure, as crowning is marked through disgust. The cultural mentality that 'if your husband sees *that*, he will never look at you the same way again' signals that birth, and especially crowning, is threatening not only to contemporary notions of maternal sexuality, but also to (heterosexual) intimate relationships. However, this rejection could be seen slightly differently. These rejections could be a form of resistance to an extreme 'male gaze', personified through the man that 'peeps'. The female participants place themselves in the women's shoes and are rejecting the (patriarchal) voyeurism, surveillance, objectification and control of the birthing process, and of birthing bodies, if momentarily.

'Natural' versus caesarean

Considering that lack of control was a prevalent feature of the participants' accounts, one might expect that attempts to gain control of the birthing process (i.e. by caesarean section) might be preferential. However, this was not the case for the majority of the participants, or in *One Born Every Minute*. Tyler and Baraitser (2013) emphasise that televisual birth is 'limited in terms of the absence of possibilities they encode for imagining, experiencing or understanding birth outside of dominant systems of control and surveillance that characterise obstetric practices in the Global North' (Tyler and Baraitser, 2013: 9). In the show, there is a distinct favouring of 'natural' birth with as little intervention as possible (O'Brien Hill, 2014). Within widespread cultural discourses of the benefits of the 'natural childbirth movement'

(Johnson, 2008) and the derision associated with caesareans (for example, 'too posh to push'), the show establishes interventions as morally questionable; interventions into birth (bar gas and air) are constructed as unnecessary, risky or as a last resort.[7] For example, within the text-in-action episodes, caesarean sections were always portrayed as an emergency procedure that was intensely dramatic and dangerous due to medical complications. As the soon-to-be mothers are rushed for a caesarean section, the filmic cues signal danger and crisis. The sound of blaring hospital alarms, close-ups of flashing red hospital lights, midwives and doctors frantically running through corridors and anxious-looking relatives are staple visual cues to signal crisis. Caesarean section is often represented as a last resort to stem the threat of death and failure.

Caesareans are not only constructed as a last resort, but any deviation from a 'natural' birth is seen as a 'bad', unnecessary choice. In one episode watched in a text-in-action session (Series 4 Episode 12), a woman wants an epidural, to the dismay of the midwives. The midwife has a disapproving conversation with the mother-to-be and subsequently, in the staffroom, discusses how unnecessary her choice of an epidural was. Moral value is imparted on how a woman 'should' give birth. From one perspective, the emphasis upon decreasing medical intervention could be seen as a positive way forward in ceasing patriarchal control of the maternal body. However, Johnson (2008) and O'Brien Hill (2014) argue that 'natural' childbirth discourses are situated within specific white, Western, middle-class concepts of the self. They argue that these discourses are imbued in power relations that privilege middle-class experience, and advocating a uniform approach to childbirth may not benefit all women.

Overall, the participants viewed giving birth 'naturally' as preferential. Reasons surrounding this were not linked to a direct rejection of medical norms. Rather, for some participants giving birth 'naturally' was linked to morality and motherhood – for example, as essential for 'bonding' (Paula, Focus Group) and a 'connection' (Nicole, Focus Group), emphasising the link of 'natural' birth with the 'good mother' myth (see O'Brien Hill, 2014; this is also evident in linking 'good' pregnancy practices to the 'good' mother present through pregnancy 'apps' (Johnson, 2014) and antenatal care (Papen, 2008)). Subsequent to their text-in-action session, Lucy and Carole similarly stressed the importance of getting a 'connection', but also that 'natural' birth 'seems loads easier' (Carole, Focus Group) and 'seems like the obvious choice' (Lucy, Focus Group). 'Choice' largely emerged in accounts of middle-class women who had not given birth. This highlights how choice is mobilised in discussions around birth with a neoliberal inflection, and how this choice is naturalised as the 'right' one (O'Brien Hill, 2014). However, considering the preference for 'natural' birth in *One Born Every Minute*, and broader sociocultural birth norms (see Johnson, 2008), how much choice there is around this is brought into question.

However, one middle-class participant, Lisa, was an exception and consistently rejected the notion that 'natural' was the 'right' way to birth. Lisa had not given birth, but throughout the fieldwork she drew on her mother's birth experiences. These experiences were upsetting for Lisa, as Lisa was premature and her mother had an emergency caesarean, resulting in a hysterectomy. She had an investment in rebutting

One Born Every Minute's claim about the 'right' type of birth. For example, when discussing *One Born Every Minute*:

> I think something that irritates me is when the woman is just like 'I want an epidural' or 'I want pain relief'. And the midwives do seem quite like resistant to it. And I think [. . .] is that kind of their training of just like trying to get out the baby as naturally as possible. If a woman's sitting there like 'I want an epidural', in my mind it's like 'well fucking give her one' [. . .] [T]hat kind of annoys me because I think that's where kind of there's a professional opinion and a personal opinion and, you know, are they dithering because they think professionally it's not a good idea [and] if so they should be saying 'well I don't think you should have that for x, y and z reasons', which is why I think it's more of a personal reason of just, you know, try and have it as naturally as possible, which I think, you know, it shouldn't be that kind of the midwives' personal choice over the patient's.
>
> *(Lisa, Interview)*

Lisa was frustrated and adamant that 'natural' birth is not always the choice of the women on *One Born Every Minute*. She felt that the midwives had another agenda to women 'naturally' birthing, which she felt was not always medically justified. Lisa valued her own and her mother's experiences of birth to challenge the dominant reading of the text. O'Brien Hill (2014) argues that in *One Born Every Minute* the 'natural' birth discourse 'encapsulates the neoliberal free agent', but 'investment in the illusion of choice [is] hugely problematic within the hospital setting' (O'Brien Hill, 2014: 190). This discourse 'positions the midwife as the expert' (ibid.: 191). Lisa mobilises choice here, in contrast to Lucy's above quote, in noting that 'natural' birth is the 'obvious choice'. Lucy utilises choice to stress that giving birth 'naturally' is the 'real' choice, whereas Lisa uses choice to argue that there is only freedom to make the 'right' (neoliberal) choice and give birth 'naturally'. Thus, birth norms are established in *One Born Every Minute* by the midwives for 'natural' birth, alongside broader sociocultural ideologies of birth; Lisa's insubordination to the midwives and their preference for 'natural' birth sees her momentarily reject these dominant ideologies.

Conclusion

This chapter has explored televisual birth via *One Born Every Minute* to see how 'returning birth to women' (Tyler and Baraitser, 2013: 10) was understood by a group of women. The exploration of these participants' opinions and reactions to *One Born Every Minute* highlighted that despite the show's efforts to inculcate dominant ideologies around birth – as unknown, abject/awesome and marked by morality – the participants' reactions were complex and unpredictable. *One Born Every Minute* offers birth as a vehicle to communicate ideas around neoliberal ideals. It was clear that the participants validated their own experiences and social positions to align themselves with, or reject, these positions offered by the text. When participants were discussing or reacting to *One Born Every Minute*, they would often do so either through their own maternal experiences or intergenerationally through their mother's experiences. While fear, anxiety and disgust of birth, as well as circulating values of birth and birthing bodies through distinctions, were prevalent in the fieldwork, the participants' reactions also highlighted momentary resistance. Some participants questioned the expertise of the midwives and the discourse of 'choice' within birth representations, and attempted to redefine the moment of crowning. There were moments whereby the participants reiterated the maternal abjection that *One Born Every Minute* offers, for example with reactions of disgust to crowning, but the responses were not always straightforward. At points, the constructed visceral nature of birthing bodies, the immediacy of television and the proximity to the participants' own experiences saw some participants redefine those moments – for example, through Alina's intergenerational discussion of crowning that attempted to re-value the maternal body through personal experience. These types of momentary resistances to the 'normative performative' (Skeggs and Wood, 2012: 49) of maternal abjection are politically significant gendered acts which rupture the normative codes of the 'good birth' and by extension the 'good mother'.

Notes

1 By using the term 'the maternal', I align myself with feminist scholarship that is concerned with exploring the subjective, psychosocial and political significance of maternal subjects, identities and practices. See the inaugural issue of *Studies in the Maternal* and www.mamsie.org.
2 The text-in-action method maps linguistic and paralinguistic reactions alongside moments of televisual drama (see Skeggs and Wood, 2012).
3 I term these 'streams', not 'groups', as some sessions only had one participant.
4 This follows a history of docusoaps leaning on the conventions of realism to present themselves as unmediated to 'justify exploitation (of unpaid participants) and voyeurism through an implied association with "documentary realism"' (Allen *et al.* 2014, n.p.).
5 Ellis (2015) notes that in 'fixed-rig' productions, over roughly two weeks, cameras are placed within a set location and crew are placed in onsite monitoring rooms to watch the multiple video feeds that result. He observes that the crew who watch these digital feeds also control the direction of the cameras as the action occurs on site (see Ellis, 2015 for a fuller explanation of 'fixed-rig' productions).
6 Kate Middleton, Duchess of Cambridge, is married to Prince William. The birth of their first child, Prince George, was covered extensively in the global press, especially when the couple brought the baby home from the hospital – with paparazzi, media commentators and an adoring public crowd present – the day before this text-in-action session.
7 This term refers to a woman who is perceived to have an elective caesarean to avoid the pain (and labour) of childbirth. It is often used to deride working-class celebrities, such as Victoria Beckham.

Bibliography

Ahmed, S. (2004) *The Cultural Politics of Emotion*. Edinburgh: Edinburgh University Press.
Allen, K. and H. Mendick (2013) 'Keeping It Real? Social Class, Young People and "Authenticity" in Reality TV', *Sociology*, 47 (3): 460–76.

Allen, K., I. Tyler and S. De Benedictis (2014) 'Thinking with "White Dee": The Gender Politics of "Austerity Porn"', *Sociological Research Online*, 19 (3), www.socresonline.org.uk/19/3/2.html (Last accessed 14 July 2016).

Aslama, M. and M. Pantti (2006) 'Talking Alone: Reality TV, Emotions and Authenticity', *European Journal of Cultural Studies*, 9 (2): 167–84.

Biressi, A. and H. Nunn (2005) *Reality TV: Realism and Revelation*. New York and Chichester: Wallflower Press.

Clissold, B.D. (2004) 'Candid Camera and the Origins of Reality TV', in S. Holmes and D. Jermyn (eds) *Understanding Reality Television*. London and New York: Routledge: 33–53.

Couldry, N. (2003) *Media Rituals: A Critical Approach*. London and New York: Routledge.

Dovey, J. (2000) *Freakshow: First Person Media and Factual Television*. London: Pluto Press.

Ellis, J. (2015) 'Fixed Rig Documentaries: How They Do It', *Critical Studies in Television Online*, http://cstonline.tv/fixed-rig-documentaries-how-they-do-it (Last accessed 1 November 2015).

Gill, R. (2007) 'Postfeminist Media Culture: Elements of a Sensibility', *European Journal of Cultural Studies*, 10 (2): 147–66.

Gray, A. (1992) *Video Playtime: The Gendering of a Leisure Technology*. London and New York: Routledge.

Gray, J. (2003) 'New Audiences, New Textualities: Anti-Fans and Non-Fans', *International Journal of Cultural Studies*, 6 (1): 64–81.

Hill, A. (2005) *Reality TV: Audiences and Popular Factual Television*. Abingdon and New York: Routledge.

Jensen, T. (2013) 'Creating Distinction: Middle-Class Viewers of Supernanny', in C. Fairclough, D. Hoffman, and L. Layne (eds) *Parenting in Global Perspective: Negotiating Ideologies of Kinship, Self and Politics*. Abingdon and New York: Routledge: 51–68.

Johnson, C. (2008) 'The Political "Nature" of Pregnancy and Childbirth'. Paper prepared for presentation at the annual meeting of the Canadian Political Science Association. Vancouver BC: University of British Columbia.

Johnson, S. (2014) '"Maternal Devices", Social Media and the Self-Management of Pregnancy, Mothering and Child Health', *Societies*, 4 (2): 330–50.

Kavka, M. (2008) *Reality Television, Affect and Intimacy: Reality Matters*. Basingstoke: Palgrave Macmillan.

Littler, J. (2013) 'The Rise of the "Yummy Mummy": Popular Conservatism and the Neoliberal Maternal in Contemporary British Culture', *Communication, Culture & Critique*, 6 (2): 227–43.

Mayer, V. (2005) 'Research Beyond the Pale: Whiteness in Audience Studies and Media Ethnography', *Communication Theory*, 15 (2): 148–67.

Nichols, B. (1983) 'The Voice of Documentary', *Film Quarterly*, 36 (3): 17–30.

O'Brien Hill, G.E. (2014) 'The Older Mother in *One Born Every Minute*', in I. Whelehan and J. Gwynne (eds) *Ageing, Popular Culture and Contemporary Feminism*. Basingstoke: Palgrave Macmillan: 187–202.

Orgad, S. and S. De Benedictis (2015) 'The "Stay-at-Home" Mother, Postfeminism and Neoliberalism: Content Analysis of UK News Coverage', *European Journal of Communication*, 30 (4): 418–36.

Papen, U. (2008) 'Pregnancy Starts with a Literacy Event: Pregnancy and Antenatal Care as Textually Mediated Experiences', *Ethnography*, 9 (3): 377–402.

Skeggs, B. (2004) *Class, Self, Culture*. London and New York: Routledge.

Skeggs, B. and H. Wood (2012) *Reacting to Reality Television: Performance, Audience and Value*. Abingdon and New York: Routledge.

Skeggs, B., N. Thumim and H. Wood (2008) '"Oh Goodness, I am Watching Reality TV": How Methods Make Class in Audience Research', *European Journal of Cultural Studies*, 11 (1): 5–24.

Tyler, I. (2008) '"Chav Mum Chav Scum": Class Disgust in Contemporary Britain', *Feminist Media Studies*, 8 (1): 17–34.

Tyler, I. (2011a) 'Pramface Girls: The Class Politics of "Maternal TV"', in B. Skeggs and H. Wood (eds) *Reality Television and Class*. London: Palgrave Macmillan: 210–24.

Tyler, I. (2011b) 'Pregnant Beauties: Maternal Femininities under Neoliberalism', in R. Gill and C. Scharff (eds) *New Femininities: Postfeminism, Neoliberalism and Subjectivity*. Hampshire and New York: Palgrave Macmillan: 21–36.

Tyler, I. and L. Baraitser (2013) 'Private View, Public Birth: Making Feminist Sense of the New Visual Culture of Childbirth', *Studies in the Maternal*, 5 (2): 1–27.

Tyler, I. and J. Clements (2009) 'The Taboo Aesthetics of the Birth Scene', *Feminist Review*, 93 (1): 134–7.

7

SEX, CLASS AND CONSUMERISM

British sitcom's negotiation of the single girl

Vicky Ball

As an undergraduate student in communication studies in the mid to late 1990s, my education in and knowledge of feminist approaches to gender and the media developed alongside my taste, as a television viewer, for the British female ensemble dramas which appeared regularly on my television screen at that time. *Band of Gold* (Granada for ITV, 1995–8), *Real Women* (BBC, 1998–9), *Playing the Field* (Tiger Aspect productions for the BBC, 1998–2002) and *Daylight Robbery* (Hewland International for ITV, 1999–2000), together with the female ensemble sitcom *Dinnerladies* (BBC, 1998–2000), were enjoyable and, indeed, valuable texts to me as a viewer because of the ways in which their narratives focused upon communities of regional, working-class femininities: positionalities which chimed with my own subject positioning during this same period.

Armed with the critical tools and concepts from my undergraduate honours programme, I was also able to theorise my viewing pleasure, acknowledging the ways in which these texts turned previous ways of representing groups of working-class women on their head. Thus, while working-class matriarchal communities have long been a celebrated feature of British soap operas such as *Coronation Street* (Granada for ITV, 1960–), these female ensemble texts were distinctive in moving to centre-stage that which is only celebrated periodically in British soap opera: women's relationships with women outside their roles as wives and mothers. Embodying the role-reversal trope *en vogue* in British 1990s 'heroine television' (Brunsdon, 1997: 34), the female ensemble drama afforded female characters the narrative terrain usually reserved for or associated with male buddy movies.[1] Narratives which privilege female friendship disrupt not only generic but also gendered cultural values, and can be seen as socially challenging in a number of ways:

> The traditional female life course is normative, socialised and supported by the ideology of compulsory marriage and motherhood [. . .] The recognition of

women's ability to enjoy themselves with other women obviously implicitly undermines a romantic-love ideology which stresses that true pleasure is only possible in the arms of a man. It challenges social controls over women's behaviour, especially their access to public areas; it undermines the equation of femininity with maternity, domesticity and the private area, and the culturally legitimated tendency for women to base their identities on such 'caring' relationships.

(O'Connor, 1992: 182)

In placing 'women on top', the female ensemble text embodies and celebrates female unruliness (Davis, 1975), flouting the codes of respectability which have historically secured the moral legitimation of British, working-class women's identity (Skeggs, 1997: 1–2). As Skeggs argues, historically, working-class women's identity and sexuality have been defined in relation to middle-class constructions of the modern family in which the behaviour of women was interpreted in relation to their role as wives and mothers and their capacity for the general surveillance of working-class men (1997: 5). It is through discourses of respectability that the 'threat' of working-class women's sexuality, constructed also as dangerous and impure, has been controlled (ibid.: 1/122). British female ensemble dramas of the 1990s can be seen to disrupt these codes of respectability, given the ways in which the working-class femininities of these texts are not exclusively white, straight, slim, honest, caring or faithful.

I was keen to discover the lineage of this particular fictional form, and a little critical digging uncovered a rich body of female ensemble texts dating back to the 1960s in the form of sitcoms such as *The Rag Trade* (BBC1, 1961–3; LWT for ITV, 1977–8), *The Liver Birds* (BBC, 1969–79) and *Birds of a Feather* (BBC, 1989–98; Alomo Productions/SelecTV for ITV, 2015–); prison dramas such as *Within These Walls* (LWT for ITV, 1974–8) and *Bad Girls* (Shed Productions for ITV, 1999–2006); historical dramas such as *Shoulder to Shoulder* (Warner Bros and BBC, 1974), *Tenko* (BBC, 1981–2, 1984–5) and *Call the Midwife* (Neal Street Productions for ITV, 2012–); crime dramas such as *Widows* (w. Lynda La Plante, Euston Films for ITV, 1983, 1985) and *Band of Gold* (w. Kay Mellor, Granada for ITV, 1995–8); 'lifestyle' dramas such as *Take Three Girls* (BBC, 1969–71) and *Mistresses* (Ecosse Films for BBC Wales, 2008–10); and a rock musical in the form of *Rock Follies* (w. Howard Schuman, Thames TV for ITV, 1976–7).

Like their counterparts in the 1990s, these older texts engage with particular class-based femininities. However, it is working-class femininities, and in some cases socialist feminist politics, that remain central to each of their narratives. Despite the dispersal of female ensemble texts across television schedules, it was regrettable to find that, with few exceptions, female ensemble texts have been the subject of critical neglect.[2] As I have detailed elsewhere, areas of culture tied to 'the feminine' have not only been marked out as gendered in comparison to the masculine norm, but have also been *class*ified, assigned low cultural status because of their association with women and femininity (Ball, 2013: 244).

My current research on the female ensemble drama addresses this critical neglect of female ensemble texts. By tracing the lineage of the female ensemble text across its various generic permutations from 1960s to the contemporary period, this research addresses specific gaps in feminist knowledge regarding British television's historical relationship between gender and class in their articulation at particular social and cultural junctures. The purpose of undertaking this research project is born out of feminist understandings of the 'personal as political'. It was the representation of working-class femininities that attracted me to this form of fiction twenty years ago. These fictions were exciting because they provided a rare opportunity to identify with subjectivities on television that replicated my own. But, given that television texts are entwined with and inextricable from broader social, cultural and political histories (Wheatley, 2007: 4), the marginalisation of these feminine texts within television historiography reinforces hierarchies of cultural value which perpetuate gendered and class-based relations in the UK.

Considering such feminine histories of television can open up the fields of British television drama and comedy studies. Across these interrelated fields of study, issues of class (politics) and gender have been discussed primarily with recourse to masculinity, leaving only question marks when it comes to television's engagement with issues of class in articulation with femininity. My study of female ensemble fictions allows us to delve into this history and ask how television drama and comedy have constructed, negotiated and mediated histories of class and femininity in the UK. For instance, how have these texts constructed and negotiated class and femininity in relation to the swinging sixties, the turbulent seventies, the Thatcherite eighties, the postfeminist nineties and noughties, as well as the current era of austerity?

Given the feminine identity of female ensemble texts – programmes which focus upon female identities and which increasingly have been written and produced by women – there is a presumption that these texts are also addressed solely to women. Drawing on archival sources such as BBC drama policy and production files, listing magazines and interviews with producers of the female ensemble texts, a central strand of my research has been to investigate this presumption, and to explore the shifting address of female ensemble texts over their fifty-year history.

In this chapter I share some of my findings regarding the address of the early British female ensemble texts of the 1960s and 1970s. Akin to the research on popular British soap operas of the 1960s such as *Coronation Street* (Granada, 1960–) and *Crossroads* (ATV, 1964–81; Central, 1981–8), I illustrate how female ensemble texts emerged within, and indeed formed part of, broader shifts in the address of British television in terms of gender and social class in articulation during this period. As a starting point, I will explore this issue with regard to the emergence of the first female ensemble sitcom, *The Rag Trade*, in 1961.

'You've never had it so good!'

The Rag Trade was a popular situation comedy that originally aired on the BBC for three series between 1961 and 1963. It followed a group of female working-class factory workers, led by the militant shop steward Paddy (Miriam Karlin), and their attempts to outwit their boss, the owner of Fenner's Fashions, Harold Fenner (Peter Jones). Frequently caught between the two parties was the flustered factory foreman, Reg (Reg Varney). Recounting the production context of *The Rag Trade*, the text's producer, Dennis Main Wilson, claimed the idea was borrowed from the Boulting Brothers film *I'm All Right Jack* (1959), a film satirising class relations in the postwar period marked by the economic boom, full employment, growing shop-floor militancy and increasing affluence. Discussing the translation to television, Main Wilson recounts how *The Rag Trade* 'was the female version of *I'm All Right Jack,* but for laughs'.[3] In dismissing *The Rag Trade* as a formulaic situation comedy ('it literally was feed line tag, feed line tag'), however, Main Wilson fails to register the extent to which the text personifies the broader shifts that television was attempting to address and negotiate during this period.

To be sure, television had, since its inception in the 1930s, sought to address a wide audience (Holmes, 2008: 12). This was increasingly so in the late 1940s and early 1950s due to the very same social shifts that are satirised in texts such as *I'm All Right Jack* and *The Rag Trade*. Significantly for my analysis, this rise in employment, affluence and increased consumer spending, coupled with the relative drop in the costs of television receivers, put ownership or rental of a television set, by the end of the 1950s, 'within reach of most' (Thumim, 2004: 28).

However, in its focus upon a group of female rather than male factory workers, *The Rag Trade* also demonstrates the shifting gendered address of television in articulation with social class. As with working–class audiences, women as a social group were key to the formation of the revised national address of television in these formative years of the 1950s and 1960s (Thumim, 2004). Thumim argues that 'television's special address to women was highly significant since their engagement was thought to be crucial to the establishment of the viewing "habit" at the centre of domestic life in the UK' (2004: 3). *The Rag Trade* exemplifies the shift in which television moved from addressing women as wives and mothers in the daytime home to being part of the general audience of evening programming. As such, the subsumption of women's interests into those of the general audience indicates the shifting social status of women (particularly that of young women) and their expanding citizenry as they began to be constructed and addressed as a new generation of workers as well as housewives during this period. However, as the following annual planning memo by then Head of Drama at the BBC, Sydney Newman, to the Director of Television, Kenneth Adam, in July 1964 illustrates, television's shifting address with regard to gender is one that is firmly bound up with social class, age and consumerism:

> We haven't enough programmes which have a strong appeal for women and we certainly don't have enough programmes which specifically appeal to the young – that is, up to 30–35. Part of this stems from the preponderance of material in which our heroes are never young or attractive to emulate. We must recognise the specific needs of the young working couple in which the man is likely to be in the skilled-worker class in new industries like plastics,

electronics and so on. In short, the new modern consumer type that commercial television sets out to get.

(WAC T16/62/3, 28 July 1964)[4]

Along with *The Rag Trade*, the attempt by television to appeal to and address shifting conceptions of 'woman' and the feminine is evident with more dramas focused on the subjectivities of women. Granada's protogenic ensemble drama *It's a Woman's World*, from 1964, is a case in point. This text consisted of a series of four plays each exploring a particular feminine archetype (the 'dolly bird', the mother, the career woman, the unmarried woman). However, it was towards the end of the decade, between 1968 and 1971, that the number of female ensemble texts began to proliferate on British television, with the sitcoms *Wild, Wild Women* (BBC1, 1968–9), *The Liver Birds* (BBC1, 1969–79), *Girls About Town* (ATV, 1969–70) and *It's Awfully Bad for Your Eyes, Darling* (BBC1, 1971), as well as the drama *Take Three Girls* (BBC1, 1969–71). As with the forerunners in the early 1960s, this cycle of ensemble texts embodied a pluralised sense of identity, with each female character representing a particular class-based position. However, these later texts also engage with discourses associated with the women's liberation movement, and more specifically with notions of women's sexual liberation that were circulating during this period. It is this later cycle of texts that I will explore for the remainder of this chapter. More specifically, I will seek to explore how, with the exception of *Wild, Wild Women*, these texts construct, or indeed are in dialogue with, new public femininities: single girls via their flat-sharing scenarios.

Single girls

The emergence of the single girl in ensemble texts can be seen as being rather delayed, given that this figure had already become the 'emblem of the 1960s' (Radner, 1999: 10) via popular cultural texts such as Helen Gurley Brown's *Sex and the Single Girl* (1962), the much-publicised Profumo affair and the cycle of Swinging London films such as *Darling* (John Schlesinger, 1965), *The Knack . . . And How to Get It* (Richard Lester, 1965), *Georgy Girl* (Silvio Narizzano, 1966), *Smashing Times* (Desmond Davis, 1967) and *Joanna* (Mike Sarne, 1968). While, as Melanie Bell suggests, sexual liberation was more imagined than real for the majority of women within this period (2012: 79), it is nonetheless the case that the constructions of the sexually liberated single girls within these ensemble texts played a crucial role in establishing 'new agendas' and 'possible realms of consciousness' (Harper, 2000: 101).

The attempt to construct and appeal to young women through the figure of the single girl is evident in the way in which the idea for each series originated with male television executives rather than the writers of these texts. While script ideas submitted to the BBC by Carla Lane and Myra Taylor were in the tradition of absurdist comedy (about a dachshund dog being interviewed about the height of pavements), it was the BBC's head of comedy, Michael Mills, who encouraged the women to write about young single girls sharing a bed-sit (Lane, 2006: 22). The pilot episode of

The Liver Birds, broadcast on a Monday evening on 14 April 1969, was the first episode in the eighth series of the *Comedy Playhouse* series.

However, *The Liver Birds* was not the first sitcom pilot by the BBC to focus upon groups of women for its narrative interests. Reviewing other sitcoms piloted under the *Comedy Playhouse* series highlights the BBC's sustained attempt to construct single-girls-in-flat-sharing scenarios, with pilots such as *The Bachelor Girls* (BBC1, 1963) and *The Hen House* (BBC1, 1964).[5] Conversely, while *Girls About Town* focused upon two thirty-something married women, its narrative dilemmas and feminine aspirations are in dialogue with the freedoms and aspirations open to the singleton heroines of *Take Three Girls*, *The Liver Birds* and *It's Awfully Bad for Your Eyes, Darling*.

Yet the narratives of mobile femininities associated with the female ensemble texts are not restricted to those which appear on our television screens; rather, the female ensemble texts also contributed to the inroads women writers have made into television production. With the exception of *Wild, Wild Women*, the other sitcoms in this cycle – *The Liver Birds* (Carla Lane and Myra Taylor), *It's Awfully Bad for Your Eyes, Darling* (Jilly Cooper) and *Girls About Town* (Adele Rose) – were all written by women. And half of the team of writers of *Take Three Girls'* first series was also female (Julia Jones and Charlotte Bingham).

The high numbers of women employed on the texts are not representative of all dramas and sitcoms at this time. Given that you had to be a member of a union in order to work in television during this period, it is interesting to note that the Association of Cinematograph Television and allied Technicians (ACTT) received zero applications from women writers to work in television until the 1960s.[6] And indeed, even in this decade, only 25 per cent (seven out of twenty-eight) of applications for the grade of writing in television were received by the ACTT from women. If the number of applications for membership as freelance writers is also taken into consideration (which would enable applicants to work across film and television) then the number falls further to 17 per cent, given that all fourteen applications to work as freelance writers were from male applicants.

Although these figures may not provide a complete picture of employment rates of female and male writers working in television during the 1960s (for instance, some writers may have opted to join the Writers' Guild of Great Britain, which was established in 1959), it does at least indicate how few women writers there still appeared to be in this decade compared with men, and thus the significance of 'feminine' dramatic forms such as ensemble fictions as places where women secured some employment. In this respect, I suggest that women's increasing mobility within television production emerges from, and indeed is reliant upon, shifts to the heterosexual contract brought about by the process of liberalisation and women's increased participation in the public sphere during this period; in short, the same set of factors which made the production of ensemble texts featuring mobile femininities attractive to broadcasters in the 1960s and 1970s.

Similarly to the cycle of Swinging London films, the city setting of each ensemble text is foregrounded as the site of 'pleasure and autonomy' (Luckett, 2000: 233) for young modern women. Despite their domestic flat-sharing premise, the opening credit sequences of both *The Liver Birds* and *Take Three Girls*, for instance, introduce the heroines separately, with each marvelling at the sites and freedoms offered by the city. The heroines' movement through the city streets foregrounds their agency, centrality and mobility within this space, while the fashionable clothing and popular music soundtracks of Pentangle (*Take Three Girls*) and The Scaffold (*The Liver Birds*) identify these spaces and identities with the contemporary youth culture. Although the capital city remains the site for fashionable and unconventional femininities to be explored in *Take Three Girls*, *It's Awfully Bad for Your Eyes, Darling* and *Girls About Town*, the Liverpool setting of *The Liver Birds* imagines the dispersal of independent femininities across other 'Swinging' cities of Britain. Liverpool in this instance mirrors the role and reputation of the capital city because of its associations with popular culture, including the 'Mersey Sound' made famous by The Beatles, Gerry and The Pacemakers and 'Swinging Cilla' Black earlier in the decade.

Whereas the earlier ensemble formats attempted to negotiate the feminine into masculine areas of social life, these new public femininities suggest 'a utopian fantasy of a woman freed from the social and sexual constraints that appeared to limit her mother' (Radner, 1999: 10). Similarly to the way in which texts of the earlier 1960s tapped into and drew upon various aspects of women's culture in an attempt to appeal to female viewers, in the domestic concerns of soap operas such as *Coronation Street* or *Crossroads* but also the worlds of women's magazines (*Compact*), fashion (*The Rag Trade*, *The Avengers*) and shopping (*Harpers West One*), the female ensemble text – like the Swinging London films – remediates the address of women's magazines such as *Honey* and *19*. As Luckett has aptly captured in relation to the Swinging London films:

> The narratives of these films heralded a new feminine perspective marked by the importance of sexual expression to self-identity; the centrality of individualised forms of glamour, to a more female-orientated public life, and London's structural role in enabling and authorizing this glamour and agency. Like the beauty and fashion spreads in women's magazines, this glamour has a feminine address, foregrounding its role in the creation of a new and powerful self.
>
> *(2000: 233)*

More so than the Swinging London films, however, the use of the ensemble format in the television texts shifts the focus of attention from the single girl to *girls*. There is still an emphasis on the individual identities of each woman, but the ensemble format allows for an exploration of the different choices available to women as a social group. However, the glaring absence of non-white femininities as central characters within such ensemble texts of the late 1960s points to the way in which revisions to feminine citizenship are constructed as being exclusive to white femininities despite the civil rights movements of the 1960s.

Luckett's observations regarding the critical reception of the Swinging London texts are pertinent to this analysis of the female ensemble text. She argues that such films have been overlooked in favour of the British 'new wave' films that provided a critique of the affluence and feminine archetypes embodied by the Swinging London texts. I argue that a similar logic accounts for the critical neglect of these female ensemble texts, as is evident in the differing critical treatment of the two sitcoms *The Liver Birds* and *The Likely Lads*.

Respondents to the BBC's Audience Research Survey suggested that *The Liver Birds* had typically been viewed as 'a sort of female answer to *The Likely Lads*' (WAC VR/69/241, 30 April 1969). Both texts focus on youthful northern identities and the camaraderie and antics of the two friends. Indeed, the friendship between the refined and aspirational Sandra and her comic foil Beryl is strongly reminiscent of Bob (Rodney Bewes) and Terry's (James Bolam) friendship in *The Likely Lads*. Yet in terms of critical attention, *The Likely Lads* has been applauded precisely for the way in which its representation of male youth culture is one which self-consciously replicates the 'new wave's' aesthetics and concerns, albeit with a more comedic bent.[7] The text resembles 'new wave' films not merely in terms of its realist, monochrome exploration of working-class masculinity but in terms of the more experimental use of montage promoted by the new generation of film and TV directors in the period.[8]

Not only had both actors (Bewes and Bolam) appeared in 'new wave' films but their characterisation and narratives in *The Likely Lads* frequently blurred with the cycle of film texts, as Wickham's research indicates: 'chasing girls, drudgery and camaraderie at work, nights at the pub – but also the pressures to settle down and the dreams of leaving' (Wickham, 2008: 14). As Wickham points out, *The Likely Lads*, similarly to 'new wave' texts, 'considers working-class English culture at a key moment in its history. It also asks what it is to be a man, what is expected of you, and what are the terms of the relationship between men and women?' (2008: 4–5).

Contrasting with *The Likely Lads*' attempt to replicate the 'serious', quality aesthetic and concerns of the British 'new wave', *The Liver Birds* works within the popular, and thus by association 'inferior', aesthetics of light entertainment in order to explore feminine identity in relation to this key moment of change. As a studio-based situation comedy, *The Liver Birds* embodies the artifice of light entertainment, from the stage-like set up and the often contrived situations to the more commercial, consumerist imperative visible in the girls' contemporary look and 'dolly gear' (WAC VR/69/241, 30 April 1969), which betray the more mundane and modest aspects of the two girls' home and jobs.[9]

In essence, The *Liver Birds* celebrates that which is feared in *The Likely Lads* and the 'new wave' films: the feminine.[10] John Hill has suggested that there was a suspicion of all things popular within this period because of their association with 'Americanisation', commercialism, consumerism and mass culture – the values aligned with the feminine within this same culture (1986: 25). In effect, the privileging of the 'new wave' film and television texts (including *The Likely Lads*) exemplifies 'that ranking what counts as culturally significant is "gendered", and thus the privileging of certain cultural forms or characteristics must also be seen as part of a struggle within patriarchal culture to define "reality"' (Gledhill, 1997: 349). It is precisely the question of *whose* reality and indeed *whose* history is being celebrated and privileged within television historiography with which this chapter is concerned.

Forming part of the feminist challenge to the masculine hegemony of television historiography, the remainder of the chapter is focused upon an analysis of *The Liver Birds*. Through analysing its generic and representational codes, the aim here is to contribute to reinstating the value of feminine programming traditions within television historiography and to provide a reading of the ways in which working-class femininities (as opposed to masculinities) have been constructed and addressed in relation to these more feminine social contexts and aesthetics.

The Liver Birds

The Liver Birds was a hugely successful series which ran for nine seasons between 1969 and 1979. In the pilot and short first series that aired in 1969, the two Liver Birds were Dawn (Pauline Collins) and Beryl (Polly James), followed by three seasons (1971–4) with Beryl and Sandra (Nerys Hughes) (see Figure 7.1). After Polly James decided to leave at the end of series four in 1974, Sandra's new flat-mate, Carol Boswell (Elizabeth Estensen), was introduced, and this pairing remained for the latter five series between 1975 and 1979. The series attracted consistently high viewing figures, with the pilot episode scoring an audience reaction index of 61 per cent and the first series 60 per cent (WAC VR/69/241, 30 April 1969).[11] Despite the changing line-up of flat-mates from the first to second series, questionnaires from the BBC viewing panel suggested they enjoyed the 'pleasant change to have a feminine angle on the battle of the sexes' and the contrast between the different girls' personalities, particularly that of the 'irrepressible Beryl', as well as the 'dolly gear' that was modelled in the series (ibid.).

The Liver Birds suggests that shifts to culture, defined in terms of liberalisation and feminisation, have been enabling for working-class women. Where *The Likely Lads* fostered a sense of anxiety via storylines regarding the lads' future, *The Liver Birds* embodied a hedonistic quality, a celebration of the 'here and now' and the lifestyle

FIGURE 7.1   *The Liver Birds*: celebrating female friendship on British television

choices opening up to women in the consumer-oriented context of the late 1960s and early 1970s. *The Likely Lads*' narratives are grounded in quotidian locales – the pub and the factory. In contrast with this, *The Liver Birds* takes pleasure in situating the girls in more unconventional and farcical situations within both the domestic context – from finding a new commode pot (series 2, episode 3 untitled) to looking after a parrot ('The Parrot') – and the work environment – from creating havoc on a farm in 'Have Hen Will Travel' to running on a conveyor belt in a factory ('Bird in the Club'). In short, *The Liver Birds* is a version of *Smashing Times* (Davis, 1967) or the much later *Absolutely Fabulous* (French and Saunders Productions for BBC, 1992–5, 2011–12) without the critique of consumer culture that was embodied by these other texts. *The Liver Birds* revels in the swinging sixties and the new freedoms that commercialised culture offered not just to women but also to young female actors on the modern medium of television.

Unruly 'birds'

The sitcom *Roseanne* has been celebrated by feminist critics for using the desiring figure of the unruly working-class housewife to expose and mock the ideologies of true womanhood, for instance, 'the perfect wife and mother' (Rowe, 1990: 413). However, the focus upon two white, working-class single girls living independent and hedonistic lives outside of the sanctioned institution of marriage similarly disturbs ideologies of femininity, albeit from the licensed, carnivalesque space of sitcom (ibid.: 410–11). While lifestyle options were perceived to be opening up for the majority of women as a social group more generally in this period, the representation of such liberated identities in relation to young working-class women is significant. This is because of the way in which working-class women's identities have been made safe historically, being structured closely in relation to the family, whether as daughters, as wives and/or as mothers (Skeggs, 1997).

Both *Roseanne* and *The Liver Birds* thus make visible the experiences of working-class women that have not previously been conceived of or sanctioned by television, whether as swinging singletons in the 1960s and 1970s in the UK or as a dissatisfied wife and mother in 1980s America. Each text works through the forms of female identity and, thus, of women making spectacles of themselves in the public sphere – in this instance on television – by bringing the work and private spaces of working-class women's lives to the screen.

Where these two texts diverge, however, is in the terms on which the feminine characters make spectacles of themselves within the public domain of television and within the parameters of their respective diegeses. Whereas *The Liver Birds* can be perceived to be working within the conventional codes of femininity, *Roseanne* works within the feminist-aligned 'grotesque'. Indeed, *Roseanne* and texts which followed, such as *Absolutely Fabulous*, have been celebrated by feminist academics for the way in which their acts involve a form of mimicry or masquerade, a parodic performance of the feminine that 'makes visible' what is supposed to remain concealed: 'the artifice of femininity' and 'the gap between an impossible role and the woman playing it' (Rowe, 1995: 6). Figures such as Roseanne 'have utilized the power already invested in women as image' (Rowe, 1990: 412) to begin to negotiate their own invisibility in the public sphere and disrupt and refuse, via the persona of the unruly grotesque woman, the codes of respectability that, historically, have governed working-class women's identities (Skeggs, 1997).

By way of contrast to the feminist-aligned *Roseanne*, *The Liver Birds* is a pro-gramme which appears rather more conventional and conservative because of its embodiment of a consumerist discourse. By aligning upwardly mobile and aspira-tional femininities with consumerism (their dolly gear and independent living) *The Liver Birds* parallels 'single girls' texts produced in the North American context, from *The Mary Tyler Moore Show* (MTM Productions 1970–7) to *Sex and the City* (HBO, 1998–2004). This is because the templates of femininity in all three texts resemble that which is exemplified by Helen Gurley Brown in her best-selling book *Sex and the Single Girl* (1962), and which informed the revamping of *Cosmopolitan* magazine in the US in 1965 and in the UK in 1972. This template of femininity, which has been preferred by consumer industries and media icons such as Gurley Brown, is one which encourages the reproduction of feminine heterosexuality and thus 'marriageability' via the consumption of goods and sexual pleasure (1993: 58). The paradox of this template of femininity is that while single women may no longer be stigmatised, and female identity may be defined in relation to the workplace rather than the home, the 'presumed goal' remains marriage (Radner, 1993: 59).

From this viewpoint, Radner dubs such shifts within women's culture as embodying 'neo-feminism' or 'commodity feminism'. This position is reinforced by the way in which discourses associated with the women's movement, such as 'empowerment' and self-fulfilment, are recuperated by cultural industries (including magazines such as *Cosmopolitan*) encouraging and reinforcing 'consumer culture practices as one of the chief means through which a woman can confirm her identity and express herself' (Radner, 2011: 3). This 'neo-feminist' discourse is one which repositions these working-class characters as feminine spectacles for the marriage market, albeit in relation to a more assertive sexuality. In so doing, *The Liver Birds* stands as testament to the way in which 'neo-feminist' discourses proliferated during the 1960s and 1970s in Britain, and historicises textual trends that have been discussed and defined in relation to the more recent postfeminist context.[12]

This consumer-based template of femininity appears to recuperate the unruly working-class characterisations of Beryl and Sandra with tropes of femininity. However, given the historical propensity for working-class women to be margin-alised or romanticised as long-suffering matriarchs across both British quality and popular television genres (which is also how they appear in *The Likely Lads*), the consumer logic of *The Liver Birds* constructs and addresses aspirational templates of working-class femininity that dare to dream of identities other than those based around maternity and the realist kitchen sink.[13]

The construction and address to working-class women via this consumer-based template of femininity is significant; it is one which, as Radner has argued, acknowledges the extent to which shifts to the heterosexual contract and women's positioning in the workplace involved a democratisation of the single girl across class lines. While this may translate as women of 'lower' social classes becoming recognised as citizens within the prescribed system, it also marks an important shift with regards to codes of femininity and respectability from which working-class women have been negated historically. As Skeggs' research has illustrated, femininity has always been a bourgeois sign. Drawing on Mary Ann Doane's account of masquerade, Skeggs argues that working-class women have never needed to manufacture any distance from the image of femininity, as 'they have always been positioned at a distance' (1997: 105). In Kirkham and Skeggs' discussion of *Absolutely Fabulous*, they argue that the text's attempt to satirise the consumer hedonism of the 1990s via its excessive characters, Edina and Patsy, is double-edged. So while it offers viewers the opportunity to mock the characters' 'vulgar hedonism', this is only successful if viewers are in a privileged position with regard to the desirable objects that are critiqued. As they suggest, '[f]or those who have yet to gain access to time and space to play, playfulness around consumption may remain unthinkable, the clear parody of excessive consumption coming up against the reality of viewers' lives and experiences' (1998: 294). Therefore the fashionable femininities in *The Liver Birds* mark working-class women's legitimation as feminine spectacles made possible by consumer culture. They mark important ways in which working-class women are 'de-essentialised' in relation to stigmatised identities – as grotesques and vulgar spectacles – and re-defined as respectable subjects with dreams and aspirations no different to those of women who have been historically deemed of higher social rank.

As with *Absolutely Fabulous*, *The Liver Birds* does not naturalise or conceal the tropes by which femininity is constructed. The foregrounding of fashions within the text as possible for emulation by audience members via consumption 'de-naturalises' women in relation to the means by which the feminine look is achieved. In other words, the foregrounding of the construction of femininity via fashionable clothes, hair and make-up is one which illustrates how femininity involves a form of masquerade, one that can be mimicked by feminine consumers in pursuit of the same look. This is particularly so given the parodic nature of the fashions that are foregrounded in *The Liver Birds*. The exaggerated lines and colours of fashion, from miniskirts, flares, patterned dungarees, platform heels and feather boas to volumised hair and false lashes, make this construction explicit. It is precisely the tropes by which young women attempt to make themselves noticeable in the crowded city space in order to stand out from the crowd (Wilson, 2003: 165) that also make visible the way in which femininity is constructed and practised as performance.

Unlike sober genres which draw upon more naturalised forms of acting, sitcom acting is a style that foregrounds its very performativity, drawing attention to its own construction in an attempt to 'make us laugh' (Mills, 2005: 83). In placing the action in a set of quotation marks, *The Liver Birds*, as sitcom, foregrounds femininity as a performance and evinces the gap between actor and character. This is particularly evident as the actors grow physically older, whereupon the gap between the youthful characters and the lifestyles they portray becomes more at odds with the mature bodies and faces they embody. As opposed to other fictional texts that encourage emotional identification with characters via close-ups and naturalistic acting styles, *The Liver Birds* (as sitcom) encourages critical distance via the stage-like setting from which to look upon and laugh at (and, indeed, with) the characters. In this respect, *The Liver Birds* may well draw upon codes of cultural verisimilitude to make 'believable' the flat-mate scenario, but it is one which eschews forms of psychological and emotional realism and identification. At times, the series even takes on a Brechtian air of distanciation in the way in which the quotation marks are displaced by direct address, which draws further attention to the performative aspects of the text. In the episode 'Promotion' (tx 25 March 1971), for example, Beryl takes elocution lessons in a bid to improve herself. However, Beryl's attempts to speak properly are taken to absurdist lengths as she fails to replicate the instructor's pro-nunciation of the phrase: 'Would you like to see my old pews'. The repetition of this phrase sees Beryl's voice grow higher and more hysterical; the scene concludes with her repeating the phrase and walking directly towards camera. Despite the possibility that this was a spontaneous act by Polly James, the breaking of the fourth wall draws attention to the artifice of the television sitcom and the way in which it is performed for our pleasure.

It is also the foregrounding of a character's physicality – similarly to other forms of 'female-centred' comedy, from *I Love Lucy* to *Roseanne* – that makes *The Liver Birds* ambivalent with regard to 're-naturalising' codes of femininity. Sandra represents the curvaceous and conventionally sexually attractive femininity. On the other hand, Beryl, with her small, pre-pubescent looking frame and coarse tongue, signals her working-class heritage, wherein bodies do not fit the template of respectable middle-class femininity. Her extremely wiry, undeveloped frame provides a fitting parody of the waif-like figure of Twiggy that was also celebrated in the 1960s. In the process Beryl draws attention to the incongruity, via comedy, of the image of the feminine ideal and the realities of this template as they are lived in articulation with 'real' women's bodies. Given the differing cultural and material economies of femininity, when working-class women try it, 'they often feel it is the wrong size' (Skeggs, 1997: 100). Yet while this 'de-naturalises' Beryl as fundamentally a working-class character in relation to codes of femininity in the text, it does realign her with discourses associated with working-class bodies. Thus the elocution lesson storyline may demonstrate how the text mocks codes of bourgeois femininity, but by re-drawing the 'unfit' between Beryl's and the signifiers of respectability – that of disposition and speech – it also risks essentialising women back into specific class-based positions.

The elocution lesson storyline also demonstrates the way in which *The Liver Birds* is similar to other, more masculine sitcoms of the 1960s such as *The Likely Lads* and *Steptoe and Son*, in the way it foregrounds anxieties around class and social mobility. As Wagg has argued, such texts, in effect, tell 'members of the lower social and cultural groups that they should know their place' (1998: 13). Such textual politics around class could be perceived to undermine and deconstruct the consumer rhetoric which poses themes of self-improvement as open to everyone with more buying power within the new meritocracy. Similarly to The *Likely Lads* and *Steptoe and Son*, in refusing Beryl and Sandra's social aspirations, the text advocates that 'while there is a working-class, then better to be in it' (1998: 13) and that 'cultural authenticity is what counts: to want to be successful does not in itself condemn a person, but to moderate your accent to please your social betters [. . .] does' (ibid.).

The 'birds' and the bees

Unlike other swinging single girl texts of the period, particularly *The Mary Tyler Moore Show*, the scriptwriters of *The Liver Birds*, as Hallam has suggested, 'preferred insinuation and innuendo rather than more realistic scenarios of sexual relationships'.[14] Representing some new active feminine sexual discourse akin to that of Helen Gurley Brown, Beryl's attempts to sleep with boyfriend Robert (Jonathan Lynn) are regularly thwarted by interruptions such as her sister Gloria (Paula Wilcox) going into labour in her flat. The latter scenario is one in which comedy is used to undermine the staged romantic evening between the young lovers and serve as a reminder of the practical consequences of sex.

This rather conservative approach to sex punctures the image of this independent and sexually active notion of femininity, demonstrating how chastity rather than permissiveness was privileged by mainstream television in the UK in the 1970s. Therefore the text is, arguably, aligned with governing ideals of working-class women's sexuality (Skeggs, 1997: 122). It is useful to compare the treatment of sexuality in *The Liver Birds* with that embodied by *It's Awfully Bad for Your Eyes, Darling*. As the sexual innuendo of the title suggests, the latter series foregrounds an explicit sexual discourse and sexually active feminine identities. The key difference here is the way in which each of the flat-mates inhabits a middle-class identity and thus fits more directly with the image of the swinging heroine of sophisticated boroughs of London.[15] Yet if in this way *The Liver Birds* may be seen as somewhat sexually conservative, by way of comparison with the desiring sexual subjects of *It's Awfully Bad for Your Eyes, Darling* and *Roseanne*, it is nonetheless the case that marriage and motherhood are reinforced as the route to women's personal fulfilment in all three texts. In this final section, then, I want to explore how the embodiment of neo-feminist discourse in *The Liver Birds* informs its treatment of discourses of feminism and heterosexual ideologies of love, marriage and family.

The 'Birds' and feminism

In keeping with other mainstream sitcoms and feminine-gendered texts more generally, *The Liver Birds* makes little explicit reference to the feminist movement. However, in 'St. Valentines Day' (tx. 7 April 1972), the girls' embodiment of neo-feminism is made explicit and validated precisely by the inclusion of their feminist workmate Jenny. At work, Sandra encounters Jenny (Diane Davis), who attempts to deconstruct the ideology of love and heterosexual romance in which both girls invest much time and energy. Characterised with shorter dark hair and red T-shirt displaying a clenched fist reminiscent of socialist iconography, Jenny is depicted as a militant feminist. This is by way of contrast to the softer and feminine Sandra, complete with pigtails, pink overall and false eyelashes; in short, the feminine girl. Jenny's mocking of Valentine's Day ('My heart is riding on a wave, marry me quick and be my slave') does not work to make explicit the sexual politics that underpin the ideologies of love and romance; rather, it is she who is made strange by her distance from these other normative femininities. As Sandra exclaims, 'Beryl and I have often talked about women's lib but we'd rather be, well, you know, women'. Consequently, the text works to undermine the women's liberation movement rather than existing gender and sexual inequalities. It perpetuates gender based upon sex-role stereotypes and renders those women who do not conform to the neo-feminist template as masculine and anti-social.

While *The Liver Birds* is quick to distance itself from radical feminism, its celebration of women's single and autonomous lives as a utopian existence filled with pleasure, fun and female friendship does resonate with some discourses associated with the women's liberation movement. For instance, the text frequently takes pleasure in contrasting the liberated existence of the female friends with the unhappy marriages of their parents and Beryl's sister Gloria (Paula Wilcox). There is an absence of happily married couples in *The Liver Birds* throughout its nine-year run and Gloria's eventual pregnancy does much to consolidate the association of marriage with drudgery, sacrifice and unhappiness for women. When both Sandra and Beryl receive marriage proposals during the same episode in series four ('Love Is'), only Beryl decides to accept. Sandra's decision not to marry may be seen as quite radical, because it undermines the institution of marriage and engages with feminist discourses regarding women's exploitation within family. However, Sandra's decision to remain single and Beryl's decision to marry her boyfriend, Robert ('I'm gasping for it') are presented as valid choices now freely available to all young single girls. In this way *The Liver Birds* is similar to other mainstream texts such as *Cagney and Lacey* (D'Acci, 1994), in the way in which lifestyle choices are individualised rather than being more directly attributed to feminism.

Yet it is also significant that it is Beryl, the more overtly working-class of the pair, who becomes married at this point in the narrative. To be sure, Polly James had wanted to leave the series; yet it is indicative that marriage was felt to be the lifestyle option that best accommodated this departure. As I have already suggested, working-class women's identities have often been represented in terms of marriage as the route to financial and social respectability (Skeggs, 1997). The marriage proposal comes at the precise moment in the text when Beryl is vulnerable, unemployed and possibly homeless. With Beryl depicted as deficient in other forms of cultural and social capital ('I think they whipped my intellect out with my adenoids'), marriage is represented as *the* life-choice for her; she can trade her femininity in this market (Skeggs, 1997: 9). As the more aspirational character, Sandra's decision is in keeping with the more individualistic middle-class template of femininity – one which delays marriage in order to foster her intellect and enjoy her freedom for four further years until she marries an upwardly mobile dentist named Derek in the final series.

These examples illustrate how in *The Liver Birds* marriage is taken for granted as the inevitable destiny for women, even if the girls themselves take pleasure in delaying their own nuptials. *The Liver Birds'* treatment of marriage is hegemonic and akin to familial melodrama and soap opera in 'the amount of dust the story raises along the road' (Mulvey, 1977: 76) before it is confirmed as a woman's destiny by the text. As this reading demonstrates, the notion of marriage may be confirmed but is also continually undermined, with reference to it as a social institution that limits women's freedom and the fun offered by the single girl's existence and friendship with other similarly positioned young women. It is the text's foregrounding of female friendship that is significant and which offers an alternative life-choice for women. It is the representations of friendship, and viewing Polly James and Nerys Hughes' enjoyment of playing the two friends, that will be remembered rather than their subsequent marriages – a fact upheld by the way in which both women are constructed as single for the reunion that was broadcast in 1996.[16]

The text's treatment of friendship is one which embodies the signifiers of the sentimental friendship text (Hollinger, 1998), one in which female friendship occupies the space of the heterosexual romance which expires when each of the girls become married. Beryl and Sandra's marriages also mark the pathways of femininity akin to the girly template of Helen Gurley Brown. Whereas marriage was the ultimate goal, work remained a key signifier of the woman's femininity, allowing her to remain independent and to afford her the girly identity. Both Sandra and Beryl swap employment and autonomy for dependence and housewifery. The turn from girlhood to womanhood, similar to the treatment of marriage, is marked by drudgery and boredom for Sandra. And 'the problem that has no name' is a feminist theme that Carla Lane took pleasure in personifying in more detail via the character of Rea in her subsequent sitcom *Butterflies*.[17]

Family, however, is reinstated in the text. Carol's family, the Boswells, come to occupy more narrative space in later series. This shift in narrative focus to accommodate the Boswell family can be read as a response to the shifting political climate, particularly the crisis in social housing in working-class areas such as Liverpool in the later 1970s. The ongoing storyline of the Boswells details their eviction from their terraced council house. When the house is eventually bulldozed ('Weeds'), the codes of sitcom are temporarily suspended as the camera sweeps to look at the demolished site, not unlike the opening credits of *Whatever Happened to the Likely Lads?* (BBC1, 1973–4), which personified the similar process of 'regeneration' that was occurring in Newcastle during the 1970s. Carol's dad likens the erosion of their communities and homes to an attempt to eradicate their class. Likening the working classes to the weeds that continue to grow between the pavements of the street that is now a building site, Carol's dad says to the councillor in charge of the demolition: 'All us weeds'll be back. We'll rise again'. The use of the national anthem over the scene of the bulldozer mocks the association of Great Britain as a 'land of hope and glory' with notions of democracy. Broadcast some ten days before Christmas, the episode packs a punch at a time of year focused upon the family.

Conclusion

In this chapter I have used female ensemble texts, particularly *The Liver Birds,* as a case study through which to explore television's address to women in the 1960s and 1970s. As this analysis has suggested, an understanding of the early address of female ensemble texts to women is one which cannot be extricated from social class. As I explored in the introduction, this is unsurprising given the ways in which class shapes and informs all aspects of social, political and cultural life, including televisual production, representation and consumption but also television historiography.

An analysis of female ensemble texts adds another layer of understanding of particular formations of class and gender with regard to the much-neglected histories of feminine-gendered fiction. While this chapter has provided a snapshot of the politics of the representation of working-class femininities in the 1960s female ensemble sitcom, the broader research project explores how class and gender intersect in subsequent ensemble texts from the late 1960s to the current period.

Notes

1 Charlotte Brunsdon defines 'heroine television' as television dramas and sitcoms that 'are all, in some fundamental way addressing feminism, or addressing the agenda that feminism has made public about the contradictory demands on women' (1997: 34). For further discussion of female ensemble texts see Ball (2013).

2 See Skirrow (1985, 1987) and Brunsdon (1987) for a discussion of the female ensemble drama *Widows*. See Hyem (1987) and Priestner (2012) for a discussion of *Tenko*. See Brunsdon (2000) and Ball (2012) for a discussion of female ensemble dramas of the 1990s. See Mahoney (2015) for a discussion of *Land Girls* (BBC, 2009–11) and *The Bletchley Circle* (World Productions for ITV, 2012–).

3 BECTU History Project, interview with Denis Main Wilson, 1991.

4 The BBC Written Archives (WAC) are held in Caversham, Reading, UK.

5 There were also other texts which focused upon the single girl in this period, including the sitcom *The Bed-Sit Girl* (BBC1, 1965–6).

6 ACTT membership application figures are from the BECTU membership application database [https://bufvc.ac.uk] (Accessed 16 January 2016).

7 See Wickham (2008) for a discussion of *The Likely Lads'* similarity to the films of the new wave.

8 For instance, the use of montage to move the narrative forward quickly in episodes such as 'Double Date' and 'The Last of the Big Spenders' is reminiscent aesthetically of Martin and McGrath's *Diary of a Young Man* (BBC, 1964).

9 The text does feature some outside broadcasts but the majority of the episodes take place within the confines of the girls' flat.

10 Only a few of the 'new wave' texts focused on female identity (*A Taste of Honey* (Richardson, 1961) and *The L Shaped Room* (Forbes, 1962)).

11 This was above the average of 54 per cent for the previous Comedy Playhouse series.

12 For a discussion of postfeminism and consumerism see Arthurs (2003), Negra (2004), Akass and McCabe (2004).

13 American single girls such as those in *The Mary Tyler Moore Show* and *Sex and the City* explore consumer templates of femininity in relation to middle-class femininities.

14 www.screenonline.org.uk/tv/id/524007/index.html. (Accessed 23 February 2012).

15 More centrally, *It's Awfully Bad for your Eyes, Darling* embodies the sexually promiscuous figure of Samantha, played by Joanna Lumley, capitalising on her recent sexualised role in

the Bond film *On Her Majesty's Secret Service* (Danjaq/Eon Productions, 1969) and fore-
shadowing her role in *The New Avengers* (Avengers Enterprises, 1976–7).

16 The reunion was considered a failure with audiences.

17 For a discussion of *Butterflies* and Carla Lane's treatment of the 'problem that has no name'
see Andrews (1998) and Hallam (2005b).

Bibliography

Akass, K. and J. McCabe (2004) (eds) *Reading Sex and the City*. London: I.B.Tauris.

Andrews, M. (1998) 'Butterflies and Caustic Asides', in S. Wagg (ed.) *Because I Tell a Joke or
Two*. London and New York: Routledge: 50–64.

Arthurs, J. (2003) 'Sex and the City and Consumer Culture: Remediating Postfeminist
Drama', *Feminist Media Studies*, 3:1: 83–98.

Ball, V. (2012) 'The "Feminization" of British Television and the Re-traditionalization of
Gender', *Feminist Media Studies*, 12:2: 248–64.

Ball, V. (2013) 'Separating the Women from the Girls: Reconfigurations of the Feminine in
Contemporary British Drama', in H. Thornham and E. Weissmann (eds) *Unfixing
Feminism: Stories, Fantasies and Futures*. London: I.B.Tauris: 155–171.

Ball, V. (forthcoming) *Heroine Television*. Manchester: Manchester University Press.

BECTU Membership Application Database [https://bufvc.ac.uk] (Last accessed 16 January
2016).

Bell, M. (2012) 'Young, Single, Disillusioned: The Screen Heroine in 1960s British Cinema',
The Yearbook of English Studies, 42: 79–96.

Brunsdon, C. (1987) 'Men's Genres for Women', in H. Baehr and G. Dyer (eds) *Boxed
In: Women and Television*. London: Pandora: 184–202.

Brunsdon, C. (1997) 'The Role of Soap Opera in the Development of Feminist Television
Criticism', in C. Brunsdon (ed.) *Screen Tastes*. London: Routledge: 29–43.

Brunsdon, C. (2000) 'Not Having It All: Women and Film in the 1990s', in R. Murphy (ed.)
British Film of the 90s. London: BFI: 167–177.

Cooke, L. (2003) *British Television Drama: A History*. London: British Film Institute.

D'Acci, J. (1994) *Defining Women: Television and the Case of Cagney and Lacey*. Chapel Hill:
University of North Carolina Press.

Davis, N.Z. (1975) 'Women on Top', in N.Z. Davis, *Society and Culture in Early Modern
France*. California: Stanford University Press: 124–151.

Doane, M.A. (1982) 'Film and the Masquerade: Theorising the Female Spectator', *Screen*.
2:3–4: 74–87.

Gledhill, C. (1997) 'Genre and Gender: the Case of Soap Opera', in S. Hall (ed.) *Representation: Cultural Representations and Signifying Practices*. London: Open University/Sage:
337–86.

Gorton, K. (2013) 'A Way to Go: Lisa Holdsworth, Freelance Writer', in V. Ball and M. Bell
(eds) 'Working Women, Women's Work: Production, History and Gender': Special Issue
of *Journal of British Cinema and Television Studies*, 10:3: 618–34.

Gurley Brown, H. (1962) *Sex and the Single Girl*. New Jersey: Barricade Books.

Hallam, J. (2005a) *Lynda La Plante*. Manchester: Manchester University Press.

Hallam, J. (2005b) 'Remembering Butterflies: The Comic Art of Housework', in S. Lacey
and J. Bignell (eds) *Popular Television Drama: New Perspectives*. Manchester: Manchester
University Press: 16–35.

Hallam, J. (2013) 'Drama Queens: Making Television Drama for Women 1990–2009', in
R. Moseley, H. Wheatley, and H. Wood, 'Television for Women' dossier, *Screen*. 54:2:
256–61.

Hallam, J. (n.d.) 'The Liver Birds'. Screenonline. [www.screenonline.org.uk/tv/id/524007/index.html] (Last accessed 23 February 2012).

Harper, S. (2000) *Women in British Cinema: Mad, Bad and Dangerous to Know*. London: Continuum.

Hill, J. (1986) *Sex, Class and Realism: British Cinema 1956–1963*. London: BFI.

Hollinger, K. (1998) *In the Company of Women: Contemporary Female Friendship Films*. Minneapolis: Minnesota University Press.

Holmes, S. (2008) *Entertaining Television: The BBC and Popular Entertainment Culture in the 1950s*. Manchester: Manchester University Press.

Hyem, J. (1987) 'Entering the Arena: Writing for Television', in H. Baehr and G. Dyer (eds) *Boxed In: Women and Television*. New York and London: Pandora: 151–63.

Kirkham, P. and B. Skeggs (1998) 'Absolutely Fabulous: Absolutely Feminist?' in C. Geraghty, and D. Lusted (eds) *The Television Studies Book*. London: Arnold: 287–98.

Lane, C. (2006) *Someday I'll Find Me*. London: Robson Books.

Luckett, M. (2000) 'Travel and Mobility: Femininity and National Identity in Swinging London Films', in J. Ashby and A. Higson (eds) *British Cinema, Past and Present*. London: Routledge: 233–45.

MacMurraugh-Kavanagh M. (1999) 'Boys on Top: Gender and Authorship in the BBC Wednesday Play, 1964–70', *Media, Culture & Society*, 21:3: 409–25.

MacMurraugh-Kavanagh, M. (2000) 'Too Secret For Words: Coded Dissent in Female-Authored Wednesday Plays', in J. Bignell, S. Lacey, and M. MacMurraugh-Kavanagh (eds) *British Television Drama: Past, Present and Future*. London: Palgrave: 150–61.

Mahoney, C. (2015) '"Not Bad for a Few Ordinary Girls in a Tin Hut": Reimagining Women's Social Experience of the Second World War through the Female Ensemble Drama', *Frames Cinema Journal* [http://framescinemajournal.com/article/page/3/] (Last accessed 12 January 2016): 7.

Main Wilson, D. (1991) BECTU History project interview, conducted by Alan Lawson and Norman Swallow, 1991 [www.screenonline.org.uk/audio/id/877635/] (Last accessed 24 February 2012).

Mills, B. (2005) *Television Sitcom*. London: BFI.

Mulvey, L. (1977) 'Notes on Sirk and Melodrama', in C. Gledhill (ed.) *Home is Where the Heart Is: Studies in Melodrama and the Woman's Film*. London: BFI: 75–9.

Negra, D. (2004) '"Quality Postfeminism?": Sex and the Single Girl on HBO'. *Genders* online journal 39 [www.genders.org/g39/g39_negra.html] (Last accessed 24 June 2013).

O'Connor, P. (1992) *Friendships Between Women: A Critical Review*. New York: Guilford Press.

Priestner, A. (2012) *Remembering Tenko*. Reading: Classic TV Press.

Radner, H. (1993) 'Pretty Is as Pretty Does: Free Enterprise and the Marriage Plot', in J. Collins, H. Radner, and A. Preacher (eds) *Film Theory Goes to the Movies*, New York: Routledge: 56–76.

Radner, H. (1999) 'Introduction: Queering the Girl', in H. Radner and M. Luckett (eds) *Swinging Single: Representing Sexuality in the 1960s*, Minneapolis: University of Minnesota Press: 1–35.

Radner, H. (2011) *Neo-Feminist Cinema: Girly Films, Chick Flicks and Consumer Culture*. Abingdon and New York: Routledge.

Rowe, K. (1990) 'Roseanne: Unruly Woman as Domestic Goddess', *Screen*, 31:4: 408–19.

Rowe, K. (1995) *The Unruly Woman: Gender and the Genres of Laughter*. Austin: University of Texas Press.

Skeggs, B. (1997) *Formations of Class and Gender*. London: Sage.

Skeggs, B. (2004) *Class, Self, Culture*. London and New York: Routledge.

Skirrow, G. (1985) 'Widows', in M. Alvarado and J. Stewart (eds) *Made for Television: Euston Films Limited*. London: BFI/Thames Television International Ltd and Methuen: 174–84.

Skirrow, G. (1987) 'Women/Acting/Power', in H. Baehr, and G. Dyer (eds) *Boxed In: Women and Television*. New York and London: Pandora: 164–83.

Thumim, J. (2004) *Inventing Television Culture: Men, Women and the Box*. Oxford: Oxford University Press.

WAC T5/2, 613/1, Take Three Girls General File. From John Henderson Assistant Head of Copyright to Richard de Vivier 11 May 1966.

WAC T16/62/3, TV Policy Drama, File 3. Annual Planning Memo from Sydney Newman to Kenneth Adam 28 July 1964.

WAC VR/69/241, Audience Reaction Report. Comedy Playhouse: The Liver Birds, 30 April 1969.

Wagg, S. (1998) *Because I Tell a Joke or Two: Comedy, Politics and Social Difference*. London and New York: Routledge.

Wheatley, H. (ed.) (2007) *Reviewing Television History: Critical Issues in Television Historiography*. London: I.B.Tauris.

Wickham, P. (2008) *The Likely Lads*. London: BFI.

Wilson, E. (1980) *Only Halfway to Paradise: Women in Post-war Britain 1946–1968*. London: Tavistock Publications.

Wilson, E. (2003) *Adorned in Dreams: Fashion and Modernity* (2nd edn). London: I.B.Tauris.

PART III

Formations of women's television

8

FEMINIST TELEVISION OR TELEVISION FOR WOMEN? REVISITING THE LAUNCH OF CANADA'S WOMEN'S TELEVISION NETWORK

Sarah A. Matheson

This chapter examines discourses surrounding women's television in Canada, focusing specifically on the launch of the Women's Television Network (WTN, now simply branded W). WTN went to air on 1 January 1995 as part of the licensing of six new English-language Canadian cable specialty channels and was branded with the slogan 'television for, by, and about women and their worlds'. As Shirley Ann Off explains, WTN was created as a channel defined by two mandates, commercial and political:

> WTN embraced two contradictory mandates. One mandate was political – to respond to the argument put forth by feminist organizations and scholars that women are objectified and stereotyped by the popular media. The other was commercial – to establish a privately owned, profit-oriented cable television channel squarely targeted at the female audience, an audience that, in turn, would be sold to advertisers.
>
> *(1999: 106)*

The programming on WTN promised to reflect its political mandate by emphasising information and current affairs programming for women. It also sought to differentiate itself from conventional broadcasters by downplaying or reframing so-called 'traditional' women's genres such as soap operas, cooking shows, fashion and décor programmes.

Off argues that the dominant narrative surrounding WTN, its launch and subsequent shifts in programming strategies has suggested that, due to commercial pressures, WTN compromised its political mandate, abandoned 'innovative and risky' forms of programming and, in an effort to increase ratings, gradually moved towards so-called conventional women's programming (ibid.: 110). WTN's original political mandate, it is implied, proved incompatible with the priorities and constraints associated with commercial television. This chapter revisits this pivotal moment and critically examines how the discourses surrounding WTN and its relationship to feminism were intertwined with ideas about gender and genre: that is, which genres were believed to be 'good' for women and why, how these forms were set in contrast to so-called 'feminine' genres and how the social and political value of specific programming types has been understood. I argue that, contrary to typical popular and academic accounts of WTN's early efforts, this moment reveals more than a simple clashing of commercial and political mandates. My analysis thus seeks to complicate and contest existing work on WTN by emphasising the importance of understanding this dialogue within a larger social and historical context, one that accounts in particular for shifts in discourses surrounding the relationship between feminism and popular culture in the mid-1990s. As this analysis demonstrates, the dialogue surrounding television for women often relies on a gendered cultural and aesthetic hierarchy that typically sets so-called 'feminine' forms of popular culture in opposition to political and seemingly more culturally valuable forms.

The growth of cable television and the proliferation of new channels in the emerging so-called '500-channel universe' through the 1980s and 1990s opened up new opportunities for an expansion of programming options directed towards niche audiences, including those targeting women viewers. In 1994, Lifetime Network in the United States shifted its focus more firmly to a female viewership and developed its successful brand identity 'Television for Women', proving the viability of a cable channel specifically devoted to women's programming (Lotz, 2006: 3). WTN's original name, 'Lifestyle Television' (which was used for its licence application), may have been an effort to align itself with an already successful channel with a similar niche market focus. However, its offerings were explicitly distinguished from existing 'mass appeal programming' aimed at a female audience and were purportedly 'created with the specific needs of women in mind' (CRTC, 1994). The argument put forward supporting the need for a women's network suggested that Canadian television wasn't adequately serving these needs, as a summary of the channel's proposal in the popular press demonstrated: 'Women have a unique perspective that is not being presented by conventional television where women's concerns are often relegated to lightweight daytime programming' (Atherton, 1994: D8).

While the channel never directly used the term 'feminism' to describe its approach or branding, there were a number of different ways in which this affiliation was made evident. For instance, in its licensing application, feminist research into 'sex-role stereotyping' from mass communications and psychology was used to make a case for the importance of a women's television channel which was further positioned in relation to the new 'equity clause' contained within Canada's 1991 Broadcasting Act (Off, 1999: 108).[1] In its licensing decision, the CRTC noted how the channel's political mandate dovetailed with key CRTC policy objectives regarding both gender portrayal and employment equity issues:

> namely, the need for more positive portrayals of women in programming, less stereotyping, and the need for more on-air representation of women,

especially when presented as experts and commentators. In addition, through its monitoring of employment equity issues, the Commission has often expressed concern regarding the need for more women in the broadcasting industry, a concern that Lifestyle Television is committed to address in a positive manner.

(CRTC, 1994)

This commitment took the form of a promise to include women in 'key decision-making roles, as hosts, as interviewers, as directors, and producers' and an employment equity plan that would specify that at least 60 per cent of its workforce would be female. In these documents women are imagined as an audience, but also as a social group whose interests are framed in relation to feminist research and developing government policies surrounding gender equality in Canada. Moreover, women's television is envisioned as playing a key role in addressing broader social and political issues. The inclusion of high-profile community and feminist activists such as June Callwood and Jean Pigott on their advisory committee on programming further bolstered the channel's association with feminism and gender equality (Off, 1996: 84–5).

The kind of feminist media research that was used to frame WTN's mandate and that informed its initial programming was specifically tied to an earlier second-wave feminist critique. In particular, it drew heavily on so-called 'Images of Women' research into 'sex-role stereotyping' that, in the context of the second-wave women's movement through the 1960s and 1970s, utilised content analysis and effects studies method-ologies and relied on the theoretical assumption that there is a direct association between sex-role stereotyping in the media and negative social effects for women (Lotz, 2006: 11); that is, the assertion that negative portrayals or lack of role models in the media have damaging effects such as limiting the scope of women's social roles and potentially hampering women's success (Thornham, 2000: 55–6). Negative media images are thus treated as 'false' and calls are made for more realistic or accurate representations (Hollows and Moseley, 2006: 4). This critique also informed and enabled various kinds of feminist activism. As Brunsdon and Spigel note,

> In this early period of second wave feminism, feminist dealings with television were often calls to action growing out of a conviction that women's oppression was very much related to mass media representations and that change was not only urgent, but possible.
>
> *(2008: 6)*

WTN's political mandate and much of its early programming were thus firmly located within this second-wave feminist ethos.

WTN's launch and early programming

WTN's licence stipulated that 70 per cent of its schedule would be dedicated to 'informational' programming and no more than 30 per cent would be 'drama or entertainment' (CRTC, 1994). In keeping with this breakdown, its initial pro-gramming schedule emphasised documentary and current affairs programming for women that included political affairs programmes such as *Jane Taber's Ottawa* and its flagship series, *POV: Women*, which was described as a series that would 'look at world events from a woman's point of view and ask what one woman can do to change the course of events' as well as 'identify the most appropriate action in terms of community, politics, healing, compromise and standing up for one's rights' ('Proposed', 1994: 16).[2] There were lecture-oriented programmes such as *Speaking Our Minds,* which featured prominent feminists such as Betty Friedan, Gloria Steinem, Catharine MacKinnon and Camille Paglia, among others. The channel also featured a range of information and advice programmes such as *Infologic* (which offered viewers help in using computers), *Bubie Break* (an advice programme for grandparents) and *Girl Talk,* which provided a discussion forum for girls aged twelve to sixteen.

Biographies and programmes that showcased women's achievements were pri-vileged in WTN's lineup. These included *Herstory* (which presented biographies of 'famous and forgotten women'); *The Creators,* which focused on women's contri-butions to art and culture; *Minding My Own Business,* which profiled the achieve-ments of female entrepreneurs; and *Sharing the Wisdom,* which focused on 'developments in math, science, history, biology and business' (ibid.). Finally, the channel presented female takes on traditionally masculine genres with *Natural Angler* (a fishing show for women), *Car Care* and *On Your Mark* (a women's sports pro-gramme). International serials, British comedies such as *French and Saunders* and 'classic and contemporary films geared to women' primarily constituted the channel's entertainment programming (ibid.).

As I have discussed elsewhere, WTN's early schedule stressed non-traditional and so-called 'serious' genres such as public affairs and documentary. More conventional women's genres such as soap opera, cooking and fashion programmes were down-played or, as I will discuss, reframed in ways seemingly designed to mitigate their problematic 'feminine' associations (Matheson, 2010). Reflecting on its launch, Barbara Barde, WTN's first VP of programming, explained: 'For many years, women's programming had been defined as third-rate, disease-of-the-week movies, dreary sitcoms and a game show in which contestants try to beat the clock while piling groceries into shopping carts' (Barde, 2000: B11). She later recalled:

> When we first got licensed, a lot of guys would call up and say, 'I've got a perfect show, a cooking show, a gardening show or a makeup show or a fashion show.' I would answer, 'We don't do cooking. We don't do gardening. I'm not doing fashion shows. We don't do makeover shows.' They'd ask, 'What do you do?'
>
> *(quoted in Seger, 2003: 146)*

Conventional women's programming is thus assumed to be of inferior quality (and, it is implied, created by men for women), and WTN promised to resist these traditional women's genres. As part of this broad critique of mainstream television for women, WTN identified a paucity of information and public affairs programmes aimed at female viewers and promised to address this problem, thereby drawing a line between 'informational' and 'lifestyle' television.

WTN's early schedule therefore relied on specific 'categories of classification' that Rachel Moseley (2001), drawing on Ib Bondebjerg, describes as 'hard' and 'soft' programming. The values associated with 'hard' programming – 'news, current affairs and serious documentary' – are contrasted with the values of so-called 'soft' programming, concerned with, 'among other things, homes, gardens and clothes' (ibid.: 33). Moseley reveals how these distinctions are culturally gendered, with 'soft' programming conventionally aligned with the feminine and domestic and associated with daytime television for women (ibid.). In defining itself against the forms and pleasures of traditional women's genres, WTN appeared to endorse these distinctions in a manner reminiscent of early second-wave feminist critiques. In her examination of feminist engagement with popular women's culture, Charlotte Brunsdon outlines three phases – 'repudiation–reinvestigation– revaluation' – which she uses as a 'way of characterizing the relationship between second-wave feminism and mass cultural feminine forms' (2000: 21). Brunsdon explains how, during this early moment of feminist 'repudiation', mass culture addressed to women consumers was viewed with hostility and critiqued as a site where patriarchal definitions of femininity were circulated and reproduced. Moreover, Brunsdon argues, '[t]raditional sites of feminine skill and interest, such as fashion, cooking, and various kinds of home-making were also regarded with great suspicion' (ibid.: 22). WTN's framing of conventional women's television recalls this early critique, which, according to Brunsdon, expressed hostility towards women's genres and involved a rejection and 'repudiation of traditionally feminine skills and media' (ibid.: 23). Developments in scholarship through the 1980s and 1990s, which embarked on a 'reinvestigation and revaluation' of women's genres and that were coterminous with WTN's launch, were noticeably absent in the channel's engagement with feminist media studies.

Canadian cultural nationalism and gendered genres

The discourses surrounding the social or political value of specific genres mirrors a persistent theme in discussions of Canadian television, particularly within a cultural nationalist tradition, which has been preoccupied with the tensions between the commercial and public service goals associated with broadcasting. These perspectives have typically expressed a bias against so-called 'popular' programming, due in large part to its association with Americanisation. Within this view, 'valuable' programming has been historically associated with resistance to commercialism, with an emphasis placed on values of education and cultural uplift, and has typically relied on a paternalistic distinction between what audiences want and what is considered good for them; that is, between good TV and 'good for you' TV (see Foster, 2009; Beaty and Sullivan, 2006: 68).

These distinctions have also informed discourses surrounding women's programming in Canada. For instance, in Mary Jane Miller's overview of Canadian television drama in *Turn Up the Contrast*, she notes the virtual absence of domestically produced soap operas on the CBC and suggests that this can be explained by the broadcasters' 'distaste' for the form, suggesting that it was 'not classy enough for the English [language] network' (1987: 116). According to Miller,

> Instead, to their credit, they spent what money they had on an alternative for women working in the home, like [news magazine shows] *Take Thirty*, and its replacement, *Midday*. The basic assumption in both cases was that women should have intelligent and stimulating material, tailored for them, and that soaps do not meet these criteria.
>
> *(1987: 116)*

Miller's assessment illustrates how discussions of women's programming have relied on ideas about taste and the cultural status of conventional women's genres. However, the historical importance of soap opera on the CBC and elsewhere on Canadian television should also be considered. The British soap opera *Coronation Street* (Granada, 1960–) is one of the most loved programmes on the CBC and has been broadcast on the network for decades. Canadian viewers have also long enjoyed popular US soaps on both Canadian and American channels. The influence of cultural nationalism is apparent in the ways in which particular genres are valued over others and, in the context of women's programming, these assessments have little to do with women's tastes and interests and more to do with ideas about what sorts of programming women 'should' have. These perspectives reflect a gendered cultural and aesthetic hierarchy that has historically viewed 'feminine' forms of popular culture as having dubious cultural value.

WTN did feature a number of soap operas and serial dramas in its entertainment offerings. In explaining WTN's approach to soap opera on the channel, founding president Linda Rankin acknowledged the supposedly problematic status of the genre in relation to representations of women. She explained,

> Women by and large are portrayed as victims in afternoon soaps. We have found some soaps from the Latin American countries where women are portrayed as being competent, in charge and smart . . . and where the men are good partners.
>
> *(quoted in Faulder 1994, D5)*

Other serials on WTN were also international, and included dramas from Britain and Australia. The emphasis placed on 'international' (that is, non-American) programming was specifically related to Canadian content regulations that placed restrictions on the percentage of US content that could be aired as part of the channel's non-Canadian programming.[3] However, comments such as Rankin's frame this international perspective as a strategy of resistance to problematic elements identified in conventional (and, it is implied, American) television for women.

Gender and public affairs programming for women

The convergence of discourses surrounding television, nation and gender draws attention to what Brunsdon has observed to be the 'masculinist' connotation of public service broadcasting (1997: 2). It may be argued that WTN presented a challenge to this gendering of programming types by insisting on the importance of public affairs TV for women and in its privileging of female voices and perspectives within these traditionally masculine-coded forms. Yet, the accompanying devaluing of traditional women's genres arguably works to reinscribe a historical gender bias about what constitutes valuable, serious or important programming; that is, programming that is considered 'good' for women. It suggests ideas about what kind of information matters and what doesn't (defined in relation to public service values), and in doing so reaffirms the gendered distinctions between 'hard' and 'soft' genres.

WTN and second-wave feminist media practice

While the discursive construction of WTN's relationship to feminism was expressed in part through this resistance to and critique of traditional women's television, the imprint of second-wave feminist perspectives can also be seen across the channel's early schedule. For example, the emphasis on women's history (*Herstory*, *The Creators*) and programming that aimed to make these histories visible (especially the stories of those who had been overlooked) recalls what Lana Rakow refers to as a 'recovery process' in feminist approaches to popular culture, which included searching for the 'lost voices of women' (Rakow, 2009: 205). In challenging male-dominated canons and by unearthing the cultural production of women that had been ignored or disregarded, this approach seeks to emphasise the importance of women's perspectives and acknowledge the value of women's stories that have been excluded or marginalised. In addition, the prominence given to biographies and aspirational stories of women's success (particularly within traditionally male-dominated fields such as business, sciences and technology) evokes associations with the so-called 'role-model' framework that often accompanies the 'Images of Women' tradition and suggests that television should present 'positive' role models for women (Lotz, 2006: 11).

Interestingly, many of the shows deemed most innovative, risky and experimental – series that reflected the channel's so-called 'mission and values' (Off, 1996: 88) – were actually programmes that, in their aesthetics and modes of address, reached back to earlier strategies associated with second-wave feminist media practice. In her discussion of the aesthetics and politics of feminist documentaries of the 1970s, for instance, Julia Lesage (1984) discusses how they developed as part of the women's movement and thus reflected its political vision and commitment to social change. Lesage specifically identifies the ways in which 'realist' feminist documentaries drew on the structure and function of women's consciousness-raising groups from the 1960s and 1970s, effectively operating as 'an artistic analogue' to these groups (Lesage, 1984: 231). Lesage notes the focus on the biographical and autobiographical and on women's collectivity in these films, as they involved women relating their personal stories and experiences as a form of 'politicized conversation among women' (ibid.: 237). According to Lesage, in keeping with the second-wave radical feminist notion that 'the personal is political', these personal stories were more than just 'slices of experience' but are situated within larger social and political contexts (ibid.: 236). Moreover, these films sought to challenge patriarchal (Hollywood) narratives and representations, as she explains: 'The biographical documentary serves as a critique of and antidote to past cinematic depictions of women's lives and women's space' (ibid.: 235).

WTN was presented as a kind of 'safe haven' for women, a place where viewers could be protected from the violence and sexism that purportedly permeated the rest of television. As Barde explained in an interview,

> It should feel like home. You can turn away to other channels but you can always come back and you know there isn't going to be gratuitous violence. There isn't going to be horrible sexual stereotyping. There aren't going to be those awful beer commercials.
>
> *(Seger, 2003: 147)*

Barde also talked about how she wanted women to think of the channel as a 'companion' and the series hosts as friends (ibid.: 150–1). This description invokes an image of the channel as a protected 'women's space', and the focus on issue-driven programming, round-table discussion, biography and autobiography, within this broader expressed aim that its programming would work to counter negative representations of women on TV, demonstrated a strong connection between WTN and second-wave feminist cultural production.

A number of television scholars have noted a correspondence between television forms directed towards women and dynamics found within consciousness-raising. In *Prime-Time Feminism*, for instance, Bonnie Dow (1996) examines the ways in which strategies of consciousness-raising were used in the representation of feminist themes in American situation comedies such as *One Day at a Time* and *Designing Women*. Jane Shattuc makes a similar connection to the talk show in *The Talking Cure*, quoting Patricia Mellencamp's assertion that 'It's not too far-fetched to imagine daytime talk as the electronic syndicated version of the consciousness-raising groups of the women's movement' (1997: 128). Shattuc describes these groups as 'part therapy and part political activism' (ibid.), but suggests that in their talk-show form in the 1980s and 1990s, they represented a depoliticised and individualised version. Many of WTN's early programmes similarly incorporated aspects of consciousness-raising, but arguably retained an emphasis on the political and collective.

There are examples of WTN's early shows that adopted the form of the consciousness-raising group quite literally. *Eavesdropping*, for example, was a programme in which a small group of women would sit in a living room and discuss issues and share their own stories, the idea being that viewers were eavesdropping on the real conversations of everyday women that unfolded in a politicised manner. Another interesting example of early programming on WTN that evidenced this connection was *Open for Discussion*. This was a series that aired popular Made-for-TV movies, a genre that has a central place within mainstream women's programming and, interestingly, has served as a pillar of the programming and brand identity of Lifetime and Lifetime Movie Network in the US. The form's typical characterisation as a women's genre at first makes it seem somewhat at odds with the channel's expressed commitment to avoid 'conventional' or 'stereotypical' women's programming. Moreover, critics such as Todd Gitlin (1985), Douglas Gomery (1999) and Elayne Rapping (1992), among others, have offered critiques of the Made-for-TV movie that point to problematic elements such as its tendencies towards sensationalism and the domestication and simplification of complex social issues.

However, the structure of *Open for Discussion* worked to reframe the genre within a format reminiscent of consciousness-raising. The films were bookended with panel discussions featuring experts who provided further information on the issue portrayed in the film. Interviews with women dealing with similar situations were conducted and the accuracy and realism of the fictional representations were often debated. Thus a critical framework was introduced that situated this more conventionally 'feminine'-coded, emotional, personal and melodramatic presentation of women's issues within a wider social and political context, one that emphasised the value of increased awareness and the importance of working towards social change. The stories and experiences offered by real women are presented as counterpoints to fictional representations and these perspectives, along with the authoritative viewpoints of professionals, serve to verify or dispute the account presented in the film.

On the one hand, *Open for Discussion* represents an acknowledgement of the appeal of this genre for women; however, it is presented within a framework seemingly designed to mitigate the problematic 'feminine' aspects of the form. The emotional, melodramatic treatment of women's issues is offset by this didactic framework that works to situate these private, domestic issues in relation to broader social contexts and political agendas in a manner that corresponds in concrete ways with the approach and objectives of second-wave consciousness-raising.

The strategies of consciousness-raising stress the importance of women's talk as part of second-wave feminist politics and activism. For example, in her discussion of feminist documentary, Lesage notes that '[t]hese films often show women in the private sphere getting together to define/redefine their experiences and to elaborate a strategy for making inroads on the public sphere' (1984: 225). WTN's early programming likewise emphasised the importance of talk in its address to women. The predominance of non-narrative, informational genres (or 'hard' programming) that highlighted documentary and public affairs placed emphasis on formal discussion and the informed debate of social issues. In the popular press, producers spoke about the difficulty in creating 'authoritative' public affairs programming for women. For instance, Sue Stranks, executive producer of *POV: Women*, commented: 'Viewers see women sitting in chairs and talking and they think that what they're talking about isn't important – just because they see women . . . That's just one of the misperceptions we're fighting' (quoted in Zerbisias, 1995: E3).

This programming tended to advocate values of education and activism, and (as in its use of consciousness-raising strategies) tied women's talk and experiences to a larger public discourse. In doing so, WTN insisted on the place of women's voices and perspectives in the public sphere and in genres where women have been historically marginalised.

However, this is also accompanied by a turn away from genres that depend on more everyday forms of talk, such as gossip, chat and confession, that scholars such as Mary Ellen Brown have associated with women's oral culture (1994: 17). As part of the turn in feminist television scholarship towards a reconsidering of previously dismissed 'women's genres' such as soap operas and magazine and chat shows, research has sought to reassess the significance and value associated with these forms in order to better understand the meanings and pleasures they may hold for women. This has included an interest in so-called 'feminine discourses' associated with the private and domestic spheres, such as the type of intimate and personal talk examined by Brown and traced to women's television genres, most notably the soap opera. Despite this aligning of soap operas and the private sphere, critics have argued that the genre can serve a public function. For instance, Christine Geraghty argues that soaps can operate as 'teacherly texts' and have the ability to raise awareness of social issues and engage viewers in public debates. Soap is, she argues, a genre 'operating on the boundary of the public and the private' (2005: 318–19). This 'didactic quality' described by Geraghty problematises underlying assumptions regarding the public service roles attributed to particular forms, assumptions that arguably informed WTN's early programming strategies, particularly in its privileging of a specific type of women's talk.

Following its launch, WTN received the lowest ratings of the new channels, and there was much speculation about its future. It also faced a harsh public backlash as many critics reacted negatively to its perceived feminist orientation and balked at the need for a women's channel. It is unclear why women didn't watch WTN, especially given that it claimed to address women's needs in a way traditional women's TV had failed to do; this is something that has not been adequately accounted for. It may be that in defining itself in contrast to the tastes and forms traditionally associated with women's culture, the channel limited its appeal. I would also suggest that the programming forms that comprised the early schedule may not only have conflicted with the tastes of the audience, but may have also been out of step with the complicated climate of feminism in the mid-1990s and the different role popular culture played therein. In her analysis of the channel's first two seasons, Off observes a notable shift in WTN's programming strategy away from documentary and 'unique women's informational programming' towards 'more familiar and conventional women's informational programming' (1999: 109). WTN's programming shift towards more traditionally feminine-identified genres was also noted in the popular press as critics pointed to an apparent softening of the WTN schedule.

These shifts began within a few months of the channel's launch and by August a number of top-level executives, including Rankin and Barde, had left their positions at the network. Some of the original series remained, such as *Girl Talk*, *Open for Discussion, Natural Angler, Herstory, Speaking Our Minds* and *Jane Taber's Ottawa*, while others were redesigned. *POV: Women,* for example, became *Take 3,* as it was transformed from a news analysis programme to a magazine show. In its new incarnation, current affairs topics and social issues were combined with lighter life-style segments (with the show now promoted as 'fun and substance'). A variety of new lifestyle programmes such as *Debbie Travis's Painted House* and *The Resourceful Renovator,* fashion and entertainment programmes such as *Metro Café* and *Flare TV* and parenting shows such as *You, Me & the Kids* were introduced. Most controversial was the decision to rerun popular American sitcoms such as *Mary Tyler Moore* and *Rhoda.* In interviews, the new director of programming, Susan Millican, explained the programming shift as a 'lightening up' and an attempt to counter the channel's 'too serious reputation' (Vale, 1995). Millican also presented this movement towards more mainstream programming as an effort to balance its schedule: 'If being main-stream means trying to address more aspects of women's lives then we're doing that' (Vale, 1995). In 'widening the scope' of its programming, these additional aspects included topics and genres that had been peripheral to or excluded from WTN's original schedule. In another interview, Millican explained:

> (With) the hard issue-driven panel discussions, interview after interview on some very serious issues . . . The mistake was that we weren't reflecting the balance we have in our lives . . . What we heard from viewers was that there were voids in our schedule . . . you are totally ignoring health, and parenting, and cooking. These are vital areas, this is part of our life. It's insulting ignoring it.
>
> *(quoted in Toupin, 1997: 115–16)*

By the end of its second year, WTN had gone from having the lowest audience ratings of the new channels to ranking second behind the Discovery Channel (Vale, 1997). Some critics attributed the network's substantial improvement to its pro-gramming of American series, as well as the move from 'too much substance to mostly giggletalk' (Vale, 1997). This shift has also been commonly interpreted an attempt to please advertisers instead of meeting viewers' needs, thereby reflecting a prioritisation of commercial values over social values (Off, 1996, 1999; Toupin, 1997). Moreover, Off asserts, this programming represented a retreat to the private realm (and away from the public sphere), towards a depoliticised, consumer-oriented individualism whereby the advice offered by this new programming presented 'coping strategies at an individual level rather than social remedies' (Off, 1996: 185).

Feminism and popular culture in the 1990s

This critique of WTN's programming shift is evocative of emerging critiques of postfeminism, specifically mirroring concerns about the disappearance of the type of politicised, collective, activist-oriented second-wave-inflected feminism that is seen to be embodied in these original programmes (and set in contrast with the individu-alism, depoliticisation and consumerism associated with conventional women's pro-gramming). WTN was launched within a well-documented shift in women's relationship to, understanding of and engagement with feminism and women's issues. The 1990s saw the arrival of contested and varied forms of feminism – postfeminism, third-wave feminism, commodity feminism, popular feminism – and the widespread proliferation of popular images and discourses around feminism and 'girl power' in popular culture. Hollows and Moseley (2006) detail shifts in the relationship between feminism and the popular in 'post second-wave feminism' since the 1980s that include a range of contradictory responses, such as a postfeminist backlash against feminism, the mainstreaming and commodification of aspects of feminism, new discourses surrounding the relationship between feminism and femininity and a return to 'traditional' femininities and aspects of domesticity (ibid.: 7–15).

In her discussion of how public discourses surrounding feminism shifted in the 1990s, Kathleen Karlyn identifies a number of key aspects, including the backlash against feminism described by Susan Faludi (1991) in *Backlash: The Undeclared War against American Women*, as well as the emergence of mainstream, media-driven 'new' feminists such as Naomi Wolf. Karlyn also describes how many young women dis-tanced themselves from aspects of second-wave feminism: 'they perceived aspects of Second Wave dogmatic, censorious and out-of-touch with their everyday lives in areas that mattered to them, including sex, romance, the pleasures of domesticity, and popular culture' (2011: 30). This, Karlyn notes, led to an embrace of girliness and other sorts of traditional femininities and a 'reclaiming [of] aspects of female culture, "be it Barbie, housekeeping or girl talk . . . that were tossed out with sexism during the Second Wave"' (Karlyn, quoting Baumgarder and Richards, ibid.: 34).

In this context, the narrowly defined feminism that informed WTN's early pro-gramming strategies was arguably out of sync with both the tastes and the conflicting discourses surrounding women, feminism and popular culture during this era. While often lauded as offering something innovative and unique for women, much of WTN's early programming drew on critical approaches, strategies and aesthetics associated with a much earlier feminist moment. As discussed, these programmes were often informed by a second-wave critique of gender portrayal and frequently incorporated aspects of second-wave feminist media practice. The refusal of elements of conventional women's culture came during a moment when trends in lifestyle programming placed renewed emphasis on the domestic realm and domestic issues (cooking, home, parenting) and when the meaning of domesticity in relation to feminism was being reassessed (Brunsdon, 2006: 41; Hollows, 2006). The channel's subsequent programming mix (which offered more varied genres, images and dis-courses around feminism and femininity) was perhaps a more accurate reflection of the ambivalent and contradictory moment within which it emerged. Moreover, as the internet was increasingly developing as a new platform for feminist activism, community and alternative women's culture, it is possible that many were no longer looking to television to serve these roles.

Double Take and *Go Girl!*

Two programmes that arrived amid these shifts, *Double Take* and *Go Girl!*, are interesting examples of WTN's succeeding programming mix and reflect its turn towards a more varied attitude towards women and popular culture. Both series take up critical positions in relation to issues surrounding women and media, but represent two vastly different responses, thus illustrating how differing perspectives coexisted. *Double Take* was clearly informed by a second-wave feminist approach and endorsed a politics of 'repudiation', while *Go Girl!* was more ironic and ambivalent in its treatment of mass culture forms addressed to women.

Double Take was produced by the feminist activist organisation MediaWatch (now Media Action), which is dedicated to promoting media literacy and raising awareness about gender stereotyping in the media. This series consisted of half-hour programmes which sought to 'challenge and change the representation and the portrayal of women in the media' (Doubletake, 1996). Each episode focused on a different issue and featured interviews with academics, cultural critics, politicians and women working in the media, as well as ordinary women, who discussed issues around gender and representation. In its focus on gender por-trayal, negative stereotyping and the socialising effects of mass media, *Double Take* generally followed an 'Images of Women' approach characteristic of a second-wave feminist approach (Thornham, 2000: 55). The series also expressed familiar second-wave attitudes towards conventional women's culture in its advocating of politics of awareness, collective resistance and the need for alternative narratives and representations. One episode, for example, focused on the ways in which media represent mothers and motherhood and profiled the 'Mom's the Word' collective, a group of women who were working to create new images of motherhood that would challenge and critique stereotypes of the passive dom-esticated housewife.

In contrast, *Go Girl!* was a sketch comedy show which parodied the topics and conventions of the daytime talk show. *Go Girl!* is the title of a fictional daytime talk show hosted by sisters Cathy and Yvonne, and sarcastically references the then ubiquitous 'girl power' cheer of the 1990s. Recurring characters include Reagan Tolliver, sullen host of the 'Teen Beat' segment, and 'professional lounge singer turned Super Mom' Fran Lawrence. The sketches spoofed typical daytime talk guests, such as romance novelist Judith Cooper Kelly (who presents a reading of her latest book) and the Gardening Lady, and common women's topics such as fitness and cooking. One episode featured Dini Petty, host of the long-running Canadian programme *The Dini Petty Show*, in a cameo in which she appeared as herself arriving to offer advice to the hopelessly inept Cathy and Yvonne. On the one hand, *Go Girl!* addressed the viewer as an audience that was well versed in the forms of popular culture marketed to women and would appreciate its intertextual address. At the same time, the sketches mocked the co-opting and commercialising of messages of women's empowerment and the hollowness of 'girl power' rhetoric. It adopted a critical stance in relation to the conventions and forms associated with women's culture that was also playful and acknowledged both women's interest in and ambivalence about these forms. In this way, *Go Girl!* can be situated within the context of the changing relationship between feminism and popular culture that developed through the 1980s and 1990s, in which new forms of feminism are seen to circulate within and through popular culture as well as in opposition to it.

Conclusion

Following these programming shifts, WTN's schedule came to be a mix of lifestyle and entertainment programming and documentary and public affairs, and presented varied and often conflicting perspectives on conventional women's issues such as motherhood, domesticity, femininity, beauty culture and so on. This shift was clearly motivated by commercial pressures. However, contrary to common critiques that the channel simply abandoned feminism for commercialism, this shift may also be productively viewed as a response to the shifting discourses surrounding feminism, femininity and popular culture in which some of the second-wave principles upon which the channel's early programming strategy was devised were being questioned, particularly in its stance towards popular forms associated with mainstream women's culture.

WTN was bought by Corus Entertainment and rebranded as W in 2001. Following this, its new programming schedule was primarily composed of lifestyle and reality-based programming. As I have discussed elsewhere, this shift was greeted as a further movement away from the channel's original political mandate, an even firmer embrace of commercial mandate and a 'dumbing down' of the channel, thus replaying these earlier discourses (Matheson, 2010). In her discussion of the expansion of lifestyle programming on British television in this period, Brunsdon describes a 'discernible feminization of prime-time terrestrial television' (Brunsdon, 2004: 78). Here, the turn to lifestyle genres and other feminine-coded forms since its launch in 1995 can likewise be read as a curious (and in some ways paradoxical) 'feminising' of Canada's Women's Television Network. It is in the interpretation of that shift that we find problematic assumptions about what the role and function of television for women should be and which genres are deemed most appropriate for serving this presumed role. It is important therefore to attend to a subtext that frequently underpins these dialogues: that is, the revival of a gendered aesthetic and taste hierarchy that often accompanies these sorts of critiques; hierarchies that rely on a public–private binary, express disdain for feminine tastes and conventional women's genres and inform the distinctions that are made between feminist television and television for women.

Notes

1 This equity clause states, 'It is hereby declared as the broadcasting policy for Canada that . . . the Canadian broadcasting system should . . . through its programming and the employment opportunities arising out of its operations, serve the needs and interests, and reflect the

circumstances and aspirations, of Canadian men, women, and children, including equal rights, the linguistic duality and multicultural and multiracial nature of Canadian society and the special place of aboriginal peoples within that society' (quoted in Off, 1999: 111).

2 Due to the context of production and the lack of formal archives, it has proved impossible to determine programme date runs. Some were produced in-house at WTN, others in partnership with small production companies. In many cases they were short-lived and not archived.

3 According to its condition of licence, no less than 70 per cent of its programming would be devoted to Canadian programmes and 'at least 25% of the foreign programming over the broadcast day will be from sources other than the U.S.' (CRTC, 1994: Appendix).

Bibliography

Atherton, T. (1994) 'Channel Hopping: Channel Proposals before the CRTC Could Change Your Lifestyle', *Ottawa Citizen*, 15 January: D8.

Barde, B. (2000) 'An Open Letter to Oprah: America's Talk-Show Maven Starts a New Network Wednesday', *The Province*, 1 February: B11.

Beaty, B. and R. Sullivan (2006) *Canadian Television Today*, Calgary: University of Calgary Press.

Brown, M.E. (1994) *Soap Opera and Women's Talk: The Pleasure of Resistance*, Thousand Oaks, London and New Delhi: Sage.

Brunsdon, C. (1997). *Screen Tastes: Soap Opera to Satellite Dishes*, London and New York: Routledge.

Brunsdon, C. (2000). *The Feminist, the Housewife, and the Soap Opera*, Oxford: Oxford University Press.

Brunsdon, C. (2004) 'Lifestyling Britain: The 8–9 Slot on British Television', in J. Olsson and L. Spigel (eds) *Television After TV: Essays on a Medium in Transition*, Durham: Duke University Press: 75–92.

Brunsdon, C. (2006). 'The Feminist in the Kitchen: Martha, Martha and Nigella', in J. Hollows and R. Moseley (eds) *Feminism in Popular Culture*, Oxford and New York: Berg: 41–56.

Brunsdon, C. and L. Spigel (2008) 'Introduction to the Second Edition', in C. Brunsdon and L. Spigel (eds) *Feminist Television Criticism: A Reader*, 2nd edn, Maidenhead and New York: Open University Press: 1–19.

CRTC (1994) 'Decision CRTC 94-282', 6 June, Ottawa, www.crtc.gc.ca/eng/archive/1994/DB94-282.HTM (Last accessed 3 January 2016).

'Doubletake: Focused Women Fight Media Myths' (1996) Simon Fraser University Media & Public Relations, 25 March, www.sfu.ca/archive-university-communications/pre2002 archive/features/1996/March96/doubletake.html (Last accessed 3 January 2016).

Dow, B. (1996) *Prime-Time Feminism: Television, Media Culture, and the Women's Movement since 1970*, Philadelphia: University of Pennsylvania Press.

Faludi, S. (1991) *Backlash: The Undeclared War against American Women*, New York: Crown Publishing.

Faulder, L. (1994). 'Sex, Truth, and Videotapes; New Lifestyle Channel Aims to Give Women What They Want; Facts on Lifestyle Television', *Edmonton Journal*, 16 June: D5.

Foster, D. (2009) 'Chasing the Public: The CBC and the Debate over Factual Entertainment on Canadian Airwaves', *Canadian Journal of Communication*, 34 (1): 61–77.

Geraghty, C. (2005) 'The Study of Soap Opera', in J. Wasko (ed.) *A Companion to Television*, Malden, Oxford and Carlton: Blackwell: 308–23.

Gitlin, T. (1985) *Inside Prime Time*, New York: Pantheon Books.

Gomery D. (1999) 'Brian's Song: Television, Hollywood, and the Evolution of the Movie Made for TV', in A. Rosenthal (ed.) *Why Docudrama? Fact-Fiction of Film and TV*, Carbondale and Edwardsville: Southern Illinois University Press: 78–100.

Hollows, J. (2006) 'Can I Go Home Yet? Feminism, Post-feminism and Domesticity', in J. Hollows and R. Moseley (eds) *Feminism in Popular Culture*, Oxford and New York: Berg: 97–118.

Hollows, J. and R. Moseley (2006) 'Popularity Contests: The Meanings of Popular Feminism', in J. Hollows and R. Moseley (eds) *Feminism in Popular Culture*, Oxford and New York: Berg: 1–22.

Karlyn, K. (2011) *Unruly Girls and Unrepentant Mothers: Redefining Feminism on Screen*, Austin: University of Texas Press.

Lesage, J. (1984) 'Feminist Documentary: Aesthetics and Politics', in T. Waugh (ed.) *Show Us Life: Toward a History and Aesthetics of the Committed Documentary*, Metuchen and London: Scarecrow Press: 223–51.

Lotz, A. (2006) *Redesigning Women: Television after the Network Era*, Urbana and Chicago: University of Illinois Press.

Matheson, S.A. (2010) 'Shopping, Makeovers, and Nationhood: Reality TV and Women's Programming in Canada', in J.A. Taddeo and K. Dvorak (eds) *The Tube Has Spoken: Reality TV and History*, Lexington: University Press of Kentucky: 145–70.

Miller, M.J. (1987) *Turn Up the Contrast: CBC Television Drama since 1952*, Vancouver: University of British Columbia Press.

Moseley, R. (2001) '"Real lads do cook . . . but some things are still hard to talk about": The Gendering of 8–9', in 'Factual Entertainment on British Television: The Midlands TV Research Group's "8–9 Project"', special issue, *European Journal of Cultural Studies*, 4(1): 29–62.

Off, S.A. (1996) 'Defining the "W" in WTN: A Feminist Analysis of the Women's Television Network (1993–96)', MA Thesis, School of Journalism and Communication, Carleton University, Ottawa, Ontario.

Off, S.A. (1999) 'The Women's Television Network: By, For and About Women . . . or Was That Ratings?' in L. Van Luven and P. Walton (eds) *Pop Can: Popular Culture in Canada*, Scarborough: Prentice Hall Allyn and Bacon Canada: 106–12.

'Proposed TV Channel to Reflect Women's Reality' (1994) *Herizons*, 8(1): 16.

Rakow, L.F. (2009) 'Feminist Approaches to Popular Culture: Giving Patriarchy its Due' in J. Storey (ed.) *Cultural Theory and Popular Culture: A Reader*, 3rd edn, Harlow: Pearson Longman: 199–214.

Rapping, E. (1992) *The Movie of the Week: Private Stories, Public Events*, Minneapolis: University of Minnesota Press.

Seger, L. (2003) *When Women Call the Shots: The Developing Power and Influence of Women in Television and Film*, Lincoln: iUniverse.

Shattuc, J.M. (1997) *The Talking Cure: TV Talk Shows and Women*, London and New York: Routledge.

Thornham, S. (2000) *Feminist Theory and Cultural Studies: Stories of Unsettled Relations*, London: Arnold.

Toupin, J.J. (1997) 'The Women's Television Network: A Canadian Compromise'. MA Thesis, School of Journalism and Communication, Carleton University, Ottawa Ontario.

Vale, A. (1995) 'WTN, Bravo! Fall Skeds', *Playback*, 11 September, http://playbackonline.ca/1995/09/11/4646-19950911/ (Last accessed 3 January 2016).

Vale, A. (1997). 'Programming', *Playback*, 10 March, http://playbackonline.ca/1997/03/10/5968-19970310/ (Last accessed 3 January 2016).

Zerbisias, A. (1995) 'The Women's TV Channel Faces Undeserved Hostility', *Toronto Star*, 28 March: E3.

9

TRADITION AND INNOVATION

Italian women's channels, factual entertainment and the significance of generation in women's viewing preferences

Cecilia Penati and Anna Sfardini

Introduction

Traditionally, Italy's television audience is mostly female: this is one reason why the television industry is continually investing in, expanding and diversifying the content, channels and formats available for women.[1] In recent years, the Italian television market has witnessed the launch and consolidation of several multi-channel platforms, which have significantly restructured the market and the entire competitive landscape. Channels explicitly dedicated to women and prominently featuring factual entertainment programming or scripted drama are an increasingly significant phenomenon on contemporary Italian television and have a pervasive presence on both free and pay-TV. Many elements combine to construct a channel's identity, calculated to target a female-only audience: these include the name of the channel, the logo, the graphics and, of course, the programming. Just as the idea of 'television for women' now encompasses a very diverse spectrum of channels, genres and programmes, so new female-gendered channels address a range of ideal viewers with very different ages, tastes and consumption styles.

The various multi-channel platforms that characterise contemporary Italian television represent a major development that reflects a general dynamic throughout Europe and America (Parks, 2004), whereby the multi-channel television environment has evolved to offer extensive choice for consumers (Scaglioni and Sfardini, 2008). As the number of available channels has grown, audiences have fragmented and the viewing figures for the main Rai and Mediaset channels have declined considerably.[2]

Since satellite pay television arrived on the Italian competitive scene in the 1990s, the programme offering has grown, with new channels constructed around specific 'themes' – mainly cinema, US television series, documentaries, sport and children's content.[3] More recently, channels have also been built around gender, as a handful of new 'male' channels have arisen (e.g. Discovery Channel, DMAX and AXN), followed by a bumper crop of 'female' channels. In fact, in Italy, gender has proved a powerful criterion for segmenting audiences and dictating channels' editorial policies. That trend has been playing out for a decade – since 2004, when the international group Fox launched Fox Life, a channel aimed at a female audience within the Sky entertainment package. It offered a mix of programmes, with television series and shows representative of what would soon become the native digital channels' principal genre: factual entertainment. Other significant cases followed, as channels whose core editorial policies revolved around a female identity and audience, and enjoyed exponential growth and a significant presence in public debate. Real Time, La7d, La5 and Lei – and previously Diva Universal, which ceased broadcasting in June 2015 – now form a set of allied, but multifaceted, channels that use gendered address as a creative response to an industrial requirement (Penati and Sfardini, 2014).[4] On one hand, this is a classic strategy in the cultural industry. The media industry has always sought to attract the female audience through specific narrative formulas and television genres. The creation of a circuit of mutual synergies between audience preferences and the offering of cultural products such as books, television programmes and films demonstrates as much. Indeed, Byars and Meehan (1994: 16) affirm, 'first, . . . culture industries target gendered audiences, aiming specific artefacts and particular genres at either men or women; second, . . . particular audiences, defined by gender, seem to have a special relationship with particular genres'. On the other hand, this strategy also highlights new ways to exploit audience fragmentation and to sell advertisers narrower audiences than those offered by mainstream television – audiences with a more relevant profile, that are more uniform and a closer match to the network brands' overall message (Lotz, 2007). Women are still the most sought-after and substantial target group for television broadcasters in Italy.[5] Indeed, television is an established habit for Italian women, who, significantly, spend on average more than four hours every day viewing.[6] Gender is also an essential and central parameter in the quantitative measurement of television ratings (for example see Auditel's monitoring efforts, broken down by gender, age group and socio-economic levels).[7]

Compared to the mainstream television monopoly of the past, where the public-service broadcaster, Rai, had three main channels plus the three main Mediaset channels, this new scenario has profoundly changed how Italian television approaches 'programmes for women'. It is not just television made *by* women or *about* women (although those are important focal points); rather, it concerns a more complex system of practices that involve all dimensions of the television medium, exploiting storytelling, branding and consumption processes.

After soap operas, romantic fiction and morning magazine programmes, women's channels are television's new product for female viewers. These channels promise to satisfy women's viewing needs and tastes, the 'daytime-isation' (Brunsdon, 2003) of their schedules attempting to harmonise with women's everyday routine. They represent a significant contemporary move, as compared to the pre-digital era of daytime as a sort of women's ghetto (Moseley, 2000). After surveying the contemporary scene of Italian digital channels for women, highlighting how each has particular editorial policies and a specific image of a 'real woman', this chapter will analyse female viewers' consumption of women's channels, focusing specifically on factual entertainment programming. The relationship between the supply and consumption of factual products for women allows us to probe the processes of consolidation and transformation in contemporary Italian television. We will identify the predominant viewing models underpinning the criteria for making choices, the means of consumption and, more generally, the meanings constructed around factual entertainment, often under the heading of 'lifestyle' programming (Moseley, 2000; Lewis, 2008). This analysis explores the results of a qualitative study carried out in Italy by the authors between 2011 and 2013. A total of twenty focus groups were organised by dividing participants into three age cohorts: 25–35 years, 36–45 years and 46–60 years. These three cohorts were selected based on a snapshot of the women's channels' core target emerging from Auditel figures. The different age cohorts also enabled us to interview people from different generations and in different spheres of life: half of them were part-time workers, and the other half housewives. Specifically, six groups took place in Naples, six in Rome and eight in Milan.[8]

The audience study was informed by the desire to understand what normative assumptions circulated about women's television between the industry and viewers within social contexts. What ideal visions of women (and what editorial policies) lie behind the programmes dedicated to so-called 'women's interests'? What images of women do the various expressive genres convey? The themes explored by most programmes on channels for women (the home, cooking, beauty, design and clothes clearly betray considerable conservatism and a certain reluctance to acknowledge and represent women's changing roles in contemporary society. Where, then, can inventive developments in television for women be found? How is innovation balanced with tradition? What creative processes characterise how the various programme and channel brands are constructed and communicated? Indeed, the different channels create distinct female brands and compete for specific (and distinct) target groups. And we must not forget the television medium's material nature – its concrete uses in today's domestic culture – which invokes the woman as a figure that, for various reasons, is still central to the household dynamics and the practices of consuming domestic media (O'Sullivan, 2005).

The strategic construction of gender

This chapter interrogates how, in using gendered address as a branding activity, there exists a continual balancing act between reference to traditional models of representing and invoking women and more creative, innovative impulses. An analysis of the main explicitly female-interest network brands shows how some strongly contrasting models emerge in what might seem at first to be a superficially uniform market. Each channel has its own case history in which conceptual, industrial and strategic factors have played a part, while other unplanned events have also been significant. Gendered address, used consciously and strategically as a brand identity tool, launched Fox Life, Diva Universal and Real Time. A feminine address in these cases played a thematic role in order to differentiate the output of these channels, while all channels have had to conform to the requirements of the Sky Italia media company, which owns the pay-TV platform and hosts them in its basic entertainment offering. Sky requires all its non-proprietary channels to meet specific requirements regarding both target audience and content: to meet the platform's audience gender and age profile and to commission the agreed television genres in order to avoid internal competition. This strict mandate has made it easy for a few channels to offer a focus on feminine genres. These have included Diva Universal (the only female channel focused on scripted content with a vintage flavour, such as British costume and period dramas, or American series from the eighties and nineties), Fox Life (which mixes factual entertainment and contemporary American television series) and Lei, owned by the RCS media company, which publishes many female magazines. Lei differs slightly from the others, as it was initially conceived as an extension of the magazines that already represented part of the media group's expertise, blending highbrow talk shows with vintage American television series such as *The Bionic Woman* (ABC, 1976–7, NBC 1977–8), *The Thorn Birds* (ABC, 1983) and *Alice* (CBS, 1976–85); it has since converted entirely to factual entertainment, as the genre became an established staple of women's television. Soon after inaugurating its programming in 2005, Real Time, a branch of Discovery Italia, began to set the standards in terms of both editorial decisions and audience ratings, as the most successful of the group of women's channels.

Factual entertainment on women's channels draws on several recurrent themes: body care, the kitchen, looking after the home, family relationships and affairs of the heart (Penati and Sfardini, 2015). Many channels' schedules are based on international programmes, mainly US or British material from the international factual genre. The Real Time channel's main hits are good examples of this trend: *Extreme Makeover* (Lighthearted Entertainment, Fox Life, 2004), *My Big Fat Gypsy Wedding* (Firecracker Films, Real Time, 2011–16), *Cake Boss* (High Noon Entertainment and Cakehouse Media, Real Time, 2009–16), *Hotel Hell* (One Potato Two Potato LLC, Real Time, 2013–14), *Little People, Big World* (Gay Rosenthal Productions, Real Time, 2015–16), *Say Yes to the Dress* (Half Yard Productions, Real Time, 2009–15) and *Hoarding: Buried Alive* (Discovery Studios, Real Time, 2012–15). These are interspersed with some Italian productions which are nearly always based on foreign (American or British) formats already in circulation. Examples include the franchises *Four Weddings* (Magnolia, Fox Life, 2014–16), *Don't Tell the Bride* (RCSMediaGroup/Lei, Lei, 2012 and La7d, 2014), *Project Runway* (FremantleMedia, Fox Life, 2014), *Bake Off* (Magnolia, Real Time, 2013–15) and *Farmer Wants a Wife* (FremantleMedia Italia, Fox Life, 2015), all adapted for the Italian market by the women's channels. Although these programmes exemplify the various methods of storytelling, from tutorials to makeovers and docu-reality shows, they all fall under the broad category of factual entertainment: for although their characters are ordinary people playing them-selves, they do so in situations and according to rules and mechanisms devised by the production team, in which they are 'free' to react while the programme structure is identical in each closed episode.

In the context of digital-terrestrial television, female channels have gone through more ad hoc, unplanned processes of change, adapting as their new arena gradually took shape and their direct competitors set out their stalls. One such channel was La7d, companion channel to the mainstream network La7, which was launched in haste to occupy a frequency in the new digital-terrestrial television environment. It was initially used as a catch-up service offering reruns of La7's main output, even-tually turning into a female channel once the competitive scenario unveiled. Another interesting case is the Mediaset-owned La5, the companion channel of commercial network Canale 5. It was launched to combat audience erosion in mainstream television and to exploit Mediaset's valuable rights library while attracting a hip young target audience that was less and less interested in what was now a dated approach to female television on the main channel, Canale 5. Especially during the daytime, Canale 5 presents various programmes for a female audience. They rep-resent a traditional approach to 'television for women', one that already existed before factual entertainment took hold: Italian-made soap operas, Latin American telenovelas and popular talk shows featuring celebrities and ordinary people with remarkable stories.

From this overview, women's channels might seem a homogeneous group, but a closer inspection of their historical development in relation to the opening up of digital competition reveals a series of more distinct variables. After a multiplatform television environment was established, the Italian television industry intensified its strategy of providing an offering based on associating particular types of pro-gramming with gender. In effect, the editorial choice of thematising a channel around an address to women always entails the same objective, namely to com-municate clearly that the programmes on offer have been designed and conceived to appeal to women, to attract them with content that always promises to reflect their interests and passions (Capecchi, 2006; Buonanno 2014; Grossi and Ruspini, 2007). Therefore, the contemporary offer of female channels tends to take the shape of a 'swarm' (Centorrino, 2006), at first glance seemingly indistinct and homo-geneous, yet also themed and specific. Closer examination of this swarm reveals different internal elements based on the profiling strategies used by the networks. For example, despite the common factual entertainment genre, the programmes on Real Time tend to involve urban and metropolitan contexts with a modern, luxurious lifestyle, as in *Cerco casa disperatamente* (Endemol, Real Time, 2006–13) and *Ma come ti vesti?!* (Magnolia, Real Time, 2009–15). Meanwhile, similar programmes on the Lei channel – *La seconda casa non si scorda mai* (FremantleMedia Italia, Lei, 2011), *Io donna – Buccia di banana,* (Magnolia, Lei, 2010–12, La7d, 2012–13) – choose to portray simpler everyday lifestyles and even provincial settings.

Italian female viewers of channels 'for women'

There exists a substantial academic literature on the differences between gendered viewing experiences (Lull, 1990; Gray, 1992), but that does not mean that women's media experience can be understood purely as a function of gender. Rather, the results obtained more easily describe a complex system of interpretations and uses of the medium that can also be attributed to other component variables of intersectional social identity or stage of life and status (for instance, female workers or housewives, mothers, single women, etc.).

Nevertheless, today, the very strategic focus on the female target group proposed by the women's channels affords the media/gender axis greater importance once again (Gauntlett, 2002), both as a space of representation of current female identities and as a place where female cultures are expressed and possibly even resisted. The relationship between women and television has been more actively studied by Italian scholars in recent years (Tota, 2008; Innocenti and Perrotta, 2013; Buonanno, 2014; Penati and Sfardini, 2015), especially given the way in which a gendered address is used by the editorial strategies promoted in the contemporary television arena. The following sections ask, given the importance that the television production world gives to gendered channels, by which actual criteria do today's female audiences choose what they watch? What viewing practices and habits characterise the experience of consuming channels for women? And finally, what difference has the rise of factual entertainment made to the viewing strategies of female viewers?

An important starting point for this study was to probe how the viewers interviewed saw the ongoing proliferation of channels dedicated to women, and what value they attributed to them. The first insight to emerge is linked to the same television approach that underpins the channels for women. That is, female viewers fully grasp the editorial strategy of thematising this area of the offering and they identify themselves as a specific target television audience, a commercial (rather than social) reference category complementing two other important target groups: men and children.

(50, Rome): My kids have their cartoons, my husband has his football, and at last I've got my channels, too.

(40, Naples): Lei, I think it's called, but for me it's all about women. A female channel. Made to measure just for us! (Even though I watch it with my husband.) It's a channel aimed squarely at women.

Channels for women are an inexhaustible source of programmes that can pique curiosity, give practical new tips (on DIY, the kitchen, how to dress, etc.), offer an escapist window on distant worlds and provide company as a backdrop to domestic work. All those motives suggest that this group of channels fulfils a desire for television entertainment that is associated with consuming and performing the right lifestyle. Factual entertainment's innovative dimension lies in the genre's language and specific formats, which lend a light-hearted rhythm to the *topics that women like.*

That means light entertainment – primarily for *escapism, amusement, relaxation* and the need to *switch off* and find *time for yourself* – that can adapt to the *different levels of attention* with which television *for women* is watched (from focused, committed and loyal viewing to distracted, intermittent and grazing viewing). This does not imply that viewers of female channels watch television only for fun or idle amusement. Rather, in the panoply of programmes on offer nowadays, the women's channels provide easy-viewing light entertainment, while more traditionally news-oriented content (e.g. current affairs) can be found elsewhere (on themed and public-service channels). Female audiences perceive and value the offer of women channels as light and entertaining. However, this kind of engagement with 'female content', strongly encouraged by the editorial lines of these channels, does not entirely satisfy all of the television preferences of women.

(41, Naples): They are all quite entertaining, because they are light-hearted pro-grammes, a bit like a dream. I actually think of them as fairytale programmes: you don't even wonder whether they're real or not.

(31, Milan): I think these channels are ideal if you want something relaxing; they're easy to watch.

(38, Milan): They are 'frivolous' channels, which is fine because they're undemanding – unlike, say, the news or a film. It's not about conveying information. They are a bit superficial in other ways: if there's something about how to dress, then I'll watch it and enjoy it, but obviously you can't watch only that!

(30, Milan): It's light, it takes your mind off the recession, off work, off the daily grind. It doesn't make you think; it's a breath of fresh air! It's not challenging like a political talk show.

While most of the women comment on the relative triviality of the genre, they nevertheless also have varying ways of associating with these feminised forms of factual entertainment, to which they attach different layers of significance. This seems to suggest distinctions between different generations of women, stressing a difference between older and younger audiences. The older viewers' approach to female content is more straight forwardly appreciative of recent shifts in feminised tele-vision, which we call a 'tactical' response, while the younger audience tend to deal directly with the 'stigma' associated with female television brands.

The tactical female viewer

The tactical viewer emerges most strongly from the views and consumption experiences articulated by the more mature group of women interviewed. Tactical viewers consider women's channels as a kind of evolutionary development, if not a triumph for female audiences. The experience of watching women's channels produces and plays on a sense of satisfaction and gratification, thus reinforcing the female viewer's identity. No longer marginalised within the confines of just a few genres, such as soaps or telenovelas, the tactical viewer feels as if a whole market of channels has been made just for her. This success is an important result in itself: the visibility in the channel menu of a television world aimed at female viewers offers women the opportunity to discuss their subordinate role in the family balance of remote-control use. Indeed, while domestic television consumption is often controlled, especially during prime-time, by what men and children want, the technological innovations introduced by the new set-top boxes have helped to change the rigid image of the familiar piece of kit that lends structure to everyday family life.

(42, Milan): There are four of us, and we have three televisions, but we only have Sky on one, the same one with the Wii and the games – basically, it's just for the kids. I watch TV mainly in the kitchen on digital terrestrial. Between 6 and 7 in the morning, if I get up to exercise, the TV is all mine; then between 5.30 and 7.30 in the evening, when I cook: those are the times when I watch 'women's' channels.

(35, Naples): In the evening, my husband watches TV in one room, while my daughters and I watch *Italia's Next Top Model*, *Ma come ti vesti?!* and *Case da incubo* in another.[9] We have Sky only on one TV, so the women of the house control that! We have a monopoly!

New interactive services have revolutionised traditional viewing models, and not just through greater personalisation. Female viewers in our study revealed how the Sky satellite TV set-top box is being used tactically, based on their direct involvement in the processes of domesticating satellite television that can alter television's social uses. For the first time, women – mature women, in particular – see themselves as makers of decisions about buying domestic technologies and introducing them into everyday usage, as they become capable users of new television services such as MySky and Sky Multivision.[10] This new role in the family balance of power is also supported by their desire to watch programmes and channels *made especially for them*. The consumption practices reported that describe television's role in family life reveal the tactical viewer's awareness that intra-family dynamics and the relations between the sexes are changing. The words with which the women describe how they have become familiar with new television technologies convey the sense of excitement about an ongoing renegotiation of their power in the home environment. They have become *free and independent; they can choose what they want* at any time. The lounge, culturally the place of television consumption par excellence, and traditionally under male control, is no longer the domestic nerve centre. The enriched digital-terrestrial offering (with the Multivision service for Sky subscribers) has transformed the other, intrinsically marginalised, rooms – like the bedroom or kitchen – into spaces that are equally important and functional for television watching.

(37, Naples): I have a Sky Multivision subscription, with two decoders; otherwise, I couldn't watch my favourite channels in the bedroom, since the TV with Sky is in the lounge. That helps to avoid problems – I hate football, for example, but my husband watches it all the time. So I watch all the programmes about the home, which I love.

The services supported by television digitalisation prompt a new form of cannibalisation of the television schedules (Rosenthal, 1985), based mainly on habitual practices of storing one's own list of favourite channels using the EPG service and recording the relevant programmes via a decoder. Therefore, these viewers are tactical in terms of meeting their entertainment needs through women's programmes, and appreciate the new technological affordances of the medium to redefine the family spaces and dynamics (Wajcman, 1991).[11]

The stigmatised female viewer

The second type of viewer to emerge from the study is the stigmatised viewer, found especially among the younger interviewees, in the range from 25 to 35 years old. Their characteristic trait is a dual perception of women's channels as *innovative yet traditional*. On one hand, the new roster of channels for women is a signal of the current innovation in the field of television formats and ways of storytelling, exemplified by the genre of factual entertainment that fills their schedules. This genre's added value springs from its use of original formulas and formats to represent the ordinary practices that shape and improve everyday life. The content catering for typically female viewing pleasure establishes a new kind of entertainment in the factual genre, where programmes can be consumed without viewers' full attention, to complement women's other activities. But the downside is a sense of shame, not so much in choosing factual entertainment content but rather in viewing channels that make it abundantly clear at whom they are exclusively aimed. Like a new kind of stigma, similar to traditional discussion of women's 'guilty pleasures' in relation to gendered tastes (Seiter, 1989; Gray, 1992; Radway, 1987), in watching women's channels women must also negotiate derision – and express strong resistance to embracing such an explicitly gendered targeted kind of channel.

(51, Milan): A downside is that there's nothing for men! They pull my leg at home when I watch Lei.
(49, Milan): Probably it's because of the name!
(49, Rome): I don't like it, myself, because it's only for women, apparently, almost as if it were a women's magazine.

The women's channels' identities seem *too feminine*, too uniform. They foster an image of housewives that has been only partially brought up to date – addressed as resourceful women full of initiative but largely confined to the house, with low-profile jobs if they work at all, who need advice on how to dress and present themselves well within their confined family setting. However, and interestingly, the viewer who seems to absorb general ideas about such programmes lacking value, thus feeling stigmatised, also seems to attach value to the viewing experience as a collective enterprise with other female family members. This kind of viewer tends to prefer watching *her programmes* with kindred family spirits (mothers/daughters/sisters), *behind the scenes* or late in the evening, when competition for the remote control has ended.

(42, Milan): I often watch the programmes about houses and about fashion with my mum. We have a great time; it's almost like going shopping together.

(42, Milan): I watch *Paint Your Life*, *Come è fatto* or sometimes even *Cerco casa disperatamente* with my children; they miss a bit now and again, then they ask me, 'Which one did they pick?' The same goes for the fashion programmes, even: they're glued to the TV, and wild horses wouldn't drag them away![12]

(49, Milan): I sometimes talk about it with a friend who watches these fashion programmes and who has a teenage daughter. We've talked about the channel, and I said 'Lucky you for having a daughter!' Because I can never share certain programmes with my son, so I watch them on my own.

Experiencing and sharing the interests and pleasures fuelled by the women's channels becomes an online pastime, on blogs, forums and chat groups about the programmes. There, female viewers feel part of a community founded on a shared semantics, sustained by discursive practices that continue to assert shared values, themes and interpretative paradigms on which to base a 'we-sense'. This sense of belonging is fostered by an exchange of experiences, advice and comments between women, in an effort to find a common thread linking different female identities.

Consuming factual entertainment: escapism and practicality

Turning from those two prevalent images of the viewers of women's channels, the actual ways of watching factual entertainment programming reveal two main models of engagement: the escapist and the practical. The former characterises the inter-viewees who likened their involvement in viewing women's programmes to a kind of daydream. Factual entertainment programmes are attractive when viewers engage with their stories to the point of abandoning or temporarily forgetting their normal routine and everyday tasks, immersing themselves in the imaginaries and fantasies of female tastes and pleasures, conforming to ideas about women's programming as distracting and escapist. The first and most traditional type of escapist content is the romantic, sentimental programming that revolves around weddings, a powerful narrative driver of many Italian and international television formats offered especially on Italian women's channels. Weddings, approached from various angles, are a magnet for eager audiences whose viewing tastes are amenable to the sentimental rhetoric of narratives centred on *true love stories* at the happy-ending stage – almost like a fairy-story spin-off or an archetypal soap opera in modern guise – typical of both international and Italian shows, such as *Don't Tell the Bride*, *Four Weddings*, *Say Yes to the Dress* and the Italian original production *Chi veste la sposa* (Zodiak Active, Lei, 2013–15). A second type of content that is oxygen for escapism comprises lifestyle and factual programmes set in exotic locations or exploiting *far-off dream destinations*. Viewers' engagement hinges on the pleasure of discovering social milieux and cultural models different from their own, of travelling in little-known lands and thus of feeling virtually transformed into a kind of media tourist or *cosmopolitan housewife* (Spigel, 2001). In this sense, the real-estate television genre is the most emblematic of this form of escapism, especially the formats that tell stories of buying, selling or renting luxury properties in the world's most exclusive locations, from deserted beaches and pristine countryside to the best-known art cities – as with *Case da sogno* (Leonardo TV Productions, Leonardo, 2013) and *Cerco casa disperatamente* and *Teen Cribs* (MTV Productions, MTV Italia, 2009–11, MTV HD, 2009–16). Similarly, makeover programmes offer escapist consumption, with top tips for how viewers can be more than just 'ordinary people'. These include overhauling their personal look, from beauty and make-up to clothes, and revamping their home, via major renovation work or sophisticated interior design. Docu-reality shows based on international celebrities' daily lives (for example, *Keeping Up with the Kardashians*, Ryan Seacrest Productions, Bunim/Murray Productions, E! Entertainment, 2007–11) are an extreme case of escapist consumption. They function primarily through viewers' suspension of disbelief, a necessary precondition for 'entering' the story. The enjoyment here comes from contrasting one's own everyday life with very different and distant situations and settings that epitomise that 'exotic' extravagance emblematic of eccentric lifestyles.

Across the research sample, the escapist-consumption model was more popular among (although not confined to) mature and elderly women. They seemed willing to consider television viewing as a chance to escape from reality, for the stories in factual entertainment programmes involve discovering different worlds to compare with their own familiar worlds and life experience. In particular, the British and American versions of the wedding formats successfully unite the pleasure of discovering different cultures and traditions with the desire to dive into fairytale worlds. An example is the great appeal of programmes centred on the wedding day and its various associated themes (like choosing the dress), presented and experienced by the protagonists in positive, indeed euphoric, fashion.

(50, Milan): I like watching wedding programmes to dream about my daughter's one day. I often say, 'Oh how lovely, that's a good idea!' You get some good tips. Watching a wedding makes you think back to your own.

(40, Naples): I think they are light channels, and their programmes don't require too much effort. They let you escape from everyday life and get your imagination running riot.

The second model of engagement that emerged from the study entails a more pragmatic approach to factual entertainment. The women's-channel formats cover a range of subjects, prominently including those claiming to offer practical information that viewers can use in their daily lives, from beauty tips to recipes, from tutorials on bringing up their children to ideas for running a better home or improving its décor.

Viewers engage pragmatically with the programmes because they consider them and their presenters deeply credible, all the more so when the stories presented 'really' seem to come from everyday life. Although still firmly confined to the television entertainment arena, female viewers appreciate tutorial and factual programmes for the information that they provide. They are seen as *trustworthy* and are especially well received when exploring light topics (from beauty and make-up to gardening) rather than weighty matters (health, sexuality, in-depth psychology, etc.). The pragmatic-consumption model thus corresponds perfectly to the narrative mechanisms used in contemporary factual entertainment, which is considered a kind of extension of the online tutorial and coaching videos which Ouellette and Hay (2008) extensively discuss as part of the neoliberal imperative of self-discipline.

Although the various formats present a wide array of female roles, the common factor identified is the continuation of women's traditional association with tasks and duties in the family, such as running the home, taking care of their appearance in order to look nicer and improving their personal relationships (with partners, children or even pets). Relatively few programmes portray women in the workplace or offer practical advice on tackling the many challenges of a professional career. Furthermore, pragmatic female viewers perceive that television continues to depict the working environment as a barrier that jeopardises women's ability to properly perform their roles as wives and mothers.

(38, Rome): There are lots of housewives in Italy, it's true, but even housewives work for a few hours or work from home. They should do programmes for women with different needs, not just puff pastry!

(47, Naples): The female channels are all right for women who iron and sew while watching TV. They're programmes for housewives; you can get up, put something on the stove, do the hoovering and still follow what's going on.

(37, Milan): I don't like it when women's channels use a baby's dummy or toys as images of the channel. Why do they have to keep bombarding us with the idea of women with little children and toys to pick up?

In response to television's failure to innovate on such a topical, sensitive subject, viewers (especially the younger interviewees) explore pathways of meaning to transcend a viewing model based on a conservative idea of women. With wedding-related programmes, for instance, the escapist approach typical of the mature women gives way to a more critical, ironic reading of the ideals of the *fairytale wedding* and *perfect dress* by the more pragmatic viewer.[13] In that sense, the formats predicated on fun and comic narratives of the best moments in life are recognised as the most valid expression of a kind of television that can articulate society's changing habits and values.

Women and television: tradition and innovation

This study has aimed to analyse the Italian approach to women's television, focusing on the dynamics that bring the worlds of production and consumption together.

The relationship between television and its female audience is a privileged perspective for analysing both the history of television, the development of its commercial strategies and programming content and the history of social change in Italy, where women's evolving role in society is a key theme. The simple approach of organising programming around women has undoubtedly proved extremely commercially effective. In terms of production, the plethora of Italian women's channels represents a well-defined offering framed by choices that focus on traditional feminine content (cooking, weddings, fashion, etc.), couched, however, in 'new' genres and formats in the form of factual entertainment.

The qualitative data from the empirical study reveal some prevalent viewing dynamics across the interview sample, where generation dictates the ways in which viewers are able to embrace women's channels. While all the women associated the channels with viewing pleasure, what differentiates the sample is how they experience the various programmes. There was a polarisation between mature women embracing the tactical-viewer model and younger women engaging with the stigmatisation of women's television, which reveals the central importance of generation in defining spectatorship identity (Colombo *et al.*, 2012). Mature women's image of themselves and their television consumption is more geared to appreciating it as progress, in a liberating break from the past, expressed through a desire to be no longer excluded from the new, from the technological innovation of television. Television is the key medium for these mature women as a 'media literacy' tool. Younger women voice more ambivalence in relation to the representation of their female condition and are reluctant to embrace the simplified images of women devised by the network brands. They express disenchantment as well as critical 'know-how' about gendered factual entertainment, while their collective viewing pleasure is insufficient to silence a sense of dissatisfaction with the feminised realm on television. Television is an 'old medium' in their media world, a medium that often seems to look more to the past, even in its more recent genres, keeping women tied to a traditional model.

Looking at the perceptions of the world portrayed in the factual entertainment programmes, the escapist and pragmatic means of engagement identified here suggest that this genre can satisfy both the quest for something different, for a dissonance between the experience of real life and the media imaginary, and the need for television to reflect the reality of women's lives. This dual consumption trend corresponds to the dual offering of factual programming, positioned to exploit the tension between innovation and tradition ingrained in the medium. On one hand, this new entertainment genre brings inventive elements bound up with new formulas and formats which create new forms of storytelling that can portray women in new contexts and roles, while on the other, the women's television brands' prefiguring of the audience's tastes also holds on to the privileged status still afforded to an image of the female viewer modelled on conventional roles and traditional value systems.

This picture of the formation of Italian women's channels and their simultaneous appeal to innovation and tradition must be seen against the backdrop of slow but constant social change. On these channels women seem both imprisoned in traditional domesticated roles and also represented by powerful new female personalities that can transform the female imaginary. This is one of the fullest expressions of Italian television's intrinsic characteristic: its continual effort to strike a balance between traditional features and innovative impulses, both for television and for women.

Notes

1   In the 2013–14 television season, female audiences represented 57.44 per cent of total viewers (6,233,000 out of 10,861,000). The figures refer to the television season from 1 September 2013 to 31 May 2014 (timeslot: entire day, i.e. 02:00–25:59). Report: Nielsen TV Audience Measurement Source: Auditel. Analysis: Geca Italia.

2   In Italy, the progressive fragmentation of audiences is clear to see from the figures recorded for the main television networks. In the Rai and Mediaset groups, over the period 2004–14, Rai1 saw its average daily audience fall from 2,138,000 individuals (a 23.01 per cent share) to 1,777,000 (17.33 per cent) and Canale 5 from 2,006,000 (22.45 per cent) to 1,558,000 (15.20 per cent). Taken together, in contrast, the many different television networks that sprang up with the transition to digital-terrestrial rose from 961,000 (a 10.34 per cent share) to 4,099,000 average viewers (40 per cent) in the same period. Report: Nielsen TV Audience Measurement. Source: Auditel. Analysis: Geca Italia.

3   As main examples of Italian thematic channels, see for instance: Rai Yoyo (kids' TV), Fox (US TV series), Animal Planet (documentaries), Sky Sport (sports and competitions).

4   There have also been some failures since 2004, such as the channels E! Entertainment and Lady Channel, now permanently off-air. In addition, some 'minor' channels – such as Arturo, La Sposa TV, and Fine Living – have emerged on digital-terrestrial TV.

5   By way of example, in the 2013–14 television season, female audiences represented 57.44 per cent of total viewers (6,233,000 out of 10,861,000). The figures refer to the television season from 1 September 2013 to 31 May 2014 (timeslot: entire day, i.e. 02:00–25:59). Report: Nielsen TV Audience Measurement. Source: Auditel. Analysis: Geca Italia.

6   Taking into consideration the average annual television consumption from 2005 to 2013 (from 1/1 to 31/12 each year), the Auditel figures show a slight but progressive rise in average consumption in minutes, from 265 minutes in 2005 to 286 in 2013. Report: Nielsen TV Audience Measurement. Source: Auditel. Analysis: Geca Italia.

7   Auditel is an independent and impartial company that measures television audiences in Italy on a national and regional level through the various broadcasting modes. The company represents the market members: RAI, private broadcasters, advertisers, 'media centres' and agencies.

8   Participant selection was structured, as regards the viewing choices of the female viewers involved, to cover the *channels for women* active during the study period: the digital-terrestrial channels Cielo, La5, La7d, Arturo and Realtime; the Sky satellite platform channels Fox Life, Diva Universal, E!, Lei, AliceTV, Wedding TV, SkyUno, Dove TV and Discovery Travel and Living.

9   *Italia's Next Top Model* (Magnolia, Sky Vivo, 2007–9; Sky Uno, 2011, Cielo, 2009–11), *Ma come ti vesti?!* and *Case da incubo*, Talkback Thames/FremantleMedia, Lei, 2011–16, Real Time, 2014–16.

10   These findings show an interesting link with the work of Morley (1986) on the dynamics of power related to family roles, in particular the male control exercised over domestic media consumption. The new television services represent an opportunity to change not only the family power dynamics, but also the use of gender-specific household technology: referring to the existence of 'pink' and 'blue' territories in the household technological geography described by Gray (1992), MySky and Sky Multivision emerge as technologies with a high potential to be a 'pink' colour, or strong appeal for female spectators.

11 This research finding confirms the relevance of the model of the *social shaping of technology* for approaching the changes in Italian broadcasting with the introduction of digital-terrestrial television and the satellite platform. In this study, the paradigm linked to the female gender.

12 *Paint Your Life* (Magnolia, Real Time, 2005–12); *Come è fatto* (Productions MAJ; CA, Ztélé, Real Time, 2005–11).

13 Similar research is described in Skeggs and Wood (2012).

Bibliography

Brunsdon, C. (2003) 'Lifestyling Britain: The 8–9 Slot on British Television', *International Journal of Cultural Studies*, 6:1: 5–23.

Buonanno, M. (ed.) (2014) *Il prisma dei generi: Immagini di donne in tv*, Milan: Angeli.

Byars, J. and E.R. Meehan (1994) 'Once in a Lifetime: Constructing "The Working Woman" through Cable Narrowcasting', *Camera Obscura*, 11–12 (33–34): 12–41.

Capecchi, S. (2006) *Identità di genere e media*, Rome: Carocci.

Centorrino, M. (2006) *La rivoluzione satellitare: Come Sky ha cambiato la televisione italiana*, Milan: Franco Angeli.

Colombo, F., G. Boccia Artieri, L. Del Grosso Destreri, F. Pasquali and M. Sorice (eds) (2012) *Media e generazioni nella società italiana*, Milan: Franco Angeli.

Deuze, M. (2007) *Media Life*, Malden, MA: Polity Press.

Gauntlett, D. (2002) *Media, Gender and Identity: An Introduction*, London and New York: Routledge.

Gray, A. (1992) *Video Playtime: The Gendering of a Leisure Technology*, London and New York: Routledge.

Grossi, G. and E. Ruspini (eds) (2007) *Ofelia e Parsifal: Modelli e differenze di genere nel mondo dei media*, Milan: Cortina.

Havens, T. and A. Lotz (2012) *Understanding Media Industries*, Oxford: Oxford University Press.

Hill, A. (2005) *Reality TV: Audiences and Popular Factual Television*, London and New York: Routledge.

Innocenti, V. and M. Perrotta (2013) *Factual, reality, makeover: Lo spettacolo della trasformazione nella televisione contemporanea*, Rome: Bulzoni Editore.

Lewis, T. (2008) *Smart Living: Lifestyle Media and Popular Expertise*, New York: Peter Lang.

Livingstone, S. (2007) 'From Family Television to Bedroom Culture: Young People's Media at Home' in E. Devereux (ed.) *Media Studies: Key Issues and Debates*, London: Sage: 302–21.

Lotz, A. (2007) *Television Will Be Revolutionized*, New York and London: New York University Press.

Lull, J. (1990) *Inside Family Viewing*, London: Routledge.

Morley, D. (1986) *Family Television: Cultural Power and Domestic Leisure*, London: Comedia.

Morley, D. (2000) *Home Territories: Media, Mobility and Identity*, London and New York: Routledge.

Moseley, R. (2000) 'Makeover Takeover on British Television', *Screen*, 41:3: 299–314.

Moseley, R. (2015) 'Television for Women. Nuovi spazi, nuove traiettorie', afterword to C. Penati and A. Sfardini, *La tv delle donne: Brand, programmi, pubblici*, Milan: Unicopli: 145–50.

O'Sullivan, T. (2005) 'From Television Lifestyle to Lifestyle Television', in D. Bell and J. Hollows (eds) *Ordinary Lifestyles: Popular Media, Consumption and Taste*, Maidenhead: Open University Press: 21–34.

Ouellette, L. and J. Hay (2008) *Better Living through Reality TV: Television and Post-Welfare Citizenship*, Malden: Blackwell.

Parks, L. (2004) 'Flexible Microcasting: Gender, Generation and Television Internet Convergence,' in L. Spigel and J. Olson (eds) *Television after TV. Essays on a Medium in Transition*, Chicago: Duke University Press: 133–56.

Penati, C. and A. Sfardini (2014) 'Contemporary TV for Women, between Standardisation and Creativity', *Comunicazioni sociali*, 3: 375–83.

Penati, C. and A. Sfardini (2015) *La tv delle donne: Brand, programmi e pubblici*, Milan: Unicopli.

Radway, J. (1987) *Reading the Romance: Women, Patriarchy and Popular Literature*, London: Verso.

Rosenthal, E.M. (1985) 'VCRs Having More Impact on Network Viewing, Negotiation', *Television/Radio Age*, 25 May.

Scaglioni, M. and A. Sfardini (2008) *Multi TV: L'esperienza televisiva nell'età della convergenza*, Rome: Carocci.

Seiter, E. (1989) *Remote Control: Television, Audiences, and Cultural Power*, London: Routledge.

Skeggs, B. and H. Wood (2012) *Reacting to Reality Television: Performance, Audience and Value*, Abingdon and New York: Routledge.

Spigel, L. (2001) 'Media Homes: Then and Now,' *International Journal of Cultural Studies*, 4:4: 385–411.

Tota, A.L. (2008) *Gender e media: Verso un immaginario sostenibile*, Rome: Meltemi.

Wajcman, J. (1991) *Feminism Confronts Technology*, Cambridge: Polity Press.

Weber, B.R. (2008) *Makeover TV: Selfhood, Citizenship, and Celebrity*, Durham and London: Duke University Press.

10

PRODUCING DOMESTIC ABUSE IN PAKISTANI TELEVISION

Between commerce, ratings and social responsibility

Munira Cheema

Before the liberalisation of television in 2000, Pakistan had one terrestrial channel. The Pakistan Television Corporation (commonly known as PTV) had been the state broadcaster since 1964 and thus PTV content reflected the policies of different governments. Liberal governments relaxed control over gender on screen – women could be seen without *dupatta* – while religiously inclined governments brought in their own agendas with restrictions on appearance of women, such as the *dupatta* policy (see, for example, Ali, 1986; Suleman, 1990; Kothari, 2005; Nasir, 2012).[1] In 2002, the Independent Media Corporation launched its channel Geo News from Pakistan, followed by other networks, marking the formal launch of the policy of liberalisation of media on television. Presently, five media groups have control of the Pakistani media industry, including electronic and print media. These are Independent Media Corporation, Pakistan Herald Publications, ARY Group, Waqt Group and Lakson Group (see for example Proffitt and Rasul, 2013). The broadcasting industry in Pakistan follows an advertiser-driven model that is run through a system of ratings. At the time of the fieldwork reported here (October–April 2011), Media Logic and Gallup were the two operators that determined the popular tastes of consumers through ratings.[2]

For those who remember Pakistani television before 2000, it is difficult *not* to have noticed the change in gender-based content in the post-liberalisation era. The idea of change requires careful consideration at this stage. In the pre-liberalisation era, gender issues did not have the same space in television broadcasting as they have now. Historically, there have been programmes on awareness of certain gender-related issues such as family planning (drama serials titled *Nijat* (1993) and *Aahat* (1991)) aired on PTV.[3] However, producers would not touch the controversial topics that are considered to be the taboos of Pakistani society.[4] Since 2002, there has been a distinct change in gendered content, whereby real-life practices such as woman's marriage to the Holy Quran, incest, honour killings (*karo kari*), stoning to death, rape, adultery, remarriage after divorce, domestic violence, marriages of minors, homosexuality and rights of women living in joint families have been raised in news, interactive genres (talk-based programming) and narrative forms (drama serials).[5]

Although gender-based content runs through both the narrative and the interactive forms of television, this chapter focuses on the imperatives behind the production of 'interactive TV' shows. It offers an attempt to understand both the commercial and the ideological motivations of producers in bringing changing forms of gendered content onto Pakistani screens. It asks questions about their perceptions of their audience, the importance of ratings and how they perceive emancipatory content in relation to 'interactive genres'.[6] Five sub-genres fall into the category of what I will call 'interactive TV', namely: breakfast shows, religion-based talk shows, social issues-based talk shows, crime shows and game shows.[7] Interactive television in the Pakistani context refers to audiences' access to television shows either by their direct presence as in-studio audiences or through letter-writing (those who do not have access to the internet), email, text messaging and telephone. This participation in the shows is varied: an in-studio audience in a panel-based discussion, for instance, contrasts with a member of the public participating in discussion of a sociopolitical nature. Those who are invited as panellists also vary with genre. For example, in the religion-based talk shows such as *Alim aur Alam* (Scholar and the Global Society, 2011–12) and *Hawa Ki Baiti* (Daughter of Eve, 2011–15), the discussion panel is composed of clergy from different sects of Islam. In these shows, women participate to seek religious counselling on matters of a private nature (divorce, conjugal rights or even domestic abuse). The social issues-based talk shows such as *Geo Hina Kay Sath* (Live with Hina, no longer on air) have in-studio audiences (mostly university students), and the panel is composed of a lawyer, a member of civil society (NGOs), a religious scholar and, at times, a doctor to provide comprehensive counselling on social issues. Participation in the breakfast shows such as *Utho Geo Pakistan* (2011–14), *Good Morning Pakistan* (2011–) and *Subah Saweray Maya Kay Sath* (2011–12) varies with daily topics (fashion, lifestyle and gender issues). In the case of gender-based issues, female viewers participate (through email, phone, letters) to voice their opinion on the ordeal of the victims who choose to appear on these shows or on discriminatory practices against women, but more importantly, these platforms are also used by the victims to report gender abuse on live television. Once reported, the host then takes up the case as a topic for the show and discusses it with the invited panel.

Access to the mediated public sphere

The inclusion of gendered issues in popular culture has made television quite different from what it was a decade ago. The change it has brought about operates at two levels: first, in terms of bringing into public view issues that had not thus far been discussed on television; second, in terms of providing access to a mediated public sphere via the new interactive genre of the talk show. Access is a vital issue in a country that defines the public/private distinction through Islam; rising religiosity in

Pakistan has strengthened this distinction further. In this historical moment, Pakistan is ranked the third most dangerous country in the world.[8] It is in this context that producers have allowed access to the mediated public sphere through interactive TV, and here I explore the dynamics of the production of such content.

Habermas' version of the 'public sphere' is 'in every conversation in which private individuals assemble to form a public body' (2006: 73), but for him this cannot be achieved through mainstream commercial media (Habermas 1991: 181–8, quoted in Butsch, 2009). Media scholars such as Dahlgren have worked with this starting point, noting that as

> the scale of modern society does not allow more than a relatively small number of citizens to be physically co-present, the mass media have become the chief institutions of the public sphere. It points to those institutional constellations of the media and other fora for information and opinion – and the social practices around them – which are relevant for political life. That these institutional constellations and practices may be anemic does not per se mean they are irrelevant.
>
> *(1995: 7–9)*

For this study, gender-based talk shows offer a space where marginalised publics (housewives and victims of gender abuse) use the mediated public sphere to discuss issues of concern to them, and there is an obvious exchange of ideas among different members of society in these talk shows. It is not possible to reach a consensus in these shows in a Habermasian sense, which mirrors discussions about the chaotic nature of talk on the Anglo-American talk show (see for example Livingstone and Lunt, 1994).

Feminist critics (Felski, 1989; Fraser, 1990; Benhabib, 1992; McLaughlin, 1993; Landes, 1998) have claimed the idea of alternative public spheres for other emancipatory projects, rearticulating the notion of common good in relation to that considered 'private' in the traditional model of the public sphere. Landes observes that the

> goals of generalizability and appeals to the common good may conceal rather than expose forms of domination, suppress rather than release concrete differences among persons or groups. Moreover, by banishing the language of particularity, the liberal public sphere has jeopardized its own bases of legitimation in the principles of accessibility, participation, and equality.
>
> *(1998: 144)*

Translating Landes' observation to the context of Pakistan, I trace issues that fall into the language of particularity. For example, issues such as the roles and rights of women under *Shariah* fall into the definition of the common good; however, homosexuality does not.[9] Ideally speaking, the common good and matters of shared concern should be decided by 'discursive contestation' (Fraser, 1990: 71). The interactive shows discussed here do allow limited or occasional discursive contestation, but Fraser also warns that public spheres are not spaces of 'a zero degree culture . . . these institutions may be understood as culturally specific rhetorical lenses that filter and alter the utterances they frame; they can accommodate some expressive modes and not others' (1990: 62). The spaces offered by talk shows in Pakistani popular culture operate through the logic of the market, where certain filtering and framing of discussions is heavily influenced by trends in ratings and other pressure groups (clergy and government). The emerging feminist public sphere here tilts more towards Islamic feminism than liberal feminism, reminding us that in Pakistan there is still no single 'unifying discourse' (to use McLaughlin's term, 1993: 610) on feminism. There is liberal feminism supported by NGOs and civil society, while on the other hand there is Islamic feminism supported by religious political parties such as Jamaat-e-Islami and other religious organisations such as Al Huda and Jamia Al-Hafsa.

As in any other media industry (see Gitlin, 1985; Baker and Hesmondhalgh, 2011), commercial broadcasters in Pakistan also work on the basis of popularity and demand for certain kinds of content, and that demand is determined through ratings. A number of scholars working in the tradition of political economy media (Smythe, 1977; Livant, 1979; Livant and Jhally, 1986: Meehan, 1984; Gitlin, 1985; Napoli, 2012) argue that like any other commercial industry, the media are also engaged in the selling and exchange of certain commodities (audiences, labour and ratings). Ratings are critical to the broadcasting industry, and the exchange of commodities depends on the circulation of ratings in the industry and is central to the television industry in Pakistan.[10] By knowing the demographic details of the sample audiences, producers have some idea of who is watching, and their viewing tastes become semi-predictable. In the sections that follow, I explore how ratings-driven media has identified women as the prime viewers for an emerging feminist public sphere in interactive shows, while influencing the kind of feminist public sphere which can emerge.

Producer perceptions of their viewers

The data used in this section is drawn from the responses of three producers (anonymised here), namely Rumaisa Khan (director of a high-profile breakfast show); Hana Farooq (a breakfast-show anchor) and Haseeb Alam (business executive for a major media group).

Breakfast shows are topic-based talk shows with interactive audiences either present in the studio or participating through phone calls, live Facebook messages and Twitter. Topics range from interviewing a celebrity to highlighting health and lifestyle, but, more importantly for my purposes here, also include gender issues. The first questions I posed to the producers, 'who are your viewers/what is your target market for an essentially gendered content?', were revealing. Khan mentions there is an understanding among the production team that their target audience is women, who are passive housewives:

> What they [broadcasters] are drilling into us or what production houses and channels are briefing to the directors is that majority of your viewers are typical

housewives who put food on stove and come sit in front of television until their husbands come back from work who have nothing beyond their kitchens and homes. These women are already there as our viewers, they have already created a market themselves, we have not produced these viewers and we know it from the surveys that are conducted by those who are in the business of advertising. And through the findings of the surveys, we eventually get this feedback that such women who have low IQ level probably not exceeding 4 on a scale of 1 to 10, and are typically dumb, are our target . . . so we should produce for them.

Evident from this excerpt is that producers believe there is an existing market for the kind of content they are producing, constituted by 'passive housewives'. Interestingly, Khan also notes that neither the producer nor the content has created the audience; rather, they identified the invisible, yet existing, audiences for a certain kind of content which they are producing. More interesting is her perception that her viewers are women who are not only confined to their homes (the kitchen in particular) but also have a limited IQ; producers' perceptions of their audience are governed by several stereotypes. When pressed further on how producers have come to appreciate that women constitute their audience group, Khan revealed that the research teams within the channels rely on surveys conducted by their clients/sponsors, but mainly on ratings. This comment suggests that the producers of breakfast shows are not seeking a public in the interests of debate, but rather pursuing content that is tailored for the rating sample obtained from Media Logic.

Hana Farooq, another breakfast-show host, replied in a similar vein. When asked how these women viewers engage with the serious nature of the issues raised on her shows, she noted in a contemptuous tone:

Oh, who are my viewers? My viewers are women who are either interested in designer wear we give away for calling or texting in these shows, or they seek pleasure in watching tragic stories about women who appear on shows; however, if you run a show on raising funds for flood victims you will get only 13,000 text messages. But if you have designer wear to give away you get 100,000, you imagine? Look at the indifference of these women and their level of intellect, so now you can make sense of who they are . . . but I don't call these women innocent, they want to live off their husband's pockets, they are stubborn.

Farooq's viewers are understood to belong to a certain class who are willing to spend on a certain lifestyle. This host had serious reservations regarding the nature of the content, since it was ratings-driven, and stated that the trends in ratings reveal that these viewers are certainly conforming to the desired expectations of the broadcasters and the advertisers who want them to engage through texting, even if it is in order to win designer wear. This is not something exclusive to the Pakistani context, for Baker and Hesmondhalgh (2011) also find similar frustration and contempt among creative workers working in the magazine industry; however, they relate their findings to the issue of impact upon the 'quality and value' of their work (2011: 200).

Holding a low opinion of the viewers or considering them intellectually deficient in certain ways is not just restricted to the producers of breakfast shows. In fact, it is a perception, originally derived from ratings and advertisers' surveys, that prevails at a higher level, filters down to the hosts and extends to the production houses, influencing the content they produce. Haseeb Alam, the business unit head of a major media organisation, who has a crucial role in influencing the content of the breakfast shows and drama serials, told me:

> You have to understand that the viewer in Pakistan is at the IQ level of an 8-year-old. They used to call Benazir a corrupt leader when she was alive; now they cry for her. So, we now talk to people with this range of IQ. We cater to the lowest common denominator in the society; we don't want to produce high art and be thrown out of the market.

The example given here is an interesting take on the power of media in manipulating the realities and/or perceptions of the audience. He is suggesting that the media manipulated audiences into believing that Benazir Bhutto was a corrupt leader but, after her death, glorified her to the extent that she is mourned by the majority. The use of words like 'IQ level' and 'lowest common denominator in the society' demonstrates that producers consider themselves more knowledgeable than and superior to their audiences. Their assignation of stereotypes such as *dumbness*, *low IQ*, *confined to kitchen* and *easily manipulated* clarifies producers' perceptions of housewives of a certain class. By and large, the producers perceive that women who are typical housewives form the core group of their audiences. Gone are the days when a minority could afford television, and therefore television producers understand themselves as having dumbed down in their content to cater to the lowest common denominator, seen as 'ordinary housewives'. Such opinions about the audience also emerge as an excuse for producing content that producers do not consider to be of a high standard. The tone and responses of the producers are condescending towards their viewership, with an explicit idea that housewives are not as informed or as knowledgeable as the producers. This idea is reinforced by representations of women on television that assign naivety to housewives in narrative forms. The derogatory connotation attached to the concept of a housewife, however, is also class-specific. Breakfast shows in particular are more popular among the lower-income groups such as SEC (socioeconomic groups) C, D and E.[11]

Ratings and gendered content

Since ratings obtained from Media Logic provide the producers with information about age, education, profession, class and ethnicity, the data can directly impact upon producers' perception of their audiences. This section attempts to understand the importance of ratings for producers and content, and the pressures they bring for those who are working in the media industry at any level. Content in general (across interactive and narrative genre), and the content of breakfast shows in particular, depends upon the system of ratings. Rumaisa Khan described how the content of breakfast shows was driven by trends in ratings:

> Daily themes on the show were mostly dictated from above by the CEO of the channel. The issue of thalassemia is close to his heart, so we run shows on it, and weddings. Wedding week [which includes weddings of victims of gendered crimes] is the essential feature of the morning shows, and it is when you gain maximum ratings for any show. Ratings have definitely told us one thing that women crave for wedding scenes whether it is in drama serial or in breakfast shows . . . We also started bringing on fake victims of domestic politics just to give a boost to our ratings, and the formula clicked.[12]

Wedding seasons run on all breakfast shows, with the programmes used to show weddings of the under-privileged such as victims of burns and girls living in shelter homes. The broadcasters and sponsors bear the expenses of these weddings. Khan reveals that most of the time the CEO dictates the themes and that this can even be a last-minute thing, where the CEO gives a directive on the topic of the show. From Khan's description of the situation, it seems the last-minute directive implies undue stress and uncertainty for the production team. She also raises the issue of running fake stories on domestic politics, which became one of the main reasons for her leaving the show.[13] Khan is not the only one to openly express her reservations over the central issue of trivialising content; a few other hosts admit that they are doing it for the sake of ratings while others alienate themselves from the practice, saying that this is common in the industry but they have not fallen for this trend. However, Fatika Ali, a morning-show host, highlights how ratings directly affect the issue of experimenting with themes in her shows:

> Because of ratings, we compromise on quality . . . Ratings bring the anchors into a lot of stress, it can even ruin their family lives, and it has done so in the past, we have examples.

There have been three cases of breakfast-show hosts being divorced. Ali also expresses her fear of reaching a point where her home life becomes disturbed due to the pressures of her show (mainly referring to survival in a competitive market). Ali, who was, at the time of the interview, a new entrant as an anchor for the morning show, defends her position, saying that she is open to bringing forth a few fake cases as it serves the purpose of highlighting an issue and hooks the audiences, which gives her show ratings. At a later point in the interview, she suggests that as a new entrant she compromises on the quality of the content but once she is more settled in her job she may dictate the content without worrying about ratings.

Another ethical issue in these shows occurs where hosts show the faces of real-life victims of gendered crimes rather than blurring them, especially in actual cases of rape, where victims unveil their faces. Producers encourage this practice in the name of drawing more ratings. Fatika Ali mentions:

> It is true that responsibility should lie with the broadcaster but we have to sell our product too, we do get selfish at times [showing actual rape victims' faces] to get ratings. We are in a market, we have to sell too ... it is a mixture of everything.

This approach towards drawing ratings, whereby hosts invite victims of gender abuse on shows with an apparent intention to facilitate the work of the law-enforcing authorities and courts to ensure speedy trials and to raise viewers' awareness of such issues, raises ethical concerns. But it emerges that despite willingness to produce something of social relevance, they are *more* (if not entirely) committed to drawing ratings, or, in other words, protecting their jobs. Imran Aziz, producer and content head of a popular crime show, defends the practice of unveiling rape victims' faces in this way:

> If there is a woman who wants to show her face, and feels that showing [her] face wouldn't affect her or would instead give her protection then we shall show her face. . . . But there is another angle to it, there is a huge difference in print and electronic media; unless you show the face, you wouldn't have the same impact you wanted for the show ... showing faces; yes, for us it is also about ratings too.

Aziz defends his strategy by stating that at times the issue is not primarily about ratings; rather, showing her face can also protect the victim's life, and many victims have sought legal protection through his show. He also draws attention to the different attributes of audiences for different media. Perhaps the point he is making is that the viewers want to see, more than they want to hear or read the ticker/crawler on screen. Victims can also suffer unduly for reporting and unveiling, however. For example, Kainat Soomro is a rape victim who has faced challenges in this regard.[14] Soomro reported her rape in the media and her story was later covered in detail by *Geo Hina Kay Sath* (Live with Hina, a social issue-based talk show); her family faced the consequences of reporting her ordeal when their elder son was murdered by the perpetrators.

The issue of ratings was followed through in interviews with those on the sales and marketing side of production. Farhan Aleem, senior director of marketing for a major channel, explains that their methodology is ratings-driven and that the department of marketing and sales directly influence content for this purpose:

> In terms of content, [the show] may be of social value, but the content does not have the factor or something that our advertisers need. We measure the efficiency of any software with revenue as well as rating; if we do see high ratings, then we increase the rates for this slot ... but this is debatable: we take our points to the table and the content side brings their points.

On *Geo Hina Kay Sath*, using a single topic (gender abuse, HIV, gay rights, marriage and divorce), the host introduced victims/sufferers with the intention to facilitate their reassimilation into society. Each case was taken before a panel of experts (mostly lawyers, doctors, religious scholars and activists) who then offered live counselling to the victim. *Geo Hina Kay Sath* was successful not only in creating debates, but also in facilitating the system on the ground for speedier trials of perpetrators. This format, with an underlying agenda to create debate/discussion and make citizens aware of gender issues in Pakistani society, was pulled from the screen because it lacked the 'sellable' factor.[15] On the basis of textual analysis and interviews with the host of this show, Hina Bayat Khwaja, I argue that this show was somewhat different from breakfast shows in its treatment of gender issues. Without sensationalising specific cases, it focused on the broader issue/topic (such as rape), but that did not deliver ratings. According to the host, for the first few years in-studio audiences were invited from different universities to participate in discussions; however, this was changed to paid audiences, and hence the motive for attending changed.

Another factor that impacted upon the ratings for this show was its rescheduling and title change – from *Uljhan Suljhan* (Problem Solution) to *Geo Hina Kay Sath*. The sales and marketing departments directly influence the scheduling of shows because their clients (sponsors) closely observe how scheduling impacts on the sales of their products. The marketing and sales team for any channel often influences decisions in the selection of the content, but if the creative side of the content is confident about delivering ratings, the marketing department does not intervene in the selection. In this way, commercial broadcasters allow interactive genres to use their air-time to seek protection for the victims of gendered violence, but in a way that engages consumers as well. In this scenario, the veiling and unveiling of rape victims becomes a 'selling factor' for commercial broadcasters. Addressing gender issues in society becomes synonymous with issues that are more profitable to address. The practice of unveiling rape victims sensationalises a case and the focus inevitably switches from the social issue to an individual's ordeal. Moreover, it limits the scope of the discussion; instead of revisiting the plight of women in society, it becomes a discussion of the plight of an individual who needs sympathy. In an already conservative society where women('s bodies) are considered to be repositories of honour, sensationalising the stories of rape victims through unveiling can further reinforce the public/private binary, with victims choosing not to report. It also raises questions about the limitations faced by a newly emerging public sphere in a commercial industry.

I move on, now, to assess the influence of religion on this content.

Television production as protective and empowering?

Despite producing for a ratings-driven market, gendered content such as that described above does highlight the plight of women in Pakistani society, raises awareness of legal rights and, by getting in touch with the law-enforcing agencies and lawyers, facilitates the system on the ground. Interactive shows in particular offer their platform to highlight individual cases. Usually, victims approach such formats to seek protection or contact with NGOs (such as the Sarim Burney Trust and Madadgar) or law-enforcing agencies. I refer to such content as 'emancipatory' or 'empowering' for women who live in a conservative society. Are there motivations/ interests beyond the commercial in producing emancipatory (real-life) content?

The director of a major Pakistani breakfast show discussed the need for such content:

> There are times when we want to do something serious on gender-based issues … For example, we had a victim on our show who was raped by a Member of National Assembly's son and she was facing some issues with FIR.[16] We followed the case on our show and it helped. But at the moment, I hardly see any agenda for emancipation; it is more of a competition for better ratings. At times, we also work closely with the Sarim Burney Welfare Trust that brings its cases in our shows and we try to facilitate the legal process with media coverage. There was a 3-year-old girl who was abandoned by her parents, and she was brought on our show by Sarim Burney and was later adopted by someone on another breakfast show. We also sponsor weddings for acid victims on our shows.

Popular demand may be one of the reasons here, but an intention to do something for society is clearly apparent in this director's reply. For gender issues it renders a *space for coordination* between the victims, NGOs and law-enforcing agencies, while on the other hand it informs viewers about gendered crimes in society. This dimension of such content in breakfast shows has the potential to give confidence to those who want to seek justice and can function to allow victims and marginalised groups to share a platform with politicians, lawyers and activists working on the ground for justice.

This practice on different interactive programmes has familiarised viewers with the trend of watching politicians, activists and law-enforcing agencies sharing a platform with victims from lower classes. As television diversified in genres with private channels, viewers from all classes were able to voice their opinions on this medium. Their presence and their ability to express their views or even share their ordeals show impulses of empowerment on-screen, even bridging the gap between different classes. Television, in this way, becomes a melting pot where viewers from the working class can watch the inside stories of the elite class in drama serials, while viewers from privileged classes get to know about the lives of the working class not only through drama serials but also in interactive genres. More importantly, it opens up a 'mediated public sphere' for debate on gender issues.

Most of the hosts I interviewed are conscious of their limitations in furthering an emancipatory agenda, in contrast to Reema Hasan, a breakfast-show host, who believes that she is a feminist and is determined to help victims of gendered crimes through her show:[17]

> I am a feminist and if rights of any individuals are violated on the basis of her gender, I raise voice for them. I do believe that woman is a weaker sex, legally,

socially, religiously and economically. Woman is weak in our society and I admit to it, I don't want any woman to get exploited on this premise.

This interviewee was the only host who was vocal on her position as a feminist with a clear intention of helping women. Her assertion that 'woman is a weaker sex legally, socially, religiously and economically' has its roots in the concept of *sinf-e-nazuk*, a term used in the national language to refer to women as the weaker sex. According to the religious texts, men are considered to be a degree superior to women (see for example the Holy Quran, chapter 2, verse 228). However, there are issues with such an approach towards feminism, which treats women as a degree lesser than men or as subservient to the male members of the family, an idea rooted in *Shariah*. In fact, Pakistani television culture actively engages in this particular form of feminism that finds answers to the problems of women within the paradigm of religion. In this way, the possibility of finding discourses other than religion has become almost impossible in interactive genres. This discourse on feminism becomes restrictive in that women struggling for identity have only one possible route available to them. In this perspective, a woman does not struggle to define herself as an individual or to find agency; rather, she ends up defining herself as a Muslim woman, where her identity as a Muslim comes a long way before her identity as an individual seeking equal rights with men. This raises the question of whether women are consciously seeking to reclaim their position as Muslim women, or rather have no other possible discourses to choose from. As talk shows are mostly driven by therapeutic and emotional conversation, they mostly thrive on religion-based solutions that operate within such realms (see for example Shattuc, 1997). This tendency suggests that such discussions on these shows are merely about reordering the roles of women within the home; on the one hand, they pull them into the public sphere, while on the other they are pushed back into the domain of the private, with a set of other roles assigned by religion. Though this feminist host's show also offers a space for the facilitation of gendered abuse cases, especially those of rape and other sexual abuse, usually there is no serious discussion on the status of women in Pakistani society; rather, it focuses on specific cases. Whether or not the discussion really opens up society for debates on domestic violence remains questionable. The discussion does not go as far as to strengthen the civil and social dimensions of female citizenship. I argue that the individualised case-based approach may be the first step towards breaking silence on gender-based issues in society, but that it detracts from the sociopolitical relevance of these issues (for a similar discussion on representation/discourses of prostitutes on TV, see McLaughlin, 1991).

The anchors of morning shows are conscious of their limitations in furthering an emancipatory agenda, but Reema Hasan stresses that her viewers 'bring their personal matters onto the show not only to seek justice, but all for the fact that their plight can become eye-opening for others'. Moreover, she describes how, through her show, political parties such as Mutahidda Qaumi Movement (MQM), the local party, get involved in seeking justice for rape victims. Only recently, Hasan highlighted the case of school van drivers sexually abusing young girls. For her, the question in such cases is: 'Have my viewers become cautious or not? If I have moved them, it is enough.' Her show's format, however, is not as serious as that of a previous show she hosted. Despite the existence of several other shows that dedicate specific space to gender issues, I cannot find another programme dedicated entirely to 'women-based crimes' which treats them in a manner as seriously as this show did. To this observation of mine, Hasan replies: 'See, channels cannot afford to run formats as serious like [the show] because many times influential names are behind such crimes and that get can risky for all involved in production.'[18]

This opens an interesting line of inquiry that is directly linked to the political culture in Pakistan. Reporting crime is one thing, and perhaps not as risky as probing the individual cases of victims on these shows. Often, in cases related to rape and other gendered crimes, perpetrators belong to influential families with a background in politics. This can land anchors in trouble, and the broadcasters are not willing to take risks. Even if the anchors are willing to take up the cases, politicians avoid commenting on cases that fall into the constituencies of their colleagues. I have examined this phenomenon in another study where I discuss the absence of gender issues in current affairs-based talk shows (Cheema, 2014).

Although it is commercially viable, the most popular religion-based talk show's host also expresses his clear agenda for empowering women through his shows. Mohsin Ahmad (ex-Minister Religious Affairs and now president of a major channel) describes his agenda in this manner:

> Gender discrimination is there in our society and has to be addressed and it is true that I fight the case for miserable women of our society, but I fight for those who need my support, I do not fight for the women who run NGOs. I fight for those who live in remote areas of Pakistan or those who are victims within their homes, who are unheard of anywhere, and I do not fight like women who are funded by foreign NGOs and who further Western agendas.

While Ahmad, through his writings and speeches, has always been vocal in disassociating himself from liberal feminist expressions in society, he has asserted his position as a brother in Islam to all Muslim women fighting for their place within the home. Moreover, the connotation he attributes to gender issues refers to women only. Invariably, all these genres and talk shows (whether therapeutic or in-studio audience-based) refer to issues related to gender as issues related to women, but the realities on the ground are also harsh to LGBT people in Pakistani society. For instance, homosexuals are not acknowledged as 'normal' people or even as a variant of the norm, and they do not have any official representation in the public sphere. The mediated public sphere, in general, is polarised between liberal women activists and conservative women activists fighting for their respective agendas on emancipating women. The media plays a role in reinforcing this polarity, where liberal women activists are represented as non-*purdah*-observing women with a Western outlook (see for example Mumtaz, 2005: 65–8). Liberal women activists have a limited presence on current affairs-based talk shows on English media, such as *Dawn TV* (see for example Talib and Idrees, 2012).

It is apparent that interactive genres are colonised by religion, where gender and sexuality remain the two plains on which to fight the battle of emancipation. Among the talk shows, the religion-based ones present some unprecedented trends in ratings; as a platform, such shows offer inoffensive, acceptable and rather popular resolutions to gender issues.[19] For Ahmad, his platform means more than just ratings for his programme; he has a huge fan following, with which he can influence public opinion. In this struggle to create a pressure group to challenge the government or to engage with policies, Ahmad's programme has been significant in pushing policies and in some cases facilitating the judiciary through moral policing. His show has played a crucial role in the case of identifying the graveyards of victims of honour killings (*Karo Kari*).

> There have been instances where our show has also facilitated the judicial process . . . we identified eight graveyards of *Karo Kari* victims [so-called honour killing victims], which were then taken under government custody. People can now go and recite *fatiha* [prayer] for the deceased, and it is no longer treated as a graveyard for the outcasts. In such cases, I get involved personally and follow it up with the government and on my shows to facilitate the process.[20]

Unlike other hosts, Ahmad has also been a Minister, as well as managing director of one of the leading channels; this places him in a position where he can work hand-in-hand with other officials. Usually, murder in the name of honour takes place within rural areas where feudal system/practices define the social fabric, and even religion becomes irrelevant in such areas. Therefore, there is simply no question of accommodating the law of the state. Interestingly, many feudal lords are members of different political parties; therefore, other members do not take initiatives against such practices. It was only when Musharraf (who belongs to the urban middle class, with no rural/feudal roots) was in power that Ahmad could utilise his platform to identify eight graveyards for the victims of so-called honour killings.

One concern that resurfaced through all the discussions around women's empowerment was that religion seems to be an elitist discourse that cannot be revisited by anyone, not even the clergy; therefore, anything that has been defined within *Shariah* cannot be retranslated in any other idiom. The president of one of the main channels explains how his channel ran a campaign on the Women's Empowerment Bill:

> We ran a campaign for more than one year, where the entire spectrum of clergy were taken on board before taking the Women's Empowerment Bill to the parliament. This way, media are facilitating consensus policies. I would not say that there is any such thing as Talibani environment in Pakistan as long as you do not step in their area [Blasphemy].[21]

Haseeb Alam, the business unit head of this channel, describes such a situation in a similar vein: 'we can contribute in changing the society but society is driven by many other external factors. We are living in a very extraordinary situation. State of fear is heightened ... can't discuss religion, these interest groups are the strongest!' By interest groups, Alam of course means religion-based pressure groups and factions that, time and again, assert their power in issues related to blasphemy. This issue cannot be seen in isolation; in fact, after a series of instances in which rage and anger have been expressed in the name of religion, society in general, and the television space in particular, have become cautious regarding issues that have recently become off-limits. Only recently (May 2014), a morning show was suspended on charges of blasphemy; the case is still in the courts.[22] This is not just a problem for creative producers in the industry; religious scholars are not exempted from the strict laws on blasphemy either. Javed Ahmed Ghamidi, a renowned Islamic scholar, has been forced to leave the country and is now seeking asylum in Malaysia.[23] His speeches and talks have become controversial for his position on apostasy and etiquettes for socialisation between men and women (popularly known as *Mard o Zan ka ikhti-laat*).[24] I argue that producing gendered television in an environment where pressure groups (such as clergy, state and the political elites) are so powerful can be very stressful for the broadcasters. In this context, producers such as Hasan and Aamir Ahmad must produce 'safe' content that does not clash with the views of any of the pressure groups.

Conclusion

This chapter finds that the television industry in Pakistan is similar to the media industries considered by Todd Gitlin (1985) and Baker and Hesmondhalgh (2011), in the sense that the commercial imperatives involved in production are more powerful than producers' grounding in ethics and their sense of social commitment. This is due to the fact that these workers lack job security and depend upon and are anxious about ratings. Yet, I argue that the ratings cannot be abstracted from the society. For example, if content around domestic politics, gendered crime or victims' weddings has better purchase, it is because these themes directly speak to the status of women in Pakistani society. The findings also inform us about how the image of a housewife is constructed in Pakistani television culture. Some producers stereotype women as naïve, ignorant and also separated from the public sphere. There is no apparent interest in either perceiving these women as intelligent (not stereotypical) or producing for women other than these (liberal or working women). Therefore, producers' perceptions become a basis for reproducing a typical kind of gendered content that, while raising gender issues, also finds the resolution of all issues in Islam.

In conclusion, I revisit the concept of the feminist public sphere and recap how this study intervenes into those debates. Feminists such as Benhabib (1992), Landes (1998) and Fraser (1990) argue that ideally, publics should arrive at common ground through discursive contestation and unconstrained discourse. The mediated public sphere in Pakistan allows limited space for unconstrained discourse. In stratified societies, the idea of the common good is also achieved through different routes. For example, it is not only about discursive contestation, but also about the issues that are reported in the mainstream news and the frequency of their reporting. Gendered crimes such as rape and honour killings have become matters of common concern through their excessive coverage across different media and different genres, for instance, but homosexuality, or whether hijab is mandatory for women, have not.

Based on the findings of this research, the kind of public sphere mobilised by these 'interactive genres' should be read in terms of a conservative feminist public sphere that is not democratic in its laws. Not all matters related to morality and sexuality can be debated freely; the logic of exclusion still operates. The project of media liberalisation has been colonised not only by commercial motives but also by religious pressure groups. These stakeholders are using the television industry for their own good. As long as the interests of religious pressure groups do not clash with the commercial interests of the media industry, they do not intervene in freedom of expression. In this sense, freedom of expression has limited scope; any expression or issue that either falls into the realm of 'blasphemy' or contests mainstream Islamic thought struggles to feature on television.

Nevertheless, the interactive genres discussed here have played a crucial role in facilitating the bureaucratic system on the ground for speedier trials (in the case of identifying graves of honour victims), building a consensus on policies (Women's Empowerment Bill) and also coordinating with civil society for the reassimilation of victims of gender abuse. It seems that it is almost inconceivable to openly challenge the hegemonic (*Shariah*-compliant) ideal of feminism and empowerment for women. At the same time, the shift described marks a transition from endorsement of culturally mandated roles of women to that of a role that is regulated as well-disciplined under *Shariah*. In this way, any project for empowerment turns into a project of disciplining women within Islam, even though, despite the pressures, television workers do try to work on projects of social value. No matter how constrained, and yet commercially viable, it may appear, the Pakistani television landscape creates partial public spheres.

Notes

1 *Dupatta* is a stole 2.5 metres long worn with the national dress. There is general acknowledgement of a broadcasting policy under which women are supposed to cover their heads on-screen. Although people refer to this policy in the industry, no one at PTV could provide me with an official document about this policy.
2 Gallup follows a diary-based system, while Media Logic operates through people-meters installed in homes across different socio-economic classes.
3 Years are drawn from Wikipedia, as no official records are available, but see: Aftab Associates (1994) 'A qualitative evaluation of the impact of "Nijaat" (a social drama) in the rural vicinity of Lahore', https://idl-bnc.idrc.ca/dspace/bitstream/10625/29143/1/123556. pdf (Last accessed 14 April 2016), p. 2; *Aahat*: Top Entity (n.d), www.topentity.com/sania-saeed/ (Last accessed 15 April 2016).
4 In the pre-liberalisation era, Pakistani television raised issues of family planning, narcotics and AIDS, but would not go so far as to highlight controversial issues in relation to gender. Similarly, the genres on PTV that highlighted these issues were either drama serials or tele-awareness campaigns on family planning, which would run for five minutes before the news.

5 This footnote explains some of the terms used here to describe family relations in Pakistan. Marriage to the Quran is also known as *Haq Bakhshish*. Women in rural Sindh can be married to the Quran, that is, they spend their life reading and memorising the Quran, rather than being married to a prospective groom of some other tribe. It is a common practice in rural Sindh to deny women the right of marriage outside their tribe. Usually male members of the family, especially brothers, force their sisters into such arrangements to retain their share in the family property that they acquire through law of inheritance. *Karo kari*, an expression that means 'black man, black woman', is used to describe couples engaged in illicit relations (cited in Pope, 2012: 22). '*Joint Family System* (JFS) comprises two or more nuclear families that form a corporate economic unit' (Levinson, Malone and Brown, 1980, quoted in Taqui, Itrat, Quadri 2007). In the case of Pakistan, *Joint Family System* refers to an arrangement of living where elderly parents live with their children and their children's families.

6 The chapter emerges from a wider project that uses a multi-method approach (textual analysis, interviews with the producers and focus groups with the viewers) to understand the production and reception of gender-based content in Pakistani television culture across interactive and narrative forms of television. The data used in this chapter includes extracts from eleven of forty-two interviews with practitioners whose work defines interactive content.

7 This study does not look at game shows. I use the term 'interactive' (a) to juxtapose the genre with narrative forms and (b) because these shows are not simply talk shows with identical formats.

8 See for example 'Pakistan ranks third on the list of most dangerous countries for women', (2011) *Express Tribune*, 15 June, http://tribune.com.pk/story/189294/pakistan-ranks-3rd-on-list-of-most-dangerous-countries-for-women/ (Last accessed 7 January 2015).

9 Because these issues are considered as prohibited under *Shariah*.

10 In Pakistan, ratings produced by Media Logic determine the popular tastes of viewers. People-meters placed near the TV set measure what is being viewed, while a handset (similar to a remote) determines who is watching in the room. Each member of the family has an assigned button on the handset which needs to be pressed before one starts watching and clicked again to sign out after watching. Both parts of the people-meter are needed to determine who is watching the channel in terms of demographics (age, sex, profession, education, locality, income). Panel homes are carefully selected by household type, demographics, TV platforms and geography to track their viewing habits.

11 Media Logic's sample audiences across socioeconomic categories (SEC A, B, C, D, E) also confirm this hierarchy.

12 Thalassemia is a genetic blood disorder. The nature of gendered abuse discussed often involved acid cases.

13 Note that domestic politics is different from domestic violence. In the case of domestic politics, the situations that are created on the interactive breakfast shows feature two aggrieved parties, such as mothers-in-law and daughters-in-law or husbands and wives. They bring their matter to these shows and a heated exchange of words takes place between them. It is similar to *The Jerry Springer Show* but varies in the issues and treatment of the topics. However, all the cases of domestic violence are genuine and real women approach these spaces to seek protection. This project is particularly interested in genuine/real cases.

14 Crilly, R. (2010) 'Pakistan's rape victim who dared to fight back', *Telegraph*, 26 December, www.telegraph.co.uk/news/worldnews/asia/pakistan/8224111/Pakistans-rape-victim-who-dared-to-fight-back.html (Last accessed 1 January 2016). For a similar discussion, also see Minhas, S.F. (2009), 'The politics of rape and honor in Pakistan' in Moorti, S. and Cuklanz, L. (eds) *Local Violence and Global Media: Feminist Analyses of Gendered Representations* (Peter Lang: New York), pp. 74–5. Also see Gabol, I. (2016) 'Lahore-girl who was gang-raped attempts suicide after pressure from prosecution', *Dawn*, 2 January, www.dawn.com/news/1230283 (Last accessed 2 January 2016).

15 I argue this on the basis of textual analysis undertaken for a wider project.
16 A complaint lodged with the police by the victim of a cognisable offence is called a First Information Report or FIR in India, Pakistan and Bangladesh.
17 See for example Walsh, D. (2012) 'For many in Pakistan television show goes too far', *New York Times*, 26 January, www.nytimes.com/2012/01/27/world/asia/for-many-in-pakistan-a-television-show-goes-too-far.html?pagewanted=all&_r=0 (Last accessed 26 July 2014).
18 See for example: Uploaded by Khan, Fawwad (2011) Aurat Khani Id Avi (Last accessed 23 July 2014); uploaded by mqmloveu (2008) 'Pakistan 6 Halala Nikah's of a Mosque Imam's wife', www.youtube.com/watch?v=6n06MaoUD4A (Last accessed 24 July 2014). This last episode features a case of a woman named Shama who was forced six times into *halala*.
19 See for example, Sulaiman, G. (2015) 'Ramzan 2015 ratings: Geo tops the ratings charts with ARY behind', BrandSynario [2 July, www.brandsynario.com/ramadan-ratings-geo-entertainment-tops-the-rating-charts-with-ary-digital-behind/ (Last accessed 2 January 2016).
20 Uploaded by Blissfulcreature (2009) 'Special program on honor killing', www.youtube.com/watch?v=WjsSlqtTskM (Last accessed 23 August 2014).
21 See Javed Ahmed Ghamidi (2012) 'Grand TV debate on Hadood Ordinence – Mufti Muneeb ur Rehman vs Javed Ahmed Ghamidi', www.youtube.com/watch?v=UFwqPu2SI6Q (Last accessed 23 August 2014).
22 See for example Hanif, M. (2012) 'How to commit blasphemy in Pakistan', *Guardian*, www.theguardian.com/world/2012/sep/05/pakistans-blasphemy-laws-colossal-absurdity (Last accessed 2 August 2014); Walsh, D. (2011) 'Islamic scholar attacks Pakistan's blasphemy laws', *Guardian*, www.theguardian.com/world/2011/jan/20/islam-ghamidi-pakistan-blasphemy-laws (Last accessed 14 May 2014). Also see Boone, J. (2014) 'Pakistan Geo News becomes latest target in blasphemy accusation trend', *Guardian*, 22 May, www.theguardian.com/world/2014/may/22/pakistan-geo-news-blasphemy-pakistan-sufi-song-wedding (Last accessed 14 May 2014).
23 See for example Walsh, n. 22.
24 Ghamidi has rearticulated the Verses on Hijab.

Bibliography

Ahmad, S. (2008) 'Identity matters, culture wars: An account of Al-Huda (re)defining identity and reconfiguring culture in Pakistan', *Culture and Religion*, 9(1): 63–80.
Ali, B. (1986) 'Pakistan Television Zia-Junejo Mullah Show', *Economic and Political Weekly*, 21(50): 2171–2.
Ang, I. (1991) 'Stalking the wild viewer', *Continuum*, 4(2): 19–35.
Babar, A. (2008) 'New "social imaginaries": The Al-Huda phenomenon', *South Asia: Journal of South Asian Studies*, 31(2): 348–63.
Baker, S. and D. Hesmondhalgh (2008) 'Creative work and emotional labour in the television industry', *Theory, Culture & Society*, 25(7–8): 97–118.
Baker, S. and D. Hesmondhalgh (2011) *Creative Labour Media Work in Three Cultural Industries*. London and New York: Routledge.
Benhabib, S. (1992) *Situating the Self: Gender, Community and Postmodernism in Contemporary Ethics*. Cambridge: Polity Press.
Butsch, R. (2009) 'Introduction: How are media public spheres?' in R. Butsch (ed.) *Media and Public Spheres*. Basingstoke: Palgrave Macmillan: 1–14.
Byrne, B. (2012) 'Qualitative interviewing' in C. Seale (ed.) *Researching Society and Culture*. 3rd edn. New Delhi, London, Singapore and Thousand Oaks: Sage: 206–26.

Cheema, M. (2014) 'Understanding gender dynamics of current affairs talk shows in Pakistani television industry' in M. Raicheva-Stover and E. Ibroscheva (eds) *Women in Politics and Media: Perspectives from Nations in Transition*. London and New York: Bloomsbury. Kindle edn.

Felski, R. (1989) *Beyond Feminist Aesthetics: Feminist Literature and Social Change*. Cambridge, MA: Harvard University Press.

Fraser, N. (1990) 'Rethinking the public sphere: A contribution to the critique of actually existing democracy', *Social Text*, 25–6: 56–80.

Gitlin, T. (1985) *Inside Prime Time*. New York: Pantheon Books.

Habermas, J. (1989) *The Structural Transformation of the Public Sphere: An Inquiry into a Category of Bourgeois Society*. Oxford: Polity Press.

Habermas, J. (1991) *The Structural Transformation of the Public Sphere: An Inquiry into a Category of Bourgeois Society* (translated by Thomas Burger with the assistance of Frederick Lawrence). Cambridge, MA: MIT Press.

Habermas, J. (2006) 'The public sphere: An encyclopedia article', in D. M. Kellner and M. G. Durham (eds) *Media and Cultural Studies: Keyworks*. 2nd edn. Malden, MA and Oxford: Blackwell: 75–9.

Hartley, J. (1996) *Popular Reality, Journalism, Modernity, Popular Culture*. London and New York: Arnold.

Hesmondhalgh, D. (2006) 'Bourdieu, the media and cultural production', *Media, Culture & Society*, 28 (2): 211–31.

Jhally, S. and B. Livant (1986) 'Watching as working: The valorization of audience consciousness', *Journal of Communication*, 36(3): 124–43.

Klein, B. (2013) 'Entertainment-education for the media-saturated: Audience perspectives on social issues in entertainment programming', *European Journal of Cultural Studies*, 16(1): 43–57.

Kothari, S. (2005) 'From genre to *zanaana*: Urdu television drama serials and women's culture in Pakistan', *Contemporary South Asia*, 14(3): 289–305.

Landes, J. B. (1998) 'The public and the private sphere: A feminist reconsideration' in J. Landes (ed.) *Feminism, the Public and the Private*. Oxford and New York: Oxford University Press: 135–63.

Levinson, D., Malone, M. J. and Brown, C. H. (1980) *Toward Explaining Human Culture: A Critical Review of the Findings of Worldwide Cross-cultural Research*. New Haven, CT: HRAF Press.

Livant, B. (1979). 'The audience commodity', *Canadian Journal of Political and Social Theory*, 3(1): 91–106.

Livingstone, S. and Lunt, P. K. (1994) *Talk on Television Audience Participation and Public Debate*. London and New York: Routledge.

McLaughlin, L. (1991) 'Discourses of prostitution/discourses of sexuality', *Critical Studies in Mass Communication* Special Issue: *Love and Sex*, 8(3): 249–72.

McLaughlin, L. (1993) 'Feminism, the public sphere, media and democracy', *Media, Culture & Society*, 15(4): 599–620.

Maududi, A. A. (2010 [1972]) *Al-Hijab Purdah and the Status of Woman in Islam*. Lahore: Metro Publishers.

Meehan, E. (1984) 'Ratings and the institutional approach: A third answer to the commodity question', *Critical Studies in Mass Communication*, 1(2): 216–25.

Moghissi, H. (2000) *Feminism and Islamic Fundamentalism: The Limits of Postmodern Analysis*. Oxford and New York: Oxford University Press.

Mumtaz, K. (2005) 'Advocacy for an end to poverty, inequality, and insecurity: Feminist social movements in Pakistan', *Gender and Development*, 13(3): 63–9.

Murdock, G. (1978) 'Blindspots about Western Marxism: A reply to Dallas Smythe', *Canadian Journal of Political and Social Theory*, 2(2) (Spring–Summer): 109–19.

Napoli, P. M. (2012) 'Audience evolution and the future of audience research', *International Journal on Media Management*, 14(2): 79–97.

Naqvi, T. H. (2011) 'Private satellite media and the geo-politics of moderation in Pakistan', in S. Banaji (ed.) *South Asian Media Cultures: Audiences, Representations, Contexts*. London: Anthem Press: 109–22.

Nasir, A. (2012) *This is PTV*, Islamabad: Pakistan Television Corporation.

Nazir, S. J. and Pintak, L. (2013) 'Pakistani journalism: At the crossroads of Muslim identity, national priorities and journalistic culture', *Media, Culture & Society*, 35(5): 640–65.

Oakley, A. (1981) 'Interviewing women: A contradiction in terms', in H. Robert (ed.) *Doing Feminist Research*. London: Routledge: 30–61.

'Pakistan ranks third on the list of most dangerous countries for women' (2011) *Express Tribune* [Online], *15* June, available on: http://tribune.com.pk/story/189294/pakistan-ranks-3rd-on-list-of-most-dangerous-countries-for-women/ (Last accessed 7 January 2015).

Pope, N. (2012) *Honor Killings in the Twenty First Century*, New York: Palgrave Macmillan.

Proffitt, J. M. and Rasul, A. (2013) 'Diversity or homogeny: Concentration of ownership and media diversity in Pakistan', *Asian Journal of Communication*, 23(6): 590–604.

Shaheed, F. (2010) 'Contested identities, gendered politics, gendered religion in Pakistan', *Third World Quarterly*, 31(6): 851–67.

Shattuc, M. J. (1997) *The Talking Cure: TV Talk Shows and Women*, London and New York: London.

Skornia, H. J. (1965) *Television and Society*, New York, London, Sydney and Toronto: McGraw-Hill.

Smythe, D. (1977) 'Communications: Blind spot of Western Marxism', *Canadian Journal of Political and Social Theory*, 1(3) (Fall/Autumn): 1–27.

Suleman, S. (1990) 'Representation of gender in prime-time television: A textual analysis of drama series of Pakistani television', PhD Thesis, University of Wisconsin-Madison.

Talib, S. and Idrees, Z. (2012) 'Pakistani media and disempowerment of women', in J. Campbell and T. Carilli (eds) *Challenging Images of Women in the Media: Reinventing Women's Lives*, Lanham, MD: Lexington Books. Kindle edn.

Taqui, A. M., Itrat, A., Qidwai, W. and Qadri, Z. (2007) 'Depression in the elderly: Does family system play a role? A cross-sectional study', *BMC Psychiatry*, 7(57): 1–12.

Walford, G. (2007) 'Classification and framing of interviews in ethnographic interviewing', *Ethnography and Education* 2(2): 145–57.

Zia, A. (2007) 'Effects of cable television on women in Pakistan: A comparative study of light and heavy viewers in Lahore', PhD Thesis, Lahore College for Women University, Punjab.

PART IV

Women and the home

11

TELEVISION IN THE IDEAL HOME

Helen Wheatley

The large-scale public exhibition in mid-twentieth-century Britain was a significant site for the demonstration of television; for many visitors, their encounter with television at exhibitions such as the National Radio Show or Radiolympia (1926–65), the Festival of Britain (1951) and the Ideal Home Exhibition (1908–) was their first. John Hartley, describing television's position as a 'popular attraction associated with crowds, spectacle, urban activity, technology and modernization' and its centrality in the 'mid-century passion for spectacular national self-aggrandizement . . . and for the public display of industrial innovation as the aesthetic of the age' (1999: 75), captures some of the excitement surrounding television at these exhibitions, and contextualises the display of television within broader exhibition practices of the time. At these sites, television was imagined as the pinnacle of domestic modernity. It was shown to be both a tool of and a reward for the housewife with new domestic responsibilities (but also more leisure time thanks to a bevy of labour-saving technologies in the rapidly shifting site of the British home). Television at the mid-century exhibition was thus presented as a spectacle of light, sound and colour, a thoroughly modern technology providing leisure and pleasure, often for a specifically female audience.

A number of feminist media historians have argued that capturing the female audience, and persuading women of the absolute necessity of television, was central to the development and take-up of the medium in the mid-twentieth-century UK (e.g. Thumim, 2004; Moseley, Wheatley and Wood, 2014). Janet Thumim suggests, for example, that

> [t]he engagement of the female audience was . . . central to at least two aspects of the emergent institution: women's support was assumed to be crucial in embedding habits of viewing into domestic routines, and the majority of early advertising was for small domestic consumables typically purchased by

women – items such as soap powders, convenience foods, and the plethora of new appliances coming to the domestic market in the later 1950s.

(2004: 25)

The exhibitions at the heart of this chapter were key, then, in underscoring this gendered address: they simultaneously demonstrated the technological development of television in Britain, highlighting television's spectacular qualities and its relationship to other non-domestic forms of entertainment (film, theatre, vaudeville, live musical and dance performance and the variety show), and explored the ways in which television might be understood as a domestic technology and how it could, or should, be integrated into the home. Thus television was presented as one among a number of other new appliances in the 'modern' home from the 1930s onwards. While Brian Winston asserts that 'barely 2,000 sets' were sold in the first year of television broadcast in the UK (1998: 112), it was reported in the *Ideal Home* magazine in November 1937 that a further 5,000 people had seen television in the past year at 'Radiolympia, or the Science Museum at Kensington, or in a shop or a friend's home' (Anon., 1937), making the large-scale public exhibition (Radiolympia in this case) one of the key locations for first encounters with television right from the outset of regular broadcasting in the UK. As I have argued elsewhere (Wheatley, 2016), the mid-century exhibition is thus an important, and largely overlooked, site in the history of British television, as it is in the US and beyond.[1]

This chapter focuses largely on the place of television at the Ideal Home Exhibition in the mid-twentieth century, particularly in the two decades that followed the re-start of the exhibition after the Second World War.[2] This exhibition has run annually at either the Olympia exhibition centre or at Earl's Court in London since 1908 up to the present day.[3] Its aims have remained constant throughout the twentieth and twenty-first centuries: to bring together the consumer goods and advice needed to construct the 'ideal home', focusing on food and cookery, furniture and decoration, showcasing both the latest inventions for the modern house, including evolving media technologies, and the latest housing designs (the centrepieces of each exhibition are model show-homes built inside these vast exhibition spaces). Television appeared at the Ideal Home Exhibition in a variety of ways during the mid-twentieth century, beginning in 1930 when the first television advertisement (for the Baird Company) appeared in the Ideal Home Exhibition catalogue. Initially, the medium was primarily brought to the exhibition by set manufacturers wishing to demonstrate their wares to those who controlled the domestic purse, but from 1956 ITV, and later the BBC, also had their own (often rather elaborate) displays at this annual exhibition, addressing potential viewers and placing each company's provision of programming firmly on display. This chapter is thus concerned with the ways in which the female consumer-citizen, as the figure at the centre of the ideal home, was targeted by broadcasters and set manufacturers alike through the complex and varied television exhibits of the mid-century exhibition. The spectacular nature of television's role at the exhibition in the postwar period can be understood in relation to theories of domestic modernity, and the ways in which modernity was lived, expressed and imagined in the private worlds of women.

This historical analysis thus draws on research conducted at the Ideal Home Exhibition archive, the British Pathé newsreel archive which covers the exhibition over successive years and the extensive files of the BBC's Publicity Department, to outline the significance of the public exhibition in tracing a history of television as a domestic object and analysing the place of television as it was presented as a gendered technology in both 'ideal' and 'future' homes.[4]

'All that is going in this very wonderful modern world': domestic modernity at the Ideal Home Exhibition

In her work on the history of the department store, Mica Nava has documented the significance of these stores in our understanding of modernity. According to Nava, 'department stores were more than just places where merchandise was bought and sold' (1997: 66); she argues that

> [t]hey formed part of the huge expansion of public space and spectacle [in the late nineteenth and early twentieth centuries, and] provided an extraordinary range of facilities, entertainments and visual pleasures . . . Visiting the stores during this period became then an excursion, an exciting adventure in the phantasmagoria of urban landscape.
>
> *(ibid.: 71)*

Similarly, David Chaney refers to department stores as functioning as 'female leisure centres' in the early twentieth century (1983: 24). The department store, like the large-scale public exhibitions at the centre of this analysis, provided a spectacular display of modernism, a 'playhouse' or 'phantasmagoria' in which the female consumer in particular might take pleasure in an encounter with all that was new and modern. This depiction of the department store as a site of spectacular leisure for the twentieth-century *flâneuse* is significant, alongside the work of others such as Penny Sparke (1995) and Judy Giles (2004), in challenging the absence of women and women's culture from histories of modernism. As Sparke has argued, 'The masculine experience of modernity dominated and eclipsed its feminine equivalent [in histories of modernism], rendering the latter trivial and marginal' (1995: 4). Contra to this, Giles develops the notion of 'domestic modernity' to refer to 'the ways in which women negotiated and understood experience and identities in terms of the complex changes that modernisation provoked in the so called private sphere' (2004: 6).

While the public spectacles of domestic modernity at the Ideal Home Exhibition are discussed at greater length below, it is clear here that in the immediate postwar period, the exhibition (like the department store) was an important site for addressing the female consumer as key proponent of domestic modernity; the exhibition thus acted as a site which the 'housewife-*flâneuse*' navigated partly as a consumer in search of the objects and technologies needed to complete her 'ideal home'. This both acknowledges her role in the reconstruction of the postwar home following a period of austerity and, for many in London at least, wartime bomb-damage to property, as well as a sense of increased leisurely mobility and freedom for women in the postwar era. Deborah Ryan's work on the Ideal Home Exhibition (1997) has shown that the exhibition in this period was very much tailored to this aspirational female visitor, confirming Judy Giles' proposal that

> The discourse of technological and scientific progress [of domestic modernity] offered the idea of a 'better' material life, symbolised in the post-Second World War figure of the housewife in her newly built, labour-saving council house freed from disease and want.
>
> *(2004: 50)*

In wartime and in the postwar decade in Britain, the notion of the ideal home became all the more pressing during a period of national reconstruction. For example, according to Harriet Atkinson, anxieties about declining birth rates and family stability were discernible

> in the 1944 Dudley Report [The Design of Dwellings], which focused on producing ideal family environments, consulting women as housewives and mothers on how these new homes should be designed, concluding that improved conditions would be important in promoting 'family life' and encouraging families to grow.
>
> *(2012: 159–60)*

While Atkinson's work traces this rhetoric of 'domestic idealism' in the exhibits of the Festival of Britain, the ideal home of the Ideal Home Exhibition took on an even greater resonance in the period of postwar reconstruction. This exhibition, which, as Giles notes, catered mainly for 'the emerging lower middle class, those for whom home ownership was becoming a very real possibility and who, it was believed, required guidance in the purchase of labour-saving domestic appliances and the creation of a home' (2004: 109), focused on the postwar reconstruction of 'ordinary' homes and families, rather than the more affluent middle classes who were reached by the displays at the Festival of Britain.

As well as offering practical advice about domestic labour-saving and the ideal design of postwar housing, the Ideal Home Exhibition picked up a focus on domestic entertainments that had been present in the exhibition from a much earlier period. The piano, the gramophone and, later, the radio had all previously been placed at the centre of home entertainment at the Ideal Home Exhibition; in the 1930 catalogue, for example, Captain J.W. Barber CBE wrote, in an article entitled 'Radio in the Ideal Home', that

> To-day the wise wife offers to her menfolk a theatre in the sitting room, she is able to bring to their minds, via the ear gate, the best plays, the best concerts, the best dramatic recitals, the best music that the Country and the Continent have to offer. Radio then, to my mind, is a woman's interest and will be increasingly so.
>
> *(p. 25)*[5]

From the mid-1930s, television was also included in the exhibition, albeit as an interesting novelty; however, by the return of the exhibition following the end of the war in 1947, television was increasingly situated at the centre of domestic leisure time for women and for the family more broadly, and its position at the exhibition shifted accordingly. Jonathan Harmsworth (Viscount Rothermere), head of the *Daily Mail* – the publication that established and sponsored the Ideal Home Exhibition until 2009 – wrote in the catalogue foreword of the first postwar exhibition in 1947:

> We in these islands have known a too long protracted era of domestic drabness and drudgery; it should be our determination that the homes of the future shall be a joy to the men and women who create them – and to the children who grow up in them.[6]

Television was therefore to play an important part in breaking up this 'domestic drabness and drudgery' at the Ideal Home Exhibition. In this year, television was situated in the 'Radio and Television' section of the exhibition and its catalogue, positioned as an item of luxury entertainment, but an aspirational consumable not yet in reach for many homes. For example, the copy by W.C. Steele in the 1947 catalogue on this section trails the Baird Grosvenor model excitedly: 'Certainly, for the sake of interest, you must see the luxury model which gives direct viewing on a screen 22 inches by 19. Destined for hotels and clubs, it is a marvel of 1947.'[7] This set, which combined a television screen with an auto-tuning eleven-band radio, a disc recording device to record radio programmes and a gramophone, was thus the height of aspirational luxury but not yet a ubiquitous domestic appliance (given that it was marketed towards installation in public, not domestic, contexts).

However, following the re-launch of the exhibition in 1947, television quite quickly began to be positioned as integral to the postwar home, and thus its position and presentation at the exhibition shifted. While the Ideal Home Exhibition, with its address to lower middle-class women, did offer advice on products and services that would aid the building of the ideal home in practical terms (rendering the domestic safe, efficient, manageable), it also simultaneously offered the promise of leisure, pleasure and (sometimes affordable) luxury for the family in the exhibitions of the immediately pre- and postwar periods. By 1949, the catalogue announced in its 'Furnishing, Decoration and Radio' section that both radio and television are 'increasingly integral to the home'.[8] This shift from aspirational luxury to integral home entertainment is also tracked in the fact that this catalogue was the first to feature furniture designed around the television set, in the form of the 'Airborne Television Suite', sectional seating designed to 'give perfect views [of the television set] all round'.

Set manufacturers, furniture designers and architects thus all played an integral part in 'normalising' the position of television in the British home via appeal to the 'modern housewife' at the Ideal Home Exhibition; this appeal was seen, for example, in a prewar advertisement for the Marconiphone Television set in the 1938 Ideal Home Exhibition catalogue, which proposed:

> The Ideal Home to-day has Television because to be really up-to-date and to enjoy all that is going in this very wonderful modern world you must have Television. There is no more thrilling entertainment than having your own stage and your own cinema screen in your own home. Think of the exciting events that you are missing – Wimbledon Tennis, Championship fights, the Boat Race, the Lord Mayor's Show, etc. etc. – seeing and hearing them just as they are happening.[9]

Television was thus positioned at the exhibition as a way to connect the public and private sphere, and as a simultaneously contemporary and futuristic technology.[10] It was both being designed into the contemporary home and imagined as a key feature of the home of the future at the precise moment when the nature of the 'ideal home' was being redefined during postwar reconstruction. This was particularly seen in the Ideal Home Exhibition in the aspirational 'homes of tomorrow' which were central to the exhibition in the mid-twentieth century, and which, almost without exception, featured television as an integral part of the 'home of the future's' interior design – from R.A. Duncan's 'Skyscraper Flat' of 1933 to the most famous and 'space-age' of the Ideal Home Exhibition's homes of the future, designed by Alison and Peter Smithson in 1956. For example, the Smithsons' house featured the following:

> The glass panel in one wall with [a] small grill . . . is the combined radio and TV set – colour TV, of course. Anne [the imagined inhabitant of the House of the Future] can switch this on from anywhere in the room, using a small short-wave transmitter with pushbutton controls.[11]

In the home of the future, then, television represented ever-present leisure and pleasure alongside domestic labour, particularly for the housewife, in the style of futuristic modernism: easy, spectacular and present at the touch of a button, sometimes even replacing traditional boundaries between rooms, as in the Smithson house, or replacing windows with a version of television as kind of ambient 'screensaver', as in the 1936 Gooch's of Knightsbridge house which was inspired by the film adaptation of H.G. Wells' *Things to Come* (1936) and had, on a band of wall, an 'animated frieze' of 'phantom clouds and waves, waving trees, clusters of flowers and the like'.[12] Lynn Spigel has explored the popularity of the 'home of the future' exhibit in the postwar period in the US in her work on the 'smart house': 'In both its upper-crust and mass-produced forms, the home of tomorrow was often the subject of women's home magazines [in the US] and was displayed with great fanfare at fairs, exhibitions and department stores' (2005: 406). She goes on to explain that 'During the 1930s and 1940s General Electric and Westinghouse opened model homes for public exhibition and began to use the concept of the home of tomorrow as a way to sell a wondrous array of electric gadgets' (ibid.). In relation to the Ideal Home Exhibition's realisations of the home of tomorrow, television was an important part of this 'wondrous array'.

Beyond these imaginary depictions of television (or versions of technologies similar to television) as central and ubiquitous in homes of the future, the archive of the Ideal Home Exhibition is a good place to look for evidence of when and how television became a feature in the real, contemporary living spaces of Britain's homes which were to be 'managed' by the British housewife. We can look, for example, at where television is placed in the exhibition and its catalogue to discern the terms by which it was understood contemporaneously. In the prewar period, where the piano and gramophone (and even, minimally, the home cinema and other home projection technologies) were treated as the centre of home entertainment at the exhibition, television appears in the Miscellaneous section of the exhibition, a kind of curious oddity. In the 1937 and 1938 exhibitions, television has its own stand, marking the beginning of regular television broadcasting in the UK, and the medium is at this time marketed in the exhibition as a spectacular, special and unusual technology, a grand novelty. The foreword to the 1938 Ideal Home Exhibition catalogue, for example, reports on 'Progress in Television too!'

> Here is a miracle the future effects of which none can adequately foresee . . . It will be fascinating to exercise your judgement upon this great achievement and to speculate about the future in your own home when the world's events are whirled before you at your fireside – in colour!
>
> *(1938: 9)*

Then, in 1939, television is shifted to the Household Services section of the exhibition for the first time, and, in the immediate postwar period, is situated in the home furnishings section (as discussed above). This means that in the space of a decade, television at the exhibition moves swiftly from being an item of miscellany, a hobbyist toy, to a spectacular new and aspirational technology, and then towards being seen as an item of household furniture, an everyday object which has become integrated within the home.

The Ideal Home Exhibition's archive contains albums full of press photographs of the exhibitions in which the placement of the television set within mock living rooms from the late 1940s onwards is shown, thus revealing the ways in which television was positioned in the imagined living spaces of the lower middle classes. In the Berg show-homes of 1949 and 1950 and the Gwen Robbins show-home of 1951, for example, television is present in the living rooms of these houses but set off to the side of the room, not a focal feature but rather an attendant technology, waiting for occasional, rather than constant, viewing; in these houses, the rooms are organised around sources of heat and light instead.[13] While the technology is still not a focal point of the living room in the latter house, it is clear from the British Pathé newsreel footage that covers this exhibit that television was being positioned as a luxury 'for the housewife' at this time. On a shot of the television set, the voice-over announcer addressing a male consumer states: 'If you want all the fittings you'll have to dig awfully deep into the old stocking.' Then, over shots of a female 'inhabitant' of the house laying the dining table, the voice continues: 'But why talk of love and money in the same breath? So long as you're only dreaming, why not do the girl proud?' This address clearly positions the heterosexual couple as the target market of the exhibition, with the woman in this partnership as the driver of consumer decisions, while her male counterpart is figured as controller of the family finances.

In the 1953 Berg house, however, television takes a more central place in the living room, with furniture organised around it – as it does in the Unity Flats in 1954, the Crouch House in 1956 and the Canada Trend House of 1957,[14] in which television is now centralised, placed next to the fireplace and enhancing, rather than replacing, the hearth as the centre of living-room design.[15] An examination of press photographs and newsreel of these exhibits thus offers a visual history of the transformation of the contemporary living room in the mid-twentieth century, and the reorganisation of a markedly gendered space, the home, around the television set. They allow us to see not only what kind of televisions were being touted as de rigueur that year, but also the role that television began to play in family life and domestic entertainment in this key period in the medium's history. By the end of the 1950s, these photographs also reveal the point at which television becomes ubiquitous enough to be 'designed into' the ideal home, as with the Davis house of 1959 – where an alcove above the fireplace provided a 'built-in' position for siting the set which might be seen as a precursor to the contemporary trend for wall-hanging, high-level flat-screen televisions – or in the Ministry of Housing Frostproof House of 1957.[16] In the British Pathé newsreel coverage of the latter, the house's imagined female occupant roams through the house, first relaxing in front of her built-in set, then laying place settings for dinner in the open-plan dining area behind the set, thus demonstrating the integral role that television played in the flow between her domestic leisure and labour.[17] The built-in set was not confined to the living room, however. In 1959, the *Guardian*'s staff reporter announced from the Ideal Home Exhibition that one of the key draws that year for the 'non-technical consumer' was 'a bathroom with perfumed water, dyed "Mediterranean blue" and three television screens controllable by the bather – one [giving] a view of the front door, one of the back, and a third [providing] just ordinary BBC and ITV' (1959: 4). Furthermore, the Caribbean House of the 1962 exhibition featured a television shelf built into the master bedroom at a high level, offering evidence of television's migration to all areas in the house.[18] The idea of built-in television, or even a television-focused room, thus becomes significant in signalling that television had 'arrived' as the central object of domestic leisure as imagined for the female visitor to the exhibition.

Television in these postwar homes thus quickly shifted from being a marginal technology, sitting awkwardly at the side of the room and waiting to be wheeled out for occasional domestic entertainment, to a built-in feature of the postwar home, and placed on permanent display. However, alongside these two placements of television in the homes of the Ideal Home Exhibition, a third possibility for television was that it would be integral in the design of new kinds of home furnishings but hidden out of sight until needed. While this impulse meant that many early sets were designed into cabinets of walnut and teak, attractive pieces of furniture in their own right, it also led to the design of built-in furniture in which television sets could be stowed away until it was time to view. As we have seen in Lynn Spigel's work on the 'history of the idea of the disappearing object' (2012: 537), and in particular her analysis of American designer George Nelson's 'Storagewall' – built-in furniture in which everything in the living space, particularly media technologies, could be tucked away from view – this was a popular design concept in the US from the mid-1940s onwards. Spigel is interested in the ways in which the Nelson-esque home renders the housewife an 'Organisation Woman' (with a nod to William H. Whyte's 'Organisation Man' (1956)), offering her mastery and control over her home and rendering her a 'kind of middle-manager for family life' (ibid.: 563). As she observes:

> Even while sociological studies and articles in women's magazines observed that women feared that TV and other home amusements would cut them off from social life in public places, the Storagewall offered housewives a pleasing sense of mastery over the privatization of everyday life by putting them in charge of hi-fis and TV sets – the new objects of home entertainment.
>
> *(ibid.: 555)*

In the UK at the 1960 Ideal Home Exhibition, this effect was achieved not only through the imitation of the sleek, clean lines of Nelson's Storagewall in the 'Rooms with a Future' exhibit, featuring a fitted, floor-to-ceiling cabinet for TV and hi-fi in the living room, but also through a nod to a much earlier era of North American design in the 'All American House' with a fireplace that 'has a simulated colonial "oven door", housing the TV and hi-fi equipment'.[19] In these houses, television is designed into the fabric of the house, a permanent feature, but hidden out of sight – waiting, as Spigel suggests, for the woman of the house to reveal it. The fact that in the latter house the television is hidden behind an 'oven door' suggests a placement in a traditionally feminine domain.

As well as being visually associated with the spaces and technologies of domestic labour, as in the above example, exhibitors at the Ideal Home Exhibition also suggested that in the mid-century ideal home in the UK, it was possible to harness 'television' to perform tasks normally associated with feminine domestic labour. For example, a press release announcing the arrival of 'TV Baby Sitting at Olympia' at the 1960 exhibition sets out this fantasy in which 'television' (actually a closed-circuit monitoring system) liberates the young mother from the home:

> We know that the days of dear old nanny have long passed away. We know that for the last ten years every mother has had to be her own nanny and that had it not been for the swift development of Television the lives of young mothers would have been shorn of all entertainment save for that which could be staged at home . . . On a stand at the Daily Mail Ideal Home Exhibition, visitors will see a competent and composed nurse seated before five television monitor

sets . . . Those who see this demonstration at Olympia may be witnessing the historic beginning of a properly organised TV Baby Sitting Organisation.

(Murphy, 1960)

Here television, in its broadcast form, is depicted as liberating the young mother from the cultural 'poverty' of home-made entertainment, while, as an audio-visual technology that can be harnessed to act as monitor rather than broadcast receiver, 'television' enables her to leave her house and her childcare responsibilities altogether. While the TV babysitting service never, in fact, caught on as a technology in widespread use in apartment blocks and housing estates, the presentation of television as the great liberator of women is significant here.

Broadcasters at the Ideal Home Exhibition

While this chapter has thus far focused on the ways in which television-set manufacturers exhibiting at the Ideal Home Exhibition focused on their products' appeals to women and families, this final section will turn to look at the presence of broadcasters at the exhibition and the ways in which they conceptualised their address to a female viewer. It is perhaps unsurprising that an exhibition staged by the *Daily Mail* – a publication largely aimed at a female readership that was owned by Associated Newspapers, a company which also had a stake in the establishment of commercial television in the UK (as co-owner of the London franchise-holder Associated Rediffusion) – would continue to place television, and the television broadcasters, at its centre. Following the start-up of ITV in September 1955, the Ideal Home Exhibition began to feature broadcasters' stands as a regular feature of its displays. While the BBC had initially focused its efforts on the public exhibition of its work at the ongoing Radiolympia/National Radio Show and took a large role in the exhibition of television at the Festival of Britain (see Wheatley, 2016), its Publicity Department took the decision that it also needed a presence at the Ideal Home Exhibition, following their assessment of ITV's stand at the 1958 exhibition. The following memo, written by the BBC's exhibition designer, Leonard Potter, and found in the BBC Publicity Department file on the Ideal Home Exhibition, offers a description of the 1958 ITV stand (which was situated in the Fashion, Beauty and Children's section of the exhibition) and sets out what the Corporation felt it was 'up against' in exhibiting as a competitor in the following year:

> [In the 1,000 square feet display] the visitor passed under three acoustic domes which were linked to three loop film projectors. These projectors were showing excerpts from some of the popular shows. The visitor then passed on to a press-button voting machine where he was invited to vote for his favourite show. His vote was registered on an electronic 'tote' which formed the background to this section. At the same time he was handed a little lapel pic of the show which he had chosen as a giveaway. Supplementing this display were a number of enlarged photographs of the glamour variety: Sabrina, Diana Dors.

The staff consisted at the time of our visit of one commissionaire and three attractive girls . . . The cost of the stand would be approximately £1,750.

(Potter, 1958)

Here we see that ITV's marketing strategy in this early period focused both on the idea of viewer choice, through its voting conceit, and on an association of television with female glamour and celebrity. In situating the ITV stand in the Fashion, Beauty and Children's section of the exhibition, its particular address to a female viewer was made all the more explicit.

The files of the BBC's Publicity Department in the late 1950s and early 1960s show that the Corporation was keenly aware that its competitor took a more populist approach to their presentation at exhibitions, an approach which was going down very well with visitors to large-scale public exhibitions. For example, Cecil McGivern's report from the Scottish Radio Show in 1957 bemoans the fact that

Our stand, in my opinion, lacked the flamboyancy and touch of showmanship necessary for exhibitions like this [in comparison to the Scottish Television stand] . . . Not only were personalities interviewed [on their stand] but performers performed, singers sang, and comedians 'gagged' to the audience.

(McGivern, 1957)

At the National Radio Show the following year, this sense of proximity to the excitement of 'show business' was further realised by the ITV companies through an immersive exhibit that gave the exhibition visitor a fully embodied experience of the excitement of television:

[The Independent Television Wonderland], staged by Associated Rediffusion and Associated Television in conjunction with the Independent Television Authority, Independent Television News and the TV Times, has been designed to transport spectators into a realm of fantasy, colour and excitement. Through a screen surrounding the entire stand, on which are depicted scenes from Lewis Carroll's beloved masterpiece, the visitor enters a dimly lit vestibule and passes on into another foyer, wrapped in complete darkness, which leads into the various halls. There are seven halls, each devoted to a particular aspect of independent television and all brightly illuminated – the idea being to heighten the sense of wonderment and to make the spectator feel that he has stumbled from a world of unreality into settings made familiar by a year's viewing.

(Anon., 1958)

These halls included the Quiz Hall,[20] the Display Hall,[21] the Hall of Music,[22] the Hall of Drama,[23] the Wild West Hall[24] and a Hall of Personalities, in which the visitor 'can see not only those who already provide his entertainment during the year but also, through various talent contests, those who might do so in the future' (ibid.), as well as being able to 'see themselves on television' via another closed-circuit TV exhibit. ITV's immersive exhibit, which presented television as a dizzying wonderland of entertainment and celebrity into which the visitor could enter, clearly emphasised the medium's spectacular qualities in order to attract viewers to the nascent commercial television service.[25] However, it also paved the way for other immersive spectacles of technological wizardry by the BBC at the Ideal Home Exhibition.

As suggested above, like the early twentieth-century department store, the large-scale, mid-century exhibition was a site in which the spectacularisation of domestic modernity was foregrounded, offering a spectacular and experiential manifestation of this in which all was new, aspirational, but also, in terms of the scale and ambition of display in these spaces, almost fantastical in their design – or phantasmagoric, in Nava's terms (1997). This phantasmagoric presentation of modernity, directed specifically towards a female audience, was particularly apparent in the BBC's immersive 'Dome of Discovery' exhibit produced for the 1961 Ideal Home Exhibition, described here in a press release prepared by George Campney, Head of Publicity for the BBC:

> The BBC display will be in the form of a sphere within which the story of the BBC will be told in light, sound and colour. Visitors enter a darkened arena and will then take a three minute journey through the many aspects of BBC broadcasting, described in graphic illustration, brilliantly lit. We have attempted, without using the written word, to provide the visitor with a narrative about the BBC. There will be taped commentary and great use will be made of ultraviolet light. As the visitor progresses round the area he will encounter . . . the electronic narrative [of] the wide range of programmes of a domestic nature that are offered by the sound and television services, particularly to women.
>
> *(Campney, 1961)*

While no photographic evidence of this design appears to have survived, the description of this exhibit offered in a radio script from the BBC's European service expands on Campney's press release, depicting the sphere thus:

> Gardening programmes for instance are represented by a flower suddenly bursting into bloom, schools programmes by a huge alphabet floating in space. The whole of this sphere eventually blossoms into a cascade of light and sound, ending in a dramatic thunderstorm.
>
> *(Patterson, 1961)*

The BBC's Radio Newsreel concluded: 'To an electronic accompaniment the illustrations pop up at you like the figures in a ghost train, it is vivid, alive and gay, like so much else at this exhibition' (Anon., 1961). In the BBC's exhibit at the 1961 Ideal Home Exhibition, then, television was presented through a display which harnessed the spectacle of lights, sound and 'special effects' to appeal directly to the female consumer (and her particular investment in educational and instructive programming), primarily, one supposes, to spur her to invest her family's money in a television set (and a television licence). This technique was revisited the following year in the BBC's 'People Make Programmes' travellator, which provided, according to the 1962 Ideal Home Exhibition catalogue, 'a kind of magic carpet from which visitors can see many of the faces of people who have made BBC programmes memorable'. We therefore see that the television exhibits at the Exhibition offered precisely the kind of immersive, phantasmagoric spectacle of modernity that Nava had previously identified in the centrepiece displays of the early twentieth-century department store. Furthermore, if, as Judy Giles notes, the Ideal Home Exhibitions, 'in all their theatricality and spectacle, constituted social spaces in which dreams and longings found visual expression for those who visited them and who, frequently, were women' (2004: 110), then these immersive television exhibits formed a significant site for such imaginings.

In this early period of competitive television broadcasting, then, it was essential for both broadcasters to appeal to the Ideal Home Exhibition's female visitors, and by extension their families, as significant potential viewers whom they needed to 'win over'. As Helen Wood (2015) has argued, women were central to the widespread take-up of television in the mid-twentieth century and negotiated the integration of the medium into the home, being particularly attentive to the tensions between domestic work and domestic leisure that surrounded the arrival of television. Both broadcasters needed to build on the image of television as an affordable luxury which had been established earlier in the exhibition's history, as discussed above. However, while this address sat easily with ITV's brand image in the late 1950s, it would seem that the BBC's Publicity Department were more comfortable touting the 'techno-logical wizardry' of television (as they had done at the National Radio Show, for example), with emphasis placed on the production and transmission of television (as told in their exhibits on the South Bank and in their Piccadilly exhibition at the Festival of Britain), than they were in appealing directly to a (predominantly) female audience at the Ideal Home Exhibition and other female-focused exhibitions.

In the documentation held in the BBC's Publicity Department's files, a distinct distaste is shown for the implied commercialisation of appealing to the housewife-consumer at the Ideal Home Exhibition. For example, John Downer, the Corporation's Exhibition and Displays officer, wrote to George Campney, Head of Publicity in 1960 (the year before the BBC displayed at the Ideal Home Exhibition), that he had the following concerns about the BBC's participation:

> The Ideal Home Exhibition is a bazaar. There are shades of quality by firms like ICI, Courtaulds, etc., but the main run of stands are usually nothing more than barker's stands. It is my belief that the corporation should not in any way compete in this sort of presentation i.e. demonstrations of cooking, housekeeping, gardening etc. Rather, the Corporation should be represented by a 'prestige' exhibit which I would refer to as an electronic delight – a fairyland of colour, shapes, lights, etc. which would excite the public's imagination.
>
> (Downer, 1960)

Downer also made further suggestions about focusing the exhibition on BBC television's twenty-fifth anniversary, thus promoting a sense of prestige and technical accomplishment over a focus on glamour, celebrity and the domestic (with its implied address to female visitors/viewers). In response, George Campney drew up a proposal stating that 'The publicity display would draw attention to the variety of programmes on sound and television which affect home life. There would be no intention to restricting the exhibition to the *Woman's Hour* type of programme' (1960). As a result, the BBC exhibits designed for this exhibition stressed the range of programmes on offer from the BBC. In 1963, for example, they presented the breadth of their programming in a market-stall conceit, designed specifically to appeal to and address a housewife skilled in the art of getting 'value for money'. This exhibit, in which each 'market stall' on the BBC's stand showcased a different genre of programming, was introduced in the 1963 catalogue under the title of 'Something for Everybody from the BBC', guiding the visitor-viewer to

> Learn about the programmes that come into your home each day. How much do they cost? What is the price of say *Compact* [a soap opera set in a the offices of a woman's magazine] or *Woman's Hour* [a topical radio discussion programme for women]?

Here the price of female-focused programming was set against the cost of the licence fee in order to stress the value for money which the Corporation offered its viewers. The BBC was therefore both uncomfortable with the gendered address of the Ideal Home Exhibition and, at the same time, mindful of it in its exhibition designs.[26]

This reluctance to engage with a female audience also directly echoes a protracted debate about whether the BBC would participate in the earlier 1957 Festival of Women at Wembley, which claimed to be 'the first exhibition for women about women ever to take place . . . intended to be a tribute to women's influence throughout every facet of the Nation's affairs' (Lewis, 1957). Doreen Stephens, Head of the Women's Programming Department at the BBC, was keen to be involved in this exhibition and stated to Mary Adams (then Controller of Television Programmes): 'I feel it would be a great pity if the BBC did not take this opportunity of putting its women's programmes across to women and to those commercial interests particularly interested in the housewife' (Stephens, 1956).[27] The idea of the BBC's participation was explored at some length, to the extent that a treatment for the display was prepared by Leonard Potter (Head of Exhibition Design):

> The BBC is in a unique position in that its programmes always get 'home' and inevitably to its women listeners and viewers in the main. Therefore the main emphasis should be on BBC programmes designed for the woman at home . . . Indeed, it may be correct to say that in recent years Television has become an essential part of the home's equipment. TV brings the world outside to the

home viewer. To the woman, who spends a great deal of her time within the home environment TV in particular has become a welcome relaxation.

(Potter, 1956)

As with almost all of the postwar exhibitions, one of the main attractions of the display was to be a 'see yourself on television' section and an opportunity for the female visitor to check whether she was 'telegenic' by appearing on-screen for the first time. Here television is figured as a technology which connected with its viewer in a particular and immediate way, with the 'see yourself' exhibit revealing something significant about television's potential to glamorise women as well as its ability to enable a form of 'magical' travel between two domains, just as it had been since Baird's demonstration of the 'Commercial Televisor' in 1930 at the Ideal Home Exhibition, where visitors were encouraged to be televised to their friends and families from a property around the corner from the exhibition on Hammersmith Road (see Wheatley, 2016, for a discussion of this demonstration). In such exhibits, the potential for television's space-binding properties and its promise of celebrity and glamour through the mediation of femininity are all demonstrated. However, ultimately the BBC refused to participate in the Festival of Women. Joyce Rowe, Sound Publicity Officer, had argued that 'the whole idea fills me with horror' (Rowe, 1956), and Michael Standing, Controller of Entertainment, agreed, writing 'it is stated that some 3 million organised women are behind the [Festival of Women] – to me a terrifying thought' (Standing, 1956). It is clear, then, that in relation to the mid-twentieth-century exhibition, the BBC was much less comfortable in embracing the notion of television as a domestic leisure technology for women than its competitor was, and than those manufacturers, designers and architects selling television as a consumable technology for the women creating the ideal home.

This chapter has thus discussed the ways in which television was situated as a technology 'for women' at the mid-twentieth-century exhibition. While most of the chapters in this book consider television programming made for, and sometimes by, women as 'television for women', the historical narrative offered in this chapter outlines the ways in which the medium, as both spectacular exhibit and everyday technology, was figured as a gendered technology at the mid-twentieth-century exhibition. This exploration of the figure of the housewife as potential television buyer/viewer at the Ideal Home Exhibition, juggling the demands of domestic labour and domestic leisure, and placing the technology at either the centre or the margins of her home, joins up to a larger set of debates about the gendering of modernity (see Felski, 1995; Nava, 1997; Giles, 2004). A history of television at the mid-twentieth-century Ideal Home Exhibition and beyond thus opens up a history of television as a gendered technology which is both aspirational and ubiquitous, spectacular and ordinary, futuristic and very much of its time.

Notes

1 See Bird Jr (1999) on television at New York's World's Fair, for example.
2 It was later the Ideal Home Show.

3　Aside from a wartime break in the exhibition between 1940 and 1946.
4　The Ideal Home Exhibition archive is held as part of the V&A Archive of Art and Design, Blythe House, London.
5　NB This catalogue, and all subsequent editions of the catalogue quoted in this chapter, are archived in the Ideal Home Exhibition files at the V&A Archive of Art and Design, Blythe House, London.
6　Viscount Rothermere, 'Foreword', 1947 Ideal Home Exhibition catalogue, p. 3.
7　W.C. Steele, 'Radio and Television Section', 1947 Ideal Home Exhibition catalogue, p. 65.
8　Anon., 'Furnishing, Decoration and Radio Section', 1949 Ideal Home Exhibition catalogue, p. 21.
9　Marconiphone advert, 1938 Ideal Home Exhibition catalogue, p. 53.
10　The idea of television connecting the public and private spheres is explored in relation to US television of the same period in the work of Lynn Spigel (1997).
11　Alison and Peter Smithson, 'The House of the Future', 1956 Ideal Home Exhibition catalogue, p. 98.
12　Gooch's of Knightsbridge, 'The Shape of Things to Come: A Panorama of Furnishing', 1936 Ideal Home Exhibition catalogue, p. 268.
13　British Pathé newsreel of the Gwen Robbins show home and its placement of television can be viewed here: www.britishpathe.com/video/how-to-make-homes-ideal (accessed 18 July 2016).
14　British Pathé newsreel of the Canada House and its placement of television can be viewed here: www.britishpathe.com/video/ideal-home-exhibition-2 (accessed 18 July 2016).
15　See Cecelia Tichi (1992) for a comparative discussion of the concept of the 'electronic hearth' in the North American home in the same period.
16　These wall-hanging sets are discussed in more detail in Wheatley (2016).
17　British Pathé newsreel of the Frostfree House and its placement of television can be viewed here: www.britishpathe.com/video/ideal-home-exhibition-2 (accessed 18 July 2016).
18　British Pathé newsreel of the Caribbean House and its placement of television can be viewed here: www.britishpathe.com/video/ideal-homes-aka-ideal-home-exhibition (accessed 18 July 2016).
19　Anon., 'All American House', 1960 Ideal Home Exhibition catalogue, p. 25.
20　With stills and exhibits from panel games and the flashing timepiece from 'Beat the Clock', the game within *Sunday Night at the London Palladium*.
21　Including the studio set from *Emergency Ward 10* (ATV, 1957–67) and back projection showing recent items from *This Week* (A-R, 1956–78).
22　Featuring stills from *The Jack Jackson Show* (ATV, 1955–9) and *Cool for Cats* (A-R, 1956–61), alongside an elaborate jukebox.
23　With an innovative costume display hung inside large 'peep-show recesses in baroque designs' (Anon., 1958).
24　Complete with stuffed bison and a tepee.
25　See my earlier discussion of the 'See Yourself on Television' exhibit in the mid-century exhibition (Wheatley, 2016).
26　The market-stall conceit was in fact thought not to have been a success. A memo from George Campney to designer Perry Guiness after the exhibition closed felt that their attempt at evoking the everyday milieu of the marketplace had come across as too high-brow/esoteric in the broader context of the exhibition (Campney, 1963).
27　See Irwin (2011) for a discussion of the significance of Stephens' role in the development of television for women.

Bibliography

Anon. (1937) 'Is television within your reach?', *Ideal Home*, November: 407.
Anon. (1958) 'The 1958 Radio Show Supplement', *The Times*, 28 August: 1.

Anon. (1961) 'Radio Newsreel Script', BBC Written Archive file 'Publicity: Ideal Home Exhibition 1952–1963' (R44/925/1), 6 March.

Atkinson, H. (2012) *The Festival of Britain: A Land and Its People*, London: I.B.Tauris.

Bird Jr, W. L. (1999) *'Better Living': Advertising, Media, and the New Vocabulary of Business Leadership, 1935–1955*, Evanston, IL: Northwestern University Press.

Campney, G. (1960) 'Ideal Home Exhibition 1961: A Proposal for BBC Participation', BBC Written Archive file 'Publicity: Ideal Home Exhibition 1952–1963' (R44/925/1), 7 November.

Campney, G. (1961) 'The BBC at the Ideal Home Exhibition', BBC Written Archive file 'Publicity: Ideal Home Exhibition 1952–1963' (R44/925/1), 6 February.

Campney, G. (1963) 'Ideal Home Exhibition', BBC Written Archive file 'Publicity: Ideal Home Exhibition 1952–1963' (R44/925/1), 12 March.

Chaney, D. (1983) 'The department store as cultural form', *Theory, Culture & Society*, 1, 3: 22–31.

Downer, J. (1960) 'Suggestions for BBC Participation in the Ideal Home Exhibition 1961', BBC Written Archive file 'Publicity: Ideal Home Exhibition 1952–1963' (R44/925/1), 5 October.

Felski, R. (1995) *The Gender of Modernity*, Cambridge, MA: Harvard University Press.

Giles, J. (2004) *The Parlour and the Suburb: Domestic Identities, Class, Femininity and Modernity*, Oxford and New York: Berg.

Guardian (1959) 'Getting down to bricks and mortar', 22 November: 4.

Irwin, M. (2011) 'What women want on television: Doreen Stephens and BBC television programmes for women, 1953–64', *Westminster Papers in Communication and Culture*, 8, 3: 99–122.

Lewis, W. (1957) 'Festival of Women: Press Release', BBC Written Archive file 'Festival of Women 1954–57' (R44/898/1), 29 June.

McGivern, C. (1957) 'Scottish Radio Show', BBC Written Archive file 'Publicity: Publicity – Scottish Radio and Television Exhibition' (R44/1255/1), 7 June.

Moseley, R., Wheatley, H. and Wood, H. (2014) 'Afternoon television: Introduction to Special Issue on afternoon television', *Critical Studies in Television*, 9, 2: 1–19.

Murphy, P. (1960) 'TV Babysitting at Olympia', BBC Written Archive file 'Publicity: Ideal Home Exhibition 1952–1963' (R44/925/1), undated.

Nava, M. (1997) 'Modernity's disavowal: Women, the city and the department store', in C. Campbell and P. Falk (eds) *The Shopping Experience*, London: Sage: 56–91.

Patterson, M. (1961) 'BBC European Division Topical Unit Script', BBC Written Archive file 'Publicity: Ideal Home Exhibition 1952–1963' (R44/925/1), undated.

Potter, L. (1956) 'Festival of Women', BBC Written Archive file 'Festival of Women 1954–57' (R44/898/1), 30 October.

Potter, L. (1958) 'Ideal Home Exhibition: ITV Display [memo to D. Russell, Head of Publicity]', BBC Written Archive file 'Publicity: Ideal Home Exhibition 1952–1963' (R44/925/1), 17 March.

Rowe, J. (1956) 'Festival of Women [memo to Miss E.M. Thomas, Assistant to the Head of Publicity]', BBC Written Archive file 'Festival of Women 1954–57' (R44/898/1), undated.

Ryan, D. S. (1997) *The Ideal Home through the Twentieth Century*, London: Hazar.

Sparke, P. (1995) *As Long as It's Pink: The Sexual Politics of Taste*, London: Pandora.

Spigel, L. (1997) 'The suburban home companion: Television and the neighbourhood ideal in post-war America', in C. Brunsdon, J. D'Acci and L. Spigel (eds) *Feminist Television Criticism: A Reader*, Oxford: Oxford University Press: 211–34.

Spigel, L. (2005) 'Designing the smart house: Post-human domesticity and conspicuous production', *European Journal of Cultural Studies*, 8, 4: 403–26.

Spigel, L. (2012) 'Object lessons for the media home: From Storagewall to invisible design', *Public Culture*, 24, 3: 535–76.

Standing, M. (1956) 'Festival of Women', BBC Written Archive file 'Festival of Women 1954–57' (R44/898/1), 14 November.

Stephens, D. (1956) 'Festival of Women', BBC Written Archive file 'Festival of Women 1954–57' (R44/898/1), 29 June.

Thumim, J. (2004) *Inventing Television Culture: Men, Women, and the Box*, Oxford: Oxford University Press.

Tichi, C. (1992) *Electronic Hearth: Creating an American Television Culture*, Oxford: Oxford University Press.

Wheatley, H. (2016) *Spectacular Television: Exploring Televisual Pleasure*, London: I.B.Tauris.

Whyte, W. H. (1956) *Organization Man*, New York: Simon & Schuster.

Winston, B. (1998) *Media Technology and Society: A History from the Telegraph to the Internet*, London and New York: Routledge.

Wood, H. (2015) 'Television – the housewife's choice? The 1949 Mass Observation Television Directive, reluctance and revision', *Media History*, 21, 3: 342–59.

12

'I'VE BEEN HAVING FANTASIES ABOUT REGAN AND CARTER THREE TIMES A WEEK'

Television, women and desire

Hazel Collie

Introduction

The word 'desire' is rarely connected with television, in contrast to the wealth of scholarship, spanning forty years, which explores it in relation to the cinema and, predominantly, the male spectator. In this chapter, I draw upon audience research which suggests a new and productive understanding of the under-explored but critical relationship between television, women and desire. As part of the 'A History of Television for Women in Britain 1947–1989' project, I carried out thirty oral history interviews with generationally and geographically dispersed British women to try to get a sense of how a female British television audience felt that television had been significant in their everyday lives.[1] The interview was designed to encourage the women to narrate their life story, separating out their television experiences into life stages, which I categorised as childhood, teenage years and adulthood.[2] Elsewhere, I have noted that the themes of these women's oral histories often gathered around familial viewing and domestic responsibility (Collie, 2013). The relational aspect of their viewing and how they used this to depict their identity, their 'self-in-relation' (Surrey, 1985), is what underpinned many of the interviews. Women's responses to questions about what they enjoyed watching were often related through what they watched with others, or even by talking about what other people in their lives enjoyed watching. Rarely did their conversation about the television programmes they watched correspond to the television that they considered to be 'for them'.

However, one key theme that did arise was the television that they had enjoyed through the lens of desire; desire for the men, both as actors and as characters, that they had found attractive and whom they took pleasure from watching in those programmes. In her work on women's pornography use, Clarissa Smith notes that the women she spoke to responded to the question 'is this magazine for women?' with responses such as 'well, I'm a woman and I liked it, therefore it is for women'

(Smith, 2007: 80). This is very different to the responses to my question about what constitutes 'television for women'. None of my interviewees made a connection between her own televisual pleasure and what this might mean for its status as 'for women'. It is significant, then, that desire is the one of the few areas in which women were enabled to talk about television 'for them'. All of the women I interviewed identified themselves as heterosexual, so these were certainly expressions of heterosexual feminine desire. Additionally, twenty-eight of the thirty women were mothers, which created a very specific relationship with television and domestic life, particularly in terms of their memories. Only the women in their forties, fifties, sixties and early seventies discussed their television viewing in relation to desire, whereas the older women in their eighties and nineties did not. This, then, is a very specific response about desire from a particular group. Throughout the interviews there were various factors which cut across the television experience along generational lines. One of these was the extent of each generational cohort's exposure to feminism, and when in their socialisation this had happened. In terms of their interest in discussing desire, we can see each generation's distinct relationship with feminism as having an impact on their entitlement to desire and on their ability to acknowledge this. In this chapter I think through the women's conversations around television and desire, considering how their responses demonstrate the ways in which the characteristic structures and rhythms of television might produce a desiring subjectivity which is different from that theorised around the film spectator, cinematic apparatus and the context of viewing.

The female spectator and the social audience

Much of the existing research on women and desire is predicated upon Laura Mulvey's formulation of the male gaze (Mulvey, 1975). The viewing processes that Mulvey identified are structured through narrative so that femininity as spectacle becomes encoded into operations of mainstream cinema, forcing the viewer to identify with the male hero and his objectification of the female. In Mulvey's somewhat hegemonic formulation, woman necessarily becomes the bearer of meaning rather than the maker of meaning. Mulvey's theorisation has since been criticised, revisited and reworked by many, including Mulvey herself (Mulvey, 1981). David Rodowick suggests that Mulvey's approach was too reductive and that her analysis did not allow space for the female subject (Rodowick, 1982). Despite these criticisms, consideration of how women look is still, to some degree, defined by Mulvey's work.

Work on the television/desire/gender nexus often proceeds around textual questions of representation of female desire in programmes with a feminine address, and with a focus on how a postfeminist climate has created a particular mode of depiction of feminine desires in programming and anticipated responses to programming created for women (Kim, 2001; Arthurs, 2003; Ouellette, 2002). Lyn Thomas' work on *Inspector Morse* (ITV, 1987–2000) concludes that it was Morse's vulnerability that made him attractive to the women she spoke to, and that 'Morse's neediness, his constant pursuit of "attractive 45-year-old women" seems here to be providing the beginnings of a feminist fantasy where female power can be combined with romance' (Thomas, 1997: 202–3). Thomas' work is an intriguing starting point for further questions around women, television and desire, drawing attention to the breadth of the female viewing experience and highlighting some of the less expected aspects of a character's traits that women might find attractive. However, Thomas also presupposes a feminist consciousness which does not pay adequate attention to the different generational positions, and associated access to feminism, that spectatorship might occupy. Media literacy, feminism and a neoliberal sensibility all cut across generation to create significantly different relationships with the medium of television. It is clearly not enough to expect that a unified spectator position can operate across generational lines.

More recently, Helen Wheatley has pointed to an emerging trend for television programmes for women which fetishise male stars' bodies. Wheatley demonstrates how dramas such as the BBC's recent re-imagining of *Poldark* or the popular *Outlander* (Starz, 2014–) series contain various textual invitations to a heterosexual, female gaze (Wheatley, 2016). In her consideration of audience responses to sex and desire on and through television, Wheatley asked television viewers to respond to an anonymous survey which dealt specifically with desire, as opposed to the more diffuse conversation generated by my interviews. Her results are quite different to mine. Wheatley's data does not display the same reluctance to discuss desire that mine does, and her respondents discussed sexual or erotic content and responses in far more explicit, physical terms than mine did. The anonymous nature of Wheatley's research has likely created a different, perhaps safer, space in which to discuss such reactions. However, the difference may also be generational, both in relation to the television programmes discussed and to my respondents. Just over 60 per cent of Wheatley's respondents were aged in their thirties and forties, as opposed to my significantly older sample. Furthermore, her focus dealt specifically with more recent programming. The differences between the two pieces of research, one historical and one contemporary, suggest that there has been a significant cultural shift in the way that sex and desire on and with television might be discussed and produced. These are the types of cultural shift which might be lost if one theoretical framework continues to be applied, uncritically, to a cultural apparatus for which it was not conceived.

The somewhat hegemonic theorisation of the gaze emerges from cinematic scholarship. In 1988 Suzanne Moore suggested that if we recognise the contradictions between public and private contexts, between the gaze of cinema and the glance of television (Ellis, 1982), we cannot be satisfied with a theory premised on a 'unified spectator sitting in a darkened studio' (Moore, 1988: 50). In the same publication, Shelagh Young noted how the processes of feminism have contributed to the construction of a female audience that knows the difference between feeling powerful and feeling powerless (1988). Both pieces highlight the difficulty of trying to explain a heterosexual female spectator's private viewing over time by an appropriation of the male gaze. Yet television's position as a domestic object, and how this plays out in female discussions of viewing desire across space and time, has not been further explored in any great detail. Little attention is paid to how far the medium's status as 'feminised', and what this means for its gendered address, might create a different space for feminine desire from that offered by the cinema or, indeed, from that offered by reading.

Accessing desire

The question of how to access women's thoughts on desire was more difficult than initial correspondence suggested. Email and written correspondence received in response to the call to interview was richer in terms of discussion of the enjoyment of watching the masculine body than the oral histories were, particularly in terms of watching the male body in sports programming.[3] In his work on the male pin-up, Richard Dyer suggests that sport is the area of life that is the most common contemporary source of male body imagery, drawing particular attention to 'the celebration of the body in sport' as a celebration of the relative affluence of Western society (Dyer, 1982: 68). This 'celebration' produces an 'acceptable' context for women to look at men on television, a fact which is attested to in the initial correspondence I received on these viewers' appreciation of physicality of the male body in sports programming. During the process of interviewing, however, the theme played out differently, with a more subtle teasing out of the women's thoughts and memories on desire. Desire emerged as a topic that my interviewees felt more able to discreetly address in the more anonymous format of the written word than in a face-to-face interview. As a means of circumventing this problem and to further illuminate the women's feelings on the subject, I contacted seven of the women who had talked about desire in their interviews (Sue E, Sue O, Tracey, Patricia, Jennie, Rachel and Carol) by email. I hoped the distance that this mode of communication would create between us might produce more detail and stimulate a dialogue which enabled a further articulation of their underlying thoughts on the question of desire and what its relationship with television might be. In fact, only three of the women – Sue E, Sue O and Tracey – responded; however, this email correspondence has been useful in pinning down some thoughts about *why* women looked to television for objects of desire. It was less successful, though, in terms of eliciting discussion of a more explicit, physical nature as found in the original correspondence, or in pinpointing what it was that women felt they were fulfilling through their televisual desires.

Such findings are indicative of a wider silence around women's desire. In conversations in which women were comfortable articulating desire, it was often reflected upon in non-physical terms. This is significantly different to the framing of responses to Helen Wheatley's Television Desire survey (2016), as discussed previously. Particular men were identified as being desirable due to displaying character traits, such as kindness, or competencies, such as a particular talent for acting. When framed in this way, desire could be justified as something other than physical and sexual. This is an extra layer of legitimation, added to an experience that they may have felt did not have legitimacy in its own right, as Janice Radway also noted in relation to women's romance reading (Radway, 1991); indeed, this may explain why only three women responded to my email request for further information, and that two of these were the only women in my sample who were not mothers. The women's reticence to go into much detail on the physicality of desire hints, perhaps, at the difficulties inherent in holding together the two separate subject positions of motherhood and the desiring woman. Work on the increasing fetishisation of the pregnant body, including naked photo shoots of celebrities such as Demi Moore and magazine voyeurism of pregnant celebrities, notes that this has not translated into acknowledgement of the desire *felt by* mothers (Tyler, 2011; Huntley, 2000).

Conversation around motherhood quickly became the dominant mode of the interviews. Part of the rapport-building of the interviews was born out of our shared experience as mothers, and in my interviews with women who were in their sixties and seventies many women extended their mothering to me. It may be, therefore, that by the time we reached questions of desire during the interview, the conversation had already been framed by motherhood, and desire had an awkward positioning within that framework. The email correspondence after the interviews was similarly limited, because by that point my relationship with them as mothers had already been established. The question of television 'for them' is also complicated by this framework, and by the question of what happens to women as mothers and as facilitators for others' comfort and wellbeing, rather than their own (Chodorow, 1994; Thompson, 1991). The two women who were most open in their narrativisation of desire, Sue E and Sue O, were, as stated above, the only women in my sample who were not mothers, suggesting that they were able to narrate their desire more openly because they did not experience the same conflict of subject positions as other women in the study.

Desire on and with television

Despite E. Ann Kaplan's warnings about the importance of distinguishing between the hypothetical spectator constructed through film's strategies and the contemporary female viewer with a feminist consciousness (Kaplan, 1983), the spectator is still more frequently inferred in film studies, whereas empirical audience studies in the consideration of television are commonplace. Although some significant reception work has been done on female cinematic audiences, the broad pattern of the theorised film spectator versus the social television audience still exists.[4]

The apparatus of television lends itself to a different looking relationship, which makes a straightforward adoption of Mulvey's cinema spectatatorship theory into discussion of television audience response difficult. John Ellis' early distinctions between cinema and television suggested that 'TV's regime of vision is less intense than cinema's: it is a regime of the glance' (Ellis, 1982: 132), rather than the overwhelming cinematic gaze. However, by prioritising the 'glance' of television, Ellis underplays the emotional labour incumbent in much television viewing. Horace Newcomb's work on the soap genre indicates why serialisations might be so involving; that the 'intimacy' and 'continuity' of the genre allow for 'greater audience involvement, a sense of becoming part of the lives and actions of the characters they see' (Newcomb, 1974: 163) as these characters' stories grow and change over time. Later feminist work considered female audiences' identification with soap operas, and the importance of the regular, reiterative relationship between viewer and serial (Brunsdon, 1981; Geraghty, 1991; Modleski, 1983; Ang, 1985). Annette Kuhn suggests that each medium constructs sexual difference through spectatorship in different ways. Cinema does so through look and spectacle while television, instead, operates through its 'capacity to insert its flow, its characteristic modes of address and the textual operations of different kinds of programmes into the rhythms and routines of domestic activities and sexual divisions of labour' (1984: 25). This correlates with how women have spoken to me about their televisual formations of desire, though I would also add the issues of television's familiarity and regularity to this definition. While the heterosexual female television audience has been well accounted for empirically (Hobson, 1982; Press, 1991; Gray, 1992; Seiter, 1999; Wood, 2009) and theoretically (Modleski, 1983), such audience work has engaged with questions of domestic labour. Within such a paradigm, questions of feminine desire have, perhaps, been lost. The domestic positioning of women and the domestication of television and its social function suggest that the medium might play a very different role in feminine desire.

Phases of desire

During interview, the women spoke about two distinct phases of attraction – their adolescent crushes and their adult pleasures – in quite different ways. This division was partly caused by my arrangement of the interview schedule, into television-viewing at different life stages, and it is clear that that this structuring of the interviews framed the way in which the women broke their memories of desire down into stages. However, their discussions of these two phases were distinct enough to suggest that they also existed, to some extent, naturally. Narratives around pop-music programming, for example, indicated a very particular adolescent 'need to belong', and in the data regarding desire we can see a similar pattern developing across the conversation about the subjects' adolescent attractions. However, their personal preferences and attractions became more individualised as they discussed their adult viewing and lives.

While the oldest women, those in their eighties and nineties, did not talk about desire at all, there *were* differences between how the two younger groups talked about desire. While women of both of these generational groups were happy to talk about youthful crushes, the women in the middle generational grouping (those in their sixties and seventies) seemed to be the most comfortable with conversation around adult desire, whereas the youngest women were, somewhat unexpectedly perhaps, more circumspect about this period of desire. One explanation might be that these youngest women (in their forties and fifties) still inhabited the day-to-day role of practical mothering, and as such the difficulty of acknowledging the previously mentioned duality in their subject positions, of desire and motherhood, might still carry a particular weight for these women.

Heart-throb time!

The teenage period of desire was characterised by reflections upon 'heart-throbs', a phrase that is very much a cultural product of its time and one which has fallen out of use in more recent years. A dismissive attitude to this stage of their viewing lives was apparent in all of the interviews, in this as in many other memories of their adolescent viewing, with the women seeking to distance themselves from the kinds of teenage crushes that as adults they can reflect upon as having been for their silly young selves. In most cases the subjects of the women's romantic fantasies were discussed in limited terms, simply naming them and drawing attention to their heart-throb status. In some cases the women did not even specify the character in a programme that they had found attractive, merely that the programme had offered something of interest in this way: 'Oh, *The Man from UNCLE*! [Arena Productions/MGM Television, 1964–9] Heart-throb time!' (Carol, 64). The tone of voice in which Carol delivered the phrase 'Heart-throb time!' was mocking, indicative of her dismissive adult attitude. Others drew attention to the vacillations of youthful attraction, again painting this disloyal characteristic of their attractions in a dismissive way:

> [I always watched] *The Man from UNCLE*. I even went to see the film *The Great Escape* (Mirisch Company, 1963) because David McCallum was in it, but came out loving Steve McQueen. Such are teenage crushes.
>
> *(Pat, 64)*

As with the example discussed above, it is Pat's final words on the matter that deliver her verdict on the foolishness of those teen pursuits from her more knowledgeable position as an adult, and she characterises her adolescent relationships with David McCallum and Steve McQueen as fleeting and somewhat fickle. However, it may not just be her life stage which leads her to dismiss the 'teenage crush' in this way. The 'one-off' experience of viewing in a cinema begins to be represented in opposition to the reliability associated with the quotidian character of television. While Sue O delivers a final, adult delivery of scorn on youthful attractions in relation to a television programme, there is a more committed quality to her memory of watching her heart-throb:

> It certainly enhanced my enjoyment of any programmes if my heart-throbs appeared. More often than not they were my main reasons for wanting to watch the programmes. I couldn't wait! I remember one, which used to be on ITV on Sunday afternoons. The programme was called *Jungle Boy* [ATV, 1957]. I think it was set in Kenya in 1959. The boy who played the lead was called Michael Carr-Hartley. I was 12, and he looked about 3 or 4 years older. He was probably a spotty youth, but I was besotted.
>
> *(Sue O, 64, email correspondence)*

Sue O's scorn seems somewhat at odds with the depth of detail of her recollection of the programme, suggesting that either she has recalled these details from over fifty years ago, and therefore the programme was more important to her than her final comment suggests, or that she researched it before she responded to me, which suggests that it still holds some fascination for her. What her recollection very clearly indicates is the commitment that she is prepared to devote to watching the object of her desire on television each week.

These were crushes that necessitated the joining of fan clubs and writing of fan letters to magazines, both activities that the women recalled with affectionate ridicule. Sylvia (52), for example, remembered joining the fan club for the enigmatic Russian spy Illya Kuryakin, played by David McCallum in *The Man from UNCLE*, because he was 'so gorgeous'. Conversation around these teenage crushes was accompanied with wry smiles, rolled eyes and shaken heads, and we see here an intimation of the way in which women are 'wearing knowledge' (Straw, 1997) that they have gained as adults to reflect upon their past selves. They have acquired a greater understanding of the world and of themselves which allows them to look back on their adolescent crushes with a mixture of scorn and affection.

In her work on teen idols, Gael Sweeney notes the differences between the contexts of television and cinema viewing. She concludes that television specifically constructs teen idols for teenage girls who are sexually unthreatening, and that teenage girls enjoy these unthreatening men during this life stage before moving on to more overtly masculine men in adulthood (Sweeney, 1994). What is notable about the men named as adolescent objects of attraction during my interviews is how often they diverged from this status as sexually unthreatening. Here, for example, Rachel lists some of the men she found attractive during her teen years:

> I fancied lots of TV stars starting with Robert Shaw in *The Buccaneers*, Clint Eastwood in *Rawhide*, *Bronco Lane*, the tall dark guy in *Compact*, *Doctor Kildare* and the leads in *Hawaii Five O* and *77 Sunset Strip*.
>
> *(Rachel, 68)*

Rachel's memory suggests that, perhaps, Sweeney has essentialised the teenage girls' desiring experience to some degree. Rachel does not recall men who fulfil the unthreatening role identified by Sweeney of, say, cheeky Davy Jones in *The Monkees* (BBC, 1967–8), who was also name-checked several times as a teen pin-up. Despite recognising some of the attendant differences between television and cinema, Sweeney's work fails to account for the familiarity and regularity, or the 'wallpaper' status (Collie, 2013), of television and how it might affect viewing relationships with programmes and stars.

Elsewhere I have drawn attention to the role that television played in women managing their adolescence (Collie and Irwin, 2013; Collie, 2014a; Collie, 2014b), and there is a different element of managing at play here. Many of the women complained about having to watch westerns or sport because their fathers insisted that was what the family would view when they were younger. Despite their dislike of such programmes, it is striking how many of their heart-throbs from that period were found in such programmes. This suggests an element of finding and creating something to enjoy in the programme to make its inevitable weekly viewing more palatable. Women thus recall finding objects of attraction in all types of programming, not just 'women's programmes'.

Tracey also indicated the multiplicity of the nature of her crushes during this period of her life:

> I used to love watching [*Top of the Pops* (BBC, 1964–2006)] for David Cassidy and David Essex. All of those. But then I discovered David Bowie, and he had my heart for ever.
>
> *(Tracey, 50)*

Like Rachel, then, Tracey was attracted to a range of idols. While David Cassidy can be seen to comfortably fill the role of sexually unthreatening, parent-pleasing heart-throb, neither David Essex nor David Bowie could be described as 'sexually unthreatening'. These adolescent memories begin to point to the diversity of heterosexual female desire. Rachel's memory makes me question how far the 'tough' and overt masculinity of many of her figures of desire is, in fact, counteracted by the regularity and everyday, domestic status of the series and serialisations in which they are found. The issues of intimacy addressed by Horace Newcomb (1974), engendered by the familiarity and regularity of teenage girls' interaction with these overtly masculine men, alter their teenage perceptions of what is threatening and unthreatening. These are overtly masculine men, but in a domestic context they are made safe by their familiar presence on television. That is, the regularity and associated intimacy of such programming stimulates a relational viewing experience with the characters *on television* as well as with those in the room with her watching television.

Adult pleasures

Viewing pleasures around desire continued into adulthood. However, as they narrated their older years the women began to describe the men they had been attracted to in quite different terms from those they had employed for the men they had been attracted to as teenager. The names that arose in conversations about adolescent desire represented a fairly standardised handful of names of men given prominence in girls' magazines and fostering a feeling of belonging and of operating in the 'field of teenage girldom' (Collie, 2014a). As older women, their objects of attraction became more diverse and diffuse. The qualities that the women related as attractive male assets also expanded considerably.

Mulvey's theorisation of the gaze assumes that spectators will always identify with the active male protagonists. In my interviews there was certainly some conversation along these lines, with characters who conform to this image, such as Richard Chamberlain's tortured priest Ralph de Bricassart in *The Thorn Birds* (ABC, 1983), and, indeed, male heroic characters from many literary adaptations, such as Colin Firth's Mr Darcy from *Pride and Prejudice* (BBC, 1995), being invoked in several interviews. However, the wider picture that emerges from my interviews is one in which women are just as likely to identify with the side-kick or anti-hero as with the hero. When they do so, they may also progress from a position of purely physical attraction to other qualities that might be more desirable in a long-term partner. Characters and actors are identified as desirable for displaying characteristics such as 'loveliness', 'kindness', 'strength' and 'capability', all of which are invoked at different times in different interviews. A much more marked conflation between character and actor also begins to emerge.

Jenny (53), for example, talks about a man and character that many might find an unusual choice as a figure of desire:

Jenny: I love *Lewis*. I love Kevin Whateley. I remember actually I came to – Kevin Whateley was in a play here once and . . . I remember asking a question at one of those question and answer things after the play, and he said 'oh that's a very good question'. And I kind of had this thing of 'Ooh, Kevin Whateley thought I asked a very good question'.

Me: Yeah, yeah.

Jenny: And so I kind of. . . I do find comfort in some of those well-known characters. There's something very nice about them, and I feel quite sort of warm and cuddly. Not because . . . I obviously know they're not real. I'm not that delusional [HC laughs] but I kind of . . . there's something comforting. You know what they're going to find amusing, you know what they're going, how their character . . . there's some familiarity.

Here, Jenny explicitly recognises how television series enable a different viewing relationship with characters on television. The regularity of television encounters allows the audience to 'know' the characters on some level. This is not just a question of the pleasure of looking, watching or gazing, but of knowing and of feeling. Both Jackie Stacey (1994) and Rachel Moseley (2002) found that 'closeness' was critical to women's relationships with female film stars in audience research. My own interview data suggests that the same might be true of women's relationships with male television stars. Jenny's memories suggest a relationship of intimacy and not one of distance, as suggested by Laura Mulvey (1975). At a later point in the interview, Jenny returns to talking about Kevin Whateley, referencing his kindness as one of his most attractive features and a reason why she particularly liked him:

> But I think someone like Kevin Whateley comes across as quite a genuine kind person in real life. And I like that. And he's talked about – cos I used to work for an organisation called The Carer Centre, where I was working with people who were looking after relatives who were disabled. And he's talked about his mum, I think it is, who's got Alzheimer's. And he's quite sort of active in getting funds for Alzheimer's societies and things like that. So I quite like seeing the human side of a person and seeing that they're actually dealing with something that's like the rest of us.
>
> (*Jenny, 53*)

On one hand, Kevin Whateley is an unlikely pin-up. However, within Jenny's broader life narrative, in which she also recounted details of a physically and verbally abusive first marriage, her need to find 'kindness' more attractive or desirable than physical strength or beauty becomes more understandable. Television's role as an agent for comfort and intimacy again emerges as central to the female viewing experience. While the question of what happens when a male is made to occupy the place of erotic object has been addressed by some (Dyer, 1982; Hansen, 1986), the focus of such work assumes that the male subject has been positioned for purposeful objectification. Richard Dyer sees the male pin-up images that he analysed as the knowing bearers of the objectifying gaze, for example. The question of what happens when the male body in programming has not been specifically imagined to appeal to women, but has nonetheless been objectified by a female viewer, has been largely neglected. Jenny's memories of Kevin Whateley, and other women's sometimes unexpected objects of desire, suggest something akin to what Helen Wheatley describes as 'accidental erotic desire' in her work on the erotics of television. She notes that scopophilic visual pleasure of the medium might be located in unlikely places (2016). Indeed, the relationship between desiring woman and television man is not entirely about comfort and intimacy. The women's narratives around their adult objects of desire reveal a more explicit suggestion of looking at men in a sexualised way than their adolescent recollections did. As Patricia put it:

> Oh God! That lovely Richard Beckinsale. Yes . . . Bless him. And to have died so young. Yes, so yes I watched that [*Porridge* (BBC1, 1974–7)]. And did I watch it for the content? No, probably not. I watched it to look at him. How shallow is that? He was lovely.
>
> *(Patricia, 64)*

Patricia's memory of Richard Beckinsale is of him as spectacle, with her choice of words a clear assertion that she was looking at him. Her gaze is 'active' (Mulvey, 1975), lingering and repetitive. Patricia made Beckinsale bear the full weight of her look. Sue E also addresses the sexualised nature of her relationship with the male characters in *The Sweeney* (ITV, 1975–8):

> *The Sweeney*. I have *The Sweeney* as my ring tone now. Well I was in love with John Thaw obviously. Um . . . there is a diary entry that says something like 'I've been having fantasies about Regan and Carter three times a week'.
>
> *(Sue E, 60)*

As well as providing a different perspective on gendered looking, Patricia and Sue E's recollections provide a different context for the hegemonic idea of the television glance (Ellis, 1982). It is clear from their comments that television is not always to be glanced at. Sue E does not recall passively glancing at Carter and Regan, but instead recounts how she took her enjoyment in watching them along with her through the rest of her week and into her diary-writing. This is what the apparatus of television offers that cinema cannot. Sue E does not have to glance at Carter and Regan, because a different spectatorial commitment has been built up over time. While Germaine Greer has concluded that women are not attracted to excessively masculine men (Greer, 2003), in my data, where the conversations around desire happened quite organically, a much more complicated picture emerges. Women are not attracted just to the 'feminised' boy but to a whole multitude of types of men, each of whom perhaps offered different parts of her ideal man. This is best demonstrated by Tracey, who responded to the first of my emails about her attraction to men on television with this list:

> Steve Hodson in *Follyfoot Farm*, Frazer Hines, he was Jamie in *Doctor Who*, Robert Powell in *Harlequin* and *Jesus of Nazareth*, Adam Faith in *Budgie*, Robert Hoffman in that French black and white 1965 series, *The Adventures of Robinson Crusoe*. David Cassidy in *The Partridge Family*, Leigh Lawson in *Travelling Man* – still gorgeous but happily married to Twiggy for years. Davy Jones from *The Monkees*. He sadly passed away last year. There was Richard O'Sullivan in *Man about the House*, but I didn't reckon much of *Robin's Nest*, though. Martin Shaw and Lewis Collins from *The Professionals*, John Thaw in *The Sweeney*, Pete Duel and Ben Murphy . . . that was *Alias Smith and Jones*. Um . . . Simon Williams, Captain James Bellamy in the original *Upstairs Downstairs*, Frank Finlay and James Aubrey from *Bouquet of Barbed Wire*, Anthony Hopkins from *A Married Man*, Philip Madoc, Roy Marsden in *The Sandbaggers*. They were most certainly the best reason for watching these shows. Their looks or charisma as an actor. You'll notice some of them weren't necessarily young and beautiful, but charisma was paramount. The dashing characters they played enhanced that to some degree, but it wasn't all about the heroics for me.
>
> *(Tracey, 50, email correspondence)*

Tracey's response shows how often she found herself attracted from the men she saw on television, how different her objects of attraction were and what her different motivations for attraction might be. The number of men listed by Tracey reflects the experience of television as more than one text. Her adult sensibility, influenced by her exposure to a society which included a visible feminism from childhood, 'allows' her to desire in this way.

Like Tracey, several other women admitted to enjoying a number of men on television, but a certain type of brand loyalty was also evident in both adolescent and adult phases of desire. Many of the women noted that they would watch everything that a certain male actor appeared in, and that sometimes he was the only reason they watched it at all:

> Patrick Mower . . . He was in a serial in the early eighties called *[The] Dark Side of the Sun* (BBC, 1983). A whole six-part serial. Unfortunately I missed some, because that was before we had our video and that was on a specific night of the

week and we went out for two or three of them. But I did see that serial and I thought, yeah definitely dishy. So I . . . um, definitely used to like seeing anything that had him in it, after that.

(Sue O, 64)

This is another very clear intimation that the men are being looked at via television and that it is women who are doing the looking. The women I talked to certainly moved on from an adolescent position to a different adult fascination, but, again, it is much more complicated than that change suggested by Gael Sweeney. Rather than moving from a position of 'feminised and unthreatening' idol to 'masculine and active' adult pleasure, their expectations of 'masculinity' in fact varied greatly. While the women all identified different facets of male television stars as desirable, their use of television stars in this way possibly stems from a similar need described here by Sue E:

Probably Roger Moore, Patrick McGoohan and, later, John Thaw. That starting with *Redcap* (ABC, 1964–6). They were my chief fancies. They were British – I don't remember having American heroes – and rather sophisticated yet good at the action stuff. In other words, unlike any of the male species I'd yet come across in real life. That was the attraction I think.

(Sue E, 60, email)

These television men offer escapism, something different from real life in terms of fantasy and wish-fulfilment. For younger women their television desires offered an opportunity to fantasise about the perceived excitement of adulthood; for older women who were acutely aware of just how unexciting adulthood could be, these men offered the chance to fantasise about the type of men missing from their very real lives.

As in Janice Radway's research on female romantic fiction readers (1984), the oral histories gathered here point to the importance of television to women's self-care. Radway uses Nancy Chodorow's psychoanalytical formations of gender to present her sample as women who are 'servicers'; women who are seen as naturally nurturing and expected to perform the task of supporting family without being formally 'reproduced' or supported themselves (Chodorow, 1994). For Radway, women's use of romantic fiction is a means of attending to their requirement for emotional sustenance and personal space. The ways in which the women whom I interviewed spoke to me about their objects of desire on television give the sense that they were not so much creating space and time for themselves within the domestic schedule as carving out a specific enjoyment within a number of programmes, as well as fulfilling a fantasy need which is not catered for in their real lives. The television series during the period between 1947 and 1989 offered something to look forward to each week.

Clarissa Smith (2007) takes issue with Julie Burchill's criticism that popular culture tends to represent sex for women as 'sex for the sex-less' (Burchill, 2000), whereby it is dressed up as a form of self-care and, therefore, not really sex. Smith reminds us that

in her own study, women were interested in *For Women* magazine for its trans-
formative possibilities and the importance of fantasy to female readers.

> The magazine enables readers' imaginative contemplations of sex without the
> risks and problems of male violence, coercion, physical, emotional and mental
> pressures. For others, the magazine also allows the sidestepping of social
> restrictions, of models of good behaviour, morality, dangers of sex, fear of
> disease and pregnancy. It enables moving outside of those injunctions that
> women don't do this, men can't let go, men will simply use you and throw
> you away.
>
> *(Smith, 2007: 225–6)*

Burchill's conclusion sanitises the notion of 'self-care' and ignores the validity of
fantasy. In fact, desire is about more than sex alone (Coward, 1984), and it represents
different things at different life stages. In this sense of comfort and escapism we can
see echoes of Janice Radway's work on women reading romantic fiction and a
re-assertion of Jane Juffer's observation that women carve out spaces for fantasy
and erotic consumption as part of their daily routines (Juffer, 1998). The transpor-
tative and escapist element of appointment viewing of men on television, a fantasy
appointment which offered something different from the men available to them in
the real world, was important to the women in my study in both adolescence and
adulthood. Television offers, as Dorothy Hobson has noted, an emotive connection
with fiction which offers an alternative to daily life (Hobson, 1980). During adolescence the fantasies offered a hint of the excitement of adulthood. During adulthood, television men offered an alternative to the men whom the women felt they
encountered in real life.

Conclusion

The domestic arena represents a different space for attraction and desire to be played
out, and television's position there creates a different viewing experience to that of
the cinema. The everydayness of television does not initially seem to lend itself to
questions of desire, but the conversations about men and their importance to the
enjoyment of certain programmes that arose from my interviews indicate the
importance of television's role in heterosexual female desire.

The types of men that women remembered attraction to were varied, but the
programmes in which these men starred typically emerged from family viewing (as,
indeed, did the majority of the women's viewing memories). This is partly due to
the workings of memory. What is remembered is what subjects ascribe value to.
When people are asked to recall something as commonplace as television, the 'value'
is often not ascribed to texts, but to contexts (Collie, 2014b). In this study I carried out
a series of oral history interviews with a group of women who generally struggled to
recall the specifics of past television programming that might have resonated with
them, instead remembering the domestic and familial contexts of that viewing.

However, the same women had no such problem remembering those programmes which featured actors and characters to whom they had been attracted and who had stimulated desire, so the difficulties of recollection were diminished by the presence of a heart-throb. Here we begin to see the construction of a heterosexual woman's television canon through desire, not entirely composed of the programmes that we might normally consider to be 'for women'; so while costume drama and other dramas are represented in the discussions coming out of this research, we also see programmes such as the 'gritty' *The Sweeney*, as well as a variety of westerns and sports programmes, being drawn upon in these recollections.

Television's domestic context also positions the medium as offering comfort as well as escapism. The narrative possibilities of the long-running or ongoing television series and serialisation (Newcomb, 1974) lend themselves to long-term, ongoing relationships with television programmes and characters, and to television pleasures which offer comfort in terms of their reliability, regularity and ease of access. Television programming and viewing, unlike a cinema trip, is regularly scheduled. The viewer's relationship with television programmes, and the characters therein, requires commitment over time, which plays out in a safe, comfortable, domestic context. Characters in those programmes become familiar and comforting through the regularity of their appearance and the viewer's interaction with them and their storylines.

These memories of looking at men through the medium of television contest hegemonic theories of female heterosexual spectatorship and desire, but also generate ideas around the differences in looking at the apparatuses of cinema and television: the differences between cinema and television, the different ways in which we invest in watching and not watching, and also how we invest our time over time to create different relationships between the viewer and what is on the screen. What is different, what television offers through its constancy and its familiarity that cinema cannot, is a particular type of feminine viewing pleasure which centres on attraction and desire. The way the women spoke to me about the regularity and familiarity of the attractive men in television programming is thus more redolent of a long-term relationship, one which offers comfort in its familiarity and requires little extra effort, versus the nerve-racking first date implied by the cinematic experience.

Notes

1 This AHRC-funded project (AHF01725/1) was jointly investigated by teams at the University of Warwick and De Montfort University. Its purpose was to begin a sustained historical analysis of television for women between 1947 (when television began a sustained broadcast post-Second World War) and 1989 (when satellite broadcasting began) from both production and reception perspectives. Dr Helen Wheatley, Dr Rachel Moseley and Dr Mary Irwin investigated the production and archival aspect of the project at Warwick, while Dr Helen Wood and I carried out the audience research at De Montfort. Adverts calling for participants were placed in *Woman's Weekly*, *Saga* and the *Lady*; these publications were targeted for their gendered and generational appeal. A number of other magazines and newspapers carried stories about the project that also led to contact with interviewees; these were *Yours*, *TV Times*, the *Guardian* and *Lincs Rural*. I also advertised my

research at the project's public engagement events at the Leicester Phoenix, the Coventry Pop-Up TV Pop Shop and the BFI, as well as through the De Montfort University intranet and through the Hedgerley branch (South Buckinghamshire) of the Women's Institute. In total, sixty-nine women contacted me, and from these a sample of thirty women who represented a generational and geographical spread was selected. The women I interviewed were aged between 42 and 95 and came from various regions of the United Kingdom. The women were exclusively white and all self-identified as heterosexual. The women's social class identification spanned working-class and middle-class backgrounds, and twenty-eight of the thirty women were mothers.

2 The questions were broad and gave the women space to explore themes around programming that they had particularly enjoyed during each stage, why they thought they had felt particular resonance with those programmes, who they watched television with, how they watched and who controlled what they watched. The middle section probed more general questions around the ways in which they perceived that television had influenced their actions and choices, who their television role models were and what other people thought of their viewing choices.

3 Many of the responses to the call to interview discussed the male stars of Wimbledon in these terms.

4 See Stacey (1994), Kuhn (2002) and Moseley (2002), for example, for greater consideration of the social female cinematic audience.

Bibliography

Ang, I. (1985) *Watching Dallas: Soap Opera and the Melodramatic Imagination*, Oxford: Routledge.

Arthurs, J. (2003) 'Sex and the City and Consumer Culture: Remediating Postfeminist Drama', *Feminist Media Studies*, 3(1): 83–98.

Arthurs, J. (2004) *Television and Sexuality: Regulation and the Politics of Taste*. Maidenhead and New York: Open University Press.

Bellour, R. (1979) 'Psychosis, Neurosis, Perversion', *Camera Obscura*, 3(4): 104–32.

Brunsdon, C. (1981) '"Crossroads": Notes on Soap Opera', *Screen*, 22(4): 32–7.

Burchill, J. (2000) 'The Word "Pampering" Means: "Have a Wash and Stop Being Such a Neurotic Cow". It is Sex for the Sex-less and Rest for the Rest-less', *Weekend Guardian*, 9 September: 3.

Chodorow, N. (1994) *Femininities, Masculinities, Sexualities: Freud and Beyond*, Lexington: University Press of Kentucky.

Collie, H. (2013) '"It's Just So Hard to Bring It to Mind": The Significance of "Wallpaper" in the Gendering of Television Memory Work', *VIEW Journal of European Television History and Culture*, 2(3): 13–21.

Collie, H. (2014a) 'From Cathy "Queen of the Mods" to Paula "Pop Princess": Women, Music Television and Adolescent Female Identity', in L. Mee and J. Walker (eds) *Cinema, Television and History: New Approaches*, Newcastle: Cambridge Scholars Press: 47–66.

Collie, H. (2014b) *Television for Women: Generation, Gender and the Everyday*. PhD thesis. De Montfort University.

Collie, H. and Irwin, M. (2013) '"The Weekend Starts Here": Young Women, Pop Music Television and Identity', *Screen*, 54(2): 262–9.

Conway, M. T. (1997) 'Spectatorship in Lesbian Porn: The Woman's Woman's Film', *Wide Angle*, 19(3): 91–113.

Coward, R. (1984) *Female Desire*, London: Paladin.

Doane, M. A. (1989) 'Masquerade Reconsidered: Further Thoughts on the Female Spectator', *Discourse*, 11(1): 42–54.

Dyer, R. (1982) 'Don't Look Now', *Screen*, 23(3–4): 61–73.

Ellis, J. (1982) *Visible Fictions: Cinema, Television, Video*, London: Routledge.

Ellis, J. (2002) *Seeing Things: Television in the Age of Uncertainty*, London: I.B.Tauris.

Geraghty, C. (1991) *Women and Soap Opera: A Study of Prime Time Soaps*, Cambridge: Polity Press.

Gray, A. (1992) *Video Playtime: The Gendering of a Leisure Technology*, London: Routledge.

Greer, G. (2003) *The Boy*, London: Thames & Hudson.

Hansen, M. (1986) 'Pleasure, Ambivalence, Identification: Valentino and Female Spectatorship', *Cinema Journal*, 25(4): 6–32.

Hobson, D. (1980) 'Housewives and the Mass Media', in S. Hall, D. Hobson, A. Lowe and P. Willis (eds) *Culture, Media, Language: Working Papers in Cultural Studies 1972–1979*, London: Hutchinson: 93–102.

Hobson, D. (1982) Crossroads: *The Drama of a Soap Opera*, London: Methuen.

Huntley, R. (2000) 'Sexing the Belly: An Exploration of Sex and the Pregnant Body', *Sexualities*, 3(3): 347–62.

Juffer, J. (1998) *At Home with Pornography: Women, Sexuality, and Everyday Life*. New York: New York University Press.

Kaplan, E. A. (1983) *Women and Film: Both Sides of the Camera*, New York: Methuen.

Kim, L. S. (2001) '"Sex and the Single Girl" in Postfeminism: The F Word on Television', *Television & New Media*, 2(4): 319–34.

Kuhn, A. (1984) 'Women's Genres', *Screen*, 25(1): 18–29.

Kuhn, A. (2002) *An Everyday Magic: Cinema and Cultural Memory*, London: I.B.Tauris.

Modleski, T. (1983) 'The Rhythms of Reception: Daytime Television and Women's Work', in E. A. Kaplan (ed.) *Regarding Television: Critical Approaches – An Anthology*, Los Angeles: American Film Institute: 67–75.

Moore, S. (1988) 'Here's Looking at You, Kid!', in L. Gamman and M. Marshment (eds) *The Female Gaze: Women as Viewers of Popular Culture*, London: Women's Press: 44–59.

Moseley, R. (2002) *Growing Up with Audrey Hepburn: Text, Audience, Resonance*, Manchester: Manchester University Press.

Mulvey, L. (1975) 'Visual Pleasure and Narrative Cinema', *Screen*, 16(3): 6–18.

Mulvey, L. (1981) 'Afterthoughts on "Visual Pleasure and Narrative Cinema": Inspired by "Duel in the Sun"', *Framework*, 15/16/17: 12–15.

Newcomb, H. (1974) *Television: The Most Popular Art*, New York: Anchor.

Ouellette, L. (2002) 'Victims No More: Postfeminism, Television, and Ally McBeal', *Communication Review*, 5(4): 315–35.

Press, A. L. (1991) *Women Watching Television: Gender, Class and Generation in the American Television Experience*, Philadelphia: University of Pennsylvania Press.

Radway, J. (1991) *Reading the Romance: Women, Patriarchy, and Popular Culture*, Chapel Hill: University of North Carolina Press.

Rodowick, D. (1982). 'The Difficulty of Difference', *Wide Angle*, 5(1): 4–15.

Seiter, E. (1999) *Television and New Media Audiences*, Oxford: Clarendon Press.

Smith, C. (2007) *One for the Girls: The Pleasures and Practices of Reading Women's Porn*, Bristol: Intellect.

Stacey, J. (1987) 'Desperately Seeking Difference', *Screen*, 28(1): 48–61.

Stacey, J. (1994) *Star Gazing: Hollywood, Cinema and Female Spectatorship*, Abingdon: Routledge.

Straw, W. (1997) 'Sizing Up Record Collections: Gender and Connoisseurship in Rock Music Culture', in S. Whiteley (ed.) *Sexing the Groove: Popular Music and Gender*, London and New York: Routledge: 3–16.

Surrey, J. (1985) 'Self in Relation: A Theory of Women's Development', in J. V. Jordan, A. G. Kaplan, J. Baker Miller, I. P. Stiver and J. L. Surrey (eds) *Women's Growth in Connection*, Cambridge, MA: Belknap Press: 51–66.

Sweeney, G. (1994) 'The Face on the Lunch Box: Television's Construction of the Teen Idol', *The Velvet Light Trap*, 33: 49–59.

Taylor, H. (1989) *Scarlett's Women: Gone with the Wind and Its Female Fans*, New Brunswick: Rutgers University Press.

Thomas, L. (1997) 'In Love with Inspector Morse: Feminist Subculture and Quality Television', in C. Brunsdon, L. Spigel, and J. D'Acci (eds) *Feminist Television Criticism: A Reader*, Oxford: Clarendon Press: 184–204.

Thompson, L. (1991) 'Family Work: Women's Sense of Fairness', *Journal of Family Issues*, 12(2): 181–96.

Tyler, I. (2011). 'Pregnant Beauty: Maternal Femininities under Neoliberalism', in R. Gill and C. Scharff (eds) *New Femininities: Postfeminism, Neoliberalism and Subjectivity*, Houndmills: Palgrave Macmillan: 21–36.

Wheatley, H. (2016) *Spectacular Television: Exploring Televisual Pleasure*, London: I.B.Tauris.

Wood, H. (2009) *Talking with Television: Women, Talk Shows and Modern Self-Reflexivity*, Urbana: University of Illinois Press.

Young, S. (1988) 'Feminism and the Politics of Power: Whose Gaze is it Anyway?', in L. Gamman and M. Marshment (eds) *The Female Gaze: Women as Viewers of Popular Culture*. London: Women's Press: 173–88.

13

DREAMING OF THE 'GOOD LIFE'

Gender, mobility and anxiety in *Wanted Down Under*

Jilly Boyce Kay and Helen Wood

Introduction

This chapter is concerned with the British daytime television programme *Wanted Down Under* (BBC1, 2007–), which presents families with the possibility of trying on a new life in Australia to test whether they would like to emigrate. Unlike the reality sub-genre of property shows, this programme takes families through issues related to work, daily life and homes, as well as the emotional trauma of leaving people behind, in order to assess whether the family want to embark on a life overhaul. In this chapter we consider how the feminised daytime address of the show encourages participants and audiences to worry over contemporary conditions of family life in Britain during a period of austerity. Here the 'good life' is figured through a relatively imaginary Australia, as an escape from financial pressure and an impossible work/life balance in which time is an increasingly precious commodity. Drawing upon Lauren Berlant's (2011) ideas around the cultural work of 'cruel optimism', we consider the ways in which the programme sets up a relationship to Australia which creates an impossible attachment to a more carefree life through which family time is delivered as leisure time. Here migration is lifted out of the racialised rhetorics which frame current debates in Europe, and is instead heralded as a relatively free and easy life-choice which of course privileges, at the same time that it normalises, whiteness. Women in the programme, and the feminised daytime audience, are encouraged to worry over what such flight means – in terms of the emotional ties to home, but also crucially in their role as 'doing the right thing for the family'. In *Wanted Down Under*, this attachment to the good life is both lauded and problematised, high-lighting its premise as a gendered structure of anxiety in the current cultural milieu.

'The good life' in *Wanted Down Under*

In her book *Cruel Optimism*, Lauren Berlant (2011) argues that, in the United States and Europe, the postwar period was characterised by a sense of optimism, and that this optimism manifested in fantasies of meritocracy and 'the good life'. The objects of optimistic attachment included 'upward mobility, job security, political and social equality, and lively, durable intimacy' (2011: 3). However, as the assurances and social protections of liberal capitalism are now fast dissolving, these fantasies are increasingly fraying. The conditions of contemporary capitalism – in which risk, debt and the management of their consequences are shunted onto the shoulders of the individual rather than the state – mean that a sense of crisis has become embedded and normalised in the everyday. Berlant terms this 'crisis ordinariness', a situation in which 'a spreading precarity' has come to provide the 'dominant *structure* and *experience* of the present moment' (ibid.: 192). Precariousness, insecurity and instability are heightened features of neoliberal states, including Britain, which has experienced the unravelling of the postwar consensus in the wake of Thatcherism and successive governments. For Berlant, people cope and deal with this spreading anxiety through what she calls 'cruel optimism', where – in place of hope for progressive structural change – we have 'an intimate public of subjects who circulate scenarios of economic and intimate contingency and trade paradigms for how best to live on, considering' (ibid.). What is 'cruel' about this optimism is that it encourages the maintenance of attachment to a problematic object that only allows for further endurance rather than change. It requires 'the strange temporalities of projection onto an enabling object that is also disabling' (Berlant, 2007: 34) – an attachment to an impossible idea of 'the good life'.

We suggest that *Wanted Down Under* can be understood within this context of 'crisis ordinariness' and the question of 'how best to live on, considering'. We focus particularly on series nine of the programme, which was broadcast in January and February of 2015. In the UK, these months are in the depths of winter, and certainly the symbolic power of sunshine and swimming pools would have a particular resonance for viewers during this season. We are most concerned with the political and economic aftermath of the financial crisis of 2007/8; by 2015, Britain had been subjected for nearly five years to an economic regime of austerity, entailing huge cuts to public services, increased privatisation of public goods and an acceleration of the already widening gap in material inequality. *Wanted Down Under* can be seen as part of a shift in lifestyle programming which accommodates post-recession culture. For instance, Heather Nunn (2011) points to the ways in which, in the aftermath of the 2008/9 recession, British property programming shifted its focus from house-buying as a speculative financial investment to the notion of a 'forever home' – a place to which one could retreat, and which would act as a sanctuary from the vagaries of neoliberal capitalism. In *Wanted Down Under*, against the backdrop of precarious post-recession life in Britain, Australia is figured as a utopian space or a 'cluster of promises' (Berlant, 2011: 23) where the dream of a good life, durable intimacy and upward mobility seems still – perhaps – within reach. This is of course an extension of the much longer history in which Australia has been figured as a place of possibility and escape for working-class and lower middle-class Britons, as A. James Hammerton and Alistair Thomson (2005) carefully detail in their book about postwar migration and 'Ten Pound Poms'. Here the fantasy of Australia as the embodiment of egalitarianism and the 'good life' within British imaginaries is renewed in the contemporary context of 'crisis ordinariness'.

Wanted Down Under is a BBC Northern Ireland production that is broadcast on BBC1 in the morning.[1] It is billed on its website as a 'series in which British families are given a look at life in Australia ahead of possible migration' (occasionally they also go to New Zealand, although our chapter focuses only on Australia, its most regular destination).[2] Broadcast since 2007, at the time of writing the programme was coming up to its tenth series; it attracts audiences of up to two million and, as of October 2015, has an active Facebook page with around 7,750 followers.[3] Research by YouGov indicates that the programme is viewed predominantly by women; certainly, the discussions and comments in its official Facebook group are overwhelmingly contributed by women.[4]

Wanted Down Under shares certain similarities with a number of British lifestyle television programmes that are concerned with buying property abroad – for example, *A Place in the Sun: Home or Away?* (Channel 4, 2004–), *Phil: Secret Agent Down Under* (Channel 4, 2012) and *Escape to the Continent* (BBC1, 2014–). However, where these shows are more centrally concerned with property acquisition, *Wanted Down Under* considers the overall impact of moving overseas on families, which fits with its daytime space in the schedule, in which there has long been a durable, albeit shifting, address to women in its attempt to synchronise with the rhythmic life of the home (Moseley, Wheatley and Wood, 2014). *Wanted Down Under* therefore emphasises the *emotional* 'costs', risks and benefits of such a move, which are framed within a broader construction of family and home that reaches beyond the materiality of property. In a BBC interview to publicise the show, its presenter, Nicki Chapman, said:

> This is I think the only show around that does this, you know we see plenty of programmes about moving abroad, buying property, but this, you're road-testing a whole new life. It isn't just about getting the home, it's about the lifestyle, can you afford it, the work opportunities, *will* you have a better way of life?[5]

The participants in *Wanted Down Under* are British families in the nuclear and heteronormative sense. These are almost always composed of a heterosexual couple and dependent children (although rarely there are exceptions; for example, in series nine, a lesbian couple without children took part). The majority of participants are white and when ethnic minority participants do take part, they are British-born, with British accents and established family ties in the country. None of the participants is *already* marked as a migrant, except for the occasional Australian or New Zealander who takes part in the programme and who wishes to return 'home'. At least one parent is in paid work – this is imperative – and most often they are homeowners. While the families must possess a certain level of economic capital and the capacity to earn a stable income, they are generally not part of a highly educated, professional middle class. In the current context, the participant demographic can perhaps best be understood as part of that group coded as 'aspirational', where home ownership, financial responsibility (read: independence from the welfare state), living in a 'good' neighbourhood and – most crucially – 'wanting the best for your family' constitute the basis for a respectable class position.

Typically, one of the adults in the couple is possessed with a desire to emigrate to Australia and the other displays reluctance, hesitance or sometimes outright resistance to the idea. Through this intimate conflict, a tension is set up between the desire for a new, 'better' way of life in Australia and an attachment to traditional structures of belonging, most particularly in the form of extended family networks in the UK. The family travels to Australia for a week to 'sample' life there. The programme is thereafter split into three segments, each of which represents one aspect of a possible new life in Australia: property, work and lifestyle. These experiences are framed as 'testing' or 'sampling' life in Australia; significantly, the family must negotiate these areas without the presence of an intervening expert. At the end of each segment, the family votes on their preference for either Australia or the UK through the use of plastic laminated flags, which they flip to reveal either the Union Jack or the Southern Cross (see Figure 13.1). After this comes the 'Reality Check', where home-owning participants watch a video of their UK house being valued by estate agents; couples are provided with a specially made spreadsheet and are seen working out the comparative costs of daily living in Australia and the UK; and then they watch video clips from loved ones back home, which typically elicit tearful reactions. Finally, they cast an overall vote on whether they want to stay in the UK or to move 'down under'.

Addressing the anxious mother

In many ways *Wanted Down Under* repeats the feminised tropes of daytime television, by addressing the viewer in ways that are reminiscent of the earlier feminist analyses of

FIGURE 13.1 Participants express their preference for a life in either Australia or the UK through 'voting' with laminated flags

the soap opera. These texts call to her responsibility for '"managing" the sphere of personal life' (Brunsdon, 1997: 17) or constitute her as 'a sort of ideal mother' because, like a mother, she must (somehow) 'sympathize with all the contradictory and competing claims of the family, while making no demands of her own' (Modleski, 1979: 14). Here, we would also argue that *Wanted Down Under* draws on traditions of immediacy and intimacy from lifestyle and reality television in which the viewer is further drawn into a personal, affective realm through which any straightforward pedagogic reading of the text can be disrupted by the workings of affect (Skeggs and Wood, 2012). Misha Kavka has pointed out how reality television has from the start been 'entangled with affective eruptions that replayed, in heightened form, the sensations of ordinary life' (2014: 261). In *Wanted Down Under*'s opening 'greetings' to the home audience, presenter Nicki Chapman is standing on a beach somewhere in Australia – we do not know specifically where – which stands in as a generic promise of sunshine, 'outdoorsiness' and pristine nature. Typical greetings have included:

> If all you wanted in life was to spend quality time with the people you love, how far would *you* go to achieve your dream? For one family, it could mean a move to the other side of the world.

> Knowing your youngest child's health could deteriorate at any time, what would you do to guarantee your family the best life possible? Would you consider uprooting them to the other side of the world?

> You've spent your life believing that you should be living on the other side of the world, in a country you've never even visited. But when push came to shove, could you actually go ahead with the move, especially when it meant potential heartbreaks?

In each case, the direct address to the audience invites but also compels us to consider anxious questions about our own lives, our children's lives and, importantly, our role as parents in struggling on behalf of our families. It presents us with the iconography of paradise and escape but alerts us to the pain necessary for us to endure in order to achieve it, as well as to the risk that is inherent in having a 'dream'. In each of these openings there is figured the promise of a better life for our families, one which it is seen to be the responsibility of the mother to provide. In the authors' own experience of watching the programme together, it elicited in both of us maternal guilt about whether we were doing 'enough' – enough to give our children 'the best life possible'; enough to take the necessary risks that might buy more 'quality time'; and, first and foremost, enough to have a 'dream' for one's family and their future.

The programme's incitement to self-responsibilisation has a clearly gendered character, and this gendering comes through in the ways in which many participants discuss their desire to become better parents through spending 'quality time' with their children, or seeking 'a better life for the kids'. For example, in episode five, we meet Lisa, whose work as an accountancy lecturer means that she spends a lot of time away from the family home. In the segment where they sample the Australian 'lifestyle' – which in this case is represented by a crazy golf course in Melbourne – she reflects:

> We don't spend a huge amount of time together as a family, and moving to Australia would offer us the opportunity to have that back, and for us to feel like a family again, and for me to feel like a wife and mum again.

In episode four we meet Sarah Bone, who is a youth worker with a husband and three children, and who already has a backstory of self-transformation worthy of the narrative logics of reality television: she was a single mother and homeless at 16, but then 'turned her life around'. As she says: 'I really wanted to show people that I had it in me, so whilst being in a hostel accommodation I started doing my degree, to turn my life about for myself and my daughter.' At this point, the camera lingers over the wedding photos displayed in her home that symbolically 'prove' she did indeed 'turn her life around', and the voiceover narrates:

> Sarah's come a long way in the past fifteen years. With financial security, a loving husband and a home of her own, everything looks perfect. But it's not. Having made a better life for herself in the past, Sarah's determined to do the same again – this time for her family.

What these two examples highlight is an incitement to an *enterprising* maternal sub-jectivity where responsibility is incumbent upon mothers to seek out and secure the best possible conditions in which to raise their children. Taken in the wider context of the classed and gendered economies of reality television, in which working-class mothers are hyper-visible and subject to intensifying levels of class disgust (Tyler, 2008; Lyle, 2008; Jensen, 2010; Skeggs and Wood, 2012), the imperative to perform respectable and enterprising motherhood arguably becomes more urgently felt. Ideals of the future-oriented good neoliberal subject are also projected onto cultural inscriptions of mothers (Littler, 2013) and Kim Allen and Yvette Taylor (2012) suggest that '[m]others, charged with rearing a generation of future-citizens, are increasingly expected to take responsibility for their own trajectories, to enterprise their way out of "traps"'. Much like the gendered labour of housework, the emotional work of self-transformation is never complete; it is not enough that Sarah transformed her life fifteen years ago, or that she has achieved all the markers of normative respectability – she must now deploy her energies to turn her family's life around. While the narrative logic is clearly driven by an orientation to the future, the temporalities of hope and optimism for the future are also partly nostalgic. So, when Lisa projects her hope onto Australia as a space offering the opportunity to have 'family time', she does this through saying she wants to feel like a mother and a wife 'again', and to have time as a family 'back'. This complex figuring of temporality and hope speaks to the contradictory ways in which Australia is constructed in *Wanted Down Under*, as both a signifier of modernity, progress and 'lifestyle' and a space in which fraying fantasies under the strain of life in Britain may be transported, revived and stitched back together – where social mobility and endurable life, remembered as fantasies from the recent past, may still be possible. In the programme, the 'challenge' or 'test' that must be met in order to achieve the dream of a better family life necessarily entails emigration. The gendering of emigration as a trope of maternal responsibility is an interesting move, especially given the current climate.[6]

The feminisation of responsible migration

The most striking aspect of the figuration of migration in *Wanted Down Under* is the total absence of, and therefore a semantic distancing from, the terms 'migrant' and 'immigrant'. Very occasionally references are made to 'expats', but the overriding conceptualisation of the participants' transnational mobility in the programme is that they are simply looking to 'make a fresh start', have 'a better quality of life' or 'get a better lifestyle'. However, the type of mobility that the programme envisages for its participants means that they can in fact quite easily be understood as 'economic migrants', the definition of which is 'a person who moves from one region, place, or country to another in order to improve his or her standard of living' (Collins English Dictionary, 2015). In this sense, the notion of having a 'dream' that is highly responsible – in that the dream entails a self-sufficient family life which is not dependent on the state for welfare support – is extremely important in differentiating the participants from what Zygmunt Bauman (1998) describes as the 'vagabond' figure, who is invoked in the broader culture to embody all that is negative about international economic migration. This rhetorical move in *Wanted Down Under* works to legitimise the capacity of (white) Britons to move unimpeded across the globe, which of course must be understood as part of a much longer history of empire, colonialism and domination. This is part of the 'continuing imperial imaginary informing British migrancy' to Australia (Schech and Haggis, 2004: 176), which also means that the participants on *Wanted Down Under* do not have to offer up displays of assimilation with the local culture: they are assumed in advance to 'fit in' and to play a part in the 'white nation fantasy' that Ghassan Hage (2000) describes as part of the cultural imaginary of Australia.

Early in each episode of *Wanted Down Under* we are shown a computerised flight path of the plane that is carrying the families to Australia, accompanied by upbeat music. This visualisation of their journey around the world underlines the huge distance between the UK and Australia, but also figures the ease with which they may travel. Similarly, upon arriving in an Australian airport, we see the families in the arrivals hall; they are pushing luggage trolleys and looking weary after their long-haul flights. However, we do not see them having to be processed through the security apparatus of immigration controls; their passage into the country goes unremarked and is therefore part of the ways in which their migrancy is symbolically erased. The programme title, *Wanted Down Under*, also references the dual aspect of migration; that is to say, those who are actually 'wanted' and those who are criminalised for wanting to move, which sets apart the terms of those for whom 'legitimate' migration is possible. Sara Ahmed points to a politics of mobility which delineates 'who gets to move with ease across the lines that divide spaces' as well as 'who gets to be at home, who gets to inhabit spaces [. . .] spaces that are inhabitable for some bodies and not others' (Ahmed, 2007: 162).

Mobility and the easy inhabitation of transnational space in *Wanted Down Under* stands in stark contrast to the regimes of security and surveillance made visible in the reality television show *Border Security: Australia's Front Line* (Seven Network, 2004–), which Mark Andrejevic (2011) discusses in relation to classed distinctions in what he terms 'mobility capital'. *Border Security* works as part of a broader discursive move in installing migration as a security issue and in subjecting different groups to 'different regimes of mobility' (ibid.: 70). What is particularly significant about *Border Security* is the way in which it incorporates 'elements of sovereign power', so that on the show travellers are subjected to invasive searches, interrogation and detention (ibid.: 61). While *Wanted Down Under* appears to operate outside the coercive practices of the security state, there are hidden ways in which sovereign power is both incorporated within and shored up by the programme: in the application procedure for appearing on the programme, the criteria clearly state that applicants must be under the age of 45 and have a job that is on the skills shortage list for Australia.[7] In this way, the selection criteria for the programme directly mirror the immigration policies of the Australian state.

Ideas about 'mobility capital' still abound in *Wanted Down Under* as the programme feminises appropriate behaviours of 'responsible' migration. In the 'Reality Check' section of the programme in the second half, the parents are seen sitting down with a specially made *Wanted Down Under* spreadsheet and a calculator so that they can work out the everyday costs of living in Australia. For example, in episode one of series nine, Kirsty and Chris, a nurse and a plumber in their mid-twenties with one young son, are seen comparing the price of milk and bananas, as well as rent, childcare and council tax. Their calculations suggest that in their outgoings they would be worse off by precisely £152.07; Nicki Chapman's voiceover says here that 'this could be where Kirsty's dream unravels'. However, they then work out that when their potential income is taken into account, they would be better off by precisely £4,715.16 per year – news which causes Kirsty to literally cry with relief, as the dream is kept 'alive' (see Figure 13.2). The minutiae of families' finances and consumption practices are laid out for intimate scrutiny as part of this performance of the responsible migrant-self. What is clearly so important, and yet never made explicit, is that the family must have a clear plan for, and a commitment to, managing their finances so that they will not be a burden on the state; they must calculate and account for every expenditure, no matter how large or small. Women's traditional roles as domestic account managers are thus prized here, at the same time that they are reconfigured as part of their new roles as responsible prospective migrants.

For the worrying mother, it's not just finances which offer a reality check to the notion of the carefree 'dream'. Also included in this section of the programme is a segment in which the families view recorded video messages from loved ones back in the UK. This is where they must factor in and negotiate what the voiceover describes

FIGURE 13.2   In the 'Reality Check' section of *Wanted Down Under*, participants must calculate the costs of everyday life in Australia to test whether their dream is tenable

as the 'emotional costs' of moving away from friends and family. In episode one, as Kirsty, Chris and their toddler son watch these emotionally charged messages, this is overlaid with instrumental music from popular love songs – such as James Blunt's *Goodbye My Lover* – and this potentially works to elicit a heightened affective response from the audience, as the families break down at the personal cost of the move. Chris says, his voice slightly choked, that 'the little man's brought everyone so much closer together and I mean, it would be a shame to move him away from everyone, really'. Kirsty, highly emotional and tearful, says: 'You know, I went through a lot with my sister and mum and to leave them would just be . . .': she is unable to finish the sentence and Chris interjects: 'harder than you imagined.'

Appearing near the end of the programme, and just before the family's final deciding vote is shown, this segment is an emotional intervention into the highly formulised decision-making process. This segment usually has the effect of shaking the participants' belief that such a move would *really* give them 'a better life'. It is at this point that the meritocratic promise of Australia is tested through bringing to the fore alternative forms of value. These are values of sentimentality, belonging and attachment to people that cannot be coded as part of the future-oriented, aspirational self. These attachments cannot be rationalised and converted into direct economic benefit, but perhaps instead hark back to older, more nostalgic, classed under-standings of a 'good life'. Skeggs and Wood (2012) have suggested that reality tele-vision texts, rather than deploying coherent ideological messages, instead mobilise 'tournaments of value' whereby volatile and often contradictory emotions and values circulate in the affective realm constructed by the text as it meets the audience. *Wanted Down Under* is here mobilising the troubling, competing values that the aspiring mother must negotiate – between enterprising futures and sentimental pasts.

Having sampled the property, work opportunities, and lifestyle of Australia – which almost always leads to the participants experiencing positive feelings and more inclination to move down under – this 'reality check' intervenes to disrupt, complicate and further responsibilise the desire to move. The 'dream' must be *audited* through a rigorous consideration of financial and emotional 'costs'. Eva Illouz (2007) has suggested that capitalism and emotion, rather than being separate spheres which operate according to fundamentally different logics, have become increasingly entwined in a 'broad sweeping movement' whereby 'affect is made an essential part of economic behaviour and [. . .] emotional life – especially that of the middle classes – follows the logic of economic relations and exchange' (Illouz, 2007: 5). As this episode of *Wanted Down Under* highlights, the emotional and economic spheres of life are subjected to the same rationalising processes in making 'life choices', which is part of a longer history of the increased rationalisation of private life under capitalism (Skeggs and Wood, 2012). Just as your finances must be responsibly audited and managed in order to justify and make possible a life-changing move, so too must your emotional resilience be tested and proven: you must demonstrate a capacity to withstand and absorb the emotional price that must be paid.

In all episodes of *Wanted Down Under*, the audience are asked to consider whether the emotional 'costs' are a 'price worth paying' in order to 'achieve the dream'. Emotion therefore operates as a form of capital: to spend it may be painful in the short term, but will, it is implied, yield benefits in the long term. Unlike other makeover programmes in which teams of experts intervene to pronounce on the direction one's life should take, in *Wanted Down Under* it is the family unit, led by the mother, that must cope with the emotional risks of their decision, producing profound anxieties and agonising over whether or not they will make the 'right' choice – and what, indeed, the 'right' choice might be. The feminised and affective realm that the text constructs draws the viewer into these anxieties and ambivalences, surrounded by the notion of the 'good life' that apparently can only be found abroad, and not – significantly – within Britain.

These emotional costs are all framed around the loss of family attachments in Britain, but not through any sense of identity or nostalgia associated with the nation that is being left behind. In *Wanted Down Under*, the emotional obstacles to emigration have nothing to do with any civic or sentimental attachment to nation, let alone with patriotism. In Hammerton and Thomson's (2005) oral history work with postwar British migrants to Australia, the 'green fields' of the British landscape that were left behind are often invoked in memories of heartbreak and loss, suggesting an affective attachment to place and nation that has receded under conditions of neo-liberalism. In *Wanted Down Under*, it is not the British state, society, or even the landscape, but only kith-and-kin whose absence will constitute loss, and for whom the participants may feel 'homesick'. This potentially further highlights the ways in which, following Berlant (2011), the state has retreated both as a locus of belonging and as a motor for optimism.

Work/life balance and the 'impossible' Australian dream

Australia has promoted itself as a 'working man's paradise' (Hogan, 2009: 109) since the mid-nineteenth century, based on its relatively favourable labour laws. However, the forces of de-industrialisation, the decline of trade unions and rising levels of inequality now mean that this claim is increasingly tenuous; and yet the idea of Australia as a 'classless' and meritocratic society still persists. While this myth is explicitly *gendered* through the figure of the male breadwinner, in *Wanted Down Under* it is just as often women who are the main visa applicants based on their employment history and professional skills. Nonetheless, this notion of fair and endurable labour is reinforced through the repetition of ideas about a 'stable' family income and a tolerable work/life balance.

The reasons that participants give for wanting to leave the UK are more or less consistently framed around the intolerable pressures of waged work and the detrimental impact it has on family life. For example, in episode four we are introduced to the Bone family from Scotland through the voiceover, which tells us that they 'are struggling to balance work and family life'. We then see a shot of the father at work in the fast-food restaurant he manages, spreading tomato sauce on a pizza base. He says, 'I've been working nights and weekends for close to twenty years now'. The scene then cuts to images of their children at home playing the violin, doing homework and sitting eating snacks at the dinner table. Sarah, the mother, says: 'Dad's not here when we come in from school, Dad's not up when we leave for school in the morning.' The voiceover: 'Desperate for a fresh start, they believe Australia could be the answer.' Sarah says, as she chops vegetables in the kitchen: 'The dream is just to have a better quality of family life.' While iconographic images of sunshine, beaches and barbecues (most of them looking as if they are stock footage from the Australian tourist board) are deployed throughout the episodes as signifiers of paradise, the discourses of 'dreams' are in fact most often expressed by the participants in terms of domestic, intimate and family life – or what Berlant might call a fantasy of 'lively, durable intimacy' (2011: 3). The 'dream', then, is more about liberating time from the all-consuming grip of work than it is about living in 'paradise'.

The idea that Australia will provide fairer working conditions, particularly for blue-collar and public-sector workers who are often under considerable pressure in their jobs, is repeated throughout the series. In episode one, Kirsty, who in the UK is a registered nurse in a prison hospital, hopes that a job in Australia will give her 'better hours, better pay, more support' and a less stressful working life. The Cornish family in episode five are introduced to us in the following terms: 'Pulling pints and being a travelling teacher means James and Lisa Cornish hardly ever see their two little boys', and, because of this, 'they're considering moving lock, stock and barrel to the other side of the world'. In the narrative logic of *Wanted Down Under,* the solution to unendurable labour or low income is never to organise collectively for better workplace rights or fair pay – it is to either endure, or to escape.

The intolerability of working life in Britain forms part of a broader discourse in the programme in which the country is regularly figured as a nation in terminal moral, economic and cultural decline. In episode seventeen, Aaron, a prison officer from Rochdale, has a fixation on moving to Australia without ever having visited the country (this is not unusual in the programme); he has been 'spellbound' by the *idea* of Australia since, as a young child, he watched camcorder footage of his grandmother who had travelled there, years ago, on a holiday. Since having his child, Aaron's dream has returned and intensified as he worries about the environment in which his daughter will be brought up. Camera shots linger on grey tower blocks, dilapidated residential buildings and a battered and grimy 'Home Watch' sign. Aaron says: 'I think obviously one of the things for pushing it now is the decline in our area in't it, with me car being stolen and the anti-social behaviour.' The area is strongly coded as gloomy, abject and in irreversible decline. Amy, his partner, who works as a teaching assistant, says: 'When we first moved here it was a lovely street, but it's changing every year.' By contrast, Aaron thinks that Australia will provide his daughter with what the voiceover suggests might be a 'perfect' upbringing – he articulates this as 'outdoor things – zoos and parks and beaches. Amelia'll love it, climbing and exploring'. When Britain is visually coded as grey, miserable and in a spiral of degeneration, and Australia is expansive, pristine and utopic, the programme mobilises a strong sense of emigration as ultimately the logical and superior option.

The Australia that is conjured here can be read as a utopia – a 'safe', suburbanised space, in which property interiors are spacious, modern and minimalist: 'open-plan' domestic design, private swimming pools in the back yard, large spaces for private entertaining and the proximity of the beach seem to be the expectations that most participants have of Australian property. In this figuration, there is precious little sense of Australia's multi-ethnic demographic make-up, or of the increasing presence of poverty in a picture which mirrors the UK's widening inequality.[8] Furthermore, any sense of Aboriginal histories and populations or of Australia's colonial history is absent, as is its current obsession with the politics of reparation. This can be understood within what Skeggs and Wood (2012) describe as evidence of 'white flight' within some property programmes – attempts to move away from multi-ethnic urban settings. Similarly, David Morley (2000: 152) has suggested that the popularity of Australian soap operas in the UK might be attached to the appeal of the 'all white society' that they depict, and for which some Britons still pine; interestingly, this idea reappears in *Wanted Down Under*. For example, Sarah Bone, in episode four, says: 'Whether it be naively from watching *Home and Away* and *Neighbours* and things like that, as a young person growing up you have these images and a vision in your head.' The attachment to Australia in the show is therefore an attachment to a nostalgic myth of Australia as the 'White Nation' that Ghassan Hage (2000) describes.

Hage has documented how Australian national culture centres on a narrative of decline and a yearning for a mythic period of pre-migration – and yet this is cleansed from *Wanted Down Under*, in which contemporary Australia is mythologised both as replete with democratic promise and as white. In his later work *Against Paranoid Nationalism* (2003), Hage explicitly discusses the rise of a paranoid nationalism in Australia as part of more embedded mainstream culture of 'worrying' which has risen in direct response to the shrinking of 'hope' at the hands of the neoliberal state. This is similar to Berlant's discussion, except for Berlant optimism is redirected away from the state through other, more local and malleable routes and attachments. We might say here that in the imaginary of *Wanted Down Under*, Australia is resurrected as a site of hope and utopia in a space characterised by a lack of emotional investment in the British nation state. The programme itself ignores the imperfect cultural repertoires from colonial history, concealing Australia's own national anxieties. For Hage the rise of paranoid nationalism is based on a guilty understanding that the nation can in fact be stolen again as it has been before, and it is this which provides the psychic backdrop of worry and anxiety. He exposes the circulation of the 'white nation fantasy', whereby fantasies are not just about an idealised good life but also about a self/subject living that good life. He says that 'people don't *have* fantasies. They inhabit fantasy spaces of which they are a part' (ibid.: 70). Therefore, Australia as a solution to contemporary cultural anxiety is misrecognised in *Wanted Down Under*, since it represents parallel forms of anxiety and attachment to fantasy via the legacy of its colonial connections to Britain. In this context, then, we would suggest that in *Wanted Down Under* Australia is mobilised as the impossible attachment to the notion of the 'good life', and it is through this that optimism or hope are cultivated as a space to live on and endure.

Conclusion

We want to return to Berlant's work here to think through how the affective relations of 'cruel optimism', 'crisis ordinariness' and the 'fraying fantasies' of the present moment play out in the intimate dramas of *Wanted Down Under*. As a feminised televisual form, *Wanted Down Under* constructs a sense of the maternal responsibilities of securing 'the good life'. It would be easy enough to read the programme as an individualistic fantasy of escape from the shared responsibilities of the social polity to 'privatized utopias' (Bauman, 2000). However, there is something more complex at play in its mobilisation of competing, contradictory values.

John Ellis (2002: 78) has suggested that television has a social function as a 'vast mechanism' for 'working through', whereby 'raw data' is processed through television into 'more narrativized, explained forms'. *Wanted Down Under*, we would suggest, is less a mechanism for *explaining* than an unstable affective site of intense gendered dreams and anxieties; these affects are *sensed* and *felt* but never fully formed. Berlant points us to the ways in which the temporal present is not an object that we can coherently perceive, grasp, explicate or scrutinise, but rather is always a 'mediated affect'. As she says, 'the present is perceived, first, affectively: the present is what makes itself present to us before it becomes anything else' (Berlant, 2011: 4). The affective 'raw data' of *Wanted Down Under* is itself still volatile, unformed and unsatisfactorily named, and it offers space to raise the tensions between our enduring present and our potential futures. Helen Wheatley's notion of television generating a position of 'worrying at' social issues better captures what she describes as the medium's participation in 'a much broader set of cultural anxieties' (Wheatley, 2006: 127). *Wanted Down Under* therefore offers up the emotional anxieties of the socio-temporal present, but it does not do the work of explaining or reconciling the sets of values it unleashes and incites. Indeed, Australia, as an imperfect site for optimism, makes any neat reconciliation impossible. Rather, the programme opens out the space for a maternal cultural anxiety in the current context and invites women to undertake the emotional labour involved in finding the space to live on, regardless.

Notes

1 Repeats of the programme are broadcast on BBC2.
2 See www.bbc.co.uk/programmes/b006s5v8 (last accessed 1 April 2016).
3 See www.bbc.co.uk/mediacentre/latestnews/2014/ni-new-year (last accessed 21 October 2015).
4 See https://yougov.co.uk/profileslite#/Wanted_Down_Under/demographics (last accessed 21 October 2015).
5 Interview clip available at: www.bbc.co.uk/news/entertainment-arts-30655042 (last accessed 21 October 2015).
6 At the time of writing Europe is currently experiencing massive migration as a result of war in Syria, which has resulted in a series of moves to reinstate Europe's borders despite the evident humanitarian crises.
7 The criteria for New Zealand are slightly different, in that you must be under the age of 55. See 'Apply to appear on Wanted Down Under', available at www.bbc.co.uk/programmes/articles/2bWPNYcQxqYj0dbCCCXN652/apply-to-appear-on-wanted-down-under (last accessed 21 October 2015).
8 A 2014 report by the Australian Council of Social Service found that poverty is increasing, with 13.9 per cent of people in Australia, and 17.7 per cent of children, living below the poverty line. See www.acoss.org.au/poverty-2/ (last accessed 21 October 2015).

Bibliography

Ahmed, S. (2007) 'A phenomenology of whiteness', *Feminist Theory*, 8(2): 149–68.

Allen, K. and Y. Taylor (2012) 'Placing parenting, locating unrest: failed femininities, troubled mothers and riotous subjects', in T. Jensen and I. Tyler (eds) *Studies in the Maternal*, 4(2): 1–25.

Andrejevic, M. (2011) 'Managing the borders: classed mobility on security-themed reality TV', in H. Wood and B. Skeggs (eds) *Reality Television and Class*, London: BFI/Palgrave Macmillan: 60–72.

Bauman, Z. (1998) *Globalization: The Human Consequences*, New York: Columbia University Press.

Bauman, Z. (2000) *Liquid Modernity*, Cambridge and Malden: Blackwell/Polity.

Berlant, L. (2007) 'Cruel optimism: on Marx, loss and the senses', *New Formations*, 63: 33–51.

Berlant, L. (2011) *Cruel Optimism*, Durham and London: Duke University Press.

Brunsdon, C. (1997) *Screen Tastes: Soap Opera to Satellite Dishes*, London and New York: Routledge.

Collins English Dictionary (2015) 'Economic migrant'. Available at www.collinsdictionary.com/dictionary/english/economic-migrant (last accessed 12 July 2016).

Ellis, J. (2002) *Seeing Things: Television in the Age of Uncertainty*, London and New York: I.B.Tauris.

Hage, G. (2000) *White Nation: Fantasies of White Supremacy in a Multicultural Society*, London and New York: Routledge.

Hage, G. (2003) *Against Paranoid Nationalism: Searching for Hope in a Shrinking Society*, Annandale and London: Pluto Press.

Hammerton, A. J. and A. Thomson (2005) *Ten Pound Poms: Australia's Invisible Migrants*, Manchester and New York: Manchester University Press.

Hogan, J. (2009) *Gender, Race and National Identity: Nations of Flesh and Blood*, Abingdon and New York: Routledge.

Illouz, E. (2007) *Cold Intimacies: The Making of Emotional Capitalism*, Cambridge and Malden: Polity.

Jensen, T. (2010) '"What kind of mum are you at the moment?" *Supernanny* and the psychologising of classed embodiment', *Subjectivity*, 3(2): 170–92.

Kavka, M. (2014) 'A matter of feeling: mediated affect in reality television', in L. Ouellette (ed.) *A Companion to Reality TV*, Oxford: Wiley: 459–77.

Littler, J. (2013) 'The rise of the "yummy mummy": popular conservatism and the neoliberal maternal in contemporary British culture', *Culture, Communication and Critique*, 6(2): 227–43.

Lyle, S. (2008) '(Mis)recognition and the middle-class/bourgeois gaze: a case study of *Wife Swap*', *Critical Discourse Studies*, 5(4): 319–30.

Modleski, T. (1979) 'The search for tomorrow in today's soap operas: notes on a feminine narrative form', *Film Quarterly*, 33(1): 12–21.

Morley, D. (2000) *Home Territories: Media, Mobility and Identity*, Abingdon and New York: Routledge.

Moseley, R., H. Wheatley and H. Wood (2014) 'Introduction: television in the afternoon', *Critical Studies in Television: The International Journal of Television Studies* 9(2): 1–19.

Nunn, H. (2011) 'Investing in the "forever home": from property programming to "retreat TV"', in H. Wood and B. Skeggs (eds) *Reality Television and Class*, New York: Palgrave Macmillan: 169–82.

Schech, S. and J. Haggis (2004) 'Terrains of migrancy and whiteness: how British migrants locate themselves in Australia', in A. Moreton-Robinson (ed.) *Whitening Race: Essays in Social and Cultural Criticism*, Canberra: Aboriginal Studies Press: 176–91.

Skeggs, B. and H. Wood (2012) *Reacting to Reality Television: Performance, Audience and Value*, Abingdon and New York: Routledge.

Tyler, I. (2008) 'Chav mum chav scum: class disgust in contemporary Britain', *Feminist Media Studies*, 8(1): 17–34.

Wheatley, H. (2006) *Gothic Television*, Manchester and New York: Manchester University Press.

Wood, H. and B. Skeggs (eds) (2011) *Reality Television and Class*, London: BFI/Palgrave Macmillan.

INDEX

Locators in *italics* refer to figures and tables.